The Creation of the Organisation for the Prohibition of Chemical Weapons

A Case Study in the Birth of an Intergovernmental Organisation

In memory of John Gee
who contributed so much

OPCW

The Creation of the Organisation for the Prohibition of Chemical Weapons

A Case Study in the Birth of an Intergovernmental Organisation

edited by

Ian R. Kenyon and Daniel Feakes

T·M·C·Asser press
The Hague

Published by T·M·C·ASSER PRESS
P.O. Box 16163, 2500 BD The Hague, The Netherlands
<www.asserpress.nl>

T·M·C·ASSER PRESS' English language books are distributed exclusively by:

Cambridge University Press, The Edinburgh Building, Shaftesbury Road,
Cambridge CB2 2RU, UK,
or
for customers in the USA, Canada and Mexico:
Cambridge University Press, 100 Brook Hill Drive, West Nyack, NY 10994-2133, USA
<www.cambridge.org>

ISBN: 978-90-6704-241-3

Summary of Contents

Preface

*Ian R. Kenyon**

As I write this it is almost fourteen years since I sat, on 15 February 1993, at a borrowed desk in the offices of the OPCW Foundation, on Noordwal in The Hague, wondering how one set about establishing the Technical Secretariat of a new international organisation, the Organisation for the Prohibition of Chemical Weapons (OPCW). The job had a particular urgency, not just because the Chemical Weapons Convention (CWC) could enter into force any time after 12 January 1995, less than two years away but, more particularly, because the Preparatory Commission, at its first meeting the previous week, had decided to start its substantive work with an expert group meeting, leaving only two weeks for me to find a conference room and to set up rudimentary conference servicing facilities. That we were able to solve this problem and the many, much larger ones that followed was due to teamwork from the group who came from all over the world to join the Provisional Technical Secretariat (PTS) (we ultimately counted 65 different nationalities) and to unstinting support from the members of national delegations on the Commission and its working bodies and from the Netherlands Government and the City of The Hague, acting through the OPCW Foundation.

How did I come to be there? For the previous four years I had been Deputy Leader of the United Kingdom Disarmament delegation in Geneva while the Conference on Disarmament was concluding its work on the CWC. My posting was at an end when I was asked if I was prepared to be the UK Government's candidate to head the secretariat of the preparatory commission which would be required to set up OPCW. I accepted and made my preparations to move to The Hague if I were to be successful in gaining the appointment.

From 13-15 January 1993 the Representatives (mostly the Foreign Ministers) of 130 states met in the UNESCO building in Paris, at the invitation of the French Government, to sign the 1993 Treaty of Paris, better known as the Chemical Weapons Convention (CWC). At this stage, by signing the text and depositing the signed copy with the United Nations Secretary-General – 'the Depositary' – they individually indicated their acceptance of the content of the Convention and their intention to become parties to it through their national constitutional processes. At the same time they collectively, through the adoption of a resolution to set up a Preparatory Commission, started the process of creation of the organisation which was to operate the CWC from its entry into force '180 days after the date of the deposit of the 65th instrument of ratification, but in no case earlier than two years after its opening for signature'.[1] Four weeks later, from

* Executive Secretary to the Preparatory Commission for the Organisation for the Prohibition of Chemical Weapons, February 1993 to May 1997.

[1] CWC Article XXI, para. 1.

8 to 12 February 1993, the PrepCom (as it became familiarly known) held its first meeting in The Hague and did indeed appoint me as Executive Secretary and 'head and chief executive officer' of the PTS.

In the end, the deposit of the required 65 ratifications took longer than the specified two years and it was a little over four years later, 29 April 1997, before the CWC entered into force. The representatives of 80 out of the then 87 States Parties met in The Hague, on 6 May 1997, for the opening of the First Conference of the States Parties of the Organisation for the Prohibition of Chemical Weapons, organised and serviced by its own Technical Secretariat. It is a source of great pride to me and to all the team that OPCW was able to 'hit the ground running' and to meet all the (very) tight deadlines set out in the CWC for receipt of declarations and for initial inspections with all the necessary infrastructure in place. I am well aware that the Preparatory Commission was unable to complete all the tasks laid upon it in the Paris Resolution and that OPCW has had to find its own solutions to some of these over its first ten years of existence but at least we provided a more than adequate launching pad.

How was this done? How were the staff recruited? Who decided how they should be trained? How was the content of the inspection equipment store decided or the layout of the laboratory planned? What did the preparations cost and who paid? What was involved in building a large new office block on a prime site and why was this not the site originally offered by the city? What were the respective roles of the Provisional Technical Secretariat and the government representatives in the Working Groups and Expert Groups? How effective were their joint efforts to solve the many issues left open by the CWC's negotiators in the Conference on Disarmament in Geneva? How much was left unfinished and what effect did this have on the first years of operation of OPCW? What lessons can be learned?

Once enough time had passed to provide a certain perspective, but while most of us were still around to remember what happened, it seemed a good time to try to capture the history and to start to analyse the lessons. It was in late 2002 that the component of the Harvard Sussex Program on CBW Armament and Arms Limitation that is based at SPRU – Science and Technology Policy Research, University of Sussex in the United Kingdom offered to support a project for this purpose under the expert supervision of Professor Julian Perry Robinson, who has made a lifetime study of CBW arms control and disarmament. Daniel Feakes, who had recently returned to Sussex after three years at OPCW as HSP Researcher in The Hague, agreed to take on the job of principal researcher.

The Director-General of OPCW, Mr Rogelio Pfirter, assured us of his support and we were able to inform the OPCW community of the project through the pages of the OPCW house journal *Chemical Disarmament*. We were provided with modest grants from the Governments of the Netherlands and the United Kingdom which made it possible for us to carry out research in the archives of OPCW and the Netherlands Foreign Ministry and to carry out preliminary interviews in Brussels and The Hague. We are particularly grateful for the assistance in this phase of the project of Harmen van Dijk, Jan Hoekema and Arend Meerburg of the Foreign Ministry; Gerko Hamming and John Heydanus, formerly of the OPCW Foundation; Bob Lagerwaard of the City of The Hague; and Rio Praaning of PA Europe NV. In February 2004 we held two witness seminars in The Hague. The first, held in the OPCW building, brought together a number of former members of the PTS and delegations and produced several hours of tape-recorded discussion of the work of that body. The second was held in the Ministry of Foreign Affairs and brought together officials of the ministry and of the City of The Hague to provide background on the campaign for The Hague to be the seat of OPCW.

The Japan Institute of International Affairs provided a grant to cover the production of a paper on *The OPCW Preparatory Commission: Preparing to Implement the CWC Industry Verification Regime* (which also provided much of the material for Chapter 9).

In early 2006 the Netherlands Ministry of Foreign Affairs offered to sponsor the production of a book encapsulating the history of the creation of OPCW as a contribution to the celebration of the tenth anniversary of entry into force of the CWC in April/May 2007; Maarten Lak and Wouter Wormgoor were helpful in this regard. The Ministry kindly provided an additional grant, part of which would be used for the purchase of a number of the books. TMC Asser Press agreed to publish the book. The actual writing was performed by a small team of those who had been most closely involved in the work of the PTS with others providing comments on the drafts at various stages.

I wish to offer my grateful thanks to all those who have given so generously of their time and writing skills: Daniel Feakes; Sergei Kisselev; Ron Manley; Hassan Mashhadi; Johan Rautenbach; Paul Ryan; Lisa Tabassi; and Ralf Trapp. We all checked, and commented upon, and provided text for each others' drafts. The text was reviewed by a group including: Sergey Batsanov; Don Clagett; Richard Guthrie; John Makhubalo; Robert Mathews; and Julian Perry Robinson.

Particular thanks are also offered to the Governments of the Netherlands, Japan and the United Kingdom for their financial support in addition to that provided by HSP and to the Director-General of OPCW for the practical assistance provided by members of that organisation.

All views expressed in this book are the opinions of the authors and do not express the views of any organisation to which they may be, or have been, affiliated. Errors and omissions are the responsibility of the editors.

Table of Contents

List of Abbreviations/Acronyms

AAA	American Arbitration Association
ABAF	Advisory Board for Administrative and Financial Matters
ACAT	Assistance Coordination and Assessment Team
ACC	American Chemistry Council (formerly CMA)
ACDA	United States Arms Control and Disarmament Agency
ACW	Abandoned chemical weapons
ASP	Abandoning State Party
BDA	Bilateral Destruction Agreement (Formal title: Agreement between the United States Of America and the Union Of Soviet Socialist Republics On Destruction and Non Production of Chemical Weapons and on Measures too Facilitate the Multilateral Convention on Banning Chemical Weapons)
Bid	Annex 3 to the Paris Resolution, incorporating the formal offer of the Kingdom of the Netherlands to host the OPCW
BSG	Building Steering Group
BWC	Biological & Toxin Weapons Convention
CBW	Chemical and Biological Warfare/Weapons
CC	Confidentiality Commission
CCD	Conference of the Committee on Disarmament
CCPA	Canadian Chemical Producers Association
CD	Conference on Disarmament (earlier Committee on Disarmament)
CEFIC	European Chemical Manufacturers Association
CIA	UK Chemical Industry Association
CMA	Chemical Manufacturers' Association (now ACC)
CRHC	Committee on Relations with the Host Country
CSP	Conference of the States Parties to the CWC
CTBTO	Comprehensive Nuclear-Test-Ban Treaty Organisation
CW	Chemical Warfare/Weapons
CWC	Convention on the Prohibition of the Development, Production, Stockpiling and Use of Chemical Weapons and on their Destruction
CWDF	Chemical Weapon Destruction Facilities
CWPF	Chemical Weapon Production Facilities
CWSF	Chemical weapon storage facilities
DG	Director-General of the TS
DOC	Discrete organic chemical

EC	Executive Council of the OPCW
EE	Eastern European regional group
EIF	Entry into force of the CWC
ENDC	Conference of the Eighteen Nation Committee on Disarmament
ES	Executive Secretary of the PTS
EU	European Union
FA	Facility Agreement
FRC	First Review Conference
FSCSP	First Session of the CSP
FTIR	Fourier Transform Infra Red
G-21	Group on non-aligned members of the CD
GC/MS	Gas chromatograph/Mass spectrometer
GICCW	Government-Industry Conference against Chemical Weapons
GPS	Global positioning system
GTS	General training scheme for inspectors
HSP	Harvard Sussex Program
IAEA	International Atomic Energy Agency
IATA	International Air Transport Association
IAU	Investigation of alleged use
ICA	International cooperation and assistance
ICAO	International Civil Aviation Organisation
ICTY	International Criminal Tribunal for former Yugoslavia
ILO	International Labour Organisation
ILOAT	International Labour Organisation Administrative Tribunal
ISO	International Organisation for Standardisation
JCIA	Japan Chemical Industry Association
KMW	Kallmann, McKinnell and Wood
LAC	Latin American and Caribbean regional Group
LOU	Letter of Understanding
MCA	US Manufacturing Chemists Association
NAM	Neutral and Non-aligned Group of Countries
NATO	North Atlantic Treaty Organisation
NDE	Non-destructive evaluation
NGO	Non-Governmental Organisation
NIST	US National Institute of Standards and Technology
NLG	Netherlands Guilders
NPT	Nuclear Non-proliferation Treaty
NSG	Nuclear Suppliers Group

OACW	Old and Abandoned Chemical Weapons
OCHA	UN Office for the Coordination of Humanitarian Affairs
OCPFs	Other chemical production facilities
OCW	Old chemical weapons
OPCW	Organisation for the Prohibition of Chemical Weapons
Paris Resolution	Resolution Establishing the Preparatory Commission for the Organisation for the Prohibition of Chemical Weapons
POE	Point of Entry/Exit
POR	Programme of Requirements
PrepCom (or PC)	Preparatory Commission for the Organisation for the Prohibition of Chemical Weapons
PSF	Phosphorus, Sulphur & Fluorine containing organic chemical
PTS	Provisional Technical Secretariat
QA/QC	Quality assurance/Quality control
SAB	Scientific Advisory Board
SIPRI	Stockholm International Peace Research Institute
SOP	Standard operating procedure
STF	Specialist Task Force
TNO/PML	Prins Maurits Laboratory of the Netherlands Organisation for Scientific Research
TS	Technical Secretariat
TSP	Territorial State Party
TVA	Transitional verification arrangement
UN	United Nations
UNESCO	United Nations Educational, Scientific and Cultural Organization
UNGA	United Nations General Assembly
UNJSPF	United Nations Joint Staff Pension Fund
UNSC	United Nations Security Council
UNSCOM	United Nations Special Commission on Iraq
VA	Verification Annex to the CWC
VERIFIN	Finnish Institute for Verification of the Chemical Weapons Convention
VIS	Verification information system
WEOG	Western European and Others regional Group
WGA	Working Group A
WGB	Working Group B
WHO	World Health Organisation
WWI	World War I
WWII	World War II
Wyoming MOU	Memorandum of Understanding between the Government of the Union of Soviet Socialist Republics and the Government of the United States of America Regarding a Bilateral Verification Experiment and Data Exchange Related to Prohibition of Chemical Weapons

Chapter 1

WHY WE NEED A CHEMICAL WEAPONS CONVENTION AND AN OPCW?

Ian R. Kenyon

1. INTRODUCTION

The Twentieth Century saw the development of progressively more deadly and sophisticated chemical weapons. It has seen their use, with significant effect in a World War, in regional conflict and by terrorists. Several attempts have been made to regulate their use through international legal instruments. The most recent of these, the Convention on the Prohibition of the Development, Production, Stockpiling and Use of Chemical Weapons and on their Destruction (hereafter the Chemical Weapons Convention or CWC), which was opened for signature at Paris in January 1993 and entered into force in April 1997, gives cause for confidence that this particular scourge can be controlled but the task is not complete.

This chapter attempts to give a reasonably complete overview of the subject of chemical weapons without entering into detail of only specialist interest. After a brief description of the weapons themselves and their modes of action it examines military and political developments divided into two periods: from the beginning of the century up to the end of the Second World War and from 1946 to the end of the twentieth century, including completion of negotiation of the CWC in 1992. It then describes the scope of the prohibitions established by the Convention and some of the means provided to deal with any future problems.

The following sections of the book review in detail the negotiation in Geneva and subsequent elaboration by the Preparatory Commission of the disarmament, verification and assistance provisions of the CWC, which provide the main work of the Organisation for the Prohibition of Chemical Weapons (OPCW) together with a description of the creation of the necessary infrastructure, both in The Hague and in the Member States.[2]

The latter part of the book describes the first ten years of operation of OPCW and goes on to draw lessons for the creation of similar treaty based regimes in the future.

[2] In this volume the term 'Member States' is used to indicate States that had signed the CWC before 29 April 1997 and thus members of the Preparatory Commission. 'States Parties' refers to States that have ratified or acceded to the Convention and only applies following the Convention's entry into force on that date.

I.R. Kenyon and D. Feakes, The Creation of the OPCW

The authors hope that the reader will be lead to the conclusion that in the case of the prohibition of chemical weapons a great deal has been achieved but that some important loose ends are yet to be tied if mankind is truly to be protected from this particular, ugly weapon system.

2. The Nature of Chemical Weapons[3]

The Chemical Weapons Convention defines a chemical weapon as 'any chemical which through its chemical action on life processes can cause death, temporary incapacitation or permanent harm to humans or animals'.[4] The weapons which have been used on the battlefield or included in major military stockpiles since the beginning of the twentieth century include harassing agents – lachrymators (tear gases), and sternutators (causing sneezing); and casualty agents – lung irritants, blood agents, vesicants (blister agents), nerve agents and psychochemicals. Harassing agents are intended to reduce the effectiveness of the enemy by forcing them to put on masks or to oblige unprotected troops to evacuate closed spaces such as bunkers. The effects typically wear off in a short time after exposure to the agent ceases but high dosages can cause death or longer term injury.[5] Casualty agents are intended to kill or produce longer term incapacitation. Of those affected around 10 percent die within the short-term, from a matter of minutes for lethal doses of nerve agent to days for phosgene or mustard gas. Many casualties, whilst making an adequate recovery in the military sense, are left with serious long-term problems such as chronic bronchitis or increased susceptibility to cancer.

Lachrymators

A wide range of chemical substances were used as lachrymators in the First World War of which the largest use was made of *bromoacetone.* Towards the end of the conflict more potent agents were discovered: *α-bromobenzyl cyanide* (CA) and *ω-chloroacetophenone* (CN). In the second half of the century the lachrymator of choice for both military use and for domestic riot control has been *2-chlorobenzalmalononitrile* (CS).

Sternutators

A group of arsenical substances of great irritancy were introduced in 1917. These are solid at ambient temperatures and, like CN and CS, need to be dispersed as aerosols to

---

[3] For a fuller treatment of the nature of chemical warfare agents and their medical aspects the reader is referred to: World Health Organisation, *Public Health Response to Biological and Chemical Weapons – WHO Guidance* (Geneva, World Health Organisation 2004). The report is available from the WHO website: <www.who.int>.

[4] Herbicides are not specifically covered but the Preamble to the CWC recognises 'the prohibition embodied ... in international law, of the use of herbicides as a method of warfare'.

[5] Some agents used in the First World War as harassing agents had a significant lethality and the distinction from casualty agents was more blurred than it has been in more modern doctrine.

have full effect. These included *diphenylchloroarsine* (DA) and *10-chloro-5,10-dihydrophenarsazine* (DM or Adamsite)

Lung irritants
The first casualty agent used on a large scale was *chlorine,* dispersed in clouds from cylinders. This acts by destroying the lining of the lungs and causes death by asphyxiation. *Phosgene* was then found to be more effective and, in the form of *diphosgene,* could be delivered effectively by artillery.

Blood agents
These act by blocking the ability of the blood to carry oxygen. The principal substance used in this way in 1916 was *hydrogen cyanide.* On the battlefield its toxicity is offset by its low vapour density which made it difficult to achieve lethal dosages at the point of action.[6]

Vesicants
1917 saw the first use of *bis-(2-chloroethyl) sulphide* (mustard gas or Yperite). This has three important areas of action on the human body: the skin, where it causes large and painful blisters which are slow to heal; the eyes, where it causes severe conjunctivitis, leading to temporary blindness; and the lungs, where it causes severe damage to the lining, frequently fatal or leading to long-term ill-effects. Similar effects are available from the arsenical vesicant *2-chlorovinyldichloroarsine* (Lewisite). Mustard gas and its variants have remained an important component of chemical arsenals up to the present day.

Nerve agents[7]
Research in Germany in the late 1930s into insecticides led to the discovery of a class of highly toxic chemicals which block the action of the enzyme *acetylcholine esterase*, essential to the transmission of signals through the nerves. These agents can enter the body either through inhalation (vapour or aerosol) or through the skin (liquid droplets). Agents include *ethyl NN-dimethylphosphoramidocyanidate* (Tabun), *O-isopropyl methylphosphonofluoridate* (Sarin), *O-pinacolyl methylphosphonofluoridate* (Soman) and the even more toxic *O-ethyl S-2-diisopropylaminoethyl methylphosphonothiolate* (VX).

Psychochemicals
Another concept which has been explored is chemicals designed to produce temporary incapacitation through action on the central nervous system. *3-Quinuclidinyl benzilate* (BZ) has been weaponised and stockpiled but there is no conclusive evidence of its use on the battlefield.

---

6 This problem was overcome in the 1960s.

7 For a comprehensive treatment of the development of the nerve agents see Jonathan B Tucker, *War of Nerves: Chemical Warfare from World War I to Al-Qaeda* (New York, Pantheon Books 2006).

Toxins **and** ***bioregulators***[8]
Toxins are chemicals produced by biological processes (but capable of being produced by chemical synthesis) which have a very high toxicity. Of those which have been considered as weapons *ricin* occurs in castor beans, *saxitoxin* in algae (sometimes resulting in lethal contamination of shellfish) and *botulinum toxin* is produced by bacteria. Bioregulators are substances used naturally by the body to turn necessary bodily functions on and off.

Binary weapons
Until the 1980s chemical warfare agents were made in chemical factories, stored in bulk containers (ranging in capacity from one ton to many) or as filled munitions, and transported to the battlefield as munitions. This resulted in the storage and transport of highly toxic substances, prone to leak out of their containers and very difficult and expensive to destroy safely if not required for use in war.[9] These problems are partly overcome in the binary concept, where two somewhat less toxic materials are transported in separate containers which are inserted in the munitions at an appropriate stage and mixed within the warhead on its way to the target.[10]

3. History until 1945

Specialists in the subject cite examples back two millennia and more of the fumes of burning sulphur and noxious smokes being used in warfare. However it was the rise of the modern chemical industry at the end of the nineteenth century which first made feasible the use of significant quantities of toxic chemicals on large scale battlefields. The end of the century also saw an attempt to keep the genie in the bottle when the 1899 Hague Peace Conference adopted its Declaration (IV,2) which banned 'the use of projectiles the sole object of which is the diffusion of asphyxiating or deleterious gases'.[11]

The use of chlorine gas released from cylinders in the Ypres salient in April 1915 was not technically a breach of this legal instrument as projectiles were not involved but all the combatants in the 1914-18 conflict soon realised the advantages of projectors,[12] mortars and artillery for the delivery of chemical agents to the target and seem to have set aside any legal scruples. Over a million casualties, up to 100,000 of them fatal, are estimated to have been caused by chemicals during the conflict, a large part following the introduction of mustard gas in 1917.

[8] Development of weapons relying on toxins, however produced, would be a breach of both the Biological Weapons Convention and the Chemical Weapons Convention.

[9] The difficulty and expense of destruction have increased dramatically in recent years with the rise in environmental protection standards.

[10] Iraq devised a simpler but much more hazardous procedure in which the two precursors were to be separately poured into Scud missile warheads by the artillerymen immediately before launch.

[11] Adam Roberts and Richard Guelff (eds.), *Documents on the Laws of War* (Oxford, Clarendon Press 1982), pp. 36-37.

[12] A primitive mortar, capable of throwing a container of 15kg of agent a distance of 1500m, used in groups of several hundred fired simultaneously by electricity.

After an unsuccessful attempt in Washington in 1921 to ban both chemical weapons and submarines, the League of Nations took up the matter of the control of chemical (and biological) weapons. The result was the Protocol for the Prohibition of the Use in War of Asphyxiating, Poisonous or Other Gases, and of Bacteriological Methods of Warfare (1925 Geneva Protocol) – which opened for signature on 17 June 1925 and entered into force on 8 February 1928. Unfortunately, many of the major powers entered reservations under which they retained the right to use chemical weapons against an adversary who initiated their use or against non-parties to the Protocol.[13] Whilst China, France, the United Kingdom and the USSR all became parties in the 1920s, Japan did not sign the protocol until 1970 and the United States Administration was unable to obtain consent from the Senate to ratification until 1975.

Following the acceptance of the Protocol there were reports of the use of chemical weapons – including in Morocco (1923-26), Tripolitania (1930), Singkiang (1934), Abyssinia (1935-40) and Manchuria (1937-42).[14] Apart from the Sino-Japanese conflict the Second World War did not see other than minor (and probably unauthorized) use of chemical warfare by any of the belligerents, despite the production and deployment of very large stockpiles of different agents, most of which were either buried or dumped at sea when the war ended. The reasons for this lack of use appear to have been primarily fear of retaliation in kind, particularly against inadequately protected civilian populations. Both Roosevelt and Hitler are known to have been personally averse to first use.[15]

4. History from 1946 to CWC Entry into Force

Despite the aforementioned experience and also despite their primary reliance on nuclear weapons to deter each other from the initiation of armed conflict, during the Cold War both the USSR and the United States built up large stockpiles of chemical weapons,[16] both nerve agents and vesicants. At the end of the Cold War period they retained stocks amounting to 40,000 and 29,000 agent tonnes[17] respectively, according to official public statements made during later stages of the CWC negotiations.

---

[13] Many of these reservations were withdrawn at the time of negotiation of the CWC.

[14] World Health Organisation, *Public Health Response to Biological and Chemical Weapons – WHO Guidance* (Geneva, WHO 2004), p. 13.

[15] It is probably also the case that the chemical weapons available did not fit well in a military doctrine based on rapid movement and use of armour and would have taken up space in transport which the military preferred to use for high explosive. The use of the atom bomb closed the war with Japan before the question of use of the large US stockpiles of CW became an issue.

[16] The United Kingdom stockpile is reported to have reached 60,000 agent tons by the end of the Second World War but was disposed of in the 1960s and 70s. This was two thirds mustard gas with the balance largely phosgene, tear gas and 7,000 tons of German tabun, which was held for a decade in the UK but then dumped in the North Atlantic. Domestic nerve gas production never went beyond the pilot plant stage in the UK and even the pilot plant had been destroyed by the time CWC negotiations started in the 1980s.

[17] 'Agent tons' refer to the weight of chemical only, neglecting the weight of the shell or other means of delivery.

The armed forces of NATO and the Warsaw Pact each maintained a high state of training and physical preparedness for chemical defence but a lower level of civil defence, suggesting that chemicals were seen at that time as principally a battlefield weapon.

Meanwhile, outside the main East/West confrontation it has been claimed that up to twenty states were taking a serious interest in acquiring a chemical weapon capability. These included South Africa, much of the Middle East and North Africa, South Asia, China and the Koreas. Concern about this level of proliferation led to cooperation in export control of key precursor[18] chemicals among the industrialised countries through the Australia Group.[19]

The use of chemical weapons in conflict in the second half of the century was limited. There have been occasional reports of small-scale use in counter-insurgency and civil war situations, mostly poorly substantiated, for example in Yemen during 1963-67.[20] The United States has been accused of using chemicals in the Vietnam War but, aside from herbicides, which fall outside the CWC definition, it seems clear that their use was limited to harassing agents, almost entirely CS. Chemical weapons, both nerve agents and mustard, were used to significant effect in the Iran/Iraq War from 1983 to the cease-fire in 1988. Iraqi success in using these weapons was in part due to the inability of Iran to supply more than a small proportion of its front line troops with modern protective equipment.

After making claims that Kurds in northern Iraq were assisting Iran during the war, Iraq also used lethal chemical agents against a number of its Kurdish villages. Pictures published in the world's media of the massacre at Halabja in 1988 played an important role in building public support for an effective chemical weapons ban.

Following the 1991 Gulf War the UN Special Commission (UNSCOM), established to eliminate Iraq's programmes for the production of weapons of mass destruction, located and destroyed 690 agent tonnes of chemical warfare agents, including the nerve agent Sarin and mustard gas, together with over 3,000 tonnes of essential raw materials.

The potential use of chemical weapons by terrorists, which had long been feared, became manifest in June 1994 when seven people died and more than 200 were injured in Matsumoto, Japan as a result of a release of the nerve agent Sarin. This received little publicity outside Japan at the time but the world took notice when the group responsible, a religious cult called Aum Shinrikyo, went on to release Sarin on the Tokyo subway system on 20 March 1995, resulting in twelve deaths, 122 serious injuries and 4,695 attending hospital for gas exposure.[21]

---

[18] Precursors are chemicals from which chemical weapon agents can be synthesised.

[19] So called because its first meeting took place in the Australian Embassy in Brussels.

[20] World Health Organisation, *Public Health Response to Biological and Chemical Weapons – WHO Guidance* (Geneva, WHO 2004), p. 13.

[21] As the CWC makes no distinction between chemical weapons production facilities owned by governments or in private hands, once the Convention entered into force, the Japanese government declared the existence of the Aum production facility and OPCW inspectors confirmed its destruction.

5. Disarmament Negotiations

In 1954 when the Federal Republic of Germany adhered to the 1948 Brussels Treaty which had created the Western European Union it accepted, through Protocol III, a ban on the production of 'atomic, biological and chemical weapons' and 'agree[d] to supervision by the competent authority of the Brussels Treaty Organisation to ensure that these undertakings are observed'. The Austrian Treaty of 1955 contains similar prohibitions but without the verification clause.

Disarmament discussions in the first twenty years after the formation of the United Nations were concentrated on nuclear weapons and proposals for 'general and complete disarmament', the latter subsuming issues related to chemical and biological weapons. The late 1960s saw an increase in concern regarding chemical and biological weapons, partly as a response to the use of herbicides and tear gas by the United States in Vietnam. The matter was raised at the UN General Assembly in 1966 and accepted as an agenda item by the disarmament conference in Geneva (at that date the ENDC[22]) in 1968. In 1969 the UN Secretary-General issued a Report on *Chemical and Bacteriological (Biological) Weapons and the Effects of Their Possible Use* which was followed in 1970 by the WHO Report *Health Aspects of Chemical and Biological Weapons*.[23]

In 1968 the United Kingdom proposed that the issues of chemical and biological weapons be treated separately and offered a draft Biological Weapons Convention (BWC) in 1969. After some initial reluctance, this approach was adopted, the CCD[24] (successor to ENDC) completed the work and the BWC was opened for signature in April 1972, entering into force in March 1975. Two factors were important in this process: the announcement by the United States in 1969 of its renunciation of biological weapons[25] and the destruction of its stockpile; and the belief, held at that time but since discarded, that a biological weapons ban would be satisfactory without elaborate provisions for verification. The BWC is designed to complement the Geneva Protocol in that the prohibition of *use* is left to the Protocol while the BWC requires each Party

> never in any circumstances to develop, produce, stockpile or otherwise acquire or retain:
>
> (1) Microbial or other biological agents, or toxins whatever their origin or method of production, of types and in quantities that have no justification for prophylactic, protective or other peaceful purposes;
> (2) Weapons, equipment or means of delivery designed to use such agents or toxins for hostile purposes or in armed conflict.

---

22 Conference of the Eighteen Nation Committee on Disarmament.

23 See also the second edition: *Public health response to biological and chemical weapons – WHO Guidance* (Geneva, WHO 2004).

24 Conference of the Committee on Disarmament.

25 Extended in 1970 to include toxin weapons.

This was to provide an important starting point for discussion of scope of a CWC. The inclusion of toxins, 'whatever their origin', brings a whole class of chemicals under the provisions of the BWC. As these chemicals were also to fall within the scope of the eventual CWC they provide an area of overlapping coverage of the two conventions.

As a concession to those who were concerned about the separation of CWC and BWC the latter contains Article IX which obliges the Parties to

> continue negotiations [on chemical weapons] in good faith with a view to reaching early agreement on effective measures for the prohibition of their development, production and stockpiling and for their destruction, and on appropriate measures concerning equipment and means of delivery specially designed for the production or use of chemical agents for weapons purposes.

It was to be another twenty years before this ambition was to be realised.

Although the CCD never established a formal negotiating group to address the chemical weapons problem it received some 14 technical papers from delegations on this subject during the four years of the BWC negotiations and a further 60 working papers over the period 1972-78. These included a suggested work programme for the negotiations introduced in 1972 by the United States,[26] draft conventions from the USSR and its allies (1972 – simply adapting the BWC text to form a CWC),[27] from the Non-Aligned members (1973),[28] from Japan (1974 – proposing a step-wise approach on scope)[29] and from the United Kingdom (1976 – proposing declarations on signature and a strong verification system).[30] The main obstacle to progress at this period was the diametrically opposed views on the subject of intrusive, on-site verification systems; rejected totally by the Eastern Group and strongly demanded by the West with the Neutral and Non-Aligned Group proposing a declaration-based system. 'Verification was the single most contentious issue in the negotiations on the Chemical Weapons Convention (CWC). Disputes about on-site inspections dominated the negotiations on the CWC for the 24 years they took.'[31] The position of the USSR is summed up in this quotation from 1977:

---

[26] USA, 'Work program regarding negotiations on prohibition of chemical weapons', CCD/360, dated 20 March 1972.

[27] Bulgaria, Czechoslovakia, Hungary, Mongolia, Poland, Romania, USSR, 'Draft convention on the prohibition of the development, production and stockpiling of chemical weapons and on their destruction', CCD/361, dated 28 March 1972.

[28] Argentina, Brazil, Burma, Egypt, Ethiopia, Mexico, Morocco, Nigeria, Sweden and Yugoslavia, 'Working paper on the prohibition of the development, production and stockpiling of chemical weapons and on their destruction', CCD/400*, dated 26 April 1973.

[29] Japan, 'Draft convention on the prohibition of the development, production and stockpiling or chemical weapons and on their destruction', CCD/420, dated 30 April 1974.

[30] UK, 'Draft convention on the prohibition of the development, production and stockpiling of chemical weapons and on their destruction', CCD/512, dated 6 August 1976.

[31] See Jessica Stern, 'All's well that ends well? Verification and the CWC', in JB Poole and R Guthrie (eds.), *Verification 1993: Arms Control, Peacekeeping and the Environment* (London, VERTIC/Brassey's 1993), pp. 33-40 at p. 33.

> [On-site verification is] inevitably associated with the disclosure of military, industrial, and commercial secrets and consequently cannot be justified from the standpoint of assuring the security and economic interests of the states parties to a future agreement.[32]

However, many ideas put on the table at this stage were to play an important role later.

In July 1974 the United States and the USSR announced that they were entering into bilateral consultations with a view to a 'joint initiative' on chemical weapons.[33] The significance of this was that most of the finished legal instruments produced by the Geneva negotiating fora to that date had been produced on the basis of US/USSR joint drafts. This series of bilaterals ended in July 1980 without producing the promised initiative but were none the less important in that many of the key provisions of the eventual CWC were agreed between the two principal possessor states during this process – the use of declarations; precursor control; Consultative Committee plus Technical Secretariat (which together led to the idea of a specialized international organisation – OPCW); 10-year destruction period; Single Small-Scale Facility (to produce small quantities of agents to test protective equipment); and verification by challenge using on-site inspection, albeit voluntary.[34]

Meanwhile the 1978 UN Special Session on Disarmament had overhauled the Geneva machinery for disarmament negotiations, expanding the membership[35] and improving the working methods. The CD,[36] as it was now known, established an Ad Hoc Working Group on Chemical Weapons in 1980, tasked to 'define, through substantive examination, issues to be dealt with in the negotiation' but not to negotiate.[37] This was upgraded to an Ad Hoc Committee in 1984 with a mandate to start the 'full and complete process of negotiations, developing and working out the convention, except for its final drafting, with a view to giving the Conference a possibility to achieve agreement as soon as possible'.[38]

In March 1984 the UN Secretary-General issued a Report confirming the use of lethal chemicals, both mustard gas and nerve agent, in the war between Iraq and Iran.[39] This re-emergence of lethal chemical weapons on a large scale on the battlefield pro-

---

32 USSR, 'Some methods of monitoring compliance with an agreement on the prohibition of chemical weapons', CCD/538, dated 3 August 1977.

33 The consultations actually began only in August 1976.

34 Julian Perry Robinson, Thomas Stock and Ronald Sutherland, 'The Chemical Weapons Convention: The success of chemical disarmament negotiations', *SIPRI Yearbook 1993: World Armaments and Disarmament* (Oxford, Oxford University Press 1993), pp. 705-734 at p. 714.

35 Including China for the first time and persuading France to take its previously vacant seat.

36 Initially the 'Committee on Disarmament' but changed to the 'Conference on Disarmament' in 1984 without change to the abbreviation.

37 Committee on Disarmament, 'Decision adopted at the 69th plenary meeting held on 17 March 1980', CD/80, dated 17 March 1980.

38 'Decision on the the Re-establishment of an Ad Hoc Subsidiary Body on Chemical Weapons', CD/440, dated 28 February 1984. Changes in the organisation of negotiations are outlined in 'Report of the Ad Hoc Committee on Chemical Weapons to the Conference on Disarmament', CD/539, dated 28 August 1984.

39 United Nations, 'Report of the specialists appointed by the Secretary-General to investigate allegations by the Islamic Republic of Iran concerning the use of chemical weapons', S/16433, dated 26 March 1984.

duced a new sense of urgency in attempts to agree a ban. In April that year then Vice-president George HW Bush of the United States introduced a working paper containing the text of a draft CWC incorporating many of the elements which were to be present in the final text as adopted in 1992.[40] Important among these was the concept of short notice challenge inspections.[41]

Negotiations continued on the basis of a 'rolling text', first introduced at the end of the 1983 session, which contained three elements: 'clean text', which represented areas of agreement already achieved; alternative proposals, within square brackets, for text not yet agreed; and footnotes and appendices indicating concerns which had not been elaborated as treaty text language.

In January 1989, the French Government, Depositary of the Geneva Protocol, hosted a high-level meeting in Paris to reaffirm the Protocol and to provide political impetus to the work of the CD on the CWC. Representatives of 149 states adopted a strong Final Declaration calling for expeditious conclusion of the Convention and calling upon all states to become parties as soon as it was concluded.[42]

The negotiators in Geneva realised the importance of engaging the chemical industry in the process of elaborating the CWC, both to ensure political endorsement and to allow their particular concerns, especially regarding confidential business information, to be addressed. In addition to each delegation's own contacts with its national industry the CD arranged informal meetings with representatives of national and international chemical industry associations. This process reached a high point in September 1989 when the Australian Government hosted a Government-Industry Conference on Chemical Weapons in Canberra (see Chapter 9).

Also in September 1989 the US Secretary of State James Baker and the USSR Foreign Minister Eduard Shevardnadze, meeting at Jackson Hole, Wyoming, signed a Memorandum of Understanding regarding bilateral verification and data exchange. In phase I there would be an exchange of general data on their respective chemical weapons capabilities and a series of visits to relevant facilities. In phase II they would exchange detailed data and permit on-site inspections to verify the accuracy of the information exchanged. In June 1990 Presidents George HW Bush and Mikhail Gorbachev signed an 'Agreement ... on Destruction and Non-production of Chemical Weapons and on Measures to Facilitate the Multi-lateral Convention on Banning Chemical Weapons' under which they would cease production immediately after ratification of the agreement; reduce their CW stockpiles to 5,000 agent tonnes each by the end of 2002 (with on site inspection to confirm); further reduce their stocks to 500 agent tonnes by eight years after entry into force of the CWC; and call for a special conference at that time to determine whether the destruction process should continue to zero over the next two years.

The 1991 Gulf War found the Coalition forces facing an Iraqi army known to have stocks of chemical weapons and a recently demonstrated willingness to use them.

---

40 USA, 'Draft convention on the prohibition of chemical weapons', CD/500, dated 18 April 1984.

41 The US proposal which restricted challenge inspections to government owned or controlled facilities was eventually expanded to include all facilities.

42 The declaration is reproduced in UN General Assembly document A/44/88, dated 20 January 1989.

It also raised the threat of civilian populations in the region being exposed to danger from Scud missiles with chemical warheads. Although, in the event, chemical weapons were not used by Iraq, these events and the collapse of the USSR and the Warsaw Pact, gave a major boost to the negotiations in the CD during the 1991-92 period. With the USSR and its former allies now more willing to accept positions advanced by some Western Group members, especially on verification, the complexion of the negotiations changed to more of a North-South confrontation than an East-West one. This shift had been underway subtly since 1987-8 when members of the Non-Aligned Movement started to get more involved, but the lessening of East-West differences made it more pronounced. The chemical industry made its own contribution to accelerating progress in 1991 by offering 'open access' to all chemical production facilities as a confidence-building measure.[43] However, it was not until a year later that the resolution of disagreements within the Western Group allowed this concept to be incorporated into what became Part IX of the CWC's Verification Annex dealing with 'other chemical production facilities'. In 1991, President George HW Bush called for completion of the negotiations by May 1992.[44]

At the end of 1991, the draft convention was still far from finalized and some of the more contentious issues, among them the verification of the chemical industry, were still unresolved. Resolution of the remaining industry issues was tied to resolution of the politically charged negotiations on challenge inspection. Challenge inspections, first proposed by the United States in its 1984 draft convention, were mandatory, anywhere, anytime short-notice inspections designed as the ultimate deterrent to violations of the CWC. Despite having introduced the concept, the US modified its position on challenge inspections and the proposal was gradually watered down, in the opinion of some of the US's Western Group partners.[45] As the potential deterrent value of challenge inspections was weakened, so a chemical industry verification regime going beyond facilities using scheduled chemicals became necessary. A broader verification regime also meant that more countries would be subject to inspections thus globalizing the regime rather than limiting it to a few technologically advanced countries.

On 21 January 1992, the CD appointed German Ambassador Adolf Ritter von Wagner as Chairman of its Ad Hoc Committee on Chemical Weapons. When he responded to his election, and mirroring the expectations and aspiration of all delegations as well as the tasking by the UN General Assembly which had urged the CD to

---

43 CEFIC and CMA, 'CEFIC and CMA positions on chemical weapons convention issues affecting the chemical industry', June 1991.

44 On 13 May 1991 President Bush stated in a speech that the US 'will call for setting a target date to conclude the Convention'. A Fact Sheet issued by the White House to accompany this speech, specifies the US 'target date' as 'resolution of all major outstanding issues' by the end of the year and 'completion of the CWC within twelve (12) months', i.e., May 1992. Both the speech and the factsheet are reproduced in Conference on Disarmament document CD/1077, dated 23 May 1991.

45 The differences among the Western Group on challenge inspections were finally resolved at a meeting in Rome in May 1992. See Jessica Stern, 'All's well that ends well? Verification and the CWC', in JB Poole and R Guthrie (eds.), *Verification 1993: Arms Control, Peacekeeping and the Environment* (London, VERTIC/Brassey's 1993), pp. 33-40 at p. 35; and Hassan Mashhadi, 'How the negotiations ended', *Chemical Weapons Convention Bulletin*, No. 17 (September 1992), pp. 1 and 28-30 at p. 1.

complete CWC negotiations in 1992, von Wagner stated 'You have my firm commitment that I will do everything to bring our common endeavour to a successful conclusion'.[46] But how he would steer the negotiations from a Rolling Text cluttered with square brackets and footnotes to a clean and agreed text was far from obvious.

During 1991 and early 1992 Australia had been working on a possible CWC text in an attempt to demonstrate that it was possible to resolve all issues still open in the Rolling Text and create a clean treaty text. Australia had worked in private with key capitals to develop its text. On submitting this text to the CD on 19 March, Foreign Minister Evans clarified that 80 percent was simply a cleaned-up, stream-lined, treaty-style version of what the CD had already agreed *ad referendum*. The remaining 20 percent he characterised as a 'model for the sort of compromises that remain to be made ... based on known positions'.[47]

Although Evans made it clear that his text was not a final package, a 'take-it-or-leave-it' offer, many of the developing countries in the CD feared that that was precisely what it might turn into. And some Western delegations may well have had the expectation that von Wagner would simply adopt the Australian draft as his own.[48]

But von Wagner had made it plain that the Australian draft would not replace or supersede the Rolling Text, nor would it prejudice the results of coming negotiations – it would be used to accelerate and refine the negotiations, nothing more. During the intersessional break in the spring of 1992, von Wagner's delegation consulted extensively with key delegations and prepared a Chairman's draft of some 80 percent of the CWC text that was considered non-controversial.[49] He used many of the suggestions, including structural changers, from the Australia draft, but the text was otherwise based on the Rolling Text. As for the remaining 20 percent of the treaty text, vision papers of the different friends of the chair who were negotiating specific issues were incorporated.

Within a week or so, a group of developing countries (initially 11, later to become 14) tabled a paper that identified a number of issues that they considered needed further negotiation in the submitted Chairman's text. In doing so, they effectively sanctioned the rest of the Chairman's text. Even more so, by delineating their concerns, they gave the Chairman an opportunity to re-shuffle and intensify his negotiation machinery and adjust it as closely as possible to those remaining issues identified by the group of 14. The level of negotiations was raised to ambassadorial, and the friends-of-the-Chair mechanisms was changed to a new negotiation modus. On certain key issues, von Wagner assigned 'proponents' and 'opponents' to pursue issues together in private. On other issues, a broader, open-ended format with the assistance

[46] CD/PV.606, p. 20.

[47] CD/PV.617, p. 9. The Australian draft treaty text is reproduced in document CD/1143, dated 12 March 1992. For more detail on the Australian draft convention see Martine Letts, Robert Mathews, Tim McCormack and Chris Moraitis, 'The conclusion of the Chemical Weapons Convention: An Australian perspective', *Arms Control*, Vol. 14, No. 3 (December 1993), pp. 311-332.

[48] Compare, for example, the statements by Ambassadors Errera of France and Kamal of Pakistan in response to the submission of Australia's draft treaty text, CD/PV.617.

[49] Chairman of the Ad Hoc Committee on Chemical Weapons, 'Working paper for the final phase of the negotiations on the Chemical Weapons Convention', CD/CW/WP.400, dated 18 May 1992.

of a 'moderator' was used. Von Wagner himself kept the issue of challenge inspection under negotiation.

This intensified negotiation phase lasted for several weeks. Based on the results achieved (some agreements, others more like clarifications of options), and proposals by the Chairman in areas where there had been no agreement, von Wagner tabled on 22 June 1992 his revised draft CWC text – this time a complete and clean text.[50]

At this stage, von Wagner famously changed the way the consensus rule would be used by his Committee: any proposed change to his text would have to command consensus before he would accept it, otherwise his text would stand as it was. The fact that none of the negotiators challenged that twist of the rules illustrated two things: the current text did in fact command a high degree of support already, and delegations really wanted to finish the work (and had accepted that von Wagner's text was more or less what could be achieved). There were no clear-cut losers or winners; the text was, again paraphrasing von Wagner, an equal distribution of pain among all delegations.[51]

From here on, fairly little happened to the text itself, short of some final adjustments and editorial corrections, and the final text[52] differed little from its predecessor. The focus of the negotiations shifted towards issues that complemented the adoption of the text, and that needed to be addressed so as to ensure that the CD would eventually reach consensus to transfer the CWC draft to the UN General Assembly (for example, the question of how to deal with the differences regarding the Australia Group, or regional issues related to the future composition of the Executive Council). Most delegations said that they were prepared to accept the Chairman's final draft and, in the end, even those who felt their concerns had not been adequately addressed did not prevent the adoption of the draft by consensus.[53] They did however, insist that their views were incorporated into the report of the ad hoc committee to which the CWC text was appended.[54] Even among such delegations, there was an awareness that agreement was unlikely to be achieved any other way.[55] However, some of the issues raised by these delegations in the final days of negotiation were to return with a vengeance once the treaty had been opened for signature.

---

[50] Chairman of the Ad Hoc Committee on Chemical Weapons, 'Draft Convention on the Prohibition of the Development, Production, Stockpiling and Use of Chemical Weapons and on Their Destruction', CD/CW/WP.400/Rev.1*, dated 22 June 1992.

[51] The Ambassador describes his work in: Adolf von Wagner, 'Lessons learned', *OPCW Synthesis* (May 2000), pp. 10-11.

[52] Chairman of the Ad Hoc Committee on Chemical Weapons, 'Draft Convention on the Prohibition of the Development, Production, Stockpiling and Use of Chemical Weapons and on their Destruction', CD/CW/WP.400/Rev.2, dated 10 August 1992.

[53] Hassan Mashhadi, 'How the negotiations ended', *Chemical Weapons Convention Bulletin*, No. 17 (September 1992), pp. 1 and 28-30.

[54] 'Report of the Ad Hoc Committee on Chemical Weapons to the Conference on Disarmament', CD/1170, dated 26 August 1992.

[55] Hassan Mashhadi, 'How the negotiations ended', *Chemical Weapons Convention Bulletin*, No. 17 (September 1992), pp. 1 and 28-30.

So, 20 years of discussion and negotiation ended on 3 September 1992 when the CD itself adopted the ad hoc committee's report.[56] Writing soon after the conclusion of the negotiations, Will Carpenter, chairman of the Chemical Weapons Disarmament Work Group of the US Chemical Manufacturers Association,[57] said:

> The sustained commitment by the Western chemical industry has been a significant factor in moving the treaty negotiations forward and improving the understanding of the negotiators about the chemical industry as it relates to the treaty. Furthermore, the effective working relationship among the many government bodies, NGOs, and industry has led to progress that would probably have been impossible without such initiative on the part of the chemical industry.[58]

The draft treaty text was then transmitted to the United Nations. On 16 December 1992 the UN General Assembly adopted Resolution 47/39, by consensus, commending the Convention and calling upon all states to become parties at the earliest possible date.[59]

On 13 January 1993 the UN Secretary-General, Boutros Boutros-Ghali, the Depositary nominated in the Convention, opened the text of the Chemical Weapons Convention for signature at a three-day meeting in Paris. Plenipotentiaries of 130 states signed the Convention and adopted a Resolution establishing a Preparatory Commission to meet at The Hague, which would be the seat of the Organisation for the Prohibition of Chemical Weapons (OPCW) when the treaty entered into force. The treaty was to enter into force '180 days after the date of deposit of the 65th instrument of ratification, but in no case earlier than two years after its opening for signature',[60] as this two year period was considered to be the minimum required to permit the Preparatory Commission to complete its task.

On 31 October 1996 Hungary became the 65th state to deposit its instrument of ratification and the CWC entered into force on 29 April 1997. A total of 87 states had ratified the Convention by its entry into force. The United States became an original State Party with less than a week to spare, depositing its instrument of ratification on 25 April after a protracted battle by the Administration to win Senate approval.[61] Russia did not meet the deadline, only ratifying in November 1997.

---

56 'Report of the Conference on Disarmament to the General Assembly of the United Nations', CD/1173, dated 3 September 1992.

57 Today the American Chemistry Council.

58 Will Carpenter, 'The perspective of the Western chemical industry', in Benoit Morel and Kyle Olson (eds.), *Shadows and Substance: The Chemical Weapons Convention*, Ridgeway Series in International Security Studies (Boulder, Westview Press 1993), pp. 115-126 at p. 118.

59 While a few international agreements require only a signature from States, most require that the states also ratify the instrument through their own constitutional procedures. Ratification usually involves the consent of a legislative body so that the agreement is reflected in national law. Once a treaty has entered into force it is normally closed for signature, but a State may accede – effectively signing and ratifying at the same time.

60 CWC, Article XXI, para. 1.

61 Michael Krepon, Amy E. Smithson and John Parachini, 'The battle to obtain US CWC ratification', *Occasional Paper 35*, The Henry L. Stimson Center, July 1997.

By October 2006, ten years after the Hungarian deposit triggered entry into force, 179 states had ratified or acceded to the CWC and were thus members of OPCW; only eight of the original Signatories had yet to ratify,[62] and only eight states remained outside the treaty regime.[63]

6. The Chemical Weapons Convention

6.1 Overview

The Biological Weapons Convention consists of a Preamble and 14 articles, the whole requiring less than four pages of print in one of the standard works on arms control.[64] By contrast, the Chemical Weapons Convention's Preamble and 24 articles need 27 pages and the 3 annexes a further 76 pages in that version.[65] In the first two years after entry into force OPCW took decisions on interpretation and implementation which require 250 pages of print in the official compilation.[66] The Convention is thus in its detail one of the most complex international arms control agreements ever adopted. However its basic provisions are straightforward. States Parties undertake not to develop, produce, otherwise acquire, stockpile or retain chemical weapons; not to transfer them; not to use them; and to destroy any they possess, together with facilities for their production. They are required to declare chemical weapons and related facilities. They are also required to declare production of chemicals for 'non-prohibited purposes' in accordance with a list of chemicals annexed to the Convention and to establish import/export controls for them. They are to permit entry for OPCW inspectors to verify these declarations, to witness destruction of prohibited items and, in case of a challenge by another Party, to investigate possible non-compliance. The Convention requires each State Party to enact legislation for the implementation of the Convention, including making it a criminal offence for persons to carry out any activity which is prohibited to the state under the Convention. The Convention provides for the establishment of a new, independent international organisation, the OPCW, to provide verification and other services to the States Parties. There is also provision for assistance to States Parties attacked, or threatened with chemical weapons and to protect the right of all parties to use chemicals for peaceful purposes.[67]

---

62 Bahamas, Central African Republic, Comoros, Congo, Dominican Republic, Guinea-Bissau, Israel and Myanmar.

63 Angola, Barbados, Democratic Peoples Republic of Korea, Egypt, Iraq, Lebanon, Somalia and Syrian Arab Republic.

64 Jozef Goldblat, *Arms Control* (Oslo, PRIO 1994).

65 The full text of the CWC and related decisions can be found on the OPCW website <http://www.opcw.org>.

66 L.W. Tabassi (ed.), *OPCW: The Legal Texts* (The Hague, TMC Asser Press 1999).

67 The Convention uses the somewhat cumbersome expression 'purposes not prohibited under this Convention' in order to include defensive activities such as testing of protective equipment.

6.2 Scope

The full title of the CWC is the 'Convention on the Prohibition of the Development, Production, Stockpiling and Use of Chemical Weapons and on Their Destruction'. This purpose is spelled out in the 'General obligations', Article I:

> 1. Each State Party to this Convention undertakes never under any circumstances:
> (a) to develop, produce, otherwise acquire, stockpile or retain chemical weapons, or transfer, directly or indirectly, chemical weapons to anyone;
> (b) to use chemical weapons;
> (c) to engage in any military preparations to use chemical weapons;
> (d) to assist, encourage or induce in any way, anyone to engage in any activity prohibited to a State Party under this Convention.
> 2. Each State Party undertakes to destroy chemical weapons it owns or possesses, or that are located in any place under its jurisdiction or control, in accordance with the provisions of this Convention.
> 3. Each State Party undertakes to destroy all chemical weapons it abandoned on the territory of another State Party, in accordance with the provisions of this Convention.
> 4. Each State Party undertakes to destroy any chemical weapons production facilities it owns or possesses, or that are located in any place under its jurisdiction or control, in accordance with the provisions of this Convention.
> 5. Each State Party undertakes not to use riot control agents as a method of warfare.

At the heart of the scope of the Convention are the definitions contained in Article II, which embody what is commonly known as the 'general purpose criterion':[68]

> For the purposes of this Convention:
> 1. 'chemical weapons' means the following, together or separately:
> (a) toxic chemicals and their precursors, except where intended for purposes not prohibited under this Convention, as long as the types and quantities are consistent with such purposes;
> (b) munitions and devices, specifically designed to cause death or other harm through the toxic properties of those toxic chemicals specified in sub-paragraph (a) which would be released as a result of the employment of such munitions and devices;
> (c) any equipment specifically designed for use directly in connection with the employment of definitions and devices specified in sub-paragraph (b).
> 2. 'toxic chemical' means:
> any chemical which through its chemical action on life processes can cause death, temporary incapacitation or permanent harm to humans or animals. This includes all such chemicals, regardless of their origin or of their method of production, and regardless of whether they are produced in facilities, in munitions or elsewhere.

This definition allows the Convention to capture future discoveries and inventions as well as the chemical weapons used or produced in the past. However, for practical

---

[68] For more on the 'general purpose criterion' see UK, Department of Trade and Industry, *Annual Report 2004: Operation of the Chemical Weapons Act 1996*, section 8, 'The general purpose criterion', pp. 26-28.

purposes of verification it was necessary to specify particular chemicals as being of particular danger to the objectives of the Convention. This has been done by placing them in 'Schedules' in an Annex to the Convention. *Schedule 1* contains toxic chemicals which have been manufactured as chemical weapons or their key precursors (chemicals which can be used as a stage in their synthesis) and for which there are no known peaceful uses, (or which are so used only in very small quantities), for example the nerve agents, the mustard gases and lewisites. The list also includes two toxins, *saxitoxin* and *ricin*. *Schedule 2* contains chemicals which can be used as precursors but which also have relatively limited use for non- prohibited purposes, for example *thiodiglycol*, which is a precursor for mustard gas but is also widely used as a solvent in printing inks. *Schedule 3* contains chemicals which have been used as weapons, such as phosgene and hydrogen cyanide, and precursors, which are used in large quantities for civil chemical industry purposes. The *Annex on Chemicals* is an integral part of the Convention as formally ratified but a simplified procedure has been provided for its amendment to take account of new discoveries.

Unlike the BWC, which in this regard relies upon the Geneva Protocol, the CWC contains an explicit prohibition of *use* of chemical weapons. Although this prohibition was in the rolling text without brackets from an early stage of the negotiation, there was some concern among those states which had made reservations when ratifying the Geneva Protocol that they would be giving up the right to use chemical weapons in retaliation if these weapons were used against them, particularly by States which had not joined the CWC regime. Finally, however, this prohibition was included without qualification and the Convention contains in its Article XXII the stipulation that 'this Convention shall not be subject to reservations'.

Another area of controversy was whether to prohibit the use in war of herbicides and riot control agents. The United States was not prepared to join an herbicide ban for two reasons: firstly that it would provide ammunition to those who argue that the massive defoliation programme in the Vietnam War had been a breach of customary international law; and, secondly, that herbicides continued to be necessary to provide clear areas around defensive perimeters. The most which could be agreed regarding herbicides was a mention in the Preamble: 'Recognising the prohibition, embodied in the pertinent agreements and relevant principles of international law, of the use of herbicides as a method of warfare'.

Each State party undertakes to destroy all chemical weapons it owns or possesses in accordance with a fixed timetable, designed to ensure that the process is started promptly[69] and completed within 10 years[70] on entry into force of the Convention, regardless of the date the State joined (thus defeating any advantage to joining late). During the negotiation it was argued by some states, France in particular, that there would be a need to retain a 'security stock' at the end of the destruction period for retaliatory purposes if there were states possessing chemical weapons who had not ratified the Convention at that stage. The United States, which had been one of those supporting this position, changed its policy in May 1991, following the Gulf War, and

[69] Start of destruction within 2 years; destruction of 1 percent of the stockpile within 3 years.

[70] Extension of this deadline to 15 years is possible in certain circumstances.

this led to the successful conclusion of this aspect of the Convention on the basis of a requirement for total destruction.

A separate undertaking 'to destroy all chemical weapons [...] abandoned on the territory of another State Party' was necessary to achieve the agreement of China, which has on its territory large quantities of chemical weapons abandoned in 1945 by Japan.

The Convention does contain the provision that: 'Each State Party undertakes not to use riot control agents as a method of warfare'. The United States argued strongly that there are occasions when the use of riot control agents could be more humane than the only alternatives, which could involve lethal weapons, for example, in rescue operations for downed aircrew. The United States has since restated its policy on the military use of riot control agents in a way which is intended to be compatible with the Convention.

6.3 **Confidentiality**

One of the most important issues to be resolved in the drafting of a Convention which relies for its effective operation on an elaborate system of declarations and intrusive on-site inspections affecting both military installations and the civil chemical industry was that of the protection of confidential information. The basic requirements are set out in Article VIII, paragraph 5:

> The Organisation shall conduct its verification activities provided for under this Convention in the least intrusive manner possible consistent with the timely and efficient accomplishment of their objectives. It shall request only the information and data necessary to fulfil its responsibilities under this Convention. It shall take every precaution to protect the confidentiality of information on civil and military activities and facilities coming to its knowledge in the implementation of this Convention and, in particular, shall abide by the provisions set forth in the Confidentiality Annex.

The Confidentiality Annex provides an outline of a strict confidentiality regime which OPCW is required to convert into a detailed set of regulations covering its own conduct and to include in agreements with States Parties governing inspection activities on their territory. The Organisation assigns levels of confidentiality, in accordance with a classification system, to items of information received from Member States, either directly or as the result of inspection activity in that state, as requested by the state. These levels then influence who within the Organisation may have access and the degree of protection to be afforded both within the Organisation and by other Member States which receive the information. Member States are notified in advance which staff members of the Technical Secretariat are to receive clearance to handle their classified data. The CWC requires the establishment of a Commission to consider disputes related to confidentiality.

6.4 Sanctions

There was a wish on the part of some participants in the negotiations to include a mechanism to ensure compliance with the Convention through the automatic application of sanctions for any breach. However, when proposals were discussed many representatives were unable to commit their governments in advance to take specific action in situations whose full circumstances could not be known before the event. The Permanent Members of the Security Council in particular were unwilling to have any provision which might seem to usurp the rights and obligations of that body. The final text provides for the possibility in cases of non-compliance to 'restrict or suspend the State Party's rights and privileges under this Convention until it takes the necessary action to conform with its obligations under this Convention'.

The most important 'rights' which might be suspended are presumably those related to trade in scheduled chemicals. The CWC also allows:

> In cases where serious damage to the object and purpose of this Convention may result from activities prohibited under this Convention, in particular by Article I, the Conference may recommend collective measures to state parties in conformity with international law.[71]

The most likely outcome, however, is covered in the next paragraph by the requirement that:

> The Conference shall, in cases of particular gravity, bring the issue, including relevant information and conclusions, to the attention of the United Nations General Assembly and the United Nations Security Council.[72]

6.5 Other provisions

Detailed expositions of the content of the main provisions of the Convention relating to verification, technical assistance, the role and functioning of the OPCW, and the requirements for national implementation are given at the head of each relevant chapter of this book and are not therefore repeated here.

[71] CWC Article XII, para. 3.
[72] CWC Article XII, para. 4.

Chapter 2

How and Why OPCW Came to The Hague

Daniel Feakes & Ian R. Kenyon

1. Netherlands Interest in the Concept of an International CWC Organisation

The Netherlands interest in chemical disarmament stretches back into the 1970s and the very early days of discussions on a chemical weapons convention. For example, in July 1973, the Netherlands introduced into the Conference of the Committee on Disarmament a Working Paper which proposed a standing organ for a chemical weapons convention based upon a plenary conference, a board and a secretariat.[73] As the negotiations for a chemical weapons convention developed over the following 19 years, the Netherlands retained its interest in the concept of an international organisation.[74] The Netherlands was not the only country to be interested in these issues,[75] but it was the one with the longest running interest. The substantial amount of thinking that had gone on in The Hague set the Netherlands up very well to go on later and bid for the seat of the organisation. The members of the team in the Ministry of Foreign Affairs and in the delegation in Geneva had considerable experience of working with the International Atomic Energy Agency (IAEA) and its safeguards system. They brought this experience to bear on consideration of the organisation which would be needed to implement the verification procedures in a chemical weapons disarmament convention.

The delegation in Geneva provided the fruits of this thinking to the Conference on Disarmament in a paper in March 1984.[76] This paper noted that 'little attention ... has

[73] Netherlands, 'Working Paper on an International Organ for the Support of a CW Convention and Other Disarmament Agreements', CCD/410, dated 31 July 1973.

[74] For example, on 30 March 1978 the Netherlands introduced CCD/565, 'Study on the Establishment of an International Disarmament Agency' which called for the establishment of an International Disarmament Agency that 'would firstly be entrusted with the verification of a treaty banning chemical weapons'.

[75] See, for example, Canada, 'Organization and Control of Verification Within a Chemical Weapons Convention', CD/113, dated 9 July 1980; Canada, 'Proposed Verification Organization for a Chemical Weapons Convention', CD/313, 16 August 1982; and UK, 'Chemical Weapons Convention: The Organs and Constitution of the Organization', CD/589, dated 11 April 1985.

[76] Netherlands, 'Size and Structure of a Chemical Disarmament Inspectorate', CD/445, dated 7 March 1984.

been paid thus far to the structure and size of the inspectorate which will have to perform the different verification functions'. The paper went on to state:

> we deem it timely and useful to devote somewhat more attention to the kind of chemical disarmament inspectorate that would be required to verify effectively the compliance with a CW Convention. The Netherlands believes that by discussing the structure and size of such an organization a clearer picture may emerge of the organizational and financial implications of certain verification provisions.

The paper described an organisation similar to that first proposed in 1973 based upon a Consultative Committee, an Executive Council and a Technical Secretariat. The main types of on-site inspection that would be carried out were identified as: 'systematic continuous'; 'systematic non-continuous (regular and random)'; and 'ad hoc (challenge)'. The paper concluded that, for the first ten years of operations, this organisation would need a maximum of 165 inspectors.

The Netherlands was not only interested in the conceptual issues surrounding a standing CWC organisation. It was also a very active participant in the whole range of issues which arose during the 20-year negotiation of the Convention. In contrast to Austria and Switzerland which were later to become their rivals in the competition for the seat of the OPCW, the Netherlands was a full member of the Conference on Disarmament. As observers, Austria and Switzerland had speaking rights within the CD but were not part of the decision-making process, whereas the Netherlands delegation enjoyed full membership and was to become one of the most active delegations within the negotiations. This active role was to be presented in a positive light when it was necessary later to put The Hague's case to become the seat of the OPCW. Behind its diplomatic profile within the CD, the Netherlands also had the advantage of being home to one of the world's most highly regarded chemical weapons defence laboratories. The Prins Maurits Laboratory in Rijswijk (TNO/PML) had a good reputation among CW experts, had previously handled the destruction of old chemical weapons in Indonesia and had been involved in trial CW inspections. Its expertise in CW issues was internationally recognised and the fact that it was only 15 minutes from The Hague was to become another important selling point in the later bid for the seat. Other examples of the Netherlands' practical commitment to the negotiations included its involvement in the international inter-laboratory 'round robin' tests that began in the late 1980s and its hosting of the first national trial inspection to be conducted at a chemical industry facility in 1986. Personalities also played a key role with two Dutchmen in particular establishing themselves in Geneva as international experts on CW, namely Arend Meerburg and Jack Ooms. Dr Ooms was the only CD delegate who continuously participated over the full twenty-year course of the CWC negotiations.[77]

---

[77] A short biography of Dr Ooms appears on the OPCW website at <http://www.opcw.org/29april/page02.html>.

2. Origins of the Netherlands' Bid for the Seat of the OPCW

From this interest came the notion that it might be a good idea to base such an organisation in The Hague. Although the negotiations were not approaching their conclusion, by 1987/88 minds were beginning to turn to more practical matters such as the location of the organisation. In July 1987, the Belgian Foreign Minister Leo Tindemans had informed the CD that Belgium 'would give favourable consideration to hosting the international organization if the Conference so requested'[78] and in April 1988 Austrian Foreign Minister Alois Mock offered Vienna as the seat of the OPCW.[79] In 1988 the then Netherlands Foreign Minister Hans van den Broek needed a theme for his speech to the United Nations General Assembly's Third Special Session on Disarmament (SSOD-III). At the suggestion of the Arms Control department in the Ministry he announced that the Netherlands would be willing to act as host to the chemical weapons treaty organisation. Minister van den Broek said:

> We should also, I believe, have another good look at the institutional aspects of the chemical-weapons convention. The convention will be a multilateral one. The machinery to be set up will have to reflect this. It will most likely consist of a general conference, an executive council and a secretariat, including an inspectorate. All this has to be worked out, including a decision as to location. In regard to the latter, I am pleased to announce that as a reflection of the importance my country attaches to making a further contribution in the field of a chemical weapons ban, the Netherlands would in principle be ready to serve as host to the institutions to be established under the chemical-weapons convention.[80]

This caused considerable interest among other delegations to the CD in Geneva and they started asking the Netherlands delegation for details of the proposal. The delegation asked for instructions, itself preparing a paper suggesting that The Hague would have advantages over Geneva or Vienna (the other expected candidates, although Geneva had yet to formally announce its interest) in that it had a world-renowned chemical defence laboratory close by (the aforementioned Prins Maurits Laboratory) and that Schiphol airport, a major intercontinental hub, could provide rapid transit for inspectors to most parts of the world. The Swiss chemical defence laboratory, whilst of similar renown to TNO/PML, was at Spiez, close to Zurich and a considerable distance away from Geneva. Austria hosted an excellent nuclear laboratory (at IAEA Siebersdorf) but no chemical defence facility. In addition, the airports in Geneva and Vienna are smaller than Schiphol. On the other hand the number of foreign diplomatic missions in The Hague is much smaller than in Geneva and the delegations in Vienna have technical expertise due to their dealings with the IAEA.

There was some debate within the various ministries concerned in The Hague about the desirability of the project but those in favour won the day. A particularly important factor was the offer in August 1990 by the Ministry of Defence to contribute a maxi-

[78] CD/PV.424, p. 15, dated 23 July 1987.

[79] CD/PV.457.

[80] A/S-15/PV.3, pp. 29-30, dated 2 June 1988.

mum of NLG 35 million to the bid. The Minister of Defence made it clear that this was a one-off contribution and that it could not be spent on the campaign but only on implementation if the bid were successful. The money was to be paid in seven equal instalments of NLG 5 million each and transferred to the Ministry of Foreign Affairs. This initial sum was supplemented by contributions from the Ministries for Economic Affairs (NLG 6 million) and from the City of The Hague (NLG 2 million).

Meanwhile, the City of The Hague, which was at that time in a difficult economic situation with high unemployment and the finances of the City itself in a bad state, enthusiastically supported the project. The feeling in City Hall was that an increase in the number of international organisations in The Hague could involve both prestige and economic benefit. However, the City could make only a token financial contribution.

After two years of slow progress in the CWC negotiations the matter of the seat of the organisation again received prominence when both the Netherlands and Austrian Foreign Ministers made reference to their countries' respective offers in their speeches to the opening session of the CD in February 1990.[81] Additionally, in August 1989 the Swiss Secretary of State in the Ministry of Foreign Affairs had told the CD that Switzerland was 'willing to make a special effort to support the work' of the projected CWC Preparatory Commission, 'and to make the necessary infrastructure available to it in Switzerland'.[82] However, it would appear that the Swiss authorities were not fully committed to bidding for the seat of the organisation in these early stages, but joined the race later with a consequent disadvantage. Nevertheless, The Hague was now up against two established UN cities. Soon after the February 1990 speeches in the CD, the Austrian permanent representative submitted an aide-memoiré setting out Austria's offer in more detail.[83] The aide-memoire detailed the Austrian bid including the provision of a provisional headquarters and a permanent one paid for by Austria and listed the city's advantages as:

> The possibility of direct communication with the United Nations system; The possibility of a close exchange of know-how with the IAEA located in Vienna since 1957, which has accumulated ample experience in the field of inspection; The possibility of cost reductions through the joint use of technical facilities; and the facilitation of work owing to Vienna's experience in organizing international conferences and the availability of the necessary personnel and technical infrastructure.

It was with Minister van den Broek's February 1990 speech that real impetus was given to the Netherlands bid. One week after his speech, a task force on the 'establishment of the CW organisation' held its first meeting in The Hague. On 21 August 1990 the Netherlands permanent representative Hendrik Wagenmakers introduced to the CD a 24-page 'Bid Book' for the 'Chemical Weapons Treaty Organization'.[84] This

---

[81] See CD/PV.532, pp. 6-13, dated 6 February 1990 and CD/PV.532, pp. 13-18, dated 6 February 1990 respectively.

[82] CD/PV.523, pp. 1-5, dated 3 August 1989.

[83] CD/972, dated 21 February 1990.

[84] CD/PV.575, p. 5, dated 21 August 1990.

well produced brochure, focused on the concept of 'the green city by the sea'. It was full of colour photographs and maps and had been adapted from an existing brochure intended to attract commercial organisations to The Hague. A message from Foreign Minister van den Broek introducing the book was enhanced by a photograph showing him standing in front of the attractive view from his office window. The next few pages showed the attractions of the city itself followed by a section on transport links, featuring Schiphol airport and Rotterdam harbour. A rough outline of the contents of the bid, the details of which had yet to be finalised, was set out on the centre pages alongside a picture of the Peace Palace, home of the International Court of Justice. The book stated that:

> The Netherlands would be prepared to bear the costs of leasing a building to house the Preparatory Committee [*sic*] and the Treaty Organisation during the preparatory phase and for a considerable period of time after the signing of the treaty, which would cover half of the transitional period. The Netherlands would also meet the costs of furnishing and equipping the accommodation.

The book also stated that the Netherlands was considering the possibility of providing training facilities for inspectors free of charge. The book focused on the strengths of the bid that had been identified earlier:

> The candidature of the Netherlands is supported by its constant commitment to the CW treaty, its high degree of involvement in the complex negotiations and the quality of its scientific input. The Hague has the qualities which would make it the perfect home for the Organisation.[85]

There then followed some maps, enhanced by aerial photos and architect's models to demonstrate some of the options for office locations for the Organisation and its Preparatory Commission. The last two pages contained facts and figures relating to population, labour force quality, conference facilities, hotel accommodation, culture and recreation, etc. Overall it was an attractive item giving a clear indication of serious intent.

3. Development of the Netherlands Bid

The drafters of the bid were aware that the Netherlands had advantages stemming from its active diplomatic and scientific input into the CW negotiations and the City's promotion of The Hague as the 'legal capital of the world' but they were also aware that this was unlikely to be enough against Vienna and later Geneva as well. They were therefore keen to highlight practical aspects referred to above relating to Schipol airport and the TNO Prins Maurits Laboratory. The team used experience gained during the national trial inspections and the inter-laboratory round-robin tests carried out during the negotiations. This was reinforced by the inclusion in the bid of funding for

[85] Bid Book 1.

the training of inspectors, to be conducted in collaboration with the Laboratory. In fact, a pilot training course took place in June 1992 at PML. Other practical aspects that were also focused on in the bid related to housing, schools and diplomatic privileges and immunities.

Owing to the multi-year nature of the project (if successful) and concerns over possible cost over-run the following scheme was agreed between the Government and the City. If The Hague was indeed chosen as the site for OPCW a foundation would be established to fulfil the terms of the bid. The full sum provided by the various donors would be provided to this OPCW Foundation and invested so as to accumulate interest in the early years as the highest expenditure would be incurred towards the end of an eight-year programme. The government liability would be limited to the initial capital sum with the City assuming responsibility for any shortfall. In return the City was to have three seats on the governing board of the Foundation to the Government's two, thus giving the City control of the project.

The primary component of the bid was accommodation: for the Organisation itself once the CWC entered into force; for the Preparatory Commission during the period between the treaty's opening for signature and entry into force; and conference facilities for the Preparatory Commission and subsequently the Conference of the States Parties of the Organisation. It would not be possible with the available funds to provide a building of sufficient size to accommodate the whole organisation in perpetuity. It was therefore decided to offer such a building rent-free for three years and then to control the subsequent level of rent to be paid by the organisation itself. For the Preparatory Commission an existing, smaller office building would be rented and provided under the bid free of charge for a maximum of five years. It was considered that it should be possible to rent a suitable conference room for the occasional meetings of the Preparatory Commission and the annual meetings of the Conference of the States Parties from existing facilities within The Hague.[86] The bid also provided for a contribution, in cooperation with TNO, towards the training of inspectors and for assistance to delegations from developing countries which had no permanent diplomatic mission in The Hague. The City was also able to enhance the bid through a deal with a commercial office supply company under which furniture would be provided free of charge for both the Preparatory Commission offices and for the OPCW building provided that all office supplies were purchased from this company (see Chapter 5).

4. The Lobbying Campaign

The concept of an international competition for the seat of an international organisation was a new one for the Netherlands. Although The Hague was already home to a number of, mainly legal, international organisations, the selection of The Hague as their home had not involved a competitive element. The most recent international organi-

[86] There was in fact a considerable underestimate of the frequency and level of meetings held by international organisations such as the Preparatory Commission (see Chapter 3).

zation to be based in The Hague, the Iran-United States Claims Tribunal had been located there because of the city's traditional role as a centre of international law. Competing against established UN cities such as Geneva and Vienna, The Hague was therefore very much the underdog and some people in The Hague thought that it was not even worth bidding for the seat. However, The Hague's position as underdog also meant that the city was not encumbered by some problems which Geneva and Vienna were both perceived to be suffering from, and it also meant that the team promoting The Hague was able to use such problems to its advantage.

The Netherlands campaign to win the seat of the organisation also needs to be seen in the context of events at the time. There was a major split in public opinion over the stationing of US cruise missiles in the Netherlands. While supporting the deployment of the missiles, the government was keen to do all it could to show that it was committed to disarmament. Playing a active and positive role in the CWC negotiations in Geneva was seen as one way of doing just that. The negotiators in the Geneva delegation and in The Hague were therefore given a large degree of latitude to make proposals and one such was that The Hague should be the seat of the organisation.

The Ministry of Foreign Affairs, supported by the delegation in Geneva and advised by a professional lobbyist (Rio Praaning of Dewe Rogerson Europe) employed for this purpose by the City of The Hague, began a process of targeted lobbying of the other Governments who formed the rest of the 40-member Conference on Disarmament. It was considered important to achieve a consensus on the seat of the Organisation in the CD, with its limited membership (not including Switzerland or Austria) and a good proportion of states with close ties to the Netherlands, rather than have the matter settled by a vote of the United Nations General Assembly with its much larger membership. In September 1991, the lobbyist prepared a strategy paper outlining the campaign by which CD delegations would be persuaded to support The Hague as the seat of the organisation. Key to the strategy was getting the support of the G-21 countries – the non-aligned countries within the CD. The Netherlands delegation in Geneva already had good relations with many of these countries and special efforts were made to become aware of and understand their concerns. A large number of G-21 countries have Islam as their main religion and it was decided that a central element of the campaign would focus on the multiracial character and tolerance of Netherlands society.

As part of this lobbying process all the heads of delegations to the CD were invited to take part in a visit to The Hague in August 1991. This was very carefully orchestrated down to the head rests on the chartered KLM aircraft featuring a design with the initials 'OPCW' and to the pilot announcing on the return journey that he would need to hurry as Geneva airport closed in the middle of the evening (Schiphol operates '24/7'). During the return trip, the ambassadors were also asked to fill in and return questionnaires on their opinion of the trip itself and on their views of The Hague as the seat of the organisation. The answers received proved very useful in ensuring that the concerns of particular countries were addressed in later lobbying activities. One of the highlights of the trip was a visit to the TNO Prins Maurits Laboratory which served to reinforce the high-quality scientific input into the Netherlands bid. A group photograph of the ambassadors, taken during this visit featured in the second bid book (see p. 303 below).

At the start of the 1992 session of the Conference on Disarmament the head of the German delegation, Ambassador von Wagner, was elected as chairman of the ad hoc committee for the negotiation of the chemical weapons convention with a mandate to complete the negotiations before the end of the year. He asked the head of the Pakistan delegation, Ambassador Ahmed Kamal, to act as 'Friend of the Chair on the question of the seat of the organisation'. The President of the CD[87] and Ambassador von Wagner took the first step on 13 February by writing to all UN Member States and observers asking all those who wished to host the organisation to put themselves forward by 9 March. The governments of Austria, the Netherlands, Switzerland and Yugoslavia responded. A questionnaire was then prepared containing 92 questions regarding the nature of the bids and the characteristics of the cities put forward and sent to the four candidate countries by Ambassador Kamal on 12 March. Responses were requested by 7 April. By that date replies had been received from the first three. Yugoslavia asked for a one-week extension and then for a further week's extension. But when they proved unable to respond even after these extensions, Yugoslavia was dropped from the list. A preliminary report detailing the responses from the three governments on behalf of the cities of Vienna, The Hague and Geneva was issued to the ad hoc committee on 28 April.[88]

As part of its campaign The Hague hosted a symposium on 'OPCW: The First Five Years' from 8 to 9 May 1992 in the Knights Hall of the Netherlands Parliament in The Hague. On 14 May, the CD ambassadors visited Vienna to consider its bid to host the organisation. From 16-24 June the TNO Prins Maurits Laboratory hosted a number of trainee inspectors.[89]

On 18 May 1992, Ambassador Wagenmakers, introduced a new bid book entitled *The Hague: For ALL Practical Purposes*. This new book was much more focused on addressing the concerns of the other CD delegations and on presenting the advantages of The Hague than its predecessor. It contained a more precise exposition of the bid and went on to compare the good points from all three countries in an attempt to prove that the best was from the Netherlands on behalf of The Hague. This book specified the building which was used to house the offices of the Preparatory Commission and the site for the 'Peace Tower' to house the OPCW in front of The Hague Central Station (a different site was later substituted, see Chapter 5).

5. The Selection of The Hague

Ambassador Kamal oversaw presentations by all three candidate cities on 2 June 1992. The Netherlands bid was introduced by the acting burgomaster of The Hague, Con-

[87] The post of President of the CD is largely administrative and rotates monthly among the members in alphabetical order of country name in English.

[88] Friend of the Chair on the Seat of the Organisation, Ad Hoc Committee on Chemical Weapons, 'Preliminary Report', Paper No. 1, dated 28 April 1992; commonly referred to as 'Kamal paper 1'.

[89] CD/CW/WP.429, dated 14 August 1992.

stant Martini, and the director of the Prins Maurits Laboratory, Marius van Zelm. Attention to detail continued in the Netherlands campaign and a photo taken during the symposium in The Hague in May was distributed at the meeting (as it happens during the Austrian presentation!).

By this stage, a number of delegations had begun publicly stating their preference for the seat of the organisation. Ambassador Kamal chose an interesting procedure to discover the consensus for a single candidate, asking each delegation to inform him privately of their preference between the three cities proposed. He then suggested that Geneva, which had received the smallest number, should withdraw. He then held a second round of informal consultations with heads of delegation on 19 June. Under the same procedure as previously, Vienna withdrew its candidacy at about 17:00 and Ambassador Kamal announced that 'sadness over the loss of weighty and worthy candidates as Vienna and Geneva was tempered only by the fact that a consensus was emerging over one single candidate'. At 17:30 Ambassador von Wagner proposed adding the words 'The Hague' to draft Article VIII. After hearing no objections, he announced that consensus had been reached on The Hague as the seat of the organisation and the name of the city was therefore added to Article VIII. Thus the ad hoc committee was able to put one more building block into the draft convention as follows:

> Article VIII (3):
>
> The seat of the headquarters of the organisation shall be The Hague, Kingdom of the Netherlands.

The lessons learned from this exercise were put to good use by the Netherlands Ministry of Foreign Affairs and the City of The Hague in subsequent campaigns to attract more international organisations to The Hague.[90] In the 10 years since 1992 they not only were the front runners in the competition for the site of the Organisation for the Prohibition of Biological Weapons, the legal instrument for which was not completed by the negotiators in Geneva,[91] but successfully attracted, among others, the International Criminal Tribunal for the former Yugoslavia, the International Criminal Court, Europol and Eurojust.

---

[90] Details of further successful bids are outside the scope of this book, but are provided in Peter J van Krieken and David McKay (eds.), *The Hague: Legal Capital of the World* (The Hague, TMC Asser Press 2005).

[91] Lisa Tabassi and Scott Spence, 'The Organisation for the Prohibition of Biological Weapons', in van Krieken and McKay, 2005, pp. 483-514.

Chapter 3

ESTABLISHING THE PREPARATORY COMMISSION AND CREATING THE OPCW TECHNICAL SECRETARIAT

Ian R. Kenyon

1. CONCEPT DEVELOPMENT

Serious development of a convention to ban chemical weapons can be dated from the opening for signature in 1972 of the Biological Weapons Convention (BWC) with its Article IX committing the parties to continued negotiations with a view to also banning chemical weapons. The weaknesses of the BWC and attempts to redress them fall outside the scope of this book but a 1972 proposal from the USSR and the Eastern European Group in the CCD[92] to start negotiation on the basis of essentially the BWC text with 'chemical weapon' in place of 'biological weapon' was immediately rejected by the Western Group as having inadequate provisions for ensuring compliance. The BWC contains only two articles dealing with this important issue: Article V, which requires the States Parties to consult with each other on such matters but provides no standing body for the purpose; and Article VI, which allows for accusations of non-compliance to be referred to the UN Security Council and requires States Parties to facilitate any investigation by that body. Given the veto power held by the five permanent members of the Security Council, this latter provision did not give confidence that action would be in any way automatic if the superpowers or their allies were accusing each other. The only Formal Consultative Meeting of States Parties to date under Article V was called in 1997 to hear accusations that the United States had deliberately released *Thrips palmi* over Cuba but was unable to reach a conclusion.[93]

Western Group ideas on verification of compliance of a CWC assumed more concrete form with the introduction into the CCD in July 1973, by the Netherlands of a Working Paper which proposed a standing organ for a chemical weapons convention based upon a plenary conference, a board and a secretariat.[94] The concept was further

---

[92] Bulgaria, Czechoslovakia, Hungary, Mongolia, Poland, Romania, USSR, Conference of the Committee on Disarmament, CCD/361, dated 28 March 1972.

[93] Amb. Ian Soutar (UK), Letter to States Parties to the BWC, 15 December 1997, as reproduced in HSP, BASIC & VERTIC *BWC Sixth Review Conference Briefing Book*, 2006.

[94] Netherlands, 'Working Paper on an International Organ for the Support of a CW Convention and Other Disarmament Agreements', CCD/410, dated 31 July 1973.

developed in a 1976 draft by the United Kingdom.[95] This called for the establishment of a 'Consultative Committee' which would receive declarations of chemical weapons stocks and of 'production facilities capable of producing chemical agents'; would arrange inspections of destruction of the stocks and, on a routine basis, of the plants capable of producing chemical agents; and would arrange 'special investigations which may involve on-site inspection' if called for by a Party suspecting another of 'acting in breach of obligations [under] the Convention'. This Committee would clearly have required a permanent secretariat to assist in performing its functions but this was not explicit in the text. This concept of a Consultative Committee with verification functions also formed part of the evolving agreement on the CWC structure emerging from ongoing bilateral discussions between the United States and USSR, reported first to the CCD in 1978.[96]

The Netherlands delegation in Geneva provided the fruits of its further thinking[97] to the Conference on Disarmament in a paper in March 1984.[98] The paper described an organisation similar to that first proposed in 1973. The main types of on-site inspection that would be carried out were identified as: 'systematic continuous'; 'systematic non-continuous (regular and random)'; and 'ad hoc (challenge)'. The paper concluded that, for the first ten years of operations, a CW organisation would need a maximum of 165 inspectors, a figure surprisingly close to the current establishment of around 200.

The idea of an independent international organisation to carry out verification activities, modelled to some extent on the Safeguards Inspectorate of the International Atomic Energy Agency, was developed in several national working papers presented to the CD in the early 1980s.

Probably the most significant and influential of the national contributions at this stage when the CD negotiations which were to lead to the CWC were just getting underway was a complete draft treaty text,[99] which was supported by a speech delivered in Geneva by the then US Vice-President George HW Bush. This continued the concept of a 'Consultative Committee' as the primary organ for operating the convention, what later came to be titled the 'Conference of the States Parties', normally meeting once per year; but also foresaw the need for an Executive Council which would meet much more frequently to carry out its responsibility for, *inter alia*;

> overseeing the activities of the other subordinate bodies of the Consultative Committee, including ensuring the proper execution of the functions of the Technical Secretariat...

---

95 UK, 'Draft convention on the prohibition of the development, production and stockpiling of chemical weapons and on their destruction', CCD/512, dated 6 August 1976. The process of drafting this text is described in: Ian Kenyon, 'The Summer of '76', *CBW Conventions Bulletin*, 71, May 2006, pp. 5-6.

96 Ian Kenyon, 'The USA/USSR Arms Control Relationship and Its Impact on the CWC', *CBW Conventions Bulletin*, 72+73, September 2006, pp. 1-3.

97 See Chapter 2.

98 Netherlands, 'Size and Structure of a Chemical Disarmament Inspectorate', CD/445, dated 7 March 1984.

99 USA, 'Draft convention on the prohibition of chemical weapons', CD/500, dated 18 April 1984.

A further section of the draft provided that:

1. The Technical Secretariat should;
    a) Conduct on-site inspections pursuant to Articles …;
    b) Provide the necessary administrative support to the Consultative Committee, the Executive Council, the Fact-Finding Panel[100] and such other subsidiary bodies as may be established;
    c) Render appropriate technical assistance to Parties and to the Executive Council in implementing the provisions of the Convention, such as reviewing Schedules […], developing technical procedures, and improving the effectiveness of verification methods;
    d) Receive from Parties and distribute to them data relevant to the implementation of the Convention;
    e) Negotiate the subsidiary arrangements for systematic international on-site inspections …; and
    f) Assist the Executive Council on such other tasks as may be agreed.
2. The composition of the Technical secretariat should be elaborated by the Preparatory Commission.
3. All inspectors should be technically qualified and acceptable to their governments.

This basic structure and division of responsibilities became the foundation for the OPCW as established in the Convention text completed in 1992.

2. Article VIII

Article VIII of the CWC, formally establishes the Organisation for the Prohibition of Chemical Weapons

> to achieve the object and purpose of this Convention, to ensure the implementation of its provisions, including those for international verification of compliance with it, and to provide a forum for consultation and cooperation among States Parties.

The article states that all States Parties to the Convention shall be members of the OPCW; that its Headquarters seat shall be in The Hague; sets out the method of financing; and establishes as the organs of the Organisation: the Conference of the States Parties (CSP), the Executive Council (EC), and the Technical Secretariat (TS). The duties, powers and methods of functioning of the (essentially annual) CSP and the 41 member EC are set out in some detail but, whilst the duties of the TS are also laid out, only two paragraphs relate to its structure:

> 41. The Technical Secretariat shall comprise a Director-General, who shall be its head and chief administrative officer, inspectors and such scientific, technical and other personnel as may be required.

---

[100] In the CWC the duties foreseen in CD/500 for a Fact-Finding Panel were added to those of the Executive Council.

42. The inspectorate shall be a unit of the Technical Secretariat and shall act under the supervision of the Director-General.

Thus the size, composition and management structure of the operational arm (and most visible part) of the new organisation was left to the PrepCom to determine. This was confirmed in the Paris Resolution[101] which required the Commission, *inter alia*, to undertake:

Elaboration of a detailed staffing pattern of the Technical Secretariat, including decision-making flow charts;
Assessments of personnel requirements;
Recruitment and training of technical personnel and support staff;
Organisation of office and administrative services;
and
Preparation of programme of work and budget of the first year of activities of the Organisation;
Preparation of detailed budgetary provisions for the Organisation taking into account that the budget shall comprise two separate chapters, one relating to administrative and other costs, and one relating to verification costs.

The last of these proved to be the key to all the rest as it was through the budget setting process, first for the PrepCom itself and then through attempts to achieve a draft first budget for the Organisation, that the shape of the Provisional Technical Secretariat and then the recruitment and training of the additional staff, including inspectors, for the transition to the Technical Secretariat at entry into force of the Convention were achieved.

3. The Transition from Geneva to The Hague

Twenty years of chemical weapons discussions and negotiations in Geneva came to an end on 3 September 1992 when the Conference on Disarmament adopted the text of the Chemical Weapons Convention (CWC). It was therefore time for the provisions of Article VIII, rooted in over 20 years of conceptual discussions, to be translated into reality. However, it had been recognised in Geneva that this would be no easy task. The complexity of the negotiations and the rapidity with which they were concluded meant that a number of issues were not entirely resolved in Geneva, while others were seen as being too technical for inclusion in the text of the Convention. In fact, it had long been argued in Geneva that not all issues could or should be settled by the negotiators but would instead be left for later resolution.[102] It has been noted that:

---

[101] Paris Resolution and Related Understandings, L.W. Tabassi (ed.), *OPCW: The Legal Texts* (The Hague, TMC Asser Press 1999), pp. 523-534.

[102] 'It would be wrong to try to pass to the Commission matters of principle which must properly be resolved as part of the main negotiations. A number of such issues have been identified in the above paragraphs. On the other hand, the United Kingdom attaches great importance to early and effective

> [D]espite the fact that the CWC was negotiated over a 20-year period, the CWC text contains a number of ambiguities, including 'creative ambiguities' (to obtain an acceptable level of agreement on difficult issues) and unintentional ambiguities. As a consequence, within the agreed provisions of the CWC, there are still a number of balances and trade-offs which need to be interpreted in concrete, practical terms.[103]

The negotiators therefore decided to establish a Preparatory Commission (PrepCom) to carry out

> the necessary preparations for the effective implementation of the [CWC], and for preparing for the first session of the Conference of the States Parties to that Convention.

The PrepCom, assisted by a Provisional Technical Secretariat (PTS), was to meet until the Convention entered into force which, according to Article XXI, could not be earlier than two years after it was opened for signature.[104]

For this reason, at the close of its 1992 session the Conference on Disarmament transmitted to the United Nations not only a completed draft for the Chemical Weapons Convention but also a complementary 'Text on the Establishment of a Preparatory Commission' which had been negotiated alongside the CWC text.[105]

Following the completion of the negotiations in Geneva there followed a four-month interval before the Convention was opened for signature. An informal meeting took place in Geneva on 2 September involving an initial exchange of views on the PrepCom. Later during this interval, further meetings to lay the groundwork for activities in the months immediately after the Convention was opened for signature were convened under Ambassador Adolf von Wagner of Germany, the former chairman of the CD's Ad Hoc Committee on Chemical Weapons, on the margins of the

---

implementation of a global ban. It will therefore be important to pass as many functions as possible to be resolved by the Preparatory Commission.' (UK, 'Making the chemical weapons ban effective', CD/769, dated 10 July 1987).

'Finally, we need not be afraid to leave certain details to the Preparatory Commission and the Technical Secretariat to be worked out under the guidance of the Executive Council. There has been a tendency in the past to stipulate all future procedures in detail. This is not our task: our present task is to work out a treaty in which we all have confidence and which includes all major obligations in detail sufficient for us not to find ourselves confronted with unpleasant surprises once the treaty enters into force. Consequently, parts of the "rolling text" can be transferred to the PrepCom for further consideration and we need not devote too much attention to them any more. The extended bureau could also develop proposals on these matters for submission to the Ad Hoc Committee.' (Netherlands, CD/PV.592, p. 4, dated 23 May 1991).

'At the same time other problems of a more technical nature could be dealt with later by the Preparatory Commission, with the assistance of the Provisional Technical Secretariat.' (Italy, CD/PV.615, p. 17, dated 5 March 1992).

[103] Robert Mathews and Antony Taubman, 'Preparing for implementation of the Chemical Weapons Convention: Progress during 1993', in JB Poole and R Guthrie (eds.), *Verification 1994: Arms Control, Peacekeeping and the Environment* (London, VERTIC/Brassey's 1994), pp. 111-128 at p. 123.

[104] The two-year timeline was agreed in Geneva more as a minimum period in which states could make their own internal arrangements for ratification of the Convention, rather than the as the maximum duration of the PrepCom.

[105] United Nations, Official Records of the 47th Session of the General Assembly, Supplement No. 27 (A/47/27), 23 September 1992.

First Committee of the United Nations General Assembly in New York among the co-sponsors of the resolution on the CWC.

At one such meeting, on 23 October 1992, it was decided to establish a consultative group to advance the consensus-building process on how the PrepCom was to be structured, and who was to fill its key positions. The group had a representative from each of the five regional groupings specified in Article VIII of the CWC, and had three main issues to resolve, all interlinked: chairmanship of the PrepCom; size and composition of the Bureau to assist the chair, which the PrepCom must also elect, and the responsibilities of individual Bureau members; and appointment of an Executive Secretary, whose tasks would include developing the Provisional Technical Secretariat.

Another group also existed; this one chaired by Australia's Permanent Representative to the CD, Ambassador Paul O'Sullivan and made up of a small number of Western Group countries who were to become the main financial contributors to the PrepCom. This group concerned itself mainly with budgetary and administrative issues and distributed numerous papers relating to the first months of the PrepCom, including the size of its budget, its staffing and the cost of its meetings. These papers, circulated under Ambassador O'Sullivan's signature, were subsequently distributed to participants in the larger meetings on the PrepCom.

Further meetings took place in Geneva on 12 December 1992 and 27 January 1993 at which additional national papers were circulated. While this preparatory work achieved consensus on some issues and helped to create support for the CWC, once the PrepCom began meeting in The Hague it soon became clear that some crucial practical issues had been overlooked and that limitations had been imposed on the on the structure and activities of the PTS before it had even been created.

4. The CWC Signing Ceremony and the Paris Resolution

The Convention was opened for signature at a ceremony in Paris on 13-15 January 1993 where it was signed by 130 States. In Paris, the Signatory States also adopted the 'Resolution Establishing the Preparatory Commission for the Organisation for the Prohibition of Chemical Weapons' (also known as the 'Paris Resolution', see Chapter 4 for more details). The Resolution mandated the PrepCom to develop a number of draft agreements, provisions and guidelines for consideration and approval by the Conference of the States Parties on those issues which had been left unresolved by the negotiators in Geneva. The expectation was that these documents could be drafted within two years. However, it was clear to many that the PrepCom had a difficult task ahead of it.

In addition to achieving the tasks mandated to it by the Paris Resolution, the PrepCom also had to ensure that it did not undo the careful balances and compromises struck by the negotiators in Geneva:

> The development of detailed regulations and procedures, and the establishment of the infrastructure for the OPCW is not a trivial task, at least in part because of the necessity of

> retaining the essential aspects of the number of carefully balanced deals which were struck in the final months of negotiation. In doing so, the PrepCom must sidestep attempts to renegotiate the treaty but allow the scope for its provisions to be coherently extrapolated into practical rules.[106]

It was partly because attempts *were* made to undo the bargains from Geneva and renegotiate certain aspects of the Convention that the PrepCom was unable to complete all the tasks laid down for it in the Paris Resolution.

Before the PrepCom could start serious work on preparing to implement the treaty and to set up the OPCW it had to organise itself. The main task was daunting – to establish a major new international organisation with some unique characteristics in, as initially believed, only two years. The initial task was almost worse – to establish a fully functioning international negotiating body with full conference services and a professional secretariat, capable of preparing position papers on complex technical and political issues, on a three month roll-out – that is to say basic services in two weeks and fully operational in twelve. What follows describes how these and the other infrastructure challenges were met.

5. First Session of the Preparatory Commission

The First Session of the Commission was convened in the Van Gogh Zaal of the Netherlands Congress Centre in The Hague on Monday 8 February 1993 and closed on the following Friday. Netherlands Foreign Minister, Dr PH Kooijmans, told delegates:

> As the precursor of the future Organization, the Preparatory Commission enshrines the collective responsibility of all Signatory States for the Convention. During the next two years, that collective responsibility will be put to the test. After all, much remains to be done if the splendid blueprint of the Convention is to be turned into a living reality. You will have to work out the technical regulations and other provisions as well as the organizational requirements needed to implement the Convention.[107]

Conference Services were provided by the United Nations in accordance with UNGA Resolution 47/39 against later repayment from PrepCom funds estimated at US$ 250,000. This operation involved flying in 45 staff from Geneva (mostly interpreters, translators and multilingual typists) and recruiting a significant number of security guards, receptionists, etc., from the local student market. Substantive policy support was provided by two officers from the UN Department of Disarmament Affairs, Abdelkader Bensmail and Hannelore Hoppe, and a finance expert J Bilger from New York (at an additional cost of US$8,404).

---

[106] Robert Mathews and Antony Taubman, 'Preparing for implementation of the Chemical Weapons Convention: Progress during 1993', in JB Poole and R Guthrie (eds.), *Verification 1994: Arms Control, Peacekeeping and the Environment* (London, VERTIC/Brassey's 1994), pp. 111-128.

[107] Quoted in: Julian Perry Robinson and Peter Herby, 'International organization for chemical disarmament begins', *Chemical Weapons Convention Bulletin*, No. 19 (March 1993), pp. 1-4.

The First Session had a relatively simple agenda: to adopt some preliminary rules to enable it to operate at all (conference procedures, finance regulations, staff rules); to appoint its own officers; to set a three-month budget and set Member States' contributions; to start the process of setting up a professional secretariat; and to set a work programme for 'government experts' for the first three months. It had been suggested that this would need a meeting of only two and a half days. However, the UN and the Host Country provided for a full five day meeting and this indeed proved necessary.

The system of chairmanship had been agreed during the consultations in New York and involved the five (UN) regional groups in alphabetical order[108] each in turn choosing a candidate to serve from 8 February to 7 August and 8 August to 7 February each year, being six monthly terms of office running from the date of opening of the First Session. The PrepCom was expected to last for only two years, which would have needed only four chairmen. In this case the fifth group, Western Europe and Others,[109] would have expected the chair of the First Session of the Conference of the States Parties (FSCSP) after entry into force of the CWC. In fact the PrepCom lasted for just over four years and had nine chairmen so WEOG indeed had the FSCSP chair.

PC	Dates	Chairman	Country	Region
I	8-12 Feb 1993	Emeka A Azikiwe	Nigeria	Africa
II	19-22 Apr 1993			
III	28 Jun – 2 Jul 1993			
IV	27 Sep – 1 Oct 1993	Sirous Nasseri	Iran	Asia
V	13-16 Dec 1993			
VI	11-15 Apr 1994	Grigory V Berdennikov	Russia	EE
VII	27 Jun – 1 Jul 1994			
VIII	26-30 Sep 1994	Miguel Marin Bosch	Mexico	LAC
IX	5-8 Dec 1994			
X	3-7 Apr 1995	Finn K Fostervoll	Norway	WEOG
XI	24-28 Jul 1995			
XII	11-14 Dec 1995	Zacharias de Beer	South Africa	Africa
XIII	18-22 Mar 1996	Dato Sallehuddin Bin Abdullah	Malaysia	Asia
XIV	22-26 Jul 1996			
XV	16-21 Dec 1996	Marin Buhoara	Romania	EE
XVI	9-15 Apr 1997	Gustavo Eduardo Figueroa	Argentina	LAC
CSP-1	6-24 May 1997	Peter Cornelius Feith	Netherlands	WEOG

The Vice-Chairmen were not elected as individuals but as incumbent heads of a particular delegation from each of the five regional groups. The head of the United States delegation served as one of the Vice-Chairmen for the whole of the life of the Commission.

The OPCW Foundation had made some preliminary arrangements to accommodate the first elements of the PTS and stood ready to increase these quite rapidly, once the detailed requirements were known, to the limits set out in the Netherlands bid. They were not, however, prepared for the scale of meeting support demanded by the Member States, immediately following the opening PrepCom Session, for intersessional

108 Africa, Asia, Eastern Europe, Latin America and the Caribbean, and WEOG.

109 The 'others' being USA, Canada, Australia and New Zealand.

work. Certain Member States had made advance payments to provide a starting fund but these sums were in various places. The First Session appointed the Executive Secretary and provided him with necessary financial and other authority but only appointed three of the five staff envisaged at the next most senior level (and none of these could be available without at least a short delay). The 45 staff brought to The Hague by the UN to service the First Session went home at the end of the week. Despite all of this the first Expert Group, meeting only two weeks after the session, was provided with a room in which to meet; ushers to distribute papers; copying and typing services; and a secretary with adequate background in the subject matter. The Second Session of the Preparatory Commission was provided with full conference services, including six language interpretation, and had for consideration a first year PrepCom budget that set the basic shape of the PTS and foreshadowed the structure of OPCW itself.

6. Preparatory Commission Negotiating Machinery

6.1 Plenary sessions

The PrepCom consisted of the PTS and all states which had signed the CWC. Each Member State had one representative, supported by as many assistants as considered necessary. At its first plenary session, the PrepCom established a three-level working structure. Its formal business was conducted in plenary sessions which each lasted for about a week and which were convened every two or three months. Sixteen such plenary sessions were held altogether. Over the course of the Commission's life, the plenary sessions established five subsidiary bodies: Working Group A; Working Group B; the Committee on Relations with the Host Country; the Committee on Preparations for the First Session of the Conference of the States Parties; and the Credentials Committee. Both working groups established a large number of subsidiary expert groups.[110]

6.2 Working groups

The first plenary established two Working Groups, A and B, on legal, budgetary and administrative matters; and verification and technical cooperation and assistance matters, respectively and appointed their Chairmen. These two groups, for most of the life of the Commission, only met during the plenary sessions of the Commission, when they received reports, on given topics from the tasks identified in the Paris Resolution, from 'Expert Groups' which they mandated to meet during the inter-sessional periods. It was suggested that Working Group A might take the Technical Assistance issues in order to balance the workload of the two Working Groups. However, this

[110] The concept of the PrepCom's working structure of two working groups supported by expert groups was elaborated in a US non-paper 'Model Structure for the Chemical Weapons Convention Preparatory Commission' circulated, but never formally published, as a discussion paper in the last quarter of 1992.

was unacceptable to the countries of the 'Non-Aligned Group' as it could have been taken to imply a different degree of importance being accorded to Technical Assistance and Verification issues.

Each working group was able to establish 'expert groups' to prepare recommendations on specific issues. The original plan had been for the working groups to meet in advance of the plenary sessions and conduct a substantive review and coordination of their expert groups' work.[111] However, due to organisational pressures the working group could only meet during the plenary sessions to take note of expert group reports, revise group mandates if necessary and pass any recommendations on to the plenary. For this reason, the expert groups became what two participants described at the time as 'the driving force of the enterprise'.[112] Given the urgent nature of their tasks, expert groups under Working Group A began soon after the first plenary session, whereas Working Group B expert groups did not begin until after the second plenary session, in May and June 1993.[113]

The first issues handled were legal questions under Working Group A which was chaired initially by Ambassador Alberto Villamizar of Colombia until September 1993, then by Ambassador Jorge Morales Pedraza of Cuba and, from April 1995, by Ambassador Carlos Enrique Nones of Venezuela. The matter of recommending Rules of Procedure for the Commission was straightforward. It was expected that the Staff and Financial Rules would be equally so. However it turned out that the Members of the Commission fell into two camps, those who believed that the UN Rules provided a 'gold standard' which should be universally applied and those who felt that, in the case of the staff regulations, UN personnel had unnecessarily generous benefits, particularly with regard to payment of education costs for older children. There was also early discussion of an issue that took OPCW itself years to resolve – the question of tenure, how long individual members of staff should be permitted to remain with the organisation. Other legal issues are the subject of a separate chapter (Chapter 4). During the lifetime of the PrepCom, Working Group A established Expert Groups on the following topics (listed chronologically by the date of the Group's first report): Rules of Procedure and Privileges and Immunities; Programme of Work (subsequently Programme of Work and Budget); Staff Regulations and Financial Regulations (subsequently split into two separate expert groups); OPCW Building; Data Systems; OPCW Headquarters Agreement (subsequently OPCW Headquarters Agreement and Other Agreements); Transitional Arrangements; and Administrative, Finance and Personnel Matters.[114]

---

[111] For example, see Robert Mikulak, 'The Chemical Weapons Convention's Preparatory Commission', in Brad Roberts (ed.), *The Chemical Weapons Convention: Implementation Issues*, Centre for Strategic and International Studies, Significant Issues Series, Vol. XIV, No. 13 (1992), pp. 12-18: 'Such working groups might be in session for approximately a week or two each month'.

[112] Robert Mathews and Antony Taubman, 'Preparing for implementation of the Chemical Weapons Convention: Progress during 1993', in JB Poole and R Guthrie (eds.), *Verification 1994: Arms Control, Peacekeeping and the Environment* (London, VERTIC/Brassey's 1994), pp. 111-128 at p. 114.

[113] 'Report of the Executive Secretary for the period from the Second to the Third Session of the Preparatory Commission (22 April to 25 June 1993)', PC-III/5, dated 25 June 1993.

[114] 'Final Report of the Preparatory Commission for the Organisation for the Prohibition of Chemical Weapons to the First Session of the Conference of the States Parties of the Organisation for the Prohibition

Verification and Technical Assistance issues fell under the auspices of Working Group B, chaired until October 1995 by Sylwin Gizowski of Poland and then by Radoslav Deyanov of Bulgaria. However, there were many linkages between issues considered by the two working groups especially as it was realised that an effective verification regime depends on a credible and efficient organisation. The expert groups were open to participation by all signatory states but given the technical nature of those under Working Group B and the absence of resident diplomatic missions for many developing countries in The Hague, they were attended mainly by those countries with local embassies and with the resources and expertise to follow such issues. Usually, no more than 20 to 30 states were represented in experts groups and often fewer than 10 made an active contribution.[115] Another factor limiting participation by less well-resourced countries was that each expert group generally met over a two-week period. During the lifetime of the PrepCom, Working Group B established the following subsidiary bodies (listed chronologically by the date of the Group's first report): Safety Procedures; Chemical Engineers; Inspection Team Composition; Technical Cooperation and Assistance; Analytical Chemists; Industrial Declarations; Equipment; Training, Chemical Weapons Destruction Facilities; Chemical Weapons Storage Facilities; Inspectorate Planning; Single Small-Scale Facilities and other Schedule 1 Production Facilities; Chemical Weapons Production Facilities; Challenge Inspection; Chemical Industry Issues; Old and Abandoned Chemical Weapons; Confidentiality; Declarations and Model Facility Agreements; Inspection Procedures; Chemical Weapons Issues (meeting in two separate Groups).[116] It should be noted that some later additions absorbed the functions of earlier experts groups, e.g., Chemical Engineers and Industrial Declarations disappeared into Chemical Industry Issues.

For the first few months after the first PrepCom plenary, the expert groups did not even have a permanent home, some took place in the Netherlands Ministry of Foreign Affairs while others took place in the Promenade and Atlantic Hotels.[117] Although many of the participants knew each other, they were not entirely clear on their role and there were few if any precedents for them to follow. So each group felt its way forward carefully under the guidance of its chairman who would rely heavily on the technical expertise of the PTS staff member serving as secretary to each group. According to two participants who were active in the expert groups: 'The expert groups normally comprise only a few who are active specialists in the field of discussion, and most participants are generalist diplomats or other capital based officials with broad

---

of Chemical Weapons and to the First Meeting of the Executive Council of the Organisation for the Prohibition of Chemical Weapons', PC-XVI/37, dated 15 April 1997.

[115] Robert Mathews and Antony Taubman, 'Preparing for implementation of the Chemical Weapons Convention: Progress during 1994', in JB Poole and R Guthrie (eds.), *Verification 1995: Arms Control, Peacekeeping and the Environment* (London/Boulder, VERTIC/Westview 1995), pp. 161-179 at p. 163.

[116] 'Final Report of the Preparatory Commission for the Organisation for the Prohibition of Chemical Weapons to the First Session of the Conference of the States Parties of the Organisation for the Prohibition of Chemical Weapons and to the First Meeting of the Executive Council of the Organisation for the Prohibition of Chemical Weapons', PC-XVI/37, dated 15 April 1997.

[117] 'Report of the Executive Secretary for the period from the First to the Second Session of the Preparatory Commission (11 February to 18 April 1993)', PREPCOM/II/3, dated 19 April 1993.

engagement in CWC issues.'[118] In addition, only a few of the delegations active in the expert groups had the authority to make decisions on the spot rather than having to refer issues back to their national capitals. Australia, Canada, Sweden and the United Kingdom were among those with the expertise and well enough briefed to take decisions without reference to capital, while China and the United States were among those delegations which had to refer issues back to Beijing or Washington for decision. An additional problem for countries like China was that all meetings were held in English and it was only occasionally possible to offer interpretation facilities to experts who were not fluent in technical issues in that language. While good progress was made in 1993, many of the really contentious issues were only superficially discussed or were rapidly deferred for later consideration.

From the beginning, the work of the expert groups was not straightforward. Issues to be dealt with in one expert group were found to be linked to those discussed in another and issues such as confidentiality ran into numerous expert groups. Issues were therefore often not addressed in a simple linear fashion by the same expert group from introduction to conclusion, but moved between expert groups in a circular movement. For example, issues related to industrial declarations started off in the expert group on industrial declarations, then moved into a group on chemical industry facilities, then into a group on declarations and model facility agreements and finally into a group on chemical industry issues. Progress in one expert group could be delayed by a lack of progress in another related group. During 1994 and 1995 it became apparent that concerns about confidentiality were one of the main obstacles to progress, but such concerns arose more in the groups on equipment and health and safety than they did in the expert group on confidentiality itself. Similarly, agreement in the expert group on confidentiality was sometimes dependent upon progress in the expert group on data systems. The realisation that so many issues were interlinked, drove the PrepCom to merge some expert groups in early 1994. The previously separate expert groups dealing with inspection-related procedures (such as the groups on equipment, safety procedures, analytical chemists and so on) were merged into an expert group on inspection procedures, which went on to issue 14 reports between May 1994 and February 1997 under the chairmanship of Sergei Kisselev of Russia.

6.3 **Other subsidiary bodies**

It was later found necessary to establish a mechanism whereby the Member States of the Commission could collectively raise with the Netherlands authorities issues arising from operation or interpretation of the Bid. The Committee on Relations with the Host Country was established at the Fifth Session of the PrepCom in December 1993[119] initially to settle questions relating the new office building to be constructed for the organisation (see Chapter 5) but was found to be more generally useful, for example

---

[118] Robert Mathews and Antony Taubman, 'Preparing for implementation of the Chemical Weapons Convention: Progress during 1993', in JB Poole and R Guthrie (eds.), *Verification 1994: Arms Control, Peacekeeping and the Environment* (London, VERTIC/Brassey's 1994), pp. 111-128 at p. 114.

[119] 'Report of the Commission', PC-V/12, dated 17 December 1993, para. 5.2(a).

discussing problems relating to the issuance of visas for experts attending meetings of the PrepCom. The Fourteenth Session of the PrepCom established a Committee on Preparations for the First Session of the Conference of the States Parties with the aim of ensuring a smooth beginning of that Session and the timely commencement of the mandated activities of the OPCW.[120] Both Committees were chaired by the Chairman of the PrepCom and were open to all Member States.

7. Administrative Issues for the Preparatory Commission

7.1 **Budget**

One output from the 'O'Sullivan Group' consultations before the First Session was convened was agreement among those states involved that the budget of the PrepCom for the first year was not to exceed US$10 million.[121] Although this amount was described as 'the estimated total cost', by February 1993 many states had prepared national budgets based on this assumption. So, the structure and activities of the PTS during that first year had to be designed so as not to exceed that imposed limit while at the same time being able to service the numerous plenaries and expert groups, a task which had not been envisaged in the 'O'Sullivan Group' discussions.

There were additional factors and assumptions which shaped the various annual budgets adopted by the PrepCom and the staffing structure of the PTS. The PrepCom began with no clear idea of how large the PTS would need to be, nor how large the Technical Secretariat would need to be after entry into force. Estimates from the CWC negotiations tended to overstate its size. A US paper from those negotiations estimated the size of the fully operational Technical Secretariat at over 1,200 and early PrepCom assumptions were based on a staff of between 500 and 800 employees.[122] The task of setting a first year budget was therefore taken in two stages: the First Session adopted a budget for the first three months of the PrepCom's existence of US$1,801,397, being the precise amount of the sum of the various calculations in the O'Sullivan letter. This budget had been produced in the first instance by Paul Ryan (United Kingdom) and developed over a series of meetings of CD delegations in the period May to November 1992.[123] Working Group A established a group of experts to

[120] 'Report of the Commission', PC-XIV/29, dated 27 July 1996, para. 7.

[121] Australian Permanent Mission Geneva, Letter from Ambassador Paul O'Sullivan, dated 9 November 1992.

[122] United States of America, 'A Chemical Weapons Convention staffing and cost estimates for a Technical Secretariat', CD/CW/WP.364, dated 21 August 1991; Working Group A, 'Group of Experts on OPCW Building: second interim report', PC-III/A/WP.7, dated 12 May 1993.

[123] This budget, as became the norm in the years that followed, was hard fought to keep costs down, including a tendency by Member States to insist that staff be graded at lower levels than were normal in the UN system for the level of responsibility. Once OPCW had been established after entry into force of the CWC and armed with a consultant's report on grading within the organisation the staff took their case for upgrading to the International Labour Organisation Administrative Tribunal and won. The judgment is reproduced in OPCW document S/203/2000, dated 4 August 2000. An OPCW calculation of the financial implications of reclassification of posts is contained in document S/209/2000, dated 28 August 2000 and S/209/2000/Add.1, dated 31 August 2000.

recommend a full budget for the year and on the basis of their work the Second Session appropriated a budget of US$8,840,796 for the calendar year 1993.[124]

The setting of a budget for 1994 was even more complex. Although the PrepCom was no longer constrained by the US$10,000,000 limit set for 1993 it had to cope with the uncertainty regarding the achievement of the 65 ratifications needed to bring the CWC into force. A two part budget system was therefore devised: Part I to be sufficient for the operation of the PrepCom and its PTS for a full year *without* the need to make final preparations for entry into force; and Part II to cover the additional expenses of the final six months before entry into force, including training the first group of inspectors. The Executive Secretary was instructed not to call for Part II funds until the 65th instrument of ratification had been deposited. Member States were required to pay their Part II assessments within one month of his call. This budget system was continued for the eventual four year life of the PrepCom with the call for Part II not being issued until late October 1996. This system, although essential for the PrepCom to carry out its function caused confusion in many capitals. Delegates reported that their Finance Ministries first asked why the money had not been spent in 1994 and then showed reluctance to agree to allocate funds again in subsequent years.

By the 1994 budget the PrepCom had switched to using the Netherlands Guilder (NLG) for its accounts but for ease of comparison the budgets (at the rate of exchange used by the PrepCom) were:

		NLG	US$	
1994	Part I	34,425 000	19,339,900	
	Part II	22,036,500	12,380,000	Not used
	Total	56,461,000	31,719,300	
1995	Part I	27,251,000	15,309,600	
	Part II	29,565,300	16,609,700	Not used
	Total	56,816,300	31.919,300	
1996	Part I	24,856,700	13,964,400	
	Part II	30,403,600	17,080,700	Activated (Oct)
	Total	55,260,300	31,045,100	
1997	Part I	13,214,800	7,424,000	Jan-Apr only

It can be seen that the total remains fairly constant but there is a progressive shift from Part I to Part II. The reduction in Part I is partly due to the reduction in recruitment costs as the PTS staffing remained stable from one year to the next. The increase in Part II in 1995 is due to refinement of the design of the Inspectorate, including equipment costs.

7.2 Insurance and superannuation

An issue which required attention from the Executive Secretary from the outset was that of health insurance, death and disability benefit and superannuation provision for

[124] This is effectively equal to US$10,000,000 for a full twelve months discounted for the early February start date of the PrepCom.

the staff. It was proposed that the Commission should provide the same cover as that received by United Nations Secretariat staff. In the case of the first two benefits this merely involved negotiating a premium with the insurance company used by the UN, J. Van Breda and Co, in nearby Antwerp, and obtaining Commission approval. Both policies were identical to those in place with the UN, but thereafter were renegotiated annually and tailored to best meet the specific needs of the Organisation; an exercise which resulted in enhanced benefits to staff members and considerable financial savings to the Organisation. The importance of the death and disability insurance was to be recognised following the death of a staff member and long-term sickness leading ultimately to separation from the Secretariat of another. Superannuation proved more complicated.

The United Nations Joint Staff Pension Fund (UNJSPF) proposed that a Provident Fund be established for PTS staff with the Commission and the individual staff members each contributing a percentage of the staff member's salary each month. A formal agreement between the Commission and the UN fund would then be negotiated followed by transfer of the full amount in the Provident Fund to the UN to purchase backdated membership in the UNJSPF for staff, effective from their date of recruitment. The Provident Fund was duly established on the terms recommended and the sums collected were placed on deposit in a bank at the best available rate of interest. However, examination of the rules of the UNJSPF showed that membership was likely to be less beneficial for PTS staff than had been assumed. PTS staff were recruited on the basis of twelve month renewable contracts with no guarantee of employment by OPCW once the Convention entered into force and the Preparatory Commission was wound up. In fact any staff member whose country of citizenship failed to ratify the Convention in time would automatically be barred from continuing in post. The UN fund, however, requires five years service before full benefits are offered. Any member leaving the scheme with less than five years service is entitled only to refund of *their own* contributions, with interest, and not those made on their behalf by the organisation. In these circumstances the Executive Secretary recommended to the Commission that the Provident Fund be maintained to provide terminal gratuities to staff, involving repayment of both individual and Commission inputs plus interest. This was agreed by the Commission. The PrepCom Staff Association proposed that the Fund be invested on the stock market in the hope of obtaining a higher return but the Executive Secretary maintained that his responsibility was to ensure the security of the moneys in the fund and he left them in the care of a highly rated bank.

7.3 **Finance**

For the period before the Executive Secretary was able to establish even an embryo accounts department within the PTS itself, financial services were provided by the OPCW Foundation. Governments had provided start-up funds, in the case of Norway by making a payment to the United Nations in New York and in most other cases by providing funds to the Netherlands government, which had placed them in a holding bank account. In this manner US$1,176,634 was immediately available with a further US$650,000 and £130,000 pledged for early delivery. Unfortunately, when it was necessary to access these funds the required signatories were either sick or on leave. The Executive Secretary did not receive any salary until after fully two months in post. A particular problem in the earliest days was that, whilst the Secretariat was to operate under United Nations staff and financial rules *mutatis mutandis*,[125] none of the staff had worked for the UN and thus had no knowledge of how to operate these rules in practice. The small administrative unit of the International Court of Justice was particularly helpful in filling this gap. The PTS Accounts Department was subsequently established by a short-term consultant, Ernest Pokorny, who was one of those retired UN staff recommended by the United Nations administration.

7.4 Accommodation for the Provisional Technical Secretariat

As described more fully in Chapter 5, the Bid included an 'office building to be provided free of charge during the preparatory phase'. This turned out to be a reasonably modern office block, offering five floors and a basement garage for a dozen vehicles, in a convenient location,[126] across the garden wall from the Peace Palace, home of the International Court of Justice, and adequately served by public transport. The first tranche of accommodation consisted of the top floor, fitted out as a suite of executive offices, half the ground floor entrance vestibule with its own front door and one of the pair of lifts, set to serve the top floor only. The initial partition on the ground floor consisted of a hedge of *Ficus benjamina*! The other floors were converted sequentially as more staff were recruited until the whole building was occupied.

By the end of 1994 the PTS consisted of 55 Professional and 57 General Service staff. The next major expansion (to a total of 369, including 140 inspector trainees) came at the time immediately following the deposit of the 65th instrument of ratification in October 1996. By this time it was clear that the permanent OPCW office building was not going to be ready in time for entry into force of the Convention and it became necessary to relocate the Verification Division into, and to prepare to house the Inspectorate in, separate temporary accommodation. Although the separation of the two locations by some 1.5 km was inconvenient the ICTY premises had the advantage of a high level of building security.

7.5 Conference accommodation

The First Session of the Preparatory Commission was held in the Netherlands Congress Centre and the Member States assumed that this facility would also house the various groups which were to meet between the sessions of the Commission. However, the OPCW Foundation pointed out that the Netherlands bid had not included funds for meetings other than those of the Preparatory Commission itself. The first week of the intersessional period was therefore spent in finding suitable conference facilities at an acceptable cost for the expert groups which were to meet in the third week.

---

125 'The necessary changes having been made'.

126 Laan van Meerdervoort 51.

The short-term solution found was to use conference rooms in hotels except on those few occasions when the only suitable conference room in the Ministry of Foreign Affairs was not required by the Ministry for its own purposes. (When it was available the Ministry provided it free of charge.) The hotels approached were very happy to provide conference facilities, free of charge, provided that they were guaranteed a certain number of bed-nights and meals purchased by delegates. The Executive Secretary, however, was not in a position to insist that delegates stay or eat in a particular hotel. Eventually the Atlantic Hotel in Kijkduin agreed to make its conference room available for a fee. In practice, quite a large group of delegates did eat in the hotel, partly because it was five kilometres out of town. This distance from the Office of the Secretariat caused considerable logistical problems for the staff in servicing meetings.

The remainder of the time to the Second Session of the Preparatory Commission was spent trying to find a more permanent solution to this problem. The OPCW Foundation discovered that the Netherlands Congress Centre had a redundant cinema, the Carel Willink Hall,[127] which was used only for a few days each year during the North Sea Jazz Festival. The Congress Centre offered to convert the cinema into a fully equipped, 357 seat conference room and to let it free of rent to the Preparatory Commission for five years if the Commission or the Foundation would provide to them the necessary capital for the conversion, which they could not find from their own resources. The total cost of the scheme was NLG 1,300,000. The Foundation budget for the cost of providing conference facilities for the Commission was NLG 1,050,000. The balance of NLG 250,000 would have to be found from the Commission's budget. The Executive Secretary persuaded the Commission that this was a good deal and was permitted to sign the necessary agreement. The new arrangements were ready in time for the Fourth Session of the Commission in September 1993, until then the sessions of the Commission were housed first in the Van Gogh Zaal and then in the Prince Willem Alexander Zaal. These two facilities, both fitted out as theatres, were not very suitable as they did not allow for easy circulation of delegates and secretariat staff during meetings.

7.6 Conference services

The Conference Services Section of the Secretariat was established by Vladimir Iossifov, initially provided on loan from the Russian delegation in Geneva, who had previous experience of working within the United Nations Secretariat. The support staff required for the first Expert Groups in the Atlantic Hotel were found by recruiting some of the university students who had been employed from a local agency by the Foundation as receptionists at the First Session of the Preparatory Commission. Providing full conference services for the second session of the Preparatory Commission in April 1993 was a much bigger challenge. The UN Secretariat staff who had serviced the First Session recommended that the UN be asked to provide services also

[127] All but one of the halls in the Netherlands Congress Centre are named after well-known Dutch painters.

for the Second Session, again on a repayment basis. The staff in Geneva made all the necessary preparations to make the resources available a second time. However, only three weeks before the session was to start, the UN Controller refused permission for the staff to be used on the grounds that Resolution 47/39 had only provided for service to the First Session. Mr Iossifov rose to the challenge and recruited two 14-person teams of interpreters, to cover all six Commission languages, from Geneva, New York and Beijing and had them on site in time for the meeting to start as planned. The provision of ushers and security staff from the local market was a lesser challenge but was only successfully met due to the willingness of all members of the staff of the Secretariat to help out in whatever capacity was needed; a spirit that was to be witnessed many times over in the life of the PTS and which undoubtedly saved considerable expenditure on temporary staff.

7.7 The language issue

Governments quite naturally expect their representatives to understand the documents and oral statements on the basis of which important decisions are to be taken. There are only two solutions to this problem: send representatives who speak the language in which the meeting is being held; or ensure high quality translation of documentation and interpretation of oral statements. Unfortunately the first becomes very difficult when specialist issues are under discussion and the second can be very expensive. For example, informal meetings in the European Union are held in French or English but formal meetings have interpretation into and out of all the official languages of all Member States!

The CWC was negotiated in Geneva within a United Nations environment, high-level meetings with interpretation services in the six UN languages – Arabic, Chinese, English, French, Russian and Spanish, lower level meetings held in English without interpretation services, and all documents relating to substantive decisions translated into all six languages. It became evident at an early stage that the PrepCom was going to have problems in this regard. The formal sessions could be provided with interpretation in the six languages by contracting interpreters to travel to The Hague from the main UN centres for the relevant weeks for which dates were fixed reasonably in advance. Even this is an expensive undertaking as a full team consists of fourteen people – two each for English, French, Russian and Spanish and three each for Arabic and Chinese. These have to be provided with travel and subsistence costs in addition to their substantial fees. One team will service a maximum of eight three-hour sessions in a week. So if there is a need to operate morning and afternoon for five days, with the possibility of evening sessions or timetable overrun, two full teams have to be contracted or the excess meetings held without interpretation. A further problem can be the specialist vocabulary needed for meetings such as those of the Commission, dealing with chemistry, industrial and military equipment and so on. However much of the real work of the Commission was carried out by groups of government experts for which it was not economically feasible to provide full interpretation services. This caused very real problems for delegations supported for the particular topic by experts from capitals who had expertise in the subject matter of the meeting but spoke only their mother tongue. The English speaking diplomats who formed the local delegations could often provide informal interpretation but sometimes they had to attend simultaneous meetings in another part of town.

It clearly made sense for the PTS to include language staff to translate the documentation, arising from the expert groups and the work of the Secretariat, required for the Commission sessions. This involved a reasonably even workload and in-house translation could allow a build-up of the necessary specialist knowledge and vocabulary. In the UN system in general, translation and interpretation, which are distinct skills, are performed by separate groups of staff. An innovation in the PTS and subsequently in OPCW itself has been the recruitment of 'linguists' whose day to day task is translation but who will provide interpretation services in an emergency. This permitted support to be given to individual experts when necessary without the expense of providing full interpretation service at this level of meetings. An incidental benefit of structuring the language services in this way is that OPCW can be confident of providing interpretation services for emergency meetings of the Executive Council which, under Article IX of the CWC, can be required to meet at a few hours notice.

7.8 Information technology

The initial office equipment provided by the Foundation for the PTS included a small office photocopier and a small number of desktop PCs with WordPerfect 5.1 English software for use as word processors. The PTS requirements, both for drafting documents and for distributing them to over 140 delegations in six languages, far exceeded the capabilities of this equipment. The original photocopier died of overwork in six weeks and was replaced by a succession of ever larger and more sophisticated machines. The Executive Secretary came to an arrangement with the Foundation that the PTS would receive a cash sum in lieu of a word processor for each staff position established and that the PTS would take responsibility for all its own computing equipment requirements. One of the first decisions of the Executive Secretary, on the strong recommendation of René Haug who was at that stage acting as IT adviser, was to base the electronic office on a combination of Microsoft Windows and Lotus Notes software. Microsoft Word was chosen for word processing in English, French, Spanish, Russian and Arabic. The choice of Chinese software was left until the Chinese typist was recruited. As she was trained to use 'Little Sparrow', this was purchased together with the necessary Apple Mac computer. For the purpose of planning inspections after 'entry into force', the United States Government announced that it would arrange and pay for the development of specialist software and equipment. Meanwhile the Commission had to start grappling with the complex issue of computer security in the new organisation.

The initial Lotus Notes installation was used: to provide internal e-mail facilities for the PTS; to provide a joint document editing facility; and to provide means whereby those delegations with the necessary software could access Commission documents through direct telephone modem connection. It was also possible for PTS staff, when travelling away from the office, to access the system from a laptop computer. It was determined from the outset that any system to be used after entry into force for sensitive data would not have any means of connection to the world outside the Secretariat and would be kept separate from the administrative, unclassified system. An early proposal to provide every work-station in the PTS with direct connection to the Internet was considered to involve unacceptable security risks and, instead, a separate computer with internet access was provided on each floor for staff use.

8. The Provisional Technical Secretariat

8.1 Establishment of the PTS

On the fourth day of its First Session the Preparatory Commission, acting in accordance with the Paris Resolution,[128] established the PTS, referred to in Commission documents as 'the Secretariat'. The decision went on to say

> The Secretariat will be composed of an Executive Secretary who shall be its head and chief executive officer, and such other staff as may be required.
> [...] in matters of staff appointments, [he shall] make recommendations to the Preparatory Commission on appointments to senior management positions, (UN Grade D-1 (Principal Officer) equivalent and above) and directly appoint all other necessary staff (subject only to appropriate reporting to and liaison with the Preparatory Commission), in both cases, in accordance with the principles contained in Article VIII, paragraph 44 of the Convention.

The relevant part of paragraph 44 states:

> The paramount consideration in the employment of the staff [...] shall be the necessity of securing the highest standards of efficiency, competence and integrity. Only citizens of States Parties shall serve [...] as members of the professional and clerical staff.[129] Due regard shall be paid to the importance of recruiting staff on as wide a geographical basis as possible.

This was interpreted to mean that only citizens of Signatory States could serve in the PTS.

This eminently reasonable set of requirements, in fact poses severe problems for a technical organisation, most of the staff of which need to be engineers, scientists and professional administrators. Many delegations wished to interpret '*on as wide a geographical basis as possible*' to be the same as '*on an equitable geographical basis*', which in the minds of many means equal representation from each of the five UN regional groups.[130] Availability of trained professionals in the different regions in the required areas of skill varies considerably and this latter interpretation was never go-

---

[128] Text on the Establishment of a Preparatory Commission, para. 8(c) (as appended to the Paris Resolution).

[129] This was interpreted to mean that only citizens of Signatory States could serve in the PTS.

[130] Africa; Asia; Eastern Europe (EE); Latin America and the Caribbean (LAC); and Western Europe and Others (US, Canada, Australia and New Zealand) (WEOG).

ing to be possible. Nonetheless, pressure on the Executive Secretary to redress perceived imbalances was unrelenting.

As part of the negotiations relating to his appointment, the Executive Secretary, Ian Kenyon (UK), gave an undertaking that 'in terms of the senior posts he would endeavour to maintain a balance between appointments of staff from developed and developing Signatory States'.[131] It was understood that this meant that 50 percent of the staff at P5 would come from EE, WEOG and Japan with the other 50 percent coming from the rest of Asia, LAC and Africa. For other, more junior staff 'best endeavours' would mean just that. At the most senior level, the six D1 posts approved by the Commission would be filled as follows: the Deputy Executive Secretary from Asia; the Legal Advisor from Latin America; the Head of External Relations from Eastern Europe (Russia); the Head of Technical Cooperation and Assistance from Africa; with WEOG having two posts – Head of Verification and Head of Administration (US). This arrangement both ensured that each region had a post and met the 50:50 rule.

The budget adopted by the Commission for the first three months was directly taken from the O'Sullivan letter mentioned earlier. This calculated the personnel funding on the basis of the following staffing:

Professional staff	**Pay level (UN equivalent)**[132]
Executive Secretary	Assistant Secretary-General
Legal Adviser	P-5 or D-1
Conference Service Manager[u]	P-5 or D-1
Budget Officer[u]	P-5 or D-1
Personnel Officer[u]	P-5 or D-1
Clerical support	
ES Secretary	Level 6
Senior Secretary	Level 5
Secretary/Accountants	Level 4
Finance Clerk	Level 4

In practice only two of these posts were filled for the whole of the intersessional period covered by this budget – the Executive Secretary and his secretary. The secretary post was filled for six months by Shirley van der Steen, supplied on loan by the Netherlands Ministry of Foreign Affairs. (Even she was not available for the first week due to a prearranged ski holiday.)

The three posts marked with the superscript [u] above had been requested from the UN on three months loan by the sponsors of UN General Assembly Resolution 47/39 (1992). This resolution not only 'calls on all States to sign [...] the Convention' but 'also requests the Secretary-General to provide such services as may be requested by the Signatory States to initiate the work of the Preparatory Commission'. The 'Programme and Budget Implications' document which accompanied the draft reso-

[131] 'Statement by the Executive Secretary on senior stereophonic [*sic*] questions', as included in: 'Report of the Preparatory Commission', PREPCOM/I-4, dated 12 February 1993.

[132] The United Nations pay grades for professional staff run (from the bottom) P1 – P5, D1-D2, ASG; there are levels G1 – G6 for clerical and other support staff. In the PTS all P staff were subject to international recruitment, GS staff were locally recruited.

lution when it came to the General Assembly for a vote specifically mentions the loan, on a full reimbursement basis of these three officers.[133] However, the UN administration pleaded that they had no suitably qualified officers to spare and recommended three recently retired staff members who might be prepared to serve in the short-term.

There were additional factors and assumptions which shaped the various annual budgets adopted by the PrepCom and the staffing structure of the PTS. The PrepCom began with no clear idea of how large the PTS would need to be, nor how large the Technical Secretariat would need to be after entry into force. Estimates from the CWC negotiations tended to overstate the size of the latter. A US paper from the CD estimated the size of the fully operational Technical Secretariat at over 1,200 staff[134] and early PrepCom assumptions were for between 500 and 800 employees.[135] In fact the first full year budget adopted by OPCW seven months after entry into force authorised an establishment of 491 for the year 1998.[136] In 2004 the TS had 431 'fixed term posts', 293 Professional and 138 General Service, together with an unspecified number of 'temporary assignments and experts'.

8.2 Senior appointments

Of the D1 officers authorised by the First Session of the PrepCom only the Director of Verification, John Gee (Australia) and the Legal Adviser, Felix Calderón (Peru) were available to start work during the first intersessional period. Serguei Batsanov, the Director of External Relations was appointed by the First Session to start work 'around the time of the Second Session'. The first person appointed as Director of Administration, after considering the terms of service offered, and considering other options open to him, declined the post. A new proposal to fill this position had to await the Second Session of the Commission when Rueben Lev (United States) was appointed. Three candidates from countries of the Asian group were offered for the position of Deputy Executive Secretary but it was not possible for the group to achieve consensus on their choice during the First Session. Li Chang-he (China) was appointed by the Second Session. The final post took even longer to fill. Four candidates, all well qualified for the post of Director of Technical Cooperation and Assistance, had been put forward by their various governments at the Second Session and the African group asked the Executive Secretary to make the selection. After interviewing them all he recommended John Makhubalo (Zimbabwe) to the Third Session for appointment.

---

133 United Nations General Assembly [47th session], Fifth Committee, 'Convention on the Prohibition of the Development, Production, Stockpiling and Use of Chemical Weapons and on Their Destruction. Programme budget implications of draft resolution A/C.1/47/L.1/Rev.2. Statement submitted by the Secretary-General in accordance with rule 153 of the rules of procedure of the General Assembly', A/C.5/47/49, dated 13 November 1992.

134 United States of America, 'A Chemical Weapons Convention staffing and cost estimates for a Technical Secretariat', CD/CW/WP.364, dated 21 August 1991.

135 Working Group A, 'Group of Experts on OPCW Building: second interim report', PC-III/A/WP.7, dated 12 May 1993.

136 C-II/6, dated 5 December 1997.

8.3 Seconded personnel

The Australian government made it possible for Mr Gee to remain after the first meeting of the Commission for two weeks before returning to Australia, bringing his family back to The Hague at the beginning of April. For the substantive work of supporting the initial Expert Group meetings and preparing the budget for the first year of the work of the Commission the Executive Secretary relied upon a small group of individuals made available to him on secondment from Governments. In some cases these were fully supported by their own governments and in other cases relied on the travel and per diem payments from the Commission. Most of them subsequently formally joined the staff of the Secretariat.

This group, which worked very long hours, was composed as follows:

- *Administration*
  Paul Ryan (United Kingdom) initially acted as Chief of Staff (pending the arrival of **Agnés Marcaillou** (France)) whilst simultaneously providing administration services until such time as the various specialists arrived to take over their respective sections. He continued as Section leader – General Services through into OPCW itself. One of his first additional (and continuing) tasks was to be secretary of the expert group on the OPCW building.
  Henk Antvelink (Netherlands) offered his services as a junior personnel officer, initially working only in the evening while he worked out his notice with NATO, his former employer.

- *Conference Services*
  Vladimir Iossifov (Russia) created the Conference Services Section (see below).
  Chantal de Haas (Netherlands) who had been a locally based member of the secretariat provided for the first session of the PrepCom, was recruited to provide clerical support to the expert group meetings. She later joined the Media Branch, where she gained a professional level appointment.

- *Information Technology Services*
  Rene Haug (Switzerland), whilst a professional diplomat, had a degree of experience with IT and with a consultant **Louis Veeger**, initially supplied by Paagman & Paagman BV, developed and installed the PTS electronic office.

- *Legal services*
  Johan Rautenbach (South Africa) provided legal services, including acting as secretary to the expert groups on legal issues, pending the arrival of **Felix Calderón** in April after which Johan took the post of Deputy Legal Adviser.

- *Planning and Budget*
  Ron Nelson (United States), briefly supported by **Axel Angély** (France), started the work he was to follow through for several years coordinating PTS input to the budget drafting process.

- *Secretarial support*
  As mentioned above **Shirley van der Steen** (Netherlands) was provided on loan by her government as the Executive Secretary's secretary. Other staff were supported by **Ms J Ramdjan** (Netherlands).

Preparation of the budget for the first twelve months included construction of a staffing plan which formed the basis for the organisation not only of the PTS itself but also of the OPCW Technical Secretariat after entry into force of the Convention.

8.4 Formal recruitment

When the United Kingdom government proposed Ian Kenyon for the post of Executive Secretary in the summer of 1992, some of the governments whose support for the CWC was going to be crucial to its success approached him with proposed candidates for posts in the PTS. Thus Don Clagett (United States),[137] Agnes Marcailliou (France),[138] Bunro Shiozawa (Japan)[139] and Ralf Trapp (Germany)[140] joined the Secretariat, Trapp immediately and the other three by mid-1993 after separation from their previous employment.

Several members of Member State delegations to the First Session of the Commission who had also formed part of their national delegations to the Conference on Disarmament (CD) in Geneva during the negotiation of the CWC and who were consequently well acquainted with its provisions and the political compromises involved were given leave by their governments to join the PTS. These included Anil Wadwha (India),[141] Hassan Mashhadi (Iran)[142] and Shahbaz (Pakistan).[143]

Kenyon and Gee identified three other experts in the field of chemical weapons who were based in governmental defense laboratories and whom they knew through their involvement with the CD or UNSCOM.[144] These were Pavel Castulik (Czech Republic),[145] Ron Manley (United Kingdom)[146] and Johan Santesson (Sweden).[147] Manley and Santesson initially served as government experts and, indeed chaired meetings of experts in the early summer of 1993 but were then persuaded to come over to the PTS side of the Commission.

Geographical balance had not been achieved by this process so the Executive Secretary approached the African and Latin American regional groups for help in finding suitable candidates for some of the remaining positions. As a result of this he was able

137 Head of Industry Operations Branch, Verification Division.

138 Special Assistant to the Executive Secretary.

139 Head of Declarations and Confidentiality Branch, Verification Division.

140 Head of Industry Concepts Branch, Verification Division.

141 Head of Public Affairs and Media Branch, External Relations Division.

142 Head of Govt. Relations and Political Affairs Branch, External Relations Division.

143 Head of Assistance Branch, Technical Cooperation and Assistance Division.

144 United Nations Special Commission for Iraq, set up under UN Security Council auspices to find and destroy Iraq's chemical, biological and nuclear weapons programmes following the 1991 war.

145 Head of Training Branch, Verification Division.

146 Head of Chemical Demilitarisation Branch, Verification Division.

147 Head of Technical Cooperation Branch, Technical Cooperation and Assistance Division.

to recruit two people with technical backgrounds, Raul Fernandez (Argentina)[148] and Marta Laudares (Brazil),[149] and a diplomat with administrative experience, Chemuta Banda (Cameroon).[150]

Two specialists had to be recruited by means of a wider search; Horst Becker (Germany)[151] was recruited from within the UN system to run the PrepCom accounts, which used the UN Financial Rules; and John Parkes (Australia)[152] filled the need for a medical doctor with training in chemical defense. (Parkes only remained with the PTS for a year and was replaced by Brian Davey (South Africa) who had been a member of the Health and Safety Expert Group.)

The PTS computer network was initially established by a diplomat, Rene Haug, on loan from the government of Switzerland, supported by short-term consultants. The first appointment as head of Information Systems Branch went to Oscar Fiestas (Peru) who was followed in the post by Chantal Quincy-Jones (France). Ron Nelson (United States) worked in the Executive Secretary's Office as a Planning Officer on loan from (and paid by) his government during the early stages of the PrepCom and then moved into the same role as a staff member.[153]

The junior positions in the various branches were mostly filled by advertising the vacancies to all delegations to the PrepCom and selecting using interview panels of appropriate senior staff. By the end of 1995 the PTS had 62 professional and higher level staff representing 35 different nationalities. Unfortunately only 11 of them were women – the geographical balance was not bad but the gender balance was woeful, despite strong efforts on the part of the PTS to find suitable female candidates.

8.5 Filling out the Secretariat structure

It was evident that, if the OPCW was to 'hit the ground running' at entry into force of the Convention, the PTS would have to transform itself into the OPCW Technical Secretariat overnight, fully staffed, trained and equipped to meet the very tight deadlines laid down for receipt and processing of declarations by Member States and for initial inspections of the chemical weapon stocks and facilities declared. Thus the initial requirement was to recruit experts to become heads of the necessary policy branches whose initial task would be assisting the respective groups of government experts in developing the role of their branch. (In fact the PTS tended to operate on a collegiate basis for the first 18 months of its existence with senior staff pooling their expertise and working together on whatever was the current problem.) As entry into force drew closer the branches would have to be filled out with additional junior staff to enable them to fulfil their operational functions. A major component of the work in the latter stages would be recruitment and training of the inspectors – more than one third of the total staff and, in a sense, the *raison d'être* of the organisation.

---

148 Head of Industry Relations Branch, External Relations Division.
149 Head of Technical Support Branch, Verification Division.
150 Head of Personnel Branch, Administration Division.
151 Head of Budget and Finance Branch, Administration Division.
152 Head of Health and Safety Branch, Verification Division.
153 Mr Nelson went on to become Director of Administration in OPCW.

As the Director of Verification post was filled immediately and John Gee remained in The Hague for two weeks after the First Session, the Executive Secretary was able to work out with him immediately the branch structure for the Division that they would propose to the Expert Group on Budget and Programme of work and which of the available candidates they would place in which posts. The reference to 'available candidates' requires explanation. Within the United Nations system the process of filling a new post from the point of identifying a need, through preparing a job description, advertising, short-listing, interviewing candidates, final selection, candidate working out notice in present employment (if necessary), and transfer to place of employment takes on average 18 months. In an organisation which initially expected to exist for only two years and with an immediate need for staff who could be effective on arrival without elaborate training this system was clearly inappropriate. (It has, of course, become the norm in OPCW itself.) Instead the Executive Secretary made use of the extensive network of contacts provided by Member State delegations.

In devising the structure of the Verification Division, one of the first problems to be overcome was the fact that Germany, Japan and the US had all put forward individuals to head the 'industry' branch. In the end the problem was solved by finding jobs for all three candidates, namely two industry branches, Industry A (Don Clagett of the US) and Industry B (Ralf Trapp of Germany) that operated cooperatively with Clagett emphasizing the technical aspects of industry concerns and Trapp addressing policy matters, and a Declarations and Confidentiality Branch (Bunro Shiozawa of Japan).[154] As with many other staff positions in the early days of the PTS, lacking more junior staff or adequate secretarial assistance, the three individuals worked as a team with each working to his own strengths. Indeed, during the first year, it was seen as more important to get capable people into the PTS than to assign them specific functions; everyone carried out multiple jobs, often beyond their formal job titles, and frequently working very long hours.

For the first year, the PTS was very much a skeleton structure – the total number of professional and higher posts by the end of 1993 was only 30.[155] An enormous workload therefore fell on the staff members particularly when the expert groups were meeting and PTS staff were expected to act as their secretaries. Although this arrangement meant a lot of work for the individuals involved, it also allowed the PTS to have a significant, if less visible, influence upon the discussions. While some delegates expected the PTS to 'be seen and not heard' and to act as a basic conference servicing operation, others were aware of the expertise possessed by its staff and were keen to allow that expertise to be taken into account. The PTS got its views across mainly through the mechanism of the 'chairman's papers' which were often drafted by the

[154] All three candidates were extremely well qualified and were the kind of experts the PTS needed to recruit. For example, Don Clagett had worked in the chemical industry and had been the representative of General Electric on the CMA chemical weapons working group. Ralf Trapp was a chemist and toxicologist and had been a scientific adviser in the CWC negotiations since 1982, first for East Germany, then for Germany following reunification.

[155] 'Note by the Executive Secretary on the breakdown of nationalities for professional and higher categories represented at the Provisional Technical Secretariat as of 14 December 1993', PC-V/A/6, dated 14 December 1993.

PTS personnel acting as secretaries to the respective chairmen. The relationship between the chairman and the secretary was thus critical and many operated 'hand in glove' with one another. In contrast to 1993 when many expert group background papers and initial drafts were prepared by national delegations, from 1994 onwards most such documentation originated from within the PTS, with the PTS trying to bring the different national views together.[156]

The use of a five division structure for the PTS was driven by the demands of the Member States of the Commission for geographical balance and for keeping the number of senior posts to the minimum compatible with operational effectiveness. It was clear that there should be a division to handle the preparations for the verification task which features so strongly in the Convention but, as the inspectors would be recruited and trained in the latter stages of the Commission's work the creation of the post of Chief Inspector could be left until entry into force. The insistence of the non-aligned Member States on equal status between the verification and technical assistance roles within the new organisation led to the creation of a division for the latter task. It was important that these two divisions concentrate on these tasks and that a division be created to handle communications with Member States; the industry bodies and other non-governmental organisations; the media and the general public. The need for a legal adviser of senior rank with his associated staff and for an administration division to handle finance, personnel and general services is common to all international organisations. It was decided for the preparatory phase to include conference services in the administration, although a different solution was appropriate after the entry into force (EIF) of the CWC (see below).

Office of the Executive Secretary

Aside from the five divisions the Executive Secretary acquired a small staff reporting directly to him. In addition to the Deputy Executive Secretary these included a Special Assistant (or *Chef de Cabinet*) and a Planning Officer (principally involved with the preparation of the successive budgets through which the OPCW was created). As the work of the Commission progressed it became useful to add an Internal Auditor, an English language document editor and, in the latter stages of the build up to EIF, a Security Officer.

Administration Division

The finances of the Commission were relatively straightforward and were handled for most of the period by a *Budget and Finance Branch* with two professional officers and three general service staff. The verification operations of OPCW, with inspectors travelling all over the globe and costs to be recovered from weapon possessing states, together with an organisation three times bigger in terms of staff, required that this branch be expanded during the final stage ('Phase II') and at EIF to include three

[156] Robert Mathews and Antony Taubman, 'Preparing for implementation of the Chemical Weapons Convention: Progress during 1994', in JB Poole and R Guthrie (eds.), *Verification 1995: Arms Control, Peacekeeping and the Environment* (London/Boulder, VERTIC/Westview 1995), pp. 161-179 at p. 164.

separate sections, *Budget*; *Accounts*; and *Disbursements* and with a substantial increase in clerical staff.

The *Conference Services Branch* of the Commission included under the branch head three sections: *Conference Support* and *Documentation and Reproduction*, each with three general service staff, and the *Language Section*, which included for each of the five languages (apart from English) one Senior Linguist,[157] one Linguist and one Bilingual Typist. At EIF this section was augmented by the addition of English capability – three Linguists and a Typist – plus an expansion of the five other languages by two Linguists each for Arabic and Chinese and one each for French, Russian and Spanish. At EIF the whole Branch was taken out of the Administration Division and put under the management control of the Secretary of the Policy Making Organs (a new senior management post).

The *General Services Branch* handled management of the office facilities; procurement; and travel, including the transport fleet and drivers. Prior to the appointment of a Security Officer in the ES office, this branch handled security issues. This workload was handled by the branch head supported by a procurement officer and a group of clerks and drivers. A Building Officer was added once construction of the OPCW building was begun (see Chapter 5) to assist the branch head in liaison with the developers.

The *Human Resources Branch* (originally known as Personnel Branch) had three professional officers, the head of branch being supported by a Staff Administration Officer and a Recruitment Officer, together with three general service staff. In Phase II as the PTS staff was rapidly increased and Inspector training began the branch was augmented by five additional general service staff.

The *Information Systems Branch* serviced the needs of the Commission with a small permanent staff of three professional and two general service staff supported by an ever changing group of short-term contracted technicians. At EIF the Branch was rebuilt with a proposed full-time contracted staff of 24, including 12 professionals. The principal reason for this change was the need to ensure a secure IT environment in the new organisation.

External Relations Division

Government Relations and Political Affairs Branch, in addition to its liaison function relative to individual Member States as well as other intergovernmental organisations and the conduct of regional workshops and seminars, initially handled protocol and visa issues. In Phase II a new branch was created to handle these latter issues as the obtaining of visas for OPCW inspectors was expected to be a much larger task than that for assisting visits to Member States by PTS staff. The roles of the heads of *Industrial Relations Branch* and *Media and Public Affairs Branch* are self explanatory. The latter was supported by an NGO, Media and Public Affairs Officer and also received valuable assistance from a researcher, financially supported by the Harvard Sussex Program (who also acted as the Executive Secretary's speech writer).

---

157 For the structure of the language services see section 7.7 above.

Office of the Legal Adviser (Legal Division)
During the life of the Commission the Legal Division was not divided into branches although it was envisaged that this would be necessary after EIF. The Legal Adviser (a Director level post) was supported initially by two and later by four professional officers, a senior general service paralegal assistant and two secretaries.

Technical Cooperation and Assistance Division
The head of the division, in addition to his secretary, was supported by two branch heads. *Assistance Branch* was concerned with Article X issues (see Chapter 12) and *Technical Cooperation Branch* with Article XI (see Chapter 13). During Phase II and at EIF both branches were to be filled out with two additional professional officers and a secretary each.

Verification Division
The Verification Division, with initially seven and in Phase II eight branches was by far the largest division, employing nearly half of the total professional staff of the Provisional Secretariat (without counting the approximately 150 inspector trainees under the division's management during Phase II). The Director therefore had a professional level Assistant in addition to his secretary.

The *Health and Safety Office* had as its head a medical doctor, supported by a Safety Officer (Industry), a records clerk and a secretary. In Phase II a Senior Medical Officer was added, together with a nurse. After EIF the Health and Safety Office was expanded to 11 personnel and detached from the Verification Division and attached to the Deputy Director-General's office.

The *Chemical Demilitarisation Branch* was charged with preparations for the inspections related to declared chemical weapons and related production, storage and destruction facilities. The head of the branch was initially supported by one professional officer and a cost-free intern provided by the Monterey Institute of International Studies. A further professional officer and GS-OL Secretary were added in Phase II. At EIF the branch was initially expanded to four professional officers and a GS-OL secretary. The staffing of this Branch, however, was predicated on the existence of the Bilateral Destruction Agreement between the United States and Russia. When this failed to materialise it proved necessary to expand the Branch to 9 professional officers and 2 GS-OL support staff.

The *Declarations and Confidentiality Branch* during Phase I consisted of the head of the branch supported by two professional level officers. This was sufficient for support of the Commission experts working out declaration procedures. However, at EIF the branch had to be ready to receive and process declarations on both chemical weapons and declarable civil chemical industry. This involved a substantial expansion during Phase II, with the creation of a *Confidentiality Section* and an *Information Validation and Evaluation Section,* involving a total of nine professional level staff as well as General Service clerks. At EIF the Confidentiality Section was separated out and attached to the Office of the Director-General.

The United States, Germany and Japan all wished to have senior staff posts involved with Article VI issues. The Japanese were satisfied through the post mentioned above. To satisfy the United States and Germany the PrepCom decided to create two branches initially titled *Industry A* and *Industry B*. These were subsequently re-titled. *A* became *Industry Verification Concepts Development Branch* (further renamed *Policy and Review Branch*) which had a head of branch supported by one professional level officer. *B*, which became *Industry Operations Branch* was initially the same size but by EIF had expanded to a total of four professional officers. These two branches worked closely together, effectively as a single unit, in the development of the inspector training manual and selection of the inspector candidates.

Technical Support Branch was created to supervise the Equipment Store and the OPCW Laboratory. The head of the branch was supported by two professional level Technical Support Officers on the equipment side and a Head of Laboratory with initially one, and at EIF two, Analytical Chemists and a general service Laboratory Technician. Once the Equipment Store started to receive equipment, ready for inspection operations to start immediately after EIF it was provided with a general service Store Supervisor and a group of eight general service staff for equipment issue and servicing duties.

Training Branch had a head of branch supported by three, later four, professional officers, one of whom was responsible for the recruitment of the inspector trainees and another of whom planned the operations room for the Inspectorate. During Phase II an *Operations and Planning Centre* was established as a separate unit. At EIF this was detached from the Verification Division and came under the Chief Inspector (a new Director level post created EIF). The Training Branch was transferred to the Administration Division at EIF.

8.6 Adjustments to the Technical Secretariat structure after entry into force

The concept for the Verification Division developed by the PTS was for it to be headed by a D2 Director supported by two D1s, one to head the Inspectorate and the other to manage the other Verification Branches. However, the newly elected Director-General, in discussing his proposed top structure found that this arrangement, putting the key 70 percent of the Organisation in the hands of one director, was unacceptable to the Member States, who preferred that the Inspectorate be separate. Compared with the PTS under the Executive Secretary, the Director-General was able to agree a top structure with an increased number of director-level posts. In addition to the Head of the Inspectorate the new directors were: the Secretary of the Policy Making Organs; and the Head of Internal Oversight (which included Internal Audit and Confidentiality).

The organisation chart for the Technical Secretariat as at entry into force is shown in Figure 1. Later in 1997, following ratification by Russia and Iran, two further senior posts were added: Director of Special Projects within the Director-General's office and Head of Emergency Assistance Branch within International Cooperation and Assistance Division, filled by staff from these two states respectively.

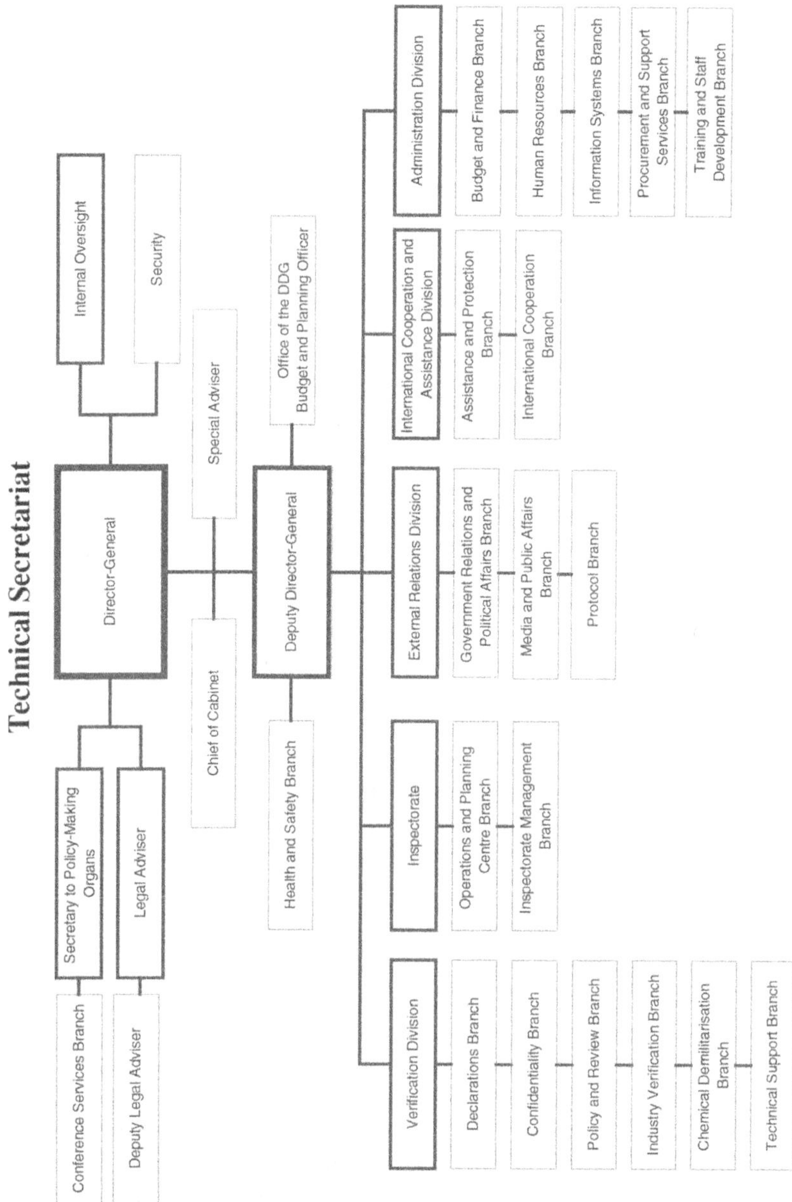
Technical Secretariat
Internal Oversight
Security
Director-General
Secretary to Policy-Making Organs
Conference Services Branch
Legal Adviser
Deputy Legal Adviser
Special Adviser
Chief of Cabinet
Office of the DDG
Budget and Planning Officer
Deputy Director-General
Health and Safety Branch
Verification Division
Declarations Branch
Confidentiality Branch
Policy and Review Branch
Industry Verification Branch
Chemical Demilitarisation Branch
Technical Support Branch
Inspectorate
Operations and Planning Centre Branch
Inspectorate Management Branch
External Relations Division
Government Relations and Political Affairs Branch
Media and Public Affairs Branch
Protocol Branch
International Cooperation and Assistance Division
Assistance and Protection Branch
International Cooperation Branch
Administration Division
Budget and Finance Branch
Human Resources Branch
Information Systems Branch
Procurement and Support Services Branch
Training and Staff Development Branch

9. Progress of the Work

The first session of the PrepCom was mainly concerned with administrative issues and the allocation of the senior posts within the PTS. Once these issues had been addressed to the extent possible, the PrepCom got down to more substantive work. By the end of 1993, the PrepCom had held five plenary sessions and progress was being made in the expert groups established to undertake its substantive work. However, work was not progressing as fast as those who saw the PrepCom as a means to provide technical elaboration of the CWC in preparation for its entry into force had foreseen. Momentum was lost partly because of the slower than expected rate of ratifications by signatory states; by the end of 1993 only four had ratified the Convention (see below). Another major factor was that some of the issues under discussion were not really technical at all, they were political. Such issues had been contentious enough in the Conference on Disarmament in Geneva to elude agreement, and they remained so in The Hague. In fact, the situation was exacerbated in the PrepCom. While the CWC negotiations had been limited to the 40 CD delegations, the discussions in the PrepCom were open to all 130-plus signatory states. Although many did not participate (in fact relative participation rates fell from 67 percent at the first plenary, to 53 percent at the fifth, although total membership did grow from 137 to 154 states), the increase meant that a greater number of interests had to be accommodated. It also meant that developing countries had a much louder voice and a great deal more attention had to be devoted to issues such as technical cooperation and assistance.

Perhaps the most important but least visible factor affecting progress was the rotation of personnel on delegations and the different mindset of many of the new diplomats. When the negotiations ended in Geneva, many of those most closely involved were left behind, either remaining in their national CD delegations or moving on to other jobs. A few moved to The Hague, and some took jobs with the PTS. A major difference between Geneva and The Hague was the background and motivation of the diplomats involved. In Geneva ministries of foreign affairs had led for most countries and, given the fact that they were involved in a negotiation, delegates were willing to look for compromises and do deals in order to achieve consensus and the completion of the CWC text. With the move to The Hague, the involvement of ministries of foreign affairs was reduced and instead ministries of defence and of industry took the lead. This switch from negotiators to implementers was inevitable but it led to a loss of collective memory and meant that the new personnel looked on the deals struck in Geneva in a very different light, focused more on how to limit the impact of the CWC nationally. In addition, the move from Geneva to The Hague had practical implications. Geneva was an international city with all the requisite resources (translators, interpreters, secretarial companies and so on) for international organisations and conferences. Delegations to the CD were staffed by diplomats with disarmament experience and multilateral expertise. By contrast, The Hague was a city without such extensive experience of hosting international conferences or organisations. There was no local pool of translators or interpreters upon which the PrepCom could call. Embassies in The Hague were mainly concerned with bilateral relations between their own countries and the Netherlands and few of the diplomats posted there were trained multilateralists. As became apparent during the first PrepCom plenary, diplomats in The Hague had no established mechanisms for discussing issues informally, there had never been a need before.

Throughout the PrepCom, and particularly from 1994 onwards, a lot of attention focused on the ratification processes in the two known possessor states, the United States and Russia. Many countries looked to Russia and the US for leadership and to them for the injection of momentum into the process. However, when it became clear during 1994 that the US Senate was not going to ratify the Convention that year, the discussions in The Hague lost some of their urgency and those who wanted to re-open issues or frustrate progress were given ample opportunity. The absence of ratification from Moscow and Washington also slowed down further ratifications as other countries waited to see what Russia and the US would do, adding to a loss of momentum in The Hague. For all of these reasons, it became apparent during 1994 that the PrepCom was moving away from a technical elaboration of the CWC and moving towards a re-run of the disagreements in Geneva, including attempts to re-interpret decisions made by the negotiators there. This led to some Western delegations seeing the PrepCom as a damage limitation exercise in which they had to hold the line against proposals which could potentially undermine the CWC as agreed in Geneva. The chairman's report of a Working Group B meeting in February 1995 stated:

> Many delegations expressed the view that, in its attempts to resolve [outstanding] issues, the Commission should attempt neither to add to the provisions of the Convention nor to interpret it. The Commission's mandate is rather to devise a mechanism for implementing the Convention in its current form.[158]

10. Rate of Deposit of Ratifications

If the OPCW was to be ready to meet the very short timelines set by the CWC for its first activities, the time available to the Preparatory Commission to complete its work was limited by Article XXI (I) of the Convention:

> This Convention shall enter into force 180 days after the date of the deposit of the 65th instrument of ratification, but in no case earlier than two years after its opening for signature.

The initial working assumption of the delegations and the PTS, given the promises of early ratification in virtually all of the speeches welcoming the conclusion of the Convention, both in the Conference on Disarmament and at the 47th UN General Assembly, was that sixty-five ratifications would be quickly exceeded and that the CWC would enter into force on 13 January 1995. This mood was reinforced by UN General Assembly resolution 47/39, adopted on 16 December 1992, which in its preamble states the conviction:

[158] Working Group B, 'Chairman's summary of the meeting on 27 February 1995', PC-X/B/WP.11, dated 27 February 1995.

> … that the Convention, particularly as adherence to it approaches universality, will contribute to the maintenance of international peace and improve the security of all States and that it therefore merits the strong support of the entire international community,

and in its operative paragraph 3:

> Calls upon all States to sign and, thereafter, according to their respective constitutional processes, to become parties to the Convention at the earliest possible date, thus contributing to its rapid entry into force and to the early achievement of universal adherence.

In fact, once the Foreign Ministers and other senior representatives of 130 states had signed the Convention in Paris, the need for ratification seemed to slip off the agenda in many countries. Also, in those countries which had chemical weapons and/or significant chemical industry, there was a realisation that implementation of the Convention would require establishment of bureaucratic procedures, drafting of regulations and, in most cases, primary legislation. This meant finding time in busy parliamentary schedules and led to inevitable delay. One exception was Sweden, where early ratification was considered to have political importance and the Parliament agreed to ratification in advance of the implementing legislation which could follow before the two year deadline. Thus it transpired that one year after the signing ceremony only four instruments of ratification had been deposited with the UN Secretary-General with only that of Sweden representing a state likely to need attention from the OPCW Inspectorate.

The ratification by Norway, deposited in April 1994, proved in retrospect to have been the first swallow of a new summer and, as can be seen from the figure below, ratifications came in fairly steadily at about two per month until the required total of sixty-five was achieved in October 1996 with the deposit of an instrument by Hungary. This fixed the date of entry into force as 29 April 1997. There was concern during the final 180 days that the CWC might enter into force without either of the known possessor states – Russia and the United States – being members. However, the US ratification was deposited in the week before EIF and that of Russia before the end of the year. Thanks to a last minute rush of deposits the Convention entered into force with 87 States Parties.

This slow progress towards the goal of entry into force and ultimately to universal adherence to the Convention led to the PTS taking a rather proactive role in supporting ratification. At first the attitude of many Member State officials was that ratification of a treaty was purely national business and that there was no role for the Secretariat. However, this reluctance in accepting help from the PTS was gradually overcome to the extent that, after entry into force, the Conference of the States Parties formally tasked the Technical Secretariat with assisting the drive for universality.

The Executive Secretary in his visits to the capitals of Member States pressed the importance of early ratification, combined with appropriate implementing legislation, not only in Foreign Ministries but, wherever possible, with senior parliamentarians. The problems stemmed not only from the need for the reengagement of political will after the gesture of signing the CWC at the Paris ceremony but from the shift of

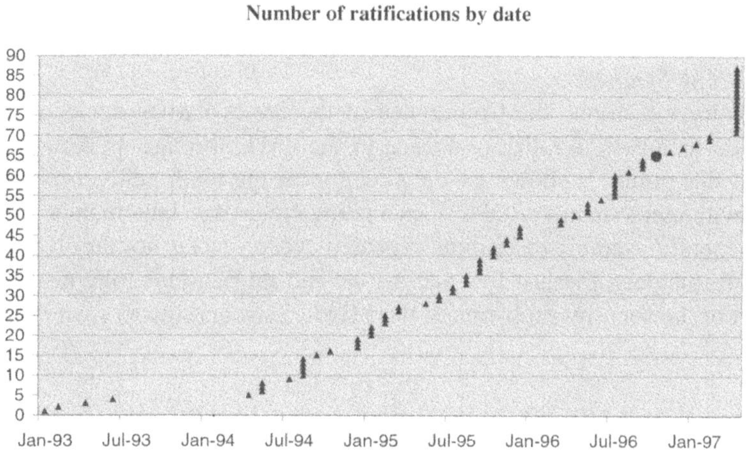

responsibility within capitals. The negotiations in Geneva had been largely the responsibility of Foreign Ministries with a lesser role for Ministries of Defence. The signatures appended to the formal copies of the treaty text were those of Foreign Ministers or accredited senior diplomats. After entry into force the main burden of assembling data for declarations and for receiving inspections would fall on Ministries of Commerce or Industry, including in many cases providing the budget and personnel to support these activities. This was even true in the chemical weapon possessor states as Ministries of Defence knew how much they had and where it was stored, whereas the data for civil chemicals needed to be collected from scratch.

Virtually all sections of the PTS contributed in one way or another. One of the main tools of the effort, gradually developed over the four year life of the Commission, was a series of workshops and seminars on the Convention held in different regions of the world. The first was difficult to organise as there was no provision in the budget for this activity but as it became accepted as useful budgets were adjusted and voluntary trust funds established to accommodate it. The PTS also organised courses for officials involved in the establishment of the National Authority which the Convention requires in every Member State. Experts from some of the Member States played an important role in all these events.

In addition to the courses and workshops the Secretariat also assisted by offering advice on legal issues related to preparations for ratification and operation of the CWC. These are fully described in Chapter 10 on Article VII.

One of the obstacles to the provision of support to many of the delegations from countries, particularly in Africa and the Caribbean, was that they had no resident representation in The Hague. This problem was partially alleviated by the appointment of a liaison officer, Mitslal Kifleyesus, based in Brussels and supported financially by funds from the Harvard Sussex Program.

Another problem for small delegations was the difficulty in following the work of the Commission when they did not have the available personnel to attend expert groups and other subsidiary meetings. The PTS therefore issued regular, so-called 'press releases', which rarely led to articles in the media but provided these small delegations with easily digested material for their reporting. The Executive Secretary also initiated the production of a regular news sheet about the Commissions activities under the title *OPCW Synthesis.*

After entry into force, the Conference of the States Parties decided to continue helping non-members to ratify or accede to the CWC through an Action Plan. The success of this policy is shown by the situation as the tenth anniversary of EIF approaches with membership of OPCW exceeding 180 states. Universality, as urged by the UN General Assembly resolution (repeated every year) is not far off in numerical terms. Unfortunately, the last few accessions and ratifications may need to await a settlement of the security problems of the Middle East and the Korean Peninsula.

11. Phase II and the Six Month Build-up to Entry into Force

Predictions of when the date of the deposit of the 65th ratification (known as the 'trigger point') would be reached came and went until Hungary's deposit on 31 October 1996 determined that the CWC would enter into force on 29 April 1997. The chairman of the PrepCom at the time, Ambassador Marin Buhoara of Romania summed up the atmosphere at a press conference:

> Despite its achievements, the Preparatory Commission faces a number of unfinished tasks in the short amount of time now available, and must roll up its sleeves to ensure that all relevant procedures are in place before the OPCW starts functioning at the entry into force of the Convention. I would like to call on all countries to exercise greater political will and urgency to resolve all the outstanding issues which have been discussed so far as quickly as possible now that the trigger point has been reached. There is now no turning back.

In order to deal with the increased workload and growth in the number of staff of the PTS in the 'ramp-up phase' (the phase from trigger point until entry into force), the annual budgets of the PrepCom since 1994 had been prepared in two phases. Phase I covered the normal operating costs of the PrepCom prior to trigger point. After this, Phase II was to be activated and was designed to cover additional costs of the 180-day period from then until entry into force. For example, phase I of the 1996 budget totalled NLG 24.8 million, while the amount to be activated under Phase II totalled NLG 30.4 million. The main additional expense was the recruitment of extra staff to bring the PTS up to the full authorised complement of 369 staff members, included among which were 140 inspector posts. Within that total, 109 were to be in the Verification Division where the Declarations and Confidentiality Branch was to be fully staffed in preparation to receive and process initial declarations, and an Operations and Planning Centre was to be created.

While the 1996 Phase II budget was activated on 31 October, the fact that neither Russia nor the US had ratified the CWC caused continuing uncertainty, as the Executive Secretary reported to the PrepCom in December 1996:

> This uncertainty leads, unavoidably, to questions about the validity of some important basic assumptions set out in various of the Commission's Budget documents. That complicates budgetary and resource planning for verification activities and the resolution of some of the outstanding issues, including the OPCW Budget, staffing requirements, etc.[159]

This uncertainty continued throughout the ramp-up phase and meant that significantly fewer staff were recruited than envisaged. For example, at the beginning of April 1997, the Verification Division had only 61 staff members, rather than the authorised 109. The Executive Secretary told the final session of the PrepCom in April 1997:

> The uncertainties which have plagued the Preparatory Commission's work in The Hague have also cast a shadow over preparations for entry into force and the mood amongst Member States. The pace of ratifications since the trigger point has accordingly been slower than was expected.

However, he added:

> Despite all these problems, the overall state of preparedness for the fulfilment of obligations under the Convention is good. Although not all tasks mandated under the Convention and the Paris Resolution have been discharged, enough has been accomplished to allow the efficient implementation of the provisions of the Convention. Much of the infrastructure needed to start the operation of the OPCW is already in place.[160]

---

159 'Report of the Executive Secretary', PC-XV/5, dated 12 December 1996.

160 'Report of the Executive Secretary', PC-XVI/12, dated 7 April 1997.

Chapter 4

LEGAL ASPECTS OF THE PREPARATORY COMMISSION FOR THE OPCW AS AN INTERNATIONAL ORGANISATION

Johan Rautenbach & Lisa Tabassi

1. INTRODUCTION

At the signing ceremony held at the headquarters of UNESCO in Paris on 13 to 15 January 1993 and opened by the President of the French Republic, François Mitterrand, two parallel processes were underway. The first and principal process was the opening for signature of a long-sought universal disarmament treaty: the Chemical Weapons Convention (CWC).[161] The second was the setting-up of a Preparatory Commission to prepare for the implementation of the Convention once it entered into force. This was done through the adoption by the Convention's Signatory States of, the 'Resolution Establishing the Preparatory Commission for the Organisation for the Prohibition of Chemical Weapons', which came to be known simply as the 'Paris Resolution'.[162]

1.1 Legal basis, constituent instrument and membership

It can be argued that the Paris Resolution, similarly to the Convention, falls within the definition of 'treaty'. As provided by the 1969 Vienna Convention on the Law of Treaties, 'Treaty' means an 'international agreement concluded between states in written form and governed by international law ... whatever its particular designation'.[163] As can be seen from the discussion below, the actions of states in respect of the provisions of the two instruments tend to support such a conclusion.

The way in which the two instruments deal with some issues is identical in a number of important respects:

---

[161] 1993 Convention on the Prohibition of the Development, Production, Stockpiling and Use of Chemical Weapons and on Their Destruction, corrected and amended text available at <www.opcw.org>.

[162] Reprinted in L. Tabassi (ed.), *OPCW: The Legal Texts* (The Hague, TMC Asser Press 1999) pp. 523-530. The 'Text on the Establishment of a Preparatory Commission', which was eventually annexed to the Paris Resolution, was drafted by the Ad Hoc Committee on Chemical Weapons in the Conference on Disarmament and transmitted to the General Assembly together with the Convention's text in the Report of the Conference on Disarmament, Official Records of the 47th Session of the General Assembly, Supplement No. 27 (A/47/27), dated 23 September 1992).

[163] Article 2, subpara. 1(a), of the 1969 Vienna Convention on the Law of Treaties.

I.R. Kenyon and D. Feakes, The Creation of the OPCW

- Both provide for the creation of an independent international organisation with legal capacity which would be established in The Hague upon the instruments' entry into force (the 'Organisation for the Prohibition of Chemical Weapons' (OPCW) and the 'Preparatory Commission for the OPCW' respectively);
- Both international organisations have a plenary organ in which the Member States take binding decisions pursuant to a stipulated procedure;
- Both international organisations have a secretariat with internationally recruited staff to support the work in accordance with regulations to be established;
- Both require a separate headquarters agreement to be negotiated and concluded with the Netherlands as host country, conferring privileges and immunities upon the respective organisations and certain categories of persons;
- Both require financial contributions by the Member States to meet the costs of the organisations;
- Both are to convene in plenary session, assisted by the United Nations Secretary-General, 30 days after the respective dates of entry into force.[164]

Beyond those similarities, the processes diverge in sharp contrast.

The Convention, by its terms, follows the formal, traditional, often cumbersome treaty procedures to enter into force and be implemented:

- Signature and ratification or accession as the means of the State's consent to be bound, implying parliamentary approval of the treaty;
- Designation of the United Nations Secretary-General as Depositary of the treaty;
- Registration with, and publication by, the United Nations Secretariat under Article 102 of the Charter of the United Nations;
- A required number of deposits of instruments of ratification (65) and a time period (at least two years) for entry into force;
- Adoption of any necessary national implementing measures and legislation by the parties; plus
- A preparatory phase in which a 'Preparatory Commission' would somehow be funded and functioning.[165]

In contrast, the undated, unsigned, 'Paris Resolution' (which contains no mention of the word 'Paris'):

- Entered into force upon adoption at the signing ceremony;
- Was never officially published and was only available as a poor-quality photocopy of what was distributed at the signing ceremony until it was eventually retyped by the Commission's Provisional Technical Secretariat two years later;

---

164 Actually, para. 2 of the Paris Resolution provides that the First Session of the Preparatory Commission would be convened 30 days after the Convention received 50 signatures – a criterion which was met immediately in Paris.

165 Implied by the reference in Convention Article VIII, para. 7, to 'financial contributions ... to the Preparatory Commission'.

- Stipulates a detailed list of tasks which the Commission should carry out in respect of the institution-building of the OPCW[166] but makes no reference to its own institution-building, except for three aspects: (a) the Commission's structure; (b) the headquarters agreement it would conclude to formalise its privileges, immunities and practical arrangements of its hosting by the Netherlands;[167] and (c) the office building, supplies, furniture, equipment and telecommunications sets it would be supplied with by the Netherlands during a maximum period of five years;[168] and
- Provides that the Commission's property, functions and recommendations would be transferred to the OPCW at the First Session of the Conference of the States Parties and the Commission would be dissolved at the conclusion of the first session.[169]

After the conclusion of the signing ceremony, the Convention remained open for signature at the headquarters of the United Nations until it entered into force. A total of 35 states signed the Convention in New York. It is at this point in time not known whether any of them received a copy of the Paris Resolution when they signed or whether any of them were surprised to learn afterwards of the existence of the Preparatory Commission when they started receiving voluminous documentation from it and requests for the annual financial contribution they were expected to make. Although the Paris Resolution, contrary to what is normally the case for binding international legal instruments, does not contain final provisions, procedures for entry into force or for ratification, the Member States of the Commission for the most part showed total commitment to the establishment and maintenance of the Commission and its institutional requirements. The Commission was able to assemble the adequate range of experts to pursue its tasks and to collect an adequate percentage of the assessed budgetary contributions to fund its operations smoothly. It can be assumed that implementation of the Paris Resolution by Signatory States moved forward uneventfully because of: (a) the commitment to realise an effective Convention; and (b) the fact that creation of preparatory commissions was not novel in international practice.[170]

In comparison to the OPCW, the only evidence that participation in the work of the Commission was not as broad as in the OPCW is the fact that, as the number of Signatory States grew, so did the corresponding quorum for sessions of the Commission ('a majority of members')[171] and it became difficult towards the end to achieve the required quorum. To ensure that the quorum could be reached, the Secretariat found it necessary to vigorously encourage the embassies located in Brussels (where

---

166 'Text on the Establishment of a Preparatory Commission', annexed to the Paris Resolution.

167 Annex 1 to the Paris Resolution.

168 Annex 3 to the Paris Resolution, paras. 5 and 8.

169 Paras. 16 and 17 of the Text on the Establishment of a Preparatory Commission, annexed to the Paris Resolution.

170 See further, Pietro Gargiulo, 'The Preparatory Commission for the Organization for the Prohibition of Chemical Weapons', in Michael Bothe et al. (eds.), *The New Chemical Weapons Convention – Implementation and Prospects* (The Hague, Kluwer Law International 1998) pp. 153-165 at pp. 153-158.

171 Rule 12 of the Rules of Procedure of the Commission.

a significant number of Signatory States which had no representation in The Hague were based) to dispatch a representative for the session and even went so far as to bus them to and fro.

The archives will show that there are, however, some Signatory States which never participated in a session of the Commission nor paid their assessed contributions. The Paris Resolution provides that the Commission shall be composed of all Signatory States and the 'expenses shall be met by those participating in the Commission'.[172] In practice, all Signatory States were assessed contributions to the budgets adopted by the Commission with no consideration given to whether a representative was being sent to the sessions or not. Three states declared that they would not be participating in the Commission (and thus do not have to contribute financially to it) but this was not accepted by the Commission since participation was viewed as an automatic consequence of signature of the Convention.[173] However, since a treaty cannot create rights or obligations for third states without their consent,[174] the states which signed the Convention after 15 January 1993 could have argued that they had never consented to the Paris Resolution. This was, however, never invoked before the Commission. Since Article VIII, paragraph 7, of the Convention provides that financial contributions made to the Commission shall be deducted in an appropriate way from the Member State's contributions to the OPCW regular budget and the annual reports of the OPCW continue to publish the outstanding amounts owed for the preparatory phase, it could have become an issue. However, that aspect of paragraph 7 remains officially unimplemented and unaddressed.

1.2 Mandate

The fundamental mandate of the Commission was to carry out the necessary preparations for the effective implementation of the Convention and to prepare for the first session of the OPCW Conference of the States Parties. That is the explicit overall purpose[175] for which the Commission was established.

Beyond that, the Paris Resolution stipulated a detailed list of tasks under three broad headings which the Commission was to carry out:[176]

- Tasks concerning the organisation and work of the OPCW Technical Secretariat and requiring immediate attention after entry into force of the Convention;
- Tasks on matters of the OPCW requiring immediate attention after entry into force of the Convention; and
- Draft agreements, provisions and guidelines regarding the substantive provisions of the Convention, for consideration and approval by the OPCW Conference of the States Parties at its first session.

---

172 Paras. 4 and 5 of the Text annexed to the Paris Resolution.

173 'Report of the Executive Secretary: Member States' Contributions and Participation in the Work of the Commission', PC-VI/9, dated 22 March 1994.

174 Article 34 of the 1969 Vienna Convention on the Law of Treaties.

175 Para. 1 of the Text annexed to the Paris Resolution.

176 Paras. 10-12 of the Text annexed to the Paris Resolution.

Finally six further tasks, formulated in general terms, were assigned to the Commission:[177]

- To establish the Provisional Technical Secretariat, appoint its officers, Executive Secretary and staff, and establish the relevant regulations;
- To make arrangements for the first session of the Conference of the States Parties;
- To develop two headquarters agreements with the Netherlands, firstly its own under which it would operate during its limited life and next a draft OPCW headquarters agreement for consideration by the OPCW Conference of the States Parties at its first session;
- To facilitate the exchange of information between Signatory States on national implementation and give advice upon request;
- To prepare studies, reports and records;
- To prepare a final report.

The Final Report[178] is the record by which the success of the Commission can be judged by scholars and historians. It describes the Commission's activities and deals with the organisational matters for the first session of the Conference of the States Parties of the OPCW. It lists the tasks it was successful in completing as 'resolved issues' and those which it could not as 'unresolved issues'. The latter were left to be taken up by the OPCW in the manner discussed further below. A comprehensive mid-term review of how the work stood in 1995 and the issues being faced in respect of each task was published[179] and analysed after entry into force.[180]

2. Legal Matters Dealt with by the Commission

In practical terms, the fact that the Commission was established as an independent international organisation with legal capacity in its own right, meant that an enormous effort had to be made from the outset, under time pressure, to put in place the Commission's detailed legal framework so that it could function and start preparing that of the OPCW's. There was a great momentum at the Convention's opening for

---

177 Paras. 9, 13-15 of the Text annexed to the Paris Resolution.

178 'Final Report of the Preparatory Commission for the Organisation for the Prohibition of Chemical Weapons to the First Session of the Conference of the States Parties of the Organisation for the Prohibition of Chemical Weapons and to the First Meeting of the Executive Council of the Organisation for the Prohibition of Chemical Weapons', PC-XVI/37, dated 15 April 1997.

179 Félix C. Calderón, 'The Preparatory Commission for the Organization for the Prohibition of Chemical Weapons', in D. Bardonnet (ed.), *The Convention on the Prohibition and Elimination of Chemical Weapons: A Breakthrough in Multilateral Disarmament,* Hague Academy Workshop in The Hague, 24-26 November 1994 (Dordrecht, Martinus Nijhoff 1995) pp. 27-150.

180 Treasa Dunworth, Ronald Sutherland and Thomas Stock, 'The Work of the Preparatory Commission, the Provisional Technical Secretariat and Preparations for Entry into Force of the Chemical Weapons Convention', in Michael Bothe et al. (eds.), *The New Chemical Weapons Convention – Implementation and Prospects* (The Hague, Kluwer Law International 1998) pp. 167-184.

signature and it was fully expected that the Convention would receive enough ratifications to enter into force at the conclusion of the minimum two-year period required by Article XXI of the Convention. Throughout its duration, the Commission met three to five times a year, interspersed with open-ended Expert Groups created to work on each of the tasks.

This meant that the Provisional Technical Secretariat worked in a high speed continuum of preparing background papers, supporting Expert Group meetings, supporting Working Group meetings and the Commission sessions, receiving Commission instructions and starting the cycle over again – with no breaks. At times it bordered on the chaotic. It also led to some curious situations, such as a new staff member being offered a standard form Letter of Appointment in which it was stated that a copy of the Commission's Staff Regulations and Rules was attached when the signer had just been in discussion with the Netherlands Ministry of Foreign Affairs to try to secure a conference room for the Expert Group to start drafting those regulations.

In any event, the necessary legal framework for the Commission and its Secretariat was created and adopted or assented to by the Commission in just over one year:

1993	
April	Rules of Procedure of the Commission[181]
June	Charter of the Provident Fund of the Commission[182]
October	Staff Regulations of the Provisional Technical Secretariat[183]
October	Financial Regulations of the Commission[184]
December	Signature of the Commission Headquarters Agreement[185]
1994	
February	Entry into force of the Commission Headquarters Agreement
April	Financial Rules of the Commission[186]
April	Administrative Rules for the Provident Fund[187]
May	Staff Rules of the Provisional Technical Secretariat[188]

[181] 'Rules of Procedure for the Preparatory Commission for the Organisation for the Prohibition of Chemical Weapons', PREPCOM/II/8, dated 22 April 1993.

[182] 'Charter of the Provident Fund of the Preparatory Commission for the Organisation for the Prohibition of Chemical Weapons', PC-VIII/5, dated 19 September 1994.

[183] 'Staff Regulations for the Provisional Technical Secretariat of the Preparatory Commission for the Organisation for the Prohibition of Chemical Weapons', PC-IV/24, dated 11 October 1993.

[184] 'Financial Regulations of the Preparatory Commission for the OPCW', PC-IV/25, dated 11 October 1993.

[185] 'Agreement between the Preparatory Commission for the Organisation for the Prohibition of Chemical Weapons and the Kingdom of the Netherlands Concerning the Headquarters of the Commission', PC-VI/6, dated 23 February 1994.

[186] 'Financial Rules for the Provisional Technical Secretariat of the Preparatory Commission for the Organisation for the Prohibition of Chemical Weapons', PC-VI/A/3, dated 25 March 1994.

[187] 'Administrative Rules for the Provident Fund of the Preparatory Commission for the Organisation for the Prohibition of Chemical Weapons', PC-VIII/6, dated 19 September 1994.

[188] 'Staff Rules of the Provisional Technical Secretariat for the Preparatory Commission for the Organisation for the Prohibition of Chemical Weapons', PC-VI/A/2, dated 18 March 1994.

As soon as each of the above steps was completed, the relevant Expert Group turned its attention to discussing the draft version of the OPCW equivalent, to be proposed to the respective working group, the Commission, and eventually recommended to the OPCW Conference of the States Parties at its first session. The drafting of the OPCW versions were viewed as completely new exercises. For example, in approving the Commission's Staff and Financial Regulations and Rules, the Commission approved the principle that the regulations and rules of the Commission did not set a precedent for the regulations and rules of the OPCW.[189]

At the same time, the Legal Division was actively participating in or observing the work being carried out by all the Expert Groups on the substantive tasks listed in the Paris Resolution. The Legal Division's involvement was routinely required in Working Group A's expert groups on institutional matters, especially on the arrangements for the OPCW building (discussed further in Chapter 5). However, a number of legal opinions were also requested by Working Group B's expert groups on a broad range of issues:

- Assumptions used in planning for the Verification Division and certain issues of security;
- Breaches of confidentiality: liability for damages and prosecution through penal action;
- Cost of verification of storage and destruction of chemical weapons, as well of destruction of production facilities;
- Definition of 'chemical weapons production facility';
- Draft understanding on the status of 'experts' in the context of investigation of alleged use and in regard to privileges and immunities;
- Legal and safety considerations regarding occupational health and safety measurements during OPCW inspections;
- Non-scheduled aircraft;
- Post-inspection procedures;
- Privileges and immunities of inspection team members;
- Provision of live chemical weapons agents as a form of technical cooperation;
- Requirements for declarations of Schedule 2 chemicals;
- Responsibility for declaration of events before a State Party became independent;
- Role of the national inspector;
- Short-term or temporary duty inspector for challenge inspections;
- The definition of 'transfer';
- The meaning of Part II(E), paragraph 43 of the Verification Annex and paragraph 12(g) of the Paris Resolution;
- The relationship between paragraph 11 of Part II of the Verification Annex and Article 36 of the Vienna Convention on Diplomatic Relations;
- The relationship between Parts X and XI of the Verification Annex if an investigation of alleged use of chemical weapons were initiated pursuant to Article IX;

[189] 'Report of the Commission', PC-VI/22, dated 15 April 1994, paras. 5.1(b) and 5.2(c).

- The respective legal status of model agreements and of facility agreements;
- The scope of paragraph 7, Part IV(B) of the Verification Annex concerning old chemical weapons.

Advice on draft national implementing legislation, as well as preparation of model legislation[190] and contribution to the development of a manual on national implementation[191] were significant projects also undertaken by and in cooperation with the Legal Division. These are discussed further in Chapter 10.

In addition to the more visible substantive work, there were of course other matters requiring legal review and advice or negotiation, such as the administrative policies, contracts for routine operations, insurance, rental and refurbishment of conference facilities and interim accommodation, procurement issues, the lease agreement and fit-up of the OPCW Laboratory, a tax reimbursement agreement and transitional arrangements for the Commission-OPCW.

Legal outreach also occupied considerable time as presentations were regularly delivered in academic meetings on legal aspects of the Convention and the OPCW and workshops on national implementation.

3. The Emergence of Unexpected Legal Issues

It would of course be unrealistic to expect that the issues that would need to be addressed during the preparatory phase could all be anticipated by the negotiators of the Convention and included in the Paris Resolution. The surprises that emerged could be said to fall into five main areas: (a) errors found in the certified copies of the Convention; (b) establishment of the OPCW Laboratory; (c) interpretation of the Paris Resolution; (d) the agreements for construction of the OPCW building; and (e) whether implementation of part of the treaty could be suspended if the treaty entered into force without the chemical weapons possessor states as members of the OPCW.

3.1 Errors in the certified copies of the Convention

The nearly 200-page text of the CWC was negotiated in English. The other five language versions were produced and proofread in the impossibly short time frame of August-September 1992 to attach to the reports of the Ad Hoc Committee and the Conference. Those translations became the authentic texts of the Convention registered with the United Nations and published as the official certified copies.

Adding to the problem, the Conference on Disarmament documents were produced using a different word processing software than that which was used by the United Nations in New York. In the transmission of the electronic texts from Geneva to New York, and the conversion from one software to another, the symbols in the Annex on Chemicals were altered.

---

190 'Model National Implementing Legislation', PC-XI/7/Rev.1, dated 31 May 1996.

191 B. Kellman et al., *Manual for National Implementation of the Chemical Weapons Convention* (Chicago, International Criminal Justice and Weapons Control Center 1993).

The discrepancies between the authentic texts of the Convention which arose during the translation and proofreading processes and the discrepancies with the text adopted by the Conference on Disarmament which arose from software incompatibility were rather quickly noticed. In June 1993, the Executive Secretary already had drawn the attention of the Commission to the problem. As a result, the Provisional Technical Secretariat undertook a painstaking scrutiny of the six language versions of the certified copies against the final negotiated text (CD/1170).[192] The procedure set forth in Article 79 of the Vienna Convention on the Law of Treaties to correct errors in treaty texts was pursued and concluded. Subsequently, during the preparatory phase, additional errors were noted and corrected in the same fashion.

3.2 **Establishment of the OPCW Laboratory**

The Convention did not explicitly provide for the establishment of an OPCW Laboratory. Annex 3 to the Paris Resolution provided that a laboratory in The Hague (TNO-PML) would provide certain services free of charge and could also perform technical functions at a price. Nevertheless, the initial report of the Expert Group on Equipment recommended that the OPCW should have its own laboratory and outlined its functions. Working Group B endorsed those recommendations.[193]

Based on points raised by Working Groups A and B, the Commission adopted the understanding that the OPCW Laboratory and Equipment Store would be an integral part of the OPCW headquarters but, for safety reasons, should be located at a separate suitable site close to The Hague, if possible in the TNO-PML facility. Furthermore, to ensure proper preparation for verification activities by the OPCW, the laboratory would need to be available before entry into force.[194] In the final report of the Expert Group on the OPCW Building, it was agreed that the floor space associated with the OPCW Laboratory would be counted in the total OPCW Building space specified in Annex 3 to the Paris Resolution,[195] but the Netherlands' authorities agreed to reimburse the OPCW for rent and other related costs of the laboratory and the associated equipment store for a period of three years.

The Commission decided that the Secretariat should take action to acquire a small standard laboratory and be equipped with items earlier identified by the Expert Group on Equipment.[196] Since it was not possible to establish the OPCW laboratory at TNO-PML, the Commission authorised the Executive Secretary to negotiate a lease agreement for an alternative site where the OPCW laboratory was established and continues to be located[197] (see also Chapter 5).

---

[192] 'Report of the Ad Hoc Committee on Chemical Weapons to the Conference on Disarmament', CD/1170, dated 26 August 1992.

[193] 'Report of Working Group B', PC-III/B/2, dated 30 June 1993, paras. 9.2 and 9.3.

[194] 'Report of the Commission', PC-V/12, dated 17 December 1993, para. 5.1.

[195] Expert Group on the OPCW Building, 'Final Report', PC-VI/A/WP.8, dated 25 February 1994, para. 6.

[196] 'Report of the Commission', PC-VII/8, dated 1 July 1994, para. 6.3.

[197] 'Report of the Commission', PC-VIII/18, dated 29 September 1994, para. 9.3.

3.3 Interpretation of the Paris Resolution

Although at first glance the terms stipulated in Annex 3 to the Paris Resolution for the hosting of the Commission and the OPCW appear to be straightforward, in practice issues arose which were eventually resolved through a series of additional understandings reached between the Commission and the Netherlands. The first concerned the Commission's rights and obligations in respect of the 'supplier designated by The Hague'. The second was considerably more complex. This concerned an array of aspects underlying the construction of the OPCW purpose-built office building, the provisions of conference facilities, the OPCW Laboratory and payment of inspector training costs. These, together with legal aspects of the agreements for the construction of the new OPCW building, are discussed in Chapter 5.

3.4 Suspension of implementation of parts of the Treaty

When the deposit of the 65th instrument of ratification occurred, neither of the two declared chemical weapons possessors, Russia and the United States, had ratified the Convention or seemed likely to do so any time soon. Russia had become apprehensive about the projected costs of destruction of its chemical weapons stockpiles. The United States had already begun destruction of its stockpiles, but internal politics in the Senate had stalled the ratification process in Washington.

As a result, the states which had deposited instruments of ratification were facing the impending prospect of the treaty entering into force without the two possessors. Although there was an assumption made by the Commission for OPCW budget and planning purposes that at least one other state might declare itself to be a possessor after entry into force, it was only a projection. Thus all the detailed treaty provisions regarding verification of the destruction of chemical weapons and their related facilities, the projected recruitment of the personnel to monitor that as well as the complex and expensive structure to supervise and administer it, would be all for naught. Why would non-possessor states subject their peaceful chemical industry to the burden of verification and invest the effort and funding to establish and support an OPCW to carry out industry inspections for non-proliferation aims, when the chemical weapons possessors remained on the outside having no obligations and no expense?

For a brief period in 1996-1997, informal discussions and research were carried out as to possible solutions to the dilemma. The precedent of the amendment of the Law of the Sea Convention before it entered into force was viewed as a possible way forward.[198] Fortunately action became unnecessary as the treaty entered into force with the United States as an original State Party and Russia following soon after.

---

198 Agreement Relating to the Implementation of Part XI of the United Nations Convention on the Law of the Sea of 10 December 1982, Annex to United Nations General Assembly resolution A/RES/48/263, dated 17 August 1994.

3.5 Dilemma faced by the original States Parties

At the opening of the First Session of the Conference of the States Parties (FSCSP), 165 states had signed the Convention but of these, only 88 had ratified it. It had entered into force for 87.[199] The FSCSP was thus confronted with the fact that the Convention had not entered into force for a number of states that were active in the preparatory phase, including one of the two declared chemical weapons possessor states. Added to this was the fact that many of the issues dealt with during the preparatory phase had remained unresolved. Although States Parties would legally have been entitled to address all unresolved issues and take action on them, this would not necessarily taken into account the known national positions of the States not party.

Two possibilities were open to States Parties. One would have been the approach that states which had not ratified the Convention had acted at their own peril, and that they would subsequently not be able to escape the sanctions in the Convention aimed at States not party. Relevant sanctions here are not only limitations on the transfer of chemicals but, more importantly (at this stage of the development of the OPCW), the fact that States that joined later would be confronted with large number of detailed interpretations of, and procedures for, the implementation of the Convention, decided by the FSCSP and subsequent Conference sessions – the OPCW *acquis*. The negative side of this would be that it could serve as a disincentive for such States to join if they found it difficult to comply with such interpretations and procedures, particularly if their positions were known from the preparatory phase and were not reflected in the decisions taken. In such cases not joining might be a preferred option to sacrificing some of their vital national interests. It was quite clear to all that the question of the effect of this on the often stated aim of universality of the Convention and the OPCW had to be addressed.

States Parties opted for the persuasion approach: allow States not party sufficient flexibility to make their positions clear, but without so much influence that the impetus for joining would be nullified.

In practical terms this boiled down to two main issues in respect of working procedures. The first was the rights of States not party regarding participation in meetings during the FSCSP. The second was how to address the unresolved issues that the FSCSP did not resolve during that session itself.[200]

3.6 Rights of States not party regarding participation in meetings during the FSCSP

The issue of rights of States not party came up during the finalisation of the Rules of Procedure of the Conference, which was itself an unresolved issue at the end of the

[199] Article XXI(2) of the Convention provides that for States whose instruments of ratification or accession are deposited subsequent to the entry into force of the Convention (i.e., 29 April 1997), it shall enter into force on the 30th day following the date of deposit of the instrument of ratification or accession.

[200] See further, Johan Rautenbach, 'Comments', in Eric P.J. Myjer (ed.), *Issues of Arms Control Law and the Chemical Weapons Convention: Obligations Inter Se and Supervisory Mechanisms* (The Hague, Martinus Nijhoff 2002), pp. 146-151.

preparatory phase. The two relevant rules eventually adopted during the FSCSP were:

> Rule 29 Signatory States
>
> Any State signatory to the Convention which has not yet deposited its instrument of ratification in accordance with Article XXI, paragraph 2, of the Convention shall be entitled, subject to prior written notification to the Director-General,[201] to participate, without taking part in the adoption of decisions, whether by consensus or by vote, in the deliberations of the Conference. This means that Signatory States shall be entitled to appoint observers to attend plenary meetings of the Conference other than those designated private meetings; to deliver statements at such meetings; to receive the documents of the Conference and to submit its views in writing to delegations.
>
> Rule 52 Public and private meetings
>
> Plenary meetings of the Conference shall be held in public unless declared private. Meetings of subsidiary bodies, including committees, shall be held in private unless designated otherwise. All decisions of the Conference taken at a private meeting shall be announced at an early public meeting. At the close of each private meeting of committees and other subsidiary bodies, the presiding officer may issue a communiqué through the Director-General.

The following elements are contained in these two rules:

- Plenary meetings of the Conference are public unless declared private;
- Meetings of subsidiary bodies are private unless designated otherwise;
- All decision of the Conference taken at a private meeting shall be announced at an early public meeting;
- Signatory States are entitled to attend public meetings;
- Signatory States are entitled to deliver statements at public plenary meetings of the Conference;
- Signatory States are entitled to receive the documents of the Conference; and
- Signatory States are entitled to circulate documents containing their views to delegations.

Owing to the particular nature of the FSCSP, States Parties considered it appropriate to have some limited informal understandings on the application of Rules 29 for the duration of the FSCSP only. These understandings were as follows:

- Contracting States[202] would have the right to participate in the debate in the Committee of the Whole without taking part in the adoption of decisions, whether by consensus or by vote;

---

[201] For the First Session of the Conference notifications were addressed to the UN Secretary-General and deposited with the Provisional Technical Secretariat of the Preparatory Commission.

[202] Article 2(1)(f) of the 1969 Vienna Convention on the Law of Treaties defines 'Contracting State' as a State which has consented to be bound by the treaty, whether or not the treaty has entered into force.

- Signatory States would be allowed to attend meetings of the Committee of the Whole. This is a clear extension of Signatory States' rights under Rule 52.
- Signatory States could provide written submissions, expressing their views in advance of meetings of the Committee of the Whole, to the Secretariat for distribution;
- The Chairman of the Committee of the Whole would announce in advance agenda items under consideration for a particular meeting of the Committee of the Whole;
- For the remainder of the Conference, there would be a number of plenary meetings to review decisions recommended by the Committee of the Whole. At the beginning of the plenary meeting there would be the possibility for all delegations, including Signatory States, to make statements under agenda item 12: 'General Debate'. Such plenaries could take place immediately preceding a meeting of the Committee of the Whole. This understanding, together with the previous two, clearly afforded Signatory States the opportunity to bring their views to the attention of States Parties at a point in time that would afford it maximum consideration.
- When the Chairman convenes a meeting of the plenary on a specific subject on which decisions are to be made, only States Parties would have the right to request the floor. This was aimed at the provision in Rule 29 that provides that participation of States not party does not include taking part in the adoption of decisions, whether by consensus or by vote. The making of statements on a specific subject on which decisions are to be made (particularly by consensus) might be construed as taking part in the adoption of such decision.

4. Conclusion

Given the relative informality of the legal basis for the Commission – an unpublished, unratified international legal instrument adopted by some but not all of those that participated in the implementation of its provisions – the ease which its operations moved forth is astonishing. The political willingness of states to carry the work forward can be the only explanation.

Some of its work was routine and totally predictable. It did what preparatory commissions do – created the necessary infrastructure and legal arrangements necessary to make the permanent institution operational from the outset. The challenges that arose unexpectedly were dealt with creatively, determinably, and solved with a lot of hard work by staff and delegates. The extent to which it was navigating uncharted territory pales in comparison with the next preparatory commission created in the field, the Preparatory Commission for the Comprehensive Nuclear-Test-Ban Treaty

---

The FSCSP used the term to refer to those States which deposited their instruments of ratification or accession after entry into force and for which the Convention would enter into force on the 30th day following the date of deposit of their instrument of ratification or accession – thus after conclusion of the FSCSP.

Organisation. Nevertheless, it served as a model for much of the initial work of that later preparatory commission; it served not only to establish the OPCW but to make a contribution in the larger field of international organisation institution building.

The bottom line was the efficiency with which the First Session of the OPCW's Conference of the States Parties functioned, the volume of decisions taken, and the subsequent ability of the OPCW to be operational from the outset – just as planned. The fact that there were unresolved issues is not completely a reflection of the Commission's effectiveness. Many of those issues were not politically ripe for resolution and needed several years of actual practice in the OPCW for their resolution. Others were discovered to be actually of no consequence to implementation of the Convention and could be dismissed, eventually.

Chapter 5

Housing the New Organisation

Paul A. Ryan

1. Introduction

Annex 3 to the Paris Resolution incorporated the formal offer of the Kingdom of the Netherlands, initially tabled at the Conference on Disarmament in 1992 in the discussions on the future seat of the Organisation and its accommodation. The 'Bid', as it was known in the Preparatory Commission, identified the accommodation needs of the future Organisation in two categories, namely the Preparatory Phase and the Full Implementation Phase and additionally addressed the conference accommodation to be provided to the new Organisation.

2. The Preparatory Phase – Interim Accommodation, Phase 1[203]

Paragraph 5 of Annex 3 to the Paris Resolution states:

> An office building of 3,300 square metres will be supplied free of charge during the preparatory phase (maximum of 5 years). The building is located in the centre of The Hague near the Peace Palace and several embassies. The Netherlands Congress Centre is 1 Km away. The modern office building was built in 1986 and consists of 3,300 square metres of office space divided over 5 floors. Office space can be made available immediately as soon as the Organisation begins working in the Hague. The building offers sufficient flexibility to allow the Organisation to grow in stages up to a maximum of 200 people. The Hague and the Netherlands will pay for the rent of the office spaces, parking places for the Organisation, maintenance costs of the buildings and installations, energy costs (heating, cooling, electricity, water) and turnkey costs (carpet, partitioning) during the preparatory phase.

The building made available to the fledgling Organisation was located at Laan van Meerdervoort 51, a modest building on a busy thoroughfare in The Hague, leased by the Municipality from the Delta Lloyd Insurance Company.

---

[203] Phase 1 refers to the period of work of the PrepCom from February 1993 to October 1996 when the 65th instrument of ratification was deposited. The six months immediately preceding entry into force in April 1997 are referred to as Phase 2.

I.R. Kenyon and D. Feakes, The Creation of the OPCW

The building was previously occupied by elements of a department of the Municipality headquartered on the opposite side of the street at Laan van Meerdervoort 70. The top two floors had been vacated some time before and the top floor (14 offices), renovated by a number of subcontractors working for the Sole Supplier, was ready for occupation. Following the first session of the PrepCom in February 1993 the newly appointed Executive Secretary and the few staff available to him were able to move in.

The remaining offices within the building were then progressively taken over, with an additional floor being taken over in April 1993 and the full building in May 1994 following the delayed transfer of the other tenants to a new location in The Hague; the delay being occasioned by the late completion of their new premises. As the future size and structure of the Provisional Technical Secretariat (PTS) was developed and agreed over the ensuing months the design of all but the top two floors was similarly discussed and agreed with the Sole Supplier, in his capacity as the internal designer and lead-contractor for the fit up and furnishing of the building.

That the building was not fully available to the PTS at the outset undoubtedly presented the Executive Secretary and the few members of the staff with additional pressures at a time when they were faced with a multitude of more important issues to resolve. That said, the progressive occupation of the building did permit the Secretariat to lay the plans with the designer which post May 1994 would lead to the Secretariat being provided with a stable working environment and one capable of absorbing additional staff members up until the major 'ramp up' in numbers following entry into force of the Convention, when as described below an additional building was required.

Although a stable office environment was provided to members of the Secretariat, this was only so, given the commitment, enthusiasm and 'can do' approach of the staff for with few exceptions the office space allocated to them did not accord to UN Standards – later to be used in the Programme of Requirements for the 'tailor made building' – nor did the building possess an adequate cooling system which given that many windows led on to Laan van Meerdervoort and could not be opened due to high noise levels from the heavy traffic on the road or for security reasons was at times needed. In mitigation it is fair to say that the high volume of publishing in house, the increasing use of IT systems, the high volume of visitors to the building and the extended working hours of members of the Secretariat throughout the six years of occupation by the Secretariat, could not have been foreseen in 1992.

One deficiency in the building that should have possibly been identified in the selection process of the building by the Netherlands authorities was the lack of space for meeting rooms; for the usable space available in the building was only 2,077 square metres. This resulted in only one designated meeting room ever being available and this on the ground floor on the road side of the building and thus noisy and in the summer months extremely hot. This deficiency was soon identified and addressed however and with the cooperation of the Netherlands Authorities alternative meeting/ conference rooms were identified and made available elsewhere to the Secretariat.

A further problem soon identified after taking over the building was that the number of parking places available to the staff of the Secretariat and to visiting delegates of the PrepCom was insufficient and strict car parking measures were dictated from the outset. Notwithstanding the best efforts of the Host Country to overcome this problem the topic remained a subject of dialogue between the PrepCom/Secretariat and departments of the Ministry of Foreign Affairs and the Municipality throughout the occupation of Laan van Meerdervoort 51, particularly after the imposition of a Car Parking Zone in the vicinity of the building in 1996 which made parking of vehicles for both visitors to and members of the Secretariat more difficult, notwithstanding the agreement of the OPCW Foundation to fund 25 parking permits.

3. The Full Implementation Phase: A Purpose-Built Headquarters Building

Paragraph 6 of Annex 3 to the Paris Resolution states:

> Before the full implementation phase, office space with a maximum of 18,000 square metres is foreseen to be made available for the Organisation in a new purpose-built office building, to be known as the 'Peace Tower'. Construction can be started as soon as the organisation can specify the required volume and further details. The building is expected to be completed two and a half years later. The Tower will be situated in the city centre business district next to Central Station.
>
> For a period of 3 years during the full implementation phase, the Hague and the Netherlands will pay for the rent of the office spaces, 110 parking places for the Organisation inside the building, maintenance costs of the building and the installations, energy costs (heating, cooling, electricity, water) and turnkey costs (carpeting, partitioning).
>
> The building is flexible enough to allow space to be made available to the Organisation in the proportion to the number of staff, up to a maximum of 18,000 square metres. After the period in which the Netherlands Government will pay for the office space as described above, office space can be leased by the Organisation at a guaranteed price of US$250 per square metres (indexed on the basis of 1992 price level, basic rent).
>
> If required expansion needs of the Organisation are known before the end of 1993, the building can be expanded to a maximum of 22,000 square metres. This expansion can be leased by the Organisation at a guaranteed price of US$250 per square metre (indexed on the basis of 1992 price levels, basic rent).

At the first session (8-12 February 1993) of the PrepCom, it was recognised that in order for the Bid of the Kingdom of the Netherlands to be realised within the time lines identified, it would be necessary for the Commission to allocate a high priority to the determination of the requirements for the OPCW permanent building. The mechanism decided upon to draw up the requirements was for an Expert Group to be formed and for the Group to report on its work to the PrepCom through Working Group A.

The first meeting of the Expert Group, chaired by Dr Radoslav Deyanov (Bulgaria) was held on 25-26 March 1993. The difficulties facing the Group were many for at the time of its creation, no decision had been taken by the PrepCom on the future size and shape of the future OPCW and in particular the future size of the Inspectorate and its associated working practices; the need for an OPCW laboratory and whether it should be within the future building; the need for Conference facilities within the building to serve the Conference of the States Parties and the Executive Council; and the level of security to be afforded the building. It was soon determined that in order for the Group to meet its remit – the preparation of a Detailed Programme of Requirements (POR) – the Expert Group would set up a Specialist Task Force (STF) to address specific issues and to undertake work between the formal meetings of the Expert Group.

Recognising the magnitude of the task facing the Expert Group and the STF, the Executive Secretary quickly recruited as consultants to the PTS a Security Adviser and a Building Adviser. The Host Country represented on the Expert Group by the OPCW Foundation similarly recruited a Project Manager and Construction Consultant (Starke Diekstra) who in July 1993 made available through the Foundation a paper entitled 'Global Programme of Requirements for the OPCW Head Office in the Hague'.[204]

With the assistance of the Consultants and following regular contact with those other Expert Groups established by the PrepCom addressing issues that would impact upon the future requirements of the building, the Expert Group progressively developed the 'global' POR provided by the OPCW Foundation into a detailed POR[205] in time for the Fifth Session of the PrepCom in December 1993. After minor corrections/changes a final consolidated version of the POR[206] was issued enabling the next stage in the building process to begin and for detailed submissions for the construction of the building to be sought from developers.

In the preparation of the POR and during the course of the many meetings of the Expert Group and STF a number of issues were raised and addressed that would ultimately result in the offer of the Kingdom of the Netherlands for the new building being subject to change. Of these perhaps the most important was the location for the new building. The offer of the Kingdom of the Netherlands had foreseen the building of the 'Peace Tower' to house the OPCW on the Koningin Julianaplein immediately adjacent to the Central railway station; part of a master plan to revitalise the centre of The Hague and to strengthen its economic structure. A detailed threat assessment and security survey of the proposed site by the Security Consultant of the PTS identified serious concerns with the site, however, and resulted in correspondence between the Executive Secretary and the City of the Hague and OPCW Foundation. Notwithstanding the importance of the development of the proposed site to the Municipality, an offer was made by the Municipality on 29 October 1993 to house the OPCW at an alternative site on the Johan de Wittlaan between the Bel Air hotel and the Netherlands Congress Centre; the offer being contingent upon the condition that any new

[204] OPCW Foundation paper, 1 July 1993, referred to in PC-IV/A/WP.1.

[205] Nieboer Gemako, 'Interim Accommodation for the OPCW', consultancy report as annexed to 'OPCW Building', PC-V/A/3, dated 10 December 1993.

[206] 'Programme of Requirements – Fifth Version – 31 March 1994', as attached to 'OPCW Building', PC-VI/A/4, dated 8 April 1994.

building on that site contribute sufficiently to the desired urban development of the city (i.e., that it be of an appropriate architectural standard).

A further issue arising from the revised offer of the Municipality for the site at Johan de Wittlaan was the matter of the land price for the new site. It was the intention of the Municipality at this stage to charge the developer the commercial value for the site and the Expert Group recognised that this would ultimately be reflected in the rental for the building to be paid by the OPCW after the first 3 years. The resolution of this matter is described below.

Following the completion of the POR by the Group of Experts, it was decided within the PrepCom that building related issues including those identified by, but not resolved, by the Expert Group should be addressed by The Committee on Host Country Relations (CRHC). In addition to building related issues, the CRHC was provided with a wide mandate covering also the facilities for the Conference of the States Parties; the privileges and immunities of representatives and experts to the PrepCom and representatives to the OPCW and the methodology for consultations with the Host Country. It was, however, to be the building issues which were to demand the focus of its attention throughout 1994 as decisions were needed on a number of issues if the accommodation required for the PTS and the OPCW were to be available in a timely and cost effective manner. Amongst the many issues relating to the permanent building to be resolved by the CRHC were:

- A determination of the land price at the Johan de Wittlaan site.
- A need to define the roles of the Commission and the Host Country in the decision making process for the new building.
- The identification of the criteria against which the design of the new building would be made.
- A decision to rent or purchase the building.
- The legal documents (Agreements) required to provide a clear definition of responsibility for the costs of the new building.
- The need to assess the availability of existing buildings in the Hague which would both satisfy the POR and be financially beneficial to the OPCW should it not pursue the option of a tailor made building.

The magnitude of the tasks facing the CRHC and the need for urgency in the decision making process for the new OPCW building two separate subsidiary bodies were created to aid the Committee, a Task Force and an Evaluation Panel.[207]

3.1 The land price

The question of the land price had not specifically been mentioned in the Bid for The Hague to host the new Organisation, unlike the unsuccessful bids of Vienna and Geneva which had both offered land in perpetuity on very favourable terms. The Commission

[207] Committee on Relations with the Host Country, 'Report of a meeting on 8 July 1994', PC-VIII/HC/1, dated 8 July 1994.

had, however, anticipated that the land for the new OPCW Headquarters Building would be made available on long lease at a nominal cost, as had been the practice with international organisations established in other cities.

The Secretariat and Commission learned that the Municipality of the Hague intended to recover from the developer of the purpose built building what they considered to be the full commercial value of the site, approximately NLG 19 million (US$ 10.75 million) and around 20 percent of the total project cost. Recognising that this cost would ultimately be reflected in the rental to be paid by the OPCW after the first three years, the Chairman and Executive Secretary jointly entered in July/August 1994 into correspondence with the Mayor of The Hague and the Minister of Foreign Affairs seeking resolution of the matter.

The response of the Minister of Foreign Affairs[208] confirmed that the land would be made available free of charge for a period of 99 years and that the payment/rent for the building would include no component for the land. This commitment of the Host Country was later to be included in the Understandings Between the Host Country and the Preparatory Commission For the OPCW concerning the Implementation of Paragraphs 6, 7, 9 and 11 of Annex 3 of the Paris Resolution.[209]

3.2 The selection process for the new OPCW building

The selection of prospective architects for the building and of developers interested in realising the project was undertaken by the OPCW Foundation. The two senior staff members of the Foundation, following extensive desk research, visited the buildings designed by architects with a reputation for fine buildings constructed in brick, which was considered necessary for the new building to fit with its surroundings. Three architects and developers were ultimately short listed. At a brief ceremony in the offices of a notary (De Brauw, Blackstone and Westbroek in The Hague) in early 1994 attended by representatives of the Commission, the Municipality, the Secretariat and the developers, the three architects were each assigned to a developer; the pairing of architect with developer being made by a draw. The draw paired:

- ProvastGoed Nederland BV (Provast) with Kallmann, McKinnell and Wood (architect based in Boston, Mass.).
- VOF C3 with Moneo (architect, based in Barcelona).
- IBC/ABN-AMRO with Snelder (architect, based in the Netherlands).

The OPCW Foundation retained the services of Starke Diekstra, the building consultant who had worked with the Group of Experts and Secretariat in developing the POR for the building, to undertake project evaluation and management, to provide advice

---

208 'Letter from the Minister for Foreign Affairs of the Netherlands concerning the OPCW Building', PC-IX/HC/4, dated 3 November 1994.

209 The 'Understandings Between the Host Country and the Preparatory Commission for the OPCW Concerning the Implementation of Paragraphs 6, 7, 9 and 11 of Annex 3 of the Paris Resolution' are contained in the annexes to the CSP decision C-1/DEC.5.

on costs and to supervise the project, including the provision of support for taking up the occupancy of the building. (Following representation by the Commission/Secretariat to the Foundation the consultancy was subsequently opened to international tender and in parallel with work starting on the building the contract was let to a Netherlands company DHV/AIB who represented the OPCW and the Foundation throughout the construction period).

Recognising the magnitude of the task of determining the submissions of the developers/architects for the new building the CRHC decided in July 1994 to establish a subordinate Task Force.[210] The initial submissions of the three developers were made available to the Task force on 16 July 1994 and following a detailed study of the proposals, an analysis of the offers and specifically of their financial and technical components was provided to the Task Force by Starke Diekstra. In late August formal presentations were then afforded the CRHC and Task Force by each of the teams of property developers and architects.

Following the presentations it was recognised that in order to compare the proposals a further analysis was required including one by the Secretariat as to the functionality of each proposal. The detailed analysis undertaken by Starke Diekstra concluded that all three designs would meet the POR and although changes and adjustments to the designs would be necessary this would not impact upon the rental levels proposed by the developers; a preference was stated however for the offer of Provast. The analysis of the Secretariat concluded that the submissions of Provast and IBC/ABN-AMRO would best serve the working needs of the OPCW. The Committee, taking due note of the report of the consultant and of the Secretariat agreed that the offer of the two property developers would best meet the needs of the Organisation, on the basis of functionality, financial considerations and other evaluations provided to it, agreed in late October 1994 to view the offer of Provast as the preferred option, subject to the provision of a suitable guarantee covering delivery date, price and quality.[211]

3.3 The decision to rent or purchase the building

The Task Force of the CRHC identified at an early stage that it could be financially beneficial for the Commission/OPCW to purchase the new building as an alternative to renting the premises as foreseen in the Bid. At the request of the CRHC, the Executive Secretary therefore commissioned an independent financial adviser, INGBank/MBO, to provide a financial analysis of the possible funding options of an OPCW tailor made building based on the approximate cost of the three proposals for the building and reflecting no cost to the OPCW of the land at the Catsheuvel Site.

The report of the financial adviser identified 3 alternatives to the renting of the building and their respective merits/disadvantages. The 3 alternatives were:

---

210 Committee on Relations with the Host Country, 'Report of a meeting on 8 July 1994', PC-VIII/HC/1, dated 8 July 1994.

211 Committee on Relations with the Host Country, 'Summary of meetings, 26–28 October 1994', PC-IX/HC/3, dated 28 October 1994.

- Purchase through mortgage. High annual costs at outset reducing over the life of the loan.
- Purchase through annuity. Fixed annual cost throughout the life of the loan
- Leasing. High annual costs but no requirement to borrow money. The OPCW could buy the building at a predetermined price at any stage.[212]

The report concluded that renting was only an attractive option if the period of occupation of the building was less than 10-15 years and flagged the need, whatever option was chosen, for a guarantor to be provided; a matter which would tax the legal departments of the PTS and the Host Country in the drawing up of the necessary legal documents (see below). Notwithstanding the comments of the financial adviser, given the many uncertainties prevailing at the time concerning the long-term future of the OPCW, a decision was reached to rent the premises and in line with the original offer of the Netherlands for the first three years rental to be paid by the Host Country.

3.4 **The legal documents**

The terms of the construction of the OPCW building, as stipulated in Annex 3 to the Paris Resolution, are rather vague:

> office space with a maximum of 18,000 square metres is foreseen to be made available for the Organisation in a new purpose-built office building to be known as the 'Peace Tower'. Construction can be started as soon as the Organisation can specify the required volume and further details...

Although goodwill was in abundance, when it came to the actual contracts and financing for realising the 'purpose-built office building', the complexity created by the Paris Resolution became sharply apparent by the multiplicity of parties, each with strict limitations on the amount of risk to be assumed. These were:

- the Commission, which was making the decisions but was not legally entitled to make commitments on behalf of the OPCW;
- the OPCW as tenant, which would come into existence at an unknown future date beyond anyone's control;
- the developer, a private company which needed a long-term tenant in order to secure financing for the building from an investment bank which demanded guarantees;
- the OPCW Foundation, which on behalf of the Host Country only had the obligation (and authority) to commit to paying the first three year's rent, maintenance, etc.; and
- delegations of Signatory States (organised as the Committee on Relations with the Host Country), which needed to prevent as far as possible a looming finan-

212 'OPCW Building – Financing Options', PC-VIII/HC/4, dated 29 August 1994.

cial responsibility for the PrepCom if the building were completed and the OPCW was nowhere near being established.

The uncertainty as to when the OPCW might actually come into existence became more worrisome as time went on. Despite the initial euphoria over the adoption of the treaty text, by 1994 the pace of ratifications had ground nearly to a halt for reasons explained elsewhere in this volume. There was a growing fear among delegations that the treaty might never enter into force, or only long after the five-year preparatory phase subsidised by the Host Country had expired.

If construction of the OPCW building was completed before the treaty entered into force and the OPCW came into existence, who would be responsible for the required payments? The Paris Resolution provided that for a period of three years during the 'full implementation phase' (in other words, after entry into force of the Convention), the Host Country would pay for the rent of the office space in the new purpose-built office building, 110 parking places inside the building, maintenance, energy and turn-key costs.[213]

Coupled with that, were the complexities of the arrangements for the construction of the OPCW building itself. Construction was to be carried out by a developer which needed to conclude a tenancy agreement with the intended tenant before construction began so as to secure financing for the construction. The PrepCom would not be the tenant. The PrepCom also had no authority to enter into commitments on behalf of the OPCW. Under the Paris Resolution the PrepCom could only make recommendations to the OPCW Conference of the States Parties, which in turn, if it wished, would authorise the OPCW Director-General to conclude the Tenancy Agreement.

It was difficult for the City of The Hague and the Netherlands to provide a guarantee beyond the terms of the bid. They were limited to their commitment to pay for the rent, maintenance, etc., for the first three years of the full implementation phase.

After protracted negotiations in the PrepCom's Committee on Relations with the Host Country in parallel with negotiations between the Provisional Technical Secretariat, the Developer and the OPCW Foundation, agreement was reached on the 'Supplementary Understandings between the Preparatory Commission for the OPCW and the Host Country relating to the Preliminary Tenancy Agreement for the New Purpose-built Office Building'.[214]

The solution found consisted of the following:

- The Commission would conclude a preliminary tenancy agreement with the developer which would enter into force upon confirmation by the Conference at its first session.
- If the building were completed before the OPCW existed, the Provisional Technical Secretariat would occupy the building and the OPCW Foundation would become the Lessee for three years. In that event, the legal relationship between the PrepCom and the OPCW Foundation would be arranged in a separate agree-

[213] Para. 6 of Annex 3 to the Paris Resolution.

[214] Confirmed by the Conference of the States Parties and published in OPCW document C-I/DEC.5, dated 14 May 1997.

ment. If the OPCW came into existence during the three-year period, the OPCW would become the Lessee and the OPCW Foundation would pay for the rent for the balance of the three year period.

- If at the end of the three-year period the OPCW still did not exist, the Provisional Technical Secretariat would have the option to take over the Tenancy Agreement on a year-to-year basis.
- If the PrepCom decided not to become the tenant, it would vacate the building and the Netherlands would assume the necessary guarantees towards the Lessor which, jointly with the Netherlands, would have the right and the obligation to look for a new tenant or otherwise dispose of the building.
- If the Conference did not confirm the Preliminary Tenancy Agreement, the OPCW would have the option to remain in the building until the end of the three-year period at which time it would either take over the tenancy or vacate the building. The Netherlands would have assumed the necessary guarantees and together with the Lessor would look for a new tenant or dispose of the building.

As a result of the conclusion of the Supplementary Understandings, and after lengthy negotiations between the Secretariat, the Developer, the OPCW Foundation and the Committee on Relations with the Host Country, followed by PrepCom approval, the Development and Realisation Agreement was concluded between the OPCW Foundation and the Developer, including annexes specifying the guarantees and ground lease agreement. At the same time, the Preliminary Tenancy Agreement was concluded by the PrepCom and the Developer. Construction began in 1996 and the building was delivered to the OPCW in 1998, nine months after the establishment of the OPCW. For the intervening period, interim accommodation was negotiated to supplement the building used during the preparatory phase.

3.5 Existing buildings

Whilst discussions within the CRHC were to be focused upon the realisation of a tailor made building, the Committee continued to see if an existing building within The Hague could serve as the future Headquarters building of the OPCW and to assess the benefits or otherwise to the organisation should such a course be followed. To this end in February 1994 the CRHC requested that the Secretariat consider the feasibility and costs associated with the option for an existing building to house the enlarged Secretariat during the 180 days preceding EIF and to forego the offer contained in the Bid for a new tailor made building. The feasibility study was also to identify the practicality and costs associated with the enlarged Secretariat pursuing an option to expand into Laan van Meerdervoort 70 and subsequently to transfer to the new building when available or alternatively to vacate Laan van Meerdervoort 51 and to occupy an existing building of approx 9,500 square metres pending occupation of the new building. The report of the Secretariat[215] concluded that whilst the study was by no

[215] 'Report by the Executive Secretary on Accommodation Options for the Provisional Technical Secretariat/Technical Secretariat', PC-VI/HC/3/Rev.1, dated 21 March 1994.

means exhaustive the option to occupy an existing building and not to pursue the 'tailor made' building offered no financial advantage to the Organisation in later years and whilst offering immediate occupancy and a single move, those advantages had to be offset by the loss of rental subsidy worth approx NLG 20 million (US$ 11.30 million) over the first five years of the existence of the Organisation. It is of interest to note here that the one building considered as an option to the tailor made building to house the OPCW was the Aegon building (see Interim Accommodation: Phase 2 below). A further study of the available buildings to house the PrepCom and subsequently OPCW was undertaken by Nieboer Gemako in June/July 1994. The study identified possible options in addition to Laan van Meerdervoort 70.[216] Of the available buildings, that at Bontekoekade 4 was identified as best meeting the future needs of the OPCW and estimated costs associated with the necessary extension and refurbishment together with the rental costs for the building were provided. Following the presentations for a new building from each of the developers and given the expense that would be incurred in expanding and refurbishing the Bontekoekade building, the CRHC recommended to the PrepCom that the Bontekoekade option should not be pursued.[217] It was only in November 1994 however that CRHC determined that the option of an existing building to house the OPCW should no longer be considered.[218]

3.6 The realisation of the new building

Following three years of deliberation, discussion and negotiation on 9 May 1996 a 'ground breaking ceremony' attended by the Secretary-General of the Ministry for Foreign Affairs, Mr D J van den Berg, the Chairman of the Commission, HE Mr Sallehaddin Abdullah (Malaysia), the Mayor of the Hague, Mr A JE Havermans, the Executive Secretary of the PrepCom, Mr Ian Kenyon, and representatives of the PrepCom, Secretariat, the OPCW Foundation, Provast and the architects took place at the Catsheuvel site and work began in earnest on the construction of the new building with a completion date for the building set for 20 January 1998.

To ensure that this deadline was met, Provast arranged for Mr Rayford Law, a representative of the architects, Kallmann, McKinnell and Wood (KMW) to be based in the Netherlands for much of the construction time and for regular visits to the site by Mr Michael Mckinnel from KMW in Boston. In parallel, the PTS in conjunction with the OPCW Foundation jointly appointed a consultancy firm (DHV/AIB) to be assist them in monitoring the realisation of the new building.

In order to provide all parties involved in the project with a forum for discussing progress on the building and to address and resolve issues in a timely manner, Frank van der Weide of Provast established and chaired a Building Steering Group (BSG).

---

216 Committee on Relations with the Host Country, 'Report by the Provisional Technical Secretariat to the Task Force on the Accommodation of the Commission/OPCW', PC-VIII/HC/WP.4, dated 22 July 1994.

217 Committee on Relations with the Host Country, 'Summary of Meetings ... 5 October-7 November 1994', PC-IX/HC/5, dated 7 November 1994, para. 2.3.

218 Committee on Relations with the Host Country, 'Summary of meetings during the intersessional period 5 October-7 November 1994', PC-IX/HC/5, dated 7 November 1994, para. 2.4.

The BSG comprised representatives of the developer, the constructor (Hillen & Roosen), the architect, the OPCW Foundation and the Secretariat (including the consultant DHV/ AIB). The BSG met weekly to discuss all aspects of the building programme including the internal design and fit up of the building. Reports on the work of the BSG and on progress of the building were subsequently provided at regular intervals to the CRHC, the PrepCom and the OPCW. Meetings of the BSG were conducted in English.

Representation of the Secretariat at meetings of the BSG included the Executive Secretary, the Legal Officer, Head of General Services (Project Officer), the Building Officer, the Security Officer, the Building and Security consultants and on occasions other members of staff. The close involvement of the Executive Secretary in the meetings of the BSG was invaluable and did much to ensure that the problems, which did arise, were quickly resolved and it was notable that following his departure at EIF meetings of the Group became more protracted and difficult.

The BSG was undoubtedly the key to ensuring that the work on site continued apace and notwithstanding that at times there were matters which resulted in heated exchanges it is to the credit of all participants, that such matters were resolved quickly without incurring a delay in the construction of the building and without a budget over run being incurred.

As the building neared completion – in December 1997 – there was an urgency on the part of the developer to bring forward the completion date of the building given the holiday break enjoyed by the contractors over the Christmas/New year period. Following detailed inspections of the building by the Consultant (DHV/AIB) and the Building Officer of the Secretariat this 'rush to closure' was resisted for the inspections revealed that a number of tasks remained to be completed and would have required the presence of a number of contractors to make good following the occupation of the building by the OPCW. As a result the OPCW did not take over the building until late January 1998 and occupancy of the building a month later. The building was formally opened by Her Majesty Queen Beatrix on 20 May 1998.

4. Additional Accommodation Issues

4.1 OPCW Laboratory

The need for an OPCW Laboratory was identified at an early stage of the work of the PrepCom and was discussed in both the Expert Groups on Equipment and on the OPCW Building. By December 1993, the PrepCom determined that the laboratory, while an integral part of the OPCW physical accommodation requirements, should be located near The Hague but not in the main OPCW Building.[219] The centre of attention was thus subsequently focused on creating a laboratory within the existing TNO-PNL facilities at Rijswijk, from whom an offer to house the facility had been received.

[219] 'Report of the Commission', PC-V/12, dated 17 December 1993.

At the same time as evaluating the offer of and facilities within TNO, an alternative site at Heulweg 28/30 was identified. This site was an industrial unit close to TNO which had been licensed for use as a laboratory. To meet the specific needs of the OPCW, both sites required considerable work and expense on refitting the premises. After a detailed analysis of the two options, it was determined on the grounds of cost and operational efficiency (including advantages of co-locating the OPCW Equipment Store with the laboratory) that the facility should be established at Heulweg 28/30.[220] The funding of the rental of these laboratory premises as well as the turnkey, utilities and maintenance costs were paid by the Host Country for three years. This was possible because the bid had allowed for a main building, including a laboratory, of 18,000 square metres whereas the agreed design for the main building was smaller and thus some funds could be released for the separate laboratory.[221]

After consultations with the local authorities in Rijswijk designed to allay concerns of local residents that 'chemical weapons' would be transported to and handled by the new laboratory, the necessary legal consent was obtained. Construction work to convert the Rijswijk premises to meet the needs of the OPCW started in 1995 and the facility was formally opened by the Mayor of Rijswijk on 11 September 1996.[222]

4.2 Conference facilities

The conference facilities used by the PrepCom and the Secretariat during the Preparatory Phase are described in Chapter 3.

Paragraph 5 of Annex 3 to the Paris Resolution states

> When needed a conference room for approximately 170 delegations will be made available, free of charge, during the maximum 8 year period of the Netherlands bid at the nearby Peace palace or Netherlands Congress Centre.

Notwithstanding the offer of the Host Country to provide facilities for the Conference of the States Parties (CSP), in the early discussions on the future OPCW building the provision of a Main Conference Room to house the CSP and the Executive Council within the future building of the Organisation was considered by the Group of Experts and the subordinate Specialist Task Force (STF). It was soon recognised however that the sites offered to house the new building of the OPCW might not be able to accommodate the construction of such a large facility whose footprint and height would be substantial. It was also recognised that the cost of maintaining such a large conference facility as would be needed to house the CSP would be considerable and given the

220 'Report of the Commission', PC-VIII/18, dated 29 September 1994.

221 OPCW Conference of the States Parties, First Session, 'Decision: Preliminary Tenancy Agreement and Related Understandings and Supplementary Understandings', C-I/DEC.5, dated 14 May 1997.

222 'Report of the Committee on Relations with the Host Country for the Period 4 July-19 December 1996', PC-XV/HC/4, dated 19 December 1996.

frequency and duration of the meetings would be an expensive and unnecessary option for the future organisation.[223]

As the discussions on the future site for the building concluded that the new building was to built on the site at Johan de Wittlaan immediately adjacent to the Netherlands Congress Centre (NCC), the Group of Experts on the OPCW Building determined that the Programme of Requirements (POR) for the new building would solely include the conference needs of the Executive Council (EC) and that the offer of the Host Country contained in the Paris Resolution to provide conference facilities for the CSP should be pursued . Given the potential need for the EC to meet at very short notice the provision of suitable conference facilities to house the Council within the building were described in detail in the POR for the new building.[224]

Recognising the interest of the Belgian authorities expressed in 1987 to house the Organisation and the subsequent interest of the city of Ieper to be associated with the new building, ite was suggested that the Executive Council Room be called the Ieper room.[225] In the years that followed discussions were to take place with the authorities in Ieper, the architect and the OPCW as to how this association could be best marked and ahead of the formal opening of the building, a wall mural was commissioned by the city, presented and mounted in the building in time for the formal opening of the building.

The decision of the PrepCom not to proceed with the provision of conference facilities within the new OPCW building determined that the offer of the Host Country (see above) to house the Conference was in need of fleshing out. Additionally it was recognised that in addition to the spatial requirements needed to house the CSP there was a need for all the logistical arrangements that would be needed to be identified and this was undertaken by the Committee on Host Country Relations and a subordinate Task Force.[226] Subsequently the needs of the OPCW to house and service the CSP were to be identified in the Supplementary.[227]

4.3 Car parking

As already indicated the matter of car parking in the buildings of the PrepCom and OPCW was a topic that was to occupy the PrepCom and Secretariat from the outset and was similarly one that would require further dialogue with the Host Country before a satisfactory solution was to be found for the new tailor made building. The Host Country Bid provided for 110 parking places within the new building but the

---

223 Working Group A, 'Groups of Experts on the OPCW Building: Third Interim Report' PC-IV/A/WP.1*, dated 30 July 1993.

224 'OPCW Building', PC-VI/A/4, dated 8 April 1994.

225 This is noted in: Working Group A, 'Groups of Experts on the OPCW Building: Third Interim Report' PC-IV/A/WP.1*, dated 30 July 1993.

226 See Committee on Relations with the Host Country, 'Summary of meetings, 26-28 October 1994', PC-IX/HC/3, dated 28 October 1994.

227 The 'Understandings Between the Host Country and the Preparatory Commission for the OPCW Concerning the Implementation of Paragraphs 6, 7, 9 and 11 of Annex 3 of the Paris Resolution' are contained in the annexes to the CSP decision C-1/DEC.5.

Programme of Requirements had identified the need for 275 spaces to be provided for use by delegates (100), the vehicles of the PrepCom/OPCW and one space per 3 staff members, assuming a staff of 500. The Bid had been based upon the national policy for car parking which restricted the number of parking spaces to be provided to company employees in order to encourage use of public transport, to reduce congestion on the roads and to encourage employees to 'take to the bicycle'. The POR on the other hand was based upon UN standards and the envisaged working practice within the OPCW. Fortuitously the location of the new building, adjacent to the Netherlands Congress Centre (NCC) with its large underground car park, enabled this particular problem to be overcome and following discussions between the Chairman of the CRHC and the Secretariat with the Director of the NCC and with the support of the OPCW Foundation, agreement was ultimately reached in November 1994 for the long-term rental of 165 car parking spaces within the NCC car park.

4.4 **Security**

The specific security needs of the OPCW had, as explained previously, dictated that an alternative site for the tailor made building from that included in the original bid of the Netherlands be provided. Security was to remain an important consideration throughout the design and construction phases of the building but it is appropriate here to describe in any detail how the security needs were satisfied; one potential 'showstopper' is however worthy of mention. Following the agreement of the PrepCom to the alternative site (the Catsheuvel site) and within months of the PrepCom deciding that a new building should be built on the site, it was learnt in November 1995 through the media that the NCC intended to construct an open-air theatre, bordering the site of the new OPCW building.[228] This resulted in the concerns of the Commission being raised with the Municipality and a formal objection to the new theatre being lodged.[229] The concerns expressed by the PrepCom can be summarised as follows:

- an open-air theatre could pose new and serious security problems to the OPCW building;
- it could mean higher costs to the commission/OPCW;
- it could imply an unacceptable increase in noise levels and traffic in the area of the OPCW building at the time that events take place; and
- the proposed design for an open-air theatre could have a negative impact on the aesthetic appearance of the immediate environs of the OPCW building.

These concerns were taken into account by the Municipality (Planning Committee). A fence and pond were to be constructed between the open air theatre and the OPCW

---

[228] The new facility was considered necessary as the North Sea Jazz Festival, a major money spinner for the NCC, had previously used the Catsheuvel site for a tented theatre.

[229] 'Report of the Committee on Relations with the Host Country for the Period 10 November-14 December 1996', PC-XV/HC/4, dated 14 December 1995 and Corr.1, dated 19 December 1995.

building and the Commission/Secretariat consulted at all stages in the development of the theatre. The number of events each year was to be very restricted and no permanent permit was to be granted; all events to be subject to a separate permit only to be issued after consultation with the Director-General. Separately, the NCC agreed to compensate the Commission/OPCW for any additional security costs resulting from events held in the open-air theatre. Provided with those assurances the CRHC agreed to withdraw the objection to the theatre. In the event the new auditorium was rarely used and has since closed.

Mention is made of the above matter for it demonstrates how a potentially serious matter was resolved by prompt action being taken by the Secretariat/Commission and the importance of maintaining excellent lines of communication with the offices of the Municipality and other government offices.

5. Interim Accommodation: Phase 2

As already identified the building provided to the Secretariat was barely adequate to house the authorised number of staff of the PTS and it was soon recognised that additional accommodation would be needed to house the expanded Secretariat during Phase 2 of the build up in staff numbers 180 days before entry into force. In November 1993 the Group of Experts on the OPCW Building identified the need for the Secretariat to undertake a review of buildings within The Hague that might be suitable for the purpose of housing the expanded Secretariat pending the availability of the tailor made building. To undertake this task the Executive Secretary commissioned a leading estate agent (Nieboer Gemako) in The Hague to undertake a survey of suitable buildings and to provide a detailed report on the possible options and likely running costs of the buildings. The report concluded that the renting of Laan van Meerdervoort 70 in combination with Laan van Meerdervoort 51 would be the most realistic option.[230]

The Expert Group prepared a POR for the Interim Accommodation of the Secretariat which identified specific functions/areas of the building which could be reduced in size, relocated or eliminated during the interim period.[231] This POR was to be an invaluable tool in the discussions on interim accommodation within the CRHC over the ensuing two years.

Following the decision of the Commission[232] in December 1994 to proceed with the tailor made building the CRHC continued to be charged with monitoring the available office accommodation in The Hague to house the enlarged Secretariat pending the new building becoming available and the focus of attention again turned to Laan van Meerdervoort 70 as the favoured solution. The uncertainty over the EIF of the

---

230 Nieboer Gemako, 'Interim Accommodation for the OPCW', consultancy report as annexed to 'OPCW Building', PC-V/A/3, dated 10 December 1993.

231 Committee on Relations with the Host Country, 'Interim Accommodation of the Commission and the OPCW', PC-VIII/HC/WP.5, dated 11 August 1994.

232 'Report of the Commission', PC-IX/11, dated 9 December 1994.

Convention would, however, result in the CRHC continuing to address the need for interim accommodation throughout 1995 and the early months of 1996. Fortuitously the delay in any decision being taken on securing an additional or alternative building to Laan van Meerdervoort 51 was to work to the advantage of the PrepCom for in early 1996 it was learnt that the Aegon Insurance Company was to vacate their premises at Churchillplein 1, adjacent to the Netherlands Congress Centre, in December that year, when responsibility for the premises would be assumed by the International Criminal Tribunal for the former Yugoslavia, who already occupied part of the building and was keen for another international organisation to share the tenancy pending a decision on the future expansion of the Tribunal. In March 1994 the Secretariat had identified the building as a possible alternative to a tailor made building for at that time the future occupation of the building by the ICTY was uncertain.[233]

Following detailed surveys of the building, the preparation of detailed estimates for the 'fit up' of the Aegon building to meet the needs of the Secretariat and an analysis of the costs to be incurred by the PrepCom for the rental and upgrade either of the two properties (the Aegon building and Laan van Meerdervoort 70) best suited to meet the needs of the expanded Secretariat at EIF, the CRHC, on behalf of the PrepCom, decided that the Aegon building was preferable for both operational and financial reasons and that a tenancy agreement should be entered with the ICTY for the lease of approximately 5,214 square metres of office space and 50 car parking spaces.[234] The Tenancy Agreement was entered on 15 January 1997 and after a few weeks during which the essential fit up of the accommodation took place the Verification Division of the Secretariat vacated Laan van Meerdervoort 51 and occupied the premises in March and were to remain there through to February 1998 when they transferred to the new tailor-made building.

5.1 The sole supplier contract

No reference to the provision of accommodation for the PrepCom, the Provisional Technical Secretariat (PTS) and subsequently Technical Secretariat of the OPCW would be complete without mention being made of the Sole Supplier Contract and of the sole supplier designated by the Municipality of The Hague. Over the period February 1993 to December 1998 the Contract and Contractor played an extremely important role in the development, fit-up and furnishing of the buildings of the Organisation.

The Bid Book of the Netherlands submitted to the Conference on Disarmament in 1992 and the subsequent Report of the Friend of the Chair (April 1992)[235] which compared the three bids to host the Organisation and which was provided to delegations at the Conference on Disarmament to facilitate a decision on the future seat of the Organisation state that the furnishing of the buildings of the new Organisation

---

[233] 'Report by the Executive Secretary on Accommodation Options for the Provisional Technical Secretariat/Technical Secretariat', PC-VI/HC/3/Rev.1, dated 21 March 1994.

[234] 'Report of the Legal Adviser on the Sublease for Interim Accommodation – Aegon Building', PC-XV/HC/3, dated 13 December 1996.

[235] Friend of the Chair on the Seat of the Organisation, Ad Hoc Committee on Chemical Weapons, 'Preliminary Report', Paper No. 1, dated 28 April 1992; commonly referred to as 'Kamal paper 1'.

would be provided free of charge in the preparatory phase for a maximum of five years and for three years thereafter subject to a number of conditions being satisfied. Subsequently, the Bid identified those conditions as follows:

> Subject to the promise that all office supplies, service contracts and other office materials for which the Organisation will pay, shall be purchased at the normal going rates from a supplier designated by the Hague, the Netherlands offers during the preparatory phase (maximum of 5 years) includes:
>
> Providing all necessary office furniture according to official European standards free of charge;
>
> Providing all the reasonably necessary office equipment, free of charge
>
> During the preparatory phase (maximum of 5 years) the Netherlands offer also includes:
>
> Providing a fully integrated digital telephone switchboard, telephones on every desk and 10 fax machines free of charge.
>
> After the preparatory phase during a period of 3 years office furniture (according to official European standards) and reasonably necessary office equipment will be supplied free of charge on a one time basis, provided that all office supplies, service contracts and other office materials for which the Organisation will pay, shall be purchased at the normal going rates from a supplier designated by The Hague.

5.2 The sole supplier

The sole supplier identified by the Municipality of The Hague, was Paagman & Paagman BV, a medium-sized company located in The Hague, which held a number of contracts with multinational companies and government offices throughout the Netherlands for the supply of office materials, equipments and furniture and ran a number of bookshops. A contract (Agreement) had been entered between the Municipality and Paagman & Paagman BV on 11 September 1992 covering the conduct of business by the latter with the OPCW. Mr Gerard Paagman was throughout the period of the contract the principal point of contact for the Organisation with the supplier.

5.3 The implementation of the sole supplier contract

Within days of the arrival of the Executive Secretary and the vanguard of the PTS in The Hague in February 1993 it became clear that the role of the Sole Supplier was not restricted to those which a cursory read through of the Bid would indicate, for Mr Paagman was also, on behalf of the OPCW Foundation, responsible for the renovation and refit of the building at Laan van Meerdervoort 51 and was to assume a similar responsibility for the internal design and fit up of the new building of the Organisation.

With few staff available within the PTS in the first few months to attend to administrative matters and with a mountain of tasks to be accomplished, the role of the sole supplier was a considerable bonus to the Secretariat for as described previously the development of the accommodation provided by the Host Country to meet the immediate needs of the Secretariat in a timely manner owed much to the total commitment and flexibility of Mr Paagman and his staff. Subsequently however the lack of clarity in the responsibilities of the sole supplier to the OPCW and the new building in particular would dictate many hours of negotiation, additional work for the decision-making bodies of the Commission/OPCW, many members of the Secretariat being diverted from their primary task and ultimately lead to a breakdown of trust between the Organisation and the sole supplier and to the termination of the contract.

Within a few months of the creation of the PTS it was found necessary to agree with the OPCW Foundation a means of ensuring that office furniture for authorized staff and an ever increasing number of temporary/contract staff be supplied in a timely manner, for initially all requests/orders had to be placed through the Foundation and delays in receiving work stations for newly recruited staff were not uncommon. The mechanism agreed with the Foundation was that NLG 4,471 was to be paid for each full time employee and that orders for furniture could be placed directly by the Secretariat with the Sole Supplier and not through the Foundation. The financial ceiling allocated was indexed each year and permitted the progressive build up of specialist items of office furniture (e.g., archives, meeting rooms, etc.) in addition to meeting the needs of each new staff member. The mechanism served the Organisation well.

With respect to the furnishing of the buildings of the PTS, it soon became apparent within the Secretariat that the level of office equipment to be provided under the Netherlands bid did not meet the demands, nor expectations of the staff of an International Organisation and that the Sole Supplier was specifically not in a position to meet the needs of the PTS for such items as computer equipments/systems, photocopiers and laboratory equipment. Initially this was resolved by the Executive Secretary reaching agreement with the Director of the OPCW Foundation (Mr GK Hamming) and the Sole Supplier and the preparation and signing (in February 1994) of a Letter of Understanding (LOU) by the Director of the OPCW Foundation, Mr GK Hamming, and the Executive Secretary. The Letter clarified the scope of the Netherlands' Bid with respect to the supply of office furniture and office equipment free of charge and identified the items to be purchased from the sole supplier.

Given the difficulties encountered in managing the existing Sole Supplier Contract and the pressing need to identify and order the furnishings for the new OPCW building which were to be provided by the sole supplier in accordance with the Bid, after some months of discussion and negotiation a separate contract for the Supply of Office Furniture and Related Equipment for the OPCW within the Netherlands was entered on 1 September 1997 between the OPCW, the OPCW Foundation and the Sole Supplier for the furnishing of the new OPCW building.

The Contract was both innovative and possibly a first of its kind for an international organisation, in that it foresaw the furniture supplied being depreciated each year and for the replacement of all furniture after eight (soft furnishings) and 16 years (hard furnishings) being provided free of charge to the Organisation subject to the sole supplier status of Paagman & Paagman BV being extended by an additional five years through to 29 April 2005 (thus eight years after Entry into Force) with thereafter automatic extension on a year by year basis unless nine months notice of termination served by either party. The agreement with the sole supplier also provided the Organisation with the right to purchase the furniture supplied free of charge by Paagman & Paagman BV at a depreciated value on the date of termination of the contract.

In retrospect the Contract did not however address in detail the mounting number of concerns with the interpretation of the LOU signed in February 1994 and reference to that document at Article 6 of the contract resulted in growing pressures for change in the relationship with the sole supplier over the ensuing months.

The mark-up of the Sole Supplier on the furniture and office supplies provided to the Commission/OPCW had been set by the OPCW Foundation and Paagman & Paagman BV at 20 percent in the previously mentioned agreement signed in 1992. Notwithstanding inclusion of this profit margin in the Contract entered in September 1997, the mark-up charged to the Organisation by the sole supplier remained a 'bone of contention' throughout the life of the contract and led to much adverse criticism of the arrangement by both the External Auditor and the Office of Internal Oversight, for by inviting and scrutinising tenders for items, the sole supplier was often found to be more expensive than alternative suppliers. This was due in part to the fact that many alternative suppliers were aware of the 'special relationship' enjoyed by Paagman & Paagman BV with the Commission/OPCW and thus any opportunity to tender for items required by the Commission/OPCW was viewed as a means of breaking into a potential lucrative market and on occasions undoubtedly led to a low bid being received in response to an invitation to tender.

As previously indicated, the relationship between the OPCW and the sole supplier was marked by recurring difficulties over the terms of the contract, the range of supplies and prices. That, in addition to a recognition by the sole supplier that the time taken to service the contract was to the detriment of his other business interests, led Mr Paagman in mid 1998 to write to the Director-General offering to terminate the Contract before 29 April 2005 subject to a payment of NLG 2.5 million. At that time the value of the furniture supplied was estimated at NLG 3,871,673 and the depreciated value of the furniture as defined in the contract – as at 29 April 2005 – estimated at NLG 1,891,637. Following a cost benefit study analysis of the offer undertaken by the consulting firm PriceWaterhouse Cooper, and discussion of the matter within the Executive Council and the Advisory Body on Administrative and Financial Matters, in November 1998 the Conference of the States Parties authorised the Director-General to terminate the contract with effect from 1 January 1999.[236]

6. Reflections

6.1 Accommodation matters

At the time that the Bid to house the OPCW was accepted, no one involved in either the preparation of the Bid nor its acceptance was fully aware of the complexity and difficulties that would be encountered in housing the PTS and OPCW. Such difficulties were compounded by the political concern over the entry into force of the Convention and thus a desire in many capitals for the new Organisation not to be allowed

236 'Report of the Third Session of the Conference of the States Parties', C-III/4, dated 20 November 1998, para. 19.5.

'to run before it could walk' and specifically to enter into a major capital commitment for a building that might never be needed if none of the key States had ratified in time. This constraint is now, sometime later, better understood but at the time was viewed as a 'thorn in the side' amidst the competing pressures to keep the commercial world (building owners, contractors, financial companies) interested in supporting the PTS/ OPCW while attending to the needs of the PTS itself and satisfying the demands of the Member States through the many committees and working groups involved in the decision-making process on accommodation issues.

One benefit of the protracted discussions on accommodation issues was that the plans drawn for the new building were well thought through and never rushed and that is now reflected in the excellent building and working environment afforded the OPCW and its staff; a building and environment which is understood to be envied by many other international organisations and one which has stood the test of time, in that changes to the internal layout of the building have been few.

The commitment and dedication of so many people (the Netherlands Authorities and particularly of the OPCW Foundation, many members of the PrepCom and of the PTS, the Developer, the architect) to the project were paramount in the success of the project. This commitment and dedication however had to be earned and for those perhaps facing a similar task in the future, must never be assumed.

Given the importance of the building project to the Organisation and the complexity of related accommodation issues, the PrepCom seriously underestimated the level and intensity of the work required to ensure not only the realisation of a new building but also the day to day building management functions necessary in the smooth running of an international headquarters and particularly one in its formative years.

Should a similar situation ever present itself again, it is imperative that a high priority be afforded the recruitment of an Infrastructure Branch including a Building Officer, a Facility Manager and sufficient support staff. The head of this branch should ideally be equipped with a knowledge of the construction industry and of facility management, have the experience of working in an International Headquarters and be equipped with good negotiating and management skills. Such a character may be a rare breed, but whatever the constraints on the finances and thus recruitment of staff, such an individual should be afforded a high priority for recruitment and afforded a grade commensurate with the task; this was not the case with the PTS. After completion of the building project such a high grade individual may no longer be necessary.

6.2 Sole supplier contract

The offer of the Kingdom of the Netherlands to provide and furnish accommodation for the PrepCom and OPCW was met in full. Notwithstanding the many difficulties encountered in administering the supply contract in the period February 1993 to January 1999 and the changing face of offices during that period due to the increasing use of personal computers and the means of storing data, that the bid was honoured owes much to the part played by the sole supplier and the OPCW Foundation. Throughout the six years of the relationship Mr Paagman and his small team at Paagman & Paagman

BV were committed to ensuring that the PrepCom and OPCW were provided with the accommodation and supplies required.

Now some years on it is clear that Mr Paagman underestimated the work that would be required of his company to service the needs of the new International organisation and failed, together with others, to recognise that the innovative agreements reached with the Netherlands authorities, to fund the furnishing of the buildings in return for the right to supply the organisation, would not stand close scrutiny by the Member States, used to open competition for the procurement of all major items of expenditure. Equally, it is now clear that the full implications of the relevant extracts of the Bid pertaining to the offer for accommodation and supplies to the PrepCom and OPCW and the many ambiguities contained in that text were not fully researched by national authorities before agreement was reached to support the bid for The Hague to host the organisation.

The concept of a sole supplier identified in the Bid has much to commend it, subject to a satisfactory pricing mechanism for items ordered by an organisation and an adequate oversight regime of the accounts of the supplier being agreed from the outset. This is particularly so in the initial period before a full administration system has been developed and staffed.

The contract signed in 1997 for the supply of furniture for the new building of the OPCW which would have seen the replacement of all furniture over a given time frame free of charge to the Organisation in exchange for an extension of the sole supplier contract had much to commend it. In other international headquarters it is noted that at times of budgetary constraint, little or no money is found for the essential replacement of the furnishings of the headquarters buildings and the working environment of staff is allowed to deteriorate. It is important in any future arrangement with a sole supplier that all parties ensure that their share understandings of its terms.

Chapter 6

RECRUITMENT AND TRAINING OF INSPECTORS

Ron G. Manley

1. INTRODUCTION

The key to gaining acceptance for the CWC's on-site inspection regime was the establishment of appropriate mechanisms to enable States Parties and their chemical industries to protect confidential information that was not relevant to the Convention. One area of particular concern to the chemical industry was the potential risk of commercial espionage being undertaken by inspectors tasked to carry out on-site inspections under the CWC. The selection and employment of inspectors was, therefore, an issue of particular concern to many delegations. Soon after the CWC negotiations were concluded a senior industry representative described hiring and training inspectors as 'perhaps the most difficult and the most critical part of implementing the treaty'. He went on: 'The inspectors must be highly qualified people with both experience and extensive formal training, which should include carrying out trial inspections. ... One of industry's biggest concerns is the quality, training and integrity of the inspectors and the process by which they will be trained'.[237]

Under many international treaties, with associated inspection regimes, the standard practice is to use inspectors, either on loan or short-term secondment, from States Parties to the treaty. This approach reduces costs and has been shown to be effective. Its major shortcoming is that it can be much more difficult to control and monitor both personnel and the flow of information. Given the high level of concern about confidentiality those states negotiating the CWC, therefore, took the view that inspectors carrying out inspections under the CWC should be members of the Technical Secretariat and full-time employees of the Organisation.[238]

It was left to the PrepCom to determine how many and what sorts of inspectors were required and how they should be trained. The first Expert Group to address this issue was the Expert Group on Inspection Team Composition, which met in The Hague from 24-28 May 1993. In its report the Group identified the kinds of skills and numbers of inspectors likely to be required for each of the different types of inspection

[237] Will Carpenter, 'The perspective of the Western chemical industry', in Benoit Morel and Kyle Olson (eds.), *Shadows and Substance: The Chemical Weapons Convention*, Ridgeway Series in International Security Studies (Boulder, Westview Press 1993), pp. 115-26, p. 124.

[238] CWC, Article VIII, para. 42.

I.R. Kenyon and D. Feakes, The Creation of the OPCW

envisaged under the CWC.[239] Building on this work it was subsequently agreed that inspectors and inspection assistants with the following professional backgrounds should be sought; chemical production technologists, chemical production logisticians, industrial chemists, chemical weapons/munitions specialists, analytical chemists, medical doctors and paramedics. There was also a debate on whether to include interpreters in this list. After further consideration it was decided that, as inspectors would be drawn from a wide geographic background, the inclusion of interpreters on the team could not be justified and they were, therefore, excluded from list. The PrepCom agreed to return to the question of the inclusion of interpreters, if it proved necessary to do so, however, no further action on this issue was in fact taken.

The Expert Group also drew the attention of the PrepCom to the need for Member States to provide some indication of the number and types of facilities to be declared. In the absence of such information, it would be difficult to make a valid assessment of the number of inspections to be undertaken and the number of inspectors required to carry them out. At the request of the PrepCom the Executive Secretary circulated a note to Member States seeking this information.[240]

The proposals of the Expert Group on Inspection Team Composition were further qualified by the Expert Group on Inspectorate Planning which met, in The Hague, from 12 – 16 July 1993. It recommended that while the inspectorate should be based on full-time inspectors it might be possible to make use of temporary (on call) inspectors, in particular during the initial period following EIF, for inspections under Articles IV and V and inspections of Schedule 1 facilities.

> Efforts shall be made to alleviate the considerable inspection workload during the first period after entry into force of the Convention, e.g. by giving first priority to inspections of facilities declared under Articles IV, V and VI, paragraph 3, during the period of initial inspections and the development of facility agreements for these facilities, by the use of temporary inspectors for certain verification activities where no considerable confidentiality problems might arise, and by use of sequential inspections of similar facilities within a region.[241]

Despite this recommendation the concept of using temporary inspectors was not pursued further during the PrepCom, or during the early years after EIF.[242] The Expert Group also drew the PrepCom's attention to the potential impact of any decision to limit the inspection of chemical weapons facilities covered by a bilateral agreement to some form of complimentary monitoring.[243] If, for example, as widely anticipated, the Executive Council were to limit the OPCW's verification activities at Russian and US chemical weapons sites and leave primary responsibility for undertaking on-site

---

[239] Report of the Combined Group of Experts: Inspection Team Composition, PC-III/B/WP.3, dated 28 May 1993.

[240] 'Note by the Executive Secretary', PC-III/4, dated 15 June 1993.

[241] Initial Report of the Expert Group on Inspectorate Planning, PC-IV/B/WP.3/Rev.1, dated 29 September 1993.

[242] It has, however, been resurrected in recent years to help deal with the very heavy workload associated with verification at chemical weapons destruction facilities.

[243] CWC, Article IV, para. 13.

verification to Russia and the United States then a much smaller number of inspectors would be required. Taking note of the recommendations of the Expert Group, Working Group B recommended that future work on planning the size and shape of the Inspectorate be addressed by the Expert Group on the Programme of Work and Budget.[244]

At its initial meeting, in September 1993, the Expert Group on the Programme of Work and Budget agreed on the following assumptions in relation to future inspections under the CWC:

> Sixty five States will deposit their instruments of ratification by 16 July 1994, thereby ensuring the entry into force (EIF) of the Convention on 13 January 1995.
>
> The United States of America and the Russian Federation will deposit their instruments of ratification prior to EIF.
>
> States which possess or have under their jurisdiction or control the large majority of declarable facilities will deposit their instruments of ratification prior to EIF.
>
> The bilateral agreement of June 1990 between the Russian Federation and the United States of America on destruction and non-production of chemical weapons will be in force and in the process of implementation. The Commission will recommend that the Organisation decide, pursuant to Articles IV and V of the Convention, to limit verification by the OPCW to measures complementary to those to be undertaken under this agreement.[245]

Taking note of these assumptions and provisional information on the number of declared facilities, the Provisional Technical Secretariat (PTS) was requested to develop a model showing the estimated number and type of inspections to be undertaken in the first year after EIF and the number of inspectors required to carry them out. The model developed by the Secretariat based on the above assumptions and that at least one other State Party in addition to Russia and the United States would declare the possession of chemical weapons indicated that approximately 260 Inspectors and inspector assistants would be required.[246] However, not all of these inspectors would be required at EIF as it was anticipated that only a small number of industry inspections would be undertaken during the first 6 months. It was, therefore, proposed that the inspectors should be trained in two groups. Training group A, with 200 trainees, would complete its training by EIF with an anticipated 180 inspectors qualifying and the second Group of 100, training group B, would complete their training approximately 6 months after EIF yielding a further 80 qualified inspectors. Further refinement of the model, over the next two years, led to a gradual reduction in these numbers. The final agreed target was for a total of 205 inspectors, 125 from training group A and 80

---

244 4th Report of Working Group B, para. 5.7, PC-IV/B/12*, dated 1 October 1993.

245 Initial Report of the Expert Group on the 1994 Programme of Work and Budget, Section II, PC-IV/A/WP.7, dated 10 September 1993.

246 Specific Assumptions and Projections for the Budget for 1994, para. 21, Attachment PB/CRP.14, 9 September 1993, to the above report.

from training group B with a few extra trainees to allow for attrition during the training course.

2. Planning Inspector Training

In Geneva, towards the end of the CWC negotiations, informal open-ended discussions on issues relating to the training of inspectors took place between interested delegations. The discussions were convened by Aapo Pölhö of Finland and took place in August, September and December 1992. The discussions were intended to produce ideas and material on training that could be presented informally to the PrepCom. By the end of 1992, several countries had already offered, or were planning to offer, OPCW related training programmes. These included: Canada, Finland, France, Germany, The Netherlands, Norway, South Africa, Switzerland, UK and US.[247] Once the PrepCom had been established in The Hague, responsibility for the development of the training programme was assigned to the Expert Group on Training, building on the discussions that had already taken place in Geneva and the courses that some states were already running or preparing. It met in The Hague for the first time, from 11 to 18 June 1993 and continued to meet at regular intervals throughout the life of the PrepCom. At its first meeting the Group developed the framework for the training course for inspectors. They agreed that the general training scheme (GTS) should be modular in form and consist of three main modules. Module 1 would be a basic foundation course to be undertaken by all trainees. Module 2 would consist of a number of specialist courses designed to enhance the skills of the different groups of inspectors. For example, sampling and analysis training for the analytical chemists or chemical engineering for the chemical engineers and industrial chemists. The courses in Module 3 would focus on the planning and undertaking of on-site inspections.[248]

While it was envisaged that the PTS/TS would provide some of this training it was recognised that a number of the courses making up each module would need to be provided by Member States. Those Member States interested in providing training courses were encouraged to provide the PTS with details of the proposed content and likely duration.[249] Over the ensuing months a number of Member States came forward with offers for training. It was considered essential that all of the individual training courses be of equivalent standard and, at the request of Working Group B the Expert Group developed guidelines for the certification of courses being offered in support of the GTS.[250] Assembling the GTS took many weeks as, in addition to identifying Member States willing to provide the individual courses, each offer had to be integrated into the overall training plan which was designed to run from start to finish

[247] 'CWC – Training courses', *UNIDIR Newsletter*, No. 20 (December 1992), pp. 36-39.

[248] Chairman's Paper annexed to the Interim Report of the Group of Experts: Training, PC-III/B/WP.10, dated 18 June 1993.

[249] 2nd Interim Report of the Experts Group on Training, para. 6, PC-IV/B/WP.8, dated 13 August 1993.

[250] 4th Interim Report of the Expert Group on Training, Appendix 1, PC-VI/B/WP.7, dated 11 February 1994.

over a period of about 20 weeks. As each course could only provide a limited number of training places it was sometimes necessary for two or more Member States to run the same course. Ensuring that each trainee received the full 20 weeks of training was not an easy task. This was particularly true of the Module 2 courses were trainees from each of the specialist groups were being offered a different training programme. The process was made even more complicated by the fact that the date of EIF was unknown and, therefore, it was not possible to tell the training centres, in the 14 Member States supporting the GTS, when their course was required to start. Eventually it became clear that, irrespective of the date of EIF, training could only begin in January or July of each year. With the deposit of the 65th ratification by Hungary, on 31 October 1996, the date of EIF finally became known and in the following month the Executive Secretary was able to inform the PrepCom that preparations for the GTS were complete. Training would commence on 13 January 1997 and end on 30 May, one month after EIF.[251]

At the very last moment, for regulatory reasons, the United States had to withdraw its offer to provide a number of the training courses. The other three Member States providing Module 1 training agreed, at very short notice, to absorb the 40 trainees scheduled to receive Module 1 training in the United States. Finding replacements for the Module 2 and 3 courses was more problematical. Russia and the United Kingdom agreed to provide two of the missing Module 2 courses and the PTS undertook to provide additional training in house.[252] It proved impossible, however, to find alternative locations for the Module 3, on-site inspection training and alternative arrangements had to be made for those trainees scheduled to receive this training in the United States.

The Expert Group on Training also considered the issue of whether training for the future TS inspectors and inspection assistants should be undertaken before or after employment by the PTS/TS. It recommended that trainees who met the relevant qualification and medical requirements should be offered a contract at the start of training with a proviso that continuing employment, following training, would be dependent on them meeting the required performance standards.[253] This approach, with the further understanding that only nationals from States Parties to the CWC could be employed by the OPCW after EIF, was the one adopted by the Organisation for the recruitment of inspectors.

3. Inspector Recruitment

An important requirement was that, in addition to being appropriately qualified and nationals of States Parties to the CWC, inspectors were recruited from as wide a geo-

---

251 Note by the Executive Secretary, 'Arrangements for Inspector Training', PC-XV/B/10, dated 6 November 1996.

252 'Report of the Executive Secretary', PC-XVI/12, dated 7 April 1997.

253 2nd Interim Report of the Experts Group on Training, para. 5, PC-IV/B/WP.8, dated 13 August 1993.

graphic base as possible. At the request of Member States, information packages – containing a brief description of the organisation and its proposed function, detailed job descriptions for each post, salary scales and provisional terms and conditions of employment – were duly prepared and circulated to all Member States in January 1994. Adverts were also placed in a number of relevant trade and professional journals and details placed on the Organisation's web site. While, in general, a satisfactory number of applications were received from Asia, North America, Western and Eastern Europe the response from Africa and Latin America was extremely low. Additional efforts were made in these regions to try and boost the number of applications and PTS staff visited a number of countries in these regions to talk directly to the relevant trade bodies and professional organisations.

By the end of this process the PTS had received more than 1,400 applications from around 70 countries for the 205 vacancies, plus a considerable number of applications for the seventy or so technical posts in the Verification Division. A total of 397 candidates were short listed and 341 were interviewed by senior PTS staff, either in The Hague or in Seoul, Stockholm, Tokyo, Beijing, Moscow, Buenos Aires, Tehran, Jakarta, Washington, Prague and New Delhi. This proved to be a complex and labour intensive task for the PTS. The initial selections were made in January 1996 but the task was made more difficult by the fact that the date of EIF was still unknown and, therefore, it was not possible to tell candidates when training would begin. The eventual outcome, however, was the identification of 128 potential trainees for training group A and a significant number of the 80 trainees required for training group B. Despite the lack of certainty over the date of EIF only a small number of candidates withdrew during the period before training eventually began in January 1997.

4. Training the Inspectors

The GTS had been designed to provide each inspector, irrespective of his background, with a solid understanding of the CWC, their rights and privileges and those of States Parties and the basic techniques involved in planning and carrying out of an inspection. Module 1 training took place at centres in France, India and the Netherlands. The specialist courses in Module 2 were designed to enhance the trainees' skills in their chosen area of expertise. As with Module 1, training was a multinational affair with trainees being dispatched to facilities in Finland, Germany, The Netherlands, Russia, Switzerland and the UK. Module 3 took place in China, the Czech Republic, Germany, Italy, Japan, Romania and Slovakia and was where the trainees put their knowledge into practice through the planning and carrying out of mock on-site inspections. The training course had results beyond the merely quantifiable: 'When you walked into the coffee bar or canteen, people were not grouped by nationality or culture but by the bonds of friendship. The sight of a table with people of six or seven nationalities sitting around it would not even warrant a second glance. Quite simply, the understandings formed during this period enabled the inspectors to function as a tight-knit and effective group. This proved to be the most valuable element of the whole training programme'.[254]

[254] Ibid., p. 39.

In addition the GTS had another important role to fill. Inspection is very much a team exercise. Once an inspection team leaves The Hague en route to the inspection site, it is basically on its own. Each member of the team not only needs to carry out his or her assigned tasks but to cooperate fully with the other team members. They of course receive support from the host country, but the success of the inspection, in the end, depends on the inspectors' ability to function as an effective team. The majority of the trainees were mid-career professionals. Many of them had held senior positions in their own countries' military or chemical industries. In many cases they were used to having numbers of subordinate staff to support them. As inspector trainees, on the other hand, everyone was on an equal footing and everyone was expected to join in and undertake their share of the tasks assigned to the team. Creating a team spirit among a group of people from very different backgrounds and cultures was, therefore, an essential goal of the GTS and, in hindsight, its greatest success.[255]

The GTS ensured that each trainee became familiar with a number of different cultures. It provided them with the opportunity to travel, live and work, for an extended period, with other trainees coming from different backgrounds and with differing levels of experience. This aided the rapid creation of a truly multicultural, multinational, corps of inspectors, which brought considerable, long-term, benefits to the OPCW and its Technical Secretariat. Thirteen Member States participated in the training programme and the majority of trainees undertook part of their training in at least three or more of these countries. Despite, the last minute setbacks the first GTS proved to be highly successful and it was successfully repeated after EIF for training group B. A total of 111 inspectors (42 chemical production technologists/industrial chemists; 29 CW-munitions specialists; 17 analytical chemists; 14 chemical production logisticians; 5 paramedics; and 4 medical specialists) from 45 States Parties from Group A were recruited to the OPCW ready to conduct inspections after entry into force.[256] Training group B underwent training from January to May 1998 and by the end of 1998 the OPCW had 205 inspectors on its staff.[257]

5. Entry into Force

The CWC entered into force on 29 April 1997. While much attention focused on the debates and discussions in the Netherlands Congress Centre during the first session of the CSP, there was much activity behind the scenes in what had now become the Technical Secretariat. The CWC contains a number of short deadlines which States Parties and the Technical Secretariat had to meet in the months immediately following entry into force, with the initial emphasis on chemical weapons and Schedule 1 facili-

---

255 Ron Manley, 'Building an International Organisation', in Rosemary Bechler (ed.), *Intercultural Dialogue*, British Council Birthday Counterpoints (London, British Council 2004), pp. 32-47.

256 OPCW, Conference of the States Parties [first session], 'Note by the Director-General: Recruitment of inspector trainees for training group B', C-I/DG.6, dated 23 May 1997.

257 OPCW, Conference of the States Parties [first review conference], 'Technical Secretariat: Background paper on the conduct of inspections under the Chemical Weapons Convention and related issues', RC-1/S/1, dated 17 April 2003.

ties. States Parties had thirty days from entry into force to submit their initial national declarations to the Technical Secretariat. By 29 May, only 30 of the over 80 States Parties had done so. The CWC requires OPCW inspectors to verify chemical weapons declarations 'promptly after a declaration is submitted'.

Once it had become clear that the US would ratify the CWC before entry into force, a number of Group A trainee inspectors left the training scheme after the end of Module 2 in order to be able to arrive in The Hague ready to commence inspections at destruction facilities in the US in June. During the first few days of June, these inspectors were dispatched to the operating destruction facilities at Tooele, Utah and Johnston Atoll in the US. In mid-June, other inspectors conducted the first Schedule 1 inspections at facilities in Sweden and the UK. The CWC requires inspectors to conduct initial inspections of all chemical weapons production facilities between 90 to 120 days following entry into force and that meant another intense burst of activity for the new inspectors in August.

Chapter 7

Preparing to Conduct Inspections

Ron G. Manley

1. Introduction

In order to get the concept of on-site inspections of both military and chemical industry facilities accepted during the negotiation of the CWC it was essential to reach a common understanding on the rules and procedures under which such inspections would be carried out. While it was accepted that, in order for the regime to be effective, the precise timing of an on-site inspection should not be predictable the rules and procedures under which it would be carried out should be. A great deal of effort, therefore, was expended on drafting those parts of the Verification Annex (VA) dealing with this issue. The general rules for the conduct of inspections are set out in Part II (E) of the VA. These, except for one or two specific exceptions, apply to all inspections and deal, for example, with the respective rights of the State Party and the inspection team, safety, communications, inspection equipment and sampling and analysis. Some provisions that are specific to particular types of inspections are contained in Part III and further, inspection specific, guidance is provided in Parts IV and V for CW related inspections, in Parts VI to IX for industry inspections and in Parts X and XI for challenge inspections and investigations of alleged use. The VA, as a whole, provides an extensive set of rules and procedures for the carrying out on-site inspections under the CWC. The drafters of the VA, however, accepted that, despite the level of detail provided, a number of areas would require further clarification and elaboration by the PrepCom. The key areas were identified in the Paris Resolution[258] and are listed in Table 1. Resolution of these issues was assigned to the PrepCom's Working Group B and the relevant Expert Groups working under it. The first of these issues 'Guidelines on detailed procedures for verification and for the conduct of inspections …' was assigned to those Expert Groups dealing specifically with either CW or industry related inspections and the results of their work has been reported in the relevant chapters dealing with these particular issues. The remaining issues were assigned to Expert Groups identified in Table 1 and the results of their work are the primary subject of this chapter.

---

[258] Paris Resolution, in L.W. Tabassi (ed.), *OPCW: The Legal Texts* (The Hague, TMC Asser Press 1999), pp. 523-530.

2. Health and Safety

The drafters of the CWC realised that in fulfilling their role OPCW inspectors would be required to operate in many different regions of the world, in a wide range of environments and frequently under potentially hazardous conditions. Development of a Health and Safety Policy for the OPCW was, therefore, assigned a high priority. The task of developing the policy and its associated regulations and guidelines was assigned to the Expert Group on Safety Procedures, which held its first meeting in The Hague from 10-21 May 1993 and met for a further seven times during the life of the PrepCom. In its first report the Group made a number of recommendations of which two were of particularly significance. The first was that the PrepCom consider the establishment of a dedicated health and safety unit within the proposed staff structure for the Technical Secretariat with, as appropriate, direct access to the Director-General. The second was that the attention of all Expert Groups be drawn to the importance of giving due consideration to health and safety aspects of recommendations arising out of their work.

Para.	Task	Expert Group
a.	Guidelines on detailed procedures for verification and for the conduct of inspections, in accordance with, inter alia, Part II, paragraph 42, of the Verification Annex;	All Industry and CW Groups
e.	A list of approved equipment, in accordance with Part II, paragraph 27, of the Verification Annex;	Equipment
f.	Procedures for the inspection of equipment, in accordance with Part II, paragraph 29, of the Verification Annex;	Equipment
g.	Procedures concerning the implementation of safety requirements for activities of inspectors and inspection assistants, in accordance with Part II, paragraph 43, of the Verification Annex;	Safety Procedures
h.	Procedures for inclusion in the inspection manual concerning the security, integrity and preservation of samples and for ensuring the protection of the confidentiality of samples transferred for analysis off-site, in accordance with Part II, paragraph 56, of the Verification Annex;	Analytical Chemists
i.	Models for facility agreements in accordance with Part III, paragraph 8, of the Verification Annex;	All CW Groups and Model FA Group
r.	Models for facility agreements covering detailed inspection procedures, in accordance with Part VI, paragraph 27, of the Verification Annex;	All Industry Groups and Model FA Group

2.1 Health and safety policy

The primary task of the Group was to draft a health and safety policy for the Organisation. Due to the potential complexity of the OPCW's operations, the Group decided that the health and safety policy would need to have a certain amount of built-in flexibility. It was, therefore, proposed that the Organisation should adopt a risk management approach to protecting the health of its employees and ensuring the safety of its operations. In accordance with this approach the health and safety policy would require, a risk assessment to be carried out, by an appropriately qualified person, prior to the undertaking of any operation and appropriate action taken to minimise any identified risks.

To facilitate the process of developing the policy a small drafting group of health and safety specialists, provided by delegations, were tasked, with the assistance of the Provisional Technical Secretariat (PTS), to draw up a draft for consideration by the Group at its second meeting. At this meeting, held from 27 September to 1 October 1993, the Group began a detailed consideration of the draft health and safety policy and associated regulations. During its consideration of this document the Group agreed and recommended to Working Group B that the OPCW Health and Safety documentation be separated into three documents. The first document would contain the health and safety policy, the second, the associated health and safety regulations; and the third, the health and safety guidelines. It proposed that the first two documents be submitted for formal approval, initially by the PrepCom and, at entry into force of the Convention (EIF), by the first Conference of the States Parties. The third document, containing the technical guidelines on health and safety, would be prepared by the PTS and circulated to Signatory States for review and comment.

At this meeting it also became clear that some delegations had serious concerns with respect to the potential, albeit inadvertent, loss of confidential information during on-site inspections and that equipment being used for health and safety purposes could contribute to this risk. For example, a respirator canister used by an inspector during an inspection could, while providing him or her with respiratory protection, also absorb and retain traces of any chemicals present in the air at the inspection site. Subsequent analysis of this canister would enable these chemicals to be identified and thus could provide information that was both confidential and not relevant to the CWC. Of particular concern for a number of delegations was the issue of ionising radiation and the dosimeters for measuring exposure to it. Some delegations argued that in order for the Organisation to be able to confirm that inspectors had not, inadvertently, been subjected to ionising radiation during their work they should be routinely issued with personal dosimeters for use during inspections. Other delegations took the view that the use of such devices could result in the loss of confidential information that was not relevant to the CWC. This issue was further complicated by the fact that one of the items of inspection equipment being considered for use at CW related inspections contained a strong neutron source and the national legislation of most countries would require personnel working in the immediate vicinity of such a source to be equipped with personal dosimeters. While these concerns, in relation to the potential loss of confidential information, applied equally to inspections of both military and industrial facilities it was the potential risks related to a challenge inspection that posed the greatest problem. The extent of the concern among some delegations with respect to the need to ensure the health and safety of OPCW personnel, while at the same time protecting the State Party's confidential information, is summarised in a working paper submitted by the delegation of Israel.[259] The relevant paragraphs of which are reproduced below.

[259] 'Israel, Safety and confidentiality', Working Paper, PC-VI/B/WP.6, 9 February 1994.

> 5. The strict preservation of confidentiality and the prevention of the disclosure of sensitive information not relevant to the Convention are essential features of all OPCW operations. As stated in Paragraph 5 of Article VIII of the Convention, 'The Organisation shall conduct its verification activities in the least intrusive manner possible consistent with the timely and efficient accomplishment of their objectives', and 'it shall take every precaution to protect the confidentiality of information on civil and military activities and facilities coming to its knowledge in the implementation of this Convention'.
>
> 6. Confidentiality is best preserved by preventing *a priori* the disclosure of unrelated information, rather than by *a posteriori* control of its distribution. Adequate measures should therefore be built into OPCW operational procedures to minimise the exposure of unrelated sensitive information in the course of inspections and other verification activities.
>
> 7. Safety equipment, including protective clothing, respirators and monitoring devices may indirectly collect information which is totally unrelated to alleged non-compliance with the Chemical Weapons Convention. This is of particular concern with regard to challenge inspections at facilities or installations not related to the Chemical Weapons Convention. Israel believes that proper measures should be taken to prevent the deliberate or inadvertent abuse of legitimate safety measures for the collection of unrelated information deemed sensitive by the inspected State Party … .

The remainder of the paper contained a number of proposals on how this potential problem might be overcome, including a proposal that a special subset of safety regulations and procedures should be developed to cover challenge inspections. While the latter proposal was not acceptable to all delegations, some of the others were and this paper and its philosophy had a major impact on the development of the Health and Safety Policy. It became very clear that the confidentiality issue would have to be addressed if consensus was to be reached on a health and safety policy for the Organisation. It was also clear that all health and safety equipment for use by inspectors during inspections would have to be included on the approved list of inspection equipment and subject to the rules and procedures governing inspection equipment.[260]

Another major issue was the question of whose safety standards should apply. While many countries and even groups of countries have various agreed standards for health and safety there are no internationally recognised standards that are accepted by all countries of the world. By its very nature the OPCW and its inspectors had to be prepared to operate, often under hazardous conditions, virtually anywhere in the world. One example of this problem was the question of occupational exposure standards for toxic chemicals. OPCW inspectors would routinely be operating at chemical weapons storage and destruction facilities. It was, therefore, essential to agree on occupational exposure standards for the most common chemical agents such as the nerve agents and mustard gas. As a basis for discussion, the two major possessors of chemical weapons Russia and the United States were asked to provide details of their occupational exposure standards for these chemicals, which they duly did. The immediate problem was that one set of standards was approximately 10 times stricter than the

[260] CWC, Verification Annex, Part II, para. 27.

other. After much heated debate about whose figures were right it turned out that the two parties concerned were measuring different parameters. The higher figure was based on short-term exposures measured in real-time, while the other was based on an average exposure, measured by continuous sampling over the full working day. This particular discussion only involved data from two players. Bearing in mind that OPCW inspectors would routinely be operating in industrial and military complexes in around 50 countries it was clear that achieving a common understanding on standards was going to be virtually impossible. It was decided to adopt a different approach to the problem. Firstly, it was agreed that the primary responsibility for the safety of inspectors during an on-site inspection rests with the inspected State Party. Secondly it was agreed that the Technical Secretariat should base its health and safety standards on the most widely accepted international standards and these would form the basis for its operations. In situations where the inspected State Party's standards were higher than those adopted by the OPCW then the inspectors would, if requested, operate to these higher standards but any additional cost or training requirements involved in doing so would be born by the inspected State Party. For example, personnel entering the toxic areas of US destruction facilities are required, by law, to do so in specially designed chemical resistant, air-fed suits. OPCW inspectors would, therefore, not be able to enter these areas using their standard approved protective equipment. To overcome this problem the US agreed, at its cost, to provide appropriate training to OPCW inspectors to enable them to use the special protective suits at US destruction facilities, should the need arise. Where the inspected State Party's standards were lower than those adopted by the OPCW then the inspectors would work to the OPCW standards.

In its final form the Health and Safety Policy begins with a brief statement, to be signed by the Director-General on behalf of the OPCW, setting out the Organisation's commitment to promoting and maintaining a high standard of health and safety in all its activities. A section that sets out the respective responsibilities of the OPCW, the Technical Secretariat staff, including its inspectors and the inspected States Parties follows this. Subsequent sections; deal with the organisation and administration of health and safety within the OPCW, the general principles for risk assessment and risk management, health and safety requirements and training.[261] The Group recommended that this draft policy document be submitted to capitals for comment and that the PrepCom's Legal Advisor be requested to review it. It further recommended that, once agreed, the Commission should adopt the draft policy and regulations for use by the PTS. After further, lengthy, discussions the draft OPCW Health and Safety Policy was finally submitted to and approved by the PrepCom, at its Sixth Session, in April 1994.[262] At this session the draft OPCW Health and Safety Policy was also adopted, *mutatis mutandis*, as the Health and Safety Policy of the Preparatory Commission.

---

[261] Working Group B, 'Revised Draft OPCW Health and Safety Policy', PC-IX/B/WP.5, dated 16 November 1994.

[262] 'Report of the Commission', PC-VI/22, dated 15 April 1994, para. 6.7.

2.2 Health and safety regulations

Having completed its work on the health and safety policy the Group turned its attention to finalising the health and safety regulations. These would set out the means by which the OPCW Health and Safety Policy would be implemented. This should have been a relatively simple task as the regulations were to be based on the policy, which had already been approved. Once again, however, the issue of confidentiality proved to be a major stumbling block. The core of the problem was the wording of section 4 of the draft regulations, which deals with health and safety during inspections and in particular paragraph 4.2 which deals with the use of detection and monitoring equipment for health and safety purposes.[263] While for some delegations the potential loss of confidential information was the driving factor others were concerned that a State Party might use health and safety as means to limit access by inspectors during an inspection. For example, if the inspection team was unable to gather sufficient data on, or to monitor the level of, any hazard present at a particular location then, in accordance with the OPCW Health and Safety Policy, the inspection at that location could not proceed. Consensus on the final wording of paragraph 4.2 of the regulations was, therefore, agreed on the following understanding.

> 3.2 The Group understood that subparagraph 4.2 of the Draft OPCW Health and Safety Regulations does not prejudice the obligation of inspected States Parties to provide available data based on detection and monitoring, to an agreed extent necessary to satisfy concerns that may exist regarding the health and safety of the inspection team. In cases where detection and monitoring, as referred to in subparagraph 5.2.2 of the Draft OPCW Health and Safety Policy (PC-IX/B/WP.5) cannot be carried out, alternative risk assessment data or information will be provided by the inspected State Party, as provided for in subparagraph 5.1.1 of the Draft OPCW Health and Safety Policy.[264]

Final agreement on the regulations was not achieved until March 1996 when the Commission, at its 13th Session, finally adopted the draft Health and Safety Regulations and applied them *mutatis mutandis* to the Preparatory Commission.[265]

2.3 Other health and safety related issues

As requested by the PrepCom the Group also devised a proposed structure for the Health and Safety Unit for the Technical Secretariat. This unit would have a staff of 13 working under a P-5 Head of Health and Safety. It would be divided into two subunits one, headed by a senior medical officer, dealing with medical issues and one, headed by a senior safety officer, dealing with safety.[266] It also recommended that the

---

263 'Draft OPCW Health and Safety Regulations', as annexed to: Expert Group on Safety Procedures, 'Eighth Report', PC-XIII/B/WP.2, dated 1 February 1996.

264 Expert Group on Safety Procedures 'Eighth Report', PC-XIII/B/WP.2, dated 1 February 1996, para. 3.2.

265 'Report of the Commission', PC-XIII/18, dated 22 March 1996, para. 7.1.

266 Expert Group on Safety Procedures, 'Second Report', PC-V/B/WP.11, dated 19 November 1993, paras. 17 to 24.

PrepCom consider filling some of these posts prior to EIF to provide health and safety support to the Commission and its Provisional Technical Secretariat. The proposed structure was eventually incorporated into the overall structure for the Technical Secretariat of the OPCW.

Having recommended that the OPCW should adopt a risk based approach to the management of Health and Safety the Group recognised that it would be essential for a number of the inspectors to receive specialist training in risk assessment and management. Under the proposed structure for the inspectorate, only 5 of the inspectors would be professional health and safety specialists and these would be primarily medical personnel. The Group, therefore, recommended that at least 25 additional inspectors should be provided with extra health and safety training. With the assistance of the Expert Group on Training it, therefore, developed the syllabus for a 4 week specialist course on health and safety.[267] In drawing up the syllabus, the Expert Group was cognisant of the fact that the majority of inspectors would be experienced chemical engineers or industrial chemists and, therefore, already likely to have a good grounding in health and safety. It also recommended that the medical personnel should receive a further 2-4 weeks specialist training in the diagnosis, management and treatment of chemical agent exposures and refresher training in field trauma care. An outline for a 3 week course covering these areas was drawn up and submitted to working Group B for further action.[268]

The Group also addressed the issue of the pre-employment medical screening of inspector candidates and OPCW headquarters staff. It recommended that in addition to a routine pre-employment medical examination the medical screening of inspector candidates should also include, a pulmonary function test and an assessment of the candidates' ability to use approved types of protective equipment. Inspector candidates were also required to be judged fit for wide geographical deployment and free from any medical conditions which might interfere with the administration of any medication or preventive treatment that might be required. While it was relatively easy to reach consensus on the precise requirements for the medical screening, reaching agreement on how and where it should be carried out was a different matter.[269] The problem was how to ensure consistency of such screening across the large number of countries involved. One option was to carry out the screening in The Hague. The cost of adopting this approach, however, was likely to be high and, therefore, unacceptable to States Parties. Equally, depending solely on medical screening undertaken by the candidate's local doctor was also unacceptable to a number of delegations. The UN maintains a list of doctors who have been certified by them as meeting an agreed standard. Many countries have medical personnel who are on this approved list. It was, therefore, proposed and accepted that UN approved medical personnel be

---

[267] 'Chairman's Paper', para. 30, as annexed to: Expert Group on Safety Procedures, 'Second Report', PC-V/B/WP.11, dated 19 November 1993.

[268] 'Chairman's Paper', Appendix 3, as annexed to: Expert Group on Safety Procedures, 'Third Report', PC-VI/B/WP.10, dated 25 February 1994.

[269] Expert Group on Safety Procedures, 'Seventh Report', PC-XII/B/WP.5, dated 1 November 1995, Annex 2, para. 8.

contracted to undertake the pre-employment medical screening on behalf of the OPCW either in the candidates home country or, where necessary, a nearby country.

Another important issue addressed by the Group was to make recommendations on the requirements for the medical treatment of persons exposed to chemical agents. The Group went on to develop general principles for the treatment of conditions caused by nerve agents, mustards, Lewisite, psychotomimetic atropine like compounds, cyanides and lung oedemagens. It recommended to the Commission that the OPCW use these as the basis for the preparation of detailed guidelines on the treatment of chemical poisoning as the latter would be dependent on the actual medications eventually selected for use by that Organisation.[270]

3. Inspection Equipment

In accordance with the CWC, equipment to be used by inspectors during on-site inspections shall be selected from a list of inspection equipment approved by the CSP.[271] The development of the draft list was one of the tasks assigned to the PrepCom under the Paris Resolution.[272] The Expert Groups dealing with each specific type of inspection were tasked to identify the types of equipment they considered might be necessary to undertake that kind of inspection. In addition the Expert Group on Safety Procedures was tasked to address the issue of health and safety related inspection equipment. The results of the deliberations of these Groups were passed to the Expert Group on Equipment, which was tasked with drawing up the draft list for consideration by Working Group B and subsequently the Commission.

The Expert Group on Equipment considered that the initial list could be subdivided into three categories: personal items to be provided to individual inspectors, items to be provided to inspection teams, and specialised items for use on particular types of inspections. Personal equipment would include items, such as personal protective equipment, flashlights, first aid kits, water bottles, etc. Team equipment would include items, such as, global positioning system (GPS), communications equipment (mobile phones, fax machines, secure phones, etc.), hand-held detectors, and flammable vapour monitors. Specialised equipment for use in selected inspections would include items such as portable x-ray equipment, Gas Chromatograph/Mass Spectrometer (GC/MS), and non-destructive evaluation (NDE) equipment.[273] While there were, subsequently, some modifications to this list and one or two additions it was, nevertheless, to form the basis for the OPCW's approved inspection equipment list. The Expert Group also provided an estimate of the numbers of each item of equipment that were likely to be required. In preparing this estimate the Expert Group noted that

---

270 Annex 1 to 7th Report of the Expert Group on Safety Procedures, PC-XII/B/WP.5, 1 November 1995.

271 CWC, Verification Annex, Part II, para. 27.

272 See the Table on page 114 above.

273 Appendix 1 to the Chairman's Paper annexed to the 2nd Interim Report of the Expert Group on Equipment, PC-V/B/WP.7, 26 October 1993.

some items of inspection equipment would be primarily for use at CW related inspections and its calculations were, therefore, based on the following assumption.

> It is explicitly assumed that the US-Russia Bilateral Treaty will be in effect and will obviate the need for the OPCW to acquire equipment to support this type of inspection in these countries. Additional procurements will be needed if CW facilities are declared in countries other than the US and Russia.[274]

While final approval of the list of inspection equipment was the responsibility of the 1st CSP the initial procurement of inspection equipment needed to take place prior to EIF. Firstly, because equipment was required for the training of inspectors and secondly, because the lead-time for the provision of some specialised items were very long and inspections were scheduled to start shortly after EIF. At the request of the Commission, therefore, the Expert Group, with the assistance of the PTS, drew up a plan for the acquisition of inspection equipment in three phases. Included in phase 1 were items that needed to be purchased as soon as practicable for training and evaluation purposes. The purchase of items included in phase 2 would begin following the deposit of the 65th ratification and the start of the 180 day run up to EIF. The procurement of items in phase 3 would take place after EIF. A copy of the equipment procurement plan with cost estimates for each phase was forwarded to the Expert Group on the Programme of Work and Budget for further action.[275]

3.1 **Operational requirements and specifications for equipment**

The first step in the procurement process was to identify the operational requirements for each item of equipment on the draft list. In the view of the Expert Group the operational requirements must be consistent with the verification aims as specified in the relevant parts of the Verification Annex to the CWC and, in particular, due consideration given to specific types of inspection, e.g., challenge inspections and investigations of alleged use. It was also essential that the operational requirement take account of confidentiality requirements as set forth in the CWC. The Group concluded that in developing these operational requirements the factors that would need to be taken into consideration were as follows:

(i) the tasks to be performed by the equipment;
(ii) the required level of performance, e.g., accuracy and reproducibility;
(iii) established provisions for the prevention of the disclosure of information not relevant to the aims of the inspection; the capability of each item of equipment;
(iv) the reliability of analytical results;
(v) the very low rate of false positive alarms;
(vi) the valid interpretation of results;

---

274 Appendix 1 of the Chairman's Paper annexed to the 2nd Interim Report of the Expert Group on Equipment, PC-V/B/WP.7, 26 October 1993, p. 31.

275 Verification Related Equipment, Expert Group on Programme of Work and Budget, PC-VIII/A/WP.1 Add.1, 20 July 1994.

(vii) the fulfilment of safety standards;
(viii) anti-tampering features; and
(ix) ease of field use, transportability and ruggedness.[276]

On the basis of these criteria, the Expert Group proceed to develop operational requirements for each item of equipment. Once again, a key factor in this process was the potential loss of confidential information and this, without question, was a major concern of delegations with respect to the development of these operational requirements. One example of this was the development of operational requirement for 'over-boots'. When entering potentially contaminated areas it is normal practice for personnel to don over-boots over their normal footwear to prevent the accidental spread of contamination outside the suspect area. Some delegations took the view that these should be disposable items, i.e., worn once and then discarded. This approach would ensure that any confidential information on surface of the over-boot could not be inadvertently carried off the site. The PTS, supported by some delegations, argued that while cheap, disposable, over-boots might be suitable for many situations in more heavily contaminated areas a much sturdier over-boot would be necessary and for economic reasons, these would need to be considered reusable. This issue was debated at considerable length and was only resolved when it was accepted that, as the reusable over-boots would, routinely, be decontaminated on leaving the contaminated area, any confidential information would also be destroyed at the same time.[277] This is just one example of many and, once again, serves to illustrate the real concern of delegations and their respective governments and industries over the protection of their non-CWC related sensitive information. In general delegations required that inspection equipment must be capable of being operated or used in a way that disclosed only information relevant to the aims of the inspection in a manner consistent with the provisions of the Confidentiality Annex of the CWC.[278]

Some delegations had serious questions relating to the specific use to which certain items of equipment might be put and wished to see this clearly spelt out in the operational requirements for these items. A good example of this was the portable x-ray equipment. The use of x-ray as a means of examining the internal structure and gathering information on the possible contents of an unknown munition is a well established process. It is routinely used as a means of screening recovered old munitions in order to determine if they are chemical weapons or high explosive rounds. A number of delegations had real concerns about the potential use of this equipment during other types of inspections, such as a challenge inspection, for example and wished to see the limitations on its use specified in the operational requirements. Other delegations considered this was an inappropriate use of the operational requirements and argued that, in any case, it was for the Technical Secretariat to decide which items on the approved list were necessary for a particular kind of inspection.

---

276 Annex to the 3rd Interim Report of the Expert Group on Equipment, para. 8, PC-VI/B/WP.4, 28 January 1994.

277 5th Report of the Commission, para. 6.4, PC-IX/11, 9 December 1994.

278 Annex to the 3rd Interim Report of the Expert Group on Equipment, para. 8, PC-VI/B/WP.4, 28 January 1994.

It took many months to resolve this issue and the operational requirements for the portable x-ray were almost the last to be agreed. The development of an agreed set of operational requirements for each item on the draft equipment list was, therefore, a difficult and lengthy process.

Once agreement on the operational requirements for a particular item of equipment were agreed the next step in the process was to draft the technical specifications for it. These specifications were not only required to identify the required performance characteristics for the given equipment item but also to address the more general inspection related questions of transportability, ruggedness, ease of maintenance, etc. Development of the technical specifications proved to be a much less controversial process and was largely undertaken without major difficulties.

3.2 Reference system for geographical coordinates

One of the declaration requirements under the CWC is to provide details of the precise location or geographical coordinates for certain declared facilities. At such facilities the inspection team will routinely carry out measurements to confirm that they are at the declared site. Normally, they would do this using a portable global positioning system (GPS) and this was the reason for the inclusion of the GPS on the approved equipment list. Even where the State Party has not provided geographic coordinates in its declaration the inspection team would still routinely take GPS readings in order to assist future inspection teams to identify the location. These instruments determine the position of a given location in relation to a reference point on the surface of globe. During the development of the operational requirements and specifications for the GPS, the Expert Group was made aware that there was more than one internationally recognised geographic reference system in routine use for determining geographical coordinates. A non-paper on this issue, tabled by the delegation of France, highlighted the fact that there were in fact, currently, 107 recognised reference systems in use around the world. The paper further recommended that the OPCW should adopt the widely used WGS 84 standard for use with the GPS. While it was possible to reach consensus on a recommendation that the WGS 84 standard should be adopted for use by the Technical Secretariat it was not possible to reach agreement for it to be adopted as the OPCW standard.[279] As software packages were available that could convert coordinates based on any of the 107 systems to WGS 84 it was finally agreed that:

> States Parties should use one of the 107 recognised reference datums for their declarations when they were required to declare the geographical co-ordinates of a facility. States Parties should state in their declarations which reference standard they had used.[280]

---

[279] 12th Report of the Expert Group on Inspection procedures, para. 7.2, PC-XIV/B/WP.5, 20 June 1996.

[280] 'Report of the Commission', PC-XIV/29, dated 27 July 1996, para. 9.4.

3.3 Procurement and evaluation of inspection equipment

While final approval of the inspection equipment list was the responsibility of the 1st CSP, as explained previously, it was necessary to begin the procurement of inspection equipment prior to EIF for training and evaluation purposes. Many delegations expressed the view that this procurement process should be fully open and transparent and should ensure that companies from all Signatory States had an equal opportunity to bid for the supply of items of inspection equipment.[281] The PTS was tasked to draw up a draft procurement policy, that would meet these aspirations, for consideration by the relevant Expert Groups. A draft policy was developed and, after modification to take into account a number of suggestions and recommendations by the Expert Groups, used by the PTS for the initial procurement of equipment.

In accordance with this draft policy the PTS circulated a list of its requirements to all Signatory States and sought expressions of interest from companies wishing to supply items of inspection equipment. Companies interested in supplying one or more items of equipment were requested to register their interest by completing a questionnaire and returning it to the PTS.[282] The PTS then produced a list of potential suppliers based on the responses to this request. This list was regularly updated and copies provided to all Signatory States. Wherever practicable, requests for tender for individual items of equipment were sought from at least three companies from the list that had expressed an interest in supplying that particular item. Procurement of the specific items of equipment then followed a normal commercial sealed bid procedure. Using this procedure the PTS successfully procured the required equipment from companies operating in a significant number of Signatory States.

In some cases offers were received for similar items of equipment each of which, on paper, appeared to meet the required operational requirements and specifications for that particular item. In these circumstances an additional evaluation step was introduced. Suppliers were either requested to provide a sample, or where necessary, one or two items were purchased for evaluation purposes. In most cases this evaluation step was undertaken solely by the PTS. For some of the more specialised items, however, it was necessary to seek support from Signatory States with the evaluation process.[283] Two examples of this were the military respirator and the GC/MS. Government laboratories in the Czech Republic and in Russia assisted with the evaluation of the former and Switzerland provided valuable input into the evaluation of the two commercially available portable GC/MS instruments.[284]

---

281 3rd Report of the Expert Group on Inspection Procedures, para. 4.4, PC-VIII/B/WP.2, 15 July 1994.

282 Note by the Executive Secretary: Procurement of Inspection Equipment for Evaluation and Training of Inspectors/ PC-VIII/B/1, 1 August 1994.

283 Note by the Executive Secretary: Evaluation of Inspection Equipment Procured for Evaluation and Training of Inspectors, PC-XIII/B/2, 2 January 1996.

284 Switzerland, 'Evaluation of portable and transportable analytical equipment for Inspections in Industry', PC-X/B/WP.18, 3 April 1995.

3.4 List of approved equipment

While reaching consensus on the inspection equipment list was by no means an easy process it should be noted that, with one or two exceptions, all of the equipment necessary to support the training of inspectors was in place prior to the start of the first training course in January 1997. One final problem, however, had to be resolved before the list could be forwarded to the CSP for formal adoption. At a late stage in the process a small number of delegations, lead by the delegation of India, expressed concerns that, due to export controls imposed by some states, they would not be able to acquire some of the items of equipment on the proposed inspection equipment list. This would mean that they would not be able to familiarise themselves with these items of equipment and would, therefore, be placed at a significant disadvantage when such items were brought to their sites by inspection teams. These delegations, therefore, proposed that a clause be added to the operating procedures for the equipment list instructing the Technical Secretariat not to acquire any item of inspection equipment that was not freely commercially available to all States Parties. Such a proposal was not acceptable to the majority of delegations who argued that, as the Technical Secretariat had no control over what was or was not commercially available to States Parties, this would put them in an untenable position. As neither faction was prepared to move on this issue final approval of the equipment list remained blocked right up until the 1st CSP. After much discussion and debate, however, the following compromise text was agreed and included in the decision document.

> the National Authority of each State Party should be able to access – in order to satisfy the inspected State Party and to enable it to familiarise itself with all the operational characteristics concerned – each item of equipment contained in the List of Approved Equipment and its use sufficiently prior to its use on the territory of the inspected State Party to ensure familiarity. In case any State Party finds that it is denied such access to any item of equipment approved for inspection purposes, it has the right to deny permission of that equipment for use on its national territory. The Director-General is requested to establish an appropriate mechanism to assist the National Authorities in their familiarisation with the approved equipment and its use.[285]

In accordance with this agreement States Parties were able to send their technical experts to the OPCW Equipment Store, at a mutually agreed time, and, under the supervision of OPCW staff, inspect the items of equipment and be briefed on their technical specifications and use. A significant number of States Parties took up this opportunity and it was to prove highly beneficial to both them and the Technical Secretariat.

[285] List of Approved Equipment with Operational Requirements and Technical Specifications, 1st Conference of the States Parties, C-1/DEC. 71, 23 May 1997.

4. Sample Collection and Analysis

Modern analytical techniques are extremely sensitive and can provide a high level of confidence of the absence or presence of specified chemicals in any given sample. The drafters of the CWC considered chemical analysis of samples collected during an on-site inspection to be the most effective means of confirming the absence or presence, at the site, of chemicals covered by the Convention and, therefore, a key component of the confidence building process. The same analytical techniques, however, are equally capable of detecting chemicals that are not relevant to the CWC and, therefore, were seen, by the Signatory States and their chemical industries, as posing a major potential challenge to their right to protect their confidential information. Reaching agreement on the section of the Verification Annex dealing with sampling and analysis was, therefore, not easy and the debate on the interpretation of the precise meaning of the paragraphs in this section continued throughout the PrepCom process.[286]

Initially, the issues related to sampling and analysis were addressed by the Expert Group on Equipment and the Combined Group of Experts: Analytical Chemists. Subsequently, both these Groups and their issues were subsumed into the Expert Group on Inspection Procedures. The Expert Group on Equipment was initially tasked to develop the following information for off-site laboratories: identify the requirements for the number and location of laboratories, laboratory specifications, laboratory equipment requirements, laboratory staff requirements, and to develop procedures for the evaluation of the performance of laboratories.[287]

4.1 OPCW laboratory

As a result of its initial deliberations the Expert Group identified the following list of analytical related tasks that would need to be carried out by the Technical Secretariat:

(a) providing technical assistance and advice to the Director-General on the certification of Designated Laboratories;
(b) handling of authentic samples taken during inspections and transported off-site, prior to their analysis by Designated Laboratories;
(c) preparation and distribution of control samples to be used in Designated Laboratories;
(d) conducting quality auditing and proficiency testing of the Designated Laboratories;
(e) organization, updating and certification of analytical databases of the OPCW;
(f) certification of analytical and other methods, of reference compounds and inspection equipment;
(g) support of maintenance and storage of inspection equipment (including protective means of the OPCW) as required; and
(h) support of training activities as required.[288]

[286] CWC, Verification Annex, Part II, paras. 52-58.

[287] Illustrative weekly schedule for meetings of Expert Groups under Working Groups A and B, p. 9, PC-II/7, dated 21 April 1993.

[288] Initial Report of the Expert Group on Equipment, para. 6, PC-III/B/WP.9, 18 June 1993.

In order for it to be able to fulfil the above tasks the Expert Group recommended that the OPCW should have its own laboratory, staffed by Technical Secretariat personnel. This view was supported by the Expert Group of Analytical Chemists and subsequently endorsed by Working Group B.[289] At the request of Working Group B the Expert Group on Equipment then addressed the question of the size and capabilities necessary for such a laboratory and the type and estimated cost of equipment that would be needed to equip it.[290] The Group also recommended that, to facilitate maintenance and calibration of the inspection equipment it would be advisable to co-locate the inspection equipment store with the OPCW Laboratory. Some delegations considered that a small high containment laboratory would be needed. The Netherlands delegation indicated that such a facility existed at its Prins Maurits Laboratory, in Rijswijk and it was possible that this could be made available to the Organisation.[291] Other delegations took the view that this level of sophistication was not necessary and a suitably adapted standard laboratory would suffice. Following a technical visit to the Prins Maurits Laboratory and after further discussion it was decided to opt for a suitably modified standard laboratory and the Commission adopted a recommendation that for the OPCW laboratory:

> the Secretariat take appropriate action to acquire a small standard laboratory designed for receiving and handling small quantities or diluted solutions of Schedule 1 (toxic) chemicals in compliance with the national standards of the host country. The laboratory should be equipped with the items identified by the Expert Group on Equipment in its Second Interim Report (PC-V/B/WP.7) and adopted by the Commission (PC-V/12, paragraph 6.4 (a)). Such a laboratory, through an adequate combination of in-house and contracted work, will perform in a cost-efficient manner the functions described in the Initial Report of the Expert Group on Equipment (PC-III/B/WP.9) and subsequently endorsed by Working Group B (PC-III/B/2).[292]

The problems associated with establishing the OPCW Laboratory and Equipment Store and staffing them are covered elsewhere in this book (Chapters 3 and 5).

The Analytical Chemists Expert Group also recommended that the OPCW laboratory should be required to obtain an internationally recognised accreditation and that a centrally controlled quality assurance/quality control programme (QA/QC) be established for the Organisation.[293] Once again, there was an extensive debate on whose standards should be used for both the laboratory accreditation and the associated QA/QC regime and the extent to which the latter should apply to the whole Organisation. Those with experience in this matter pointed out that establishing such a regime and acquiring accreditation is a time consuming and expensive business. Many delegations took the view that while a QA/QC regime for the Verification Division might be

---

[289] 3rd Report of Working Group B, para. 9.2, PC-III/B/2, 30 June 1993.

[290] Chairman's Paper annexed to the 2nd Interim Report of the Expert Group on Equipment, PC-V/B/WP.7, 26 October 1993.

[291] Group of Experts on the OPCW Building, 'Fourth Interim Report', PC-V/B/WP.4, dated 11 November 1993, Annex 2, para. 4.

[292] 'Report of the Commission', PC-VII/8, dated 1 July 1994, para. 6.3.

[293] Combined Group of Experts: Analytical Chemists, 'Report', PC-III/B/WP.7, 15 June 1993, para. 4.

desirable the application of such a regime to the whole Organisation would be difficult to justify. After further debate it was decided that the PTS should adopt the following assumptions in relation to the type of quality assurance (QA) for the Organisation:

(a) for the Verification Division: an over arching 'light' quality assurance regime of the ISO (International Organisation for Standardisation) Guide 9000 series; and
(b) for the OPCW Laboratory, including the network of designated laboratories, and the sampling assistants and analysts: a QA regime of the ISO Guide 25 type.[294]

4.2 Designation and testing of laboratories

In accordance with the CWC inspectors have the right to request that samples be taken. Normally, for health and safety reasons, the inspected State Party will take the samples in the presence of the inspectors. The inspectors will then divide the samples into an agreed number of aliquots, at least one of which will be passed to the State Party for its retention. Where possible, analysis of the samples will be carried out on-site either by the inspectors using their approved equipment or, subject to agreement, by the inspected State Party in the presence of the inspectors. In situations where the inspection team deems it necessary samples may be taken off-site for analysis at laboratories specifically designated for the purpose by the Organisation.[295] The task of certifying designated laboratories and ensuring that they maintain the level of proficiency necessary to perform the off-site analysis of samples falls on the Director-General.[296] The CWC provides no further guidance on this matter and, therefore, it was left to the PrepCom to develop detailed procedures and guidance on the designation and testing of laboratories.

The analysis of samples taken off-site for analysis has the potential to be highly contentious. It is essential, therefore, that any laboratory undertaking such analysis should be able to demonstrate that it operates to the highest standards and has the necessary competence to perform the task. It also needs to have a well established expertise in the analysis of schedule 1 chemicals, as these are the chemicals of principal interest to the CWC. While there are many high quality analytical laboratories scattered across the globe only a very limited number have experience in the analysis of schedule 1 chemicals. The initial pool of laboratories for potential designation was, therefore, very small and restricted to only a few countries.

A number of the laboratories with the requisite expertise had already begun to participate, during the closing years of the CWC negotiations, in a programme of sample exchange organised by the Finnish laboratory VERIFIN. Between 1989 and 1993 four of these analytical 'round robins' as they were known took place. Each involved one of the participating laboratories preparing a set of samples that were then shipped to the other laboratories for analysis. Each laboratory was required to

[294] 'Report of Working Group B', PC-VII/B/2*, 1 July 1994, para. 2.7.
[295] CWC, Verification Annex, Part II, para. 55.
[296] CWC, Verification Annex, Part II, para. 56.

submit its results, within a defined timeframe, along with the necessary supporting data for evaluation and scoring. A meeting of all the participating laboratories to discuss the results was then held. Sixteen laboratories participated in the third and fourth round robins.[297] Through this process these laboratories were able to establish a high level of competency and consistency in the analysis of chemical weapons related materials. A number of the experts from these laboratories subsequently participated in the Expert Groups on Equipment and Analytical Chemists and their experience formed the basis for the development of the laboratory proficiency test regime to be used by the OPCW. In accordance with this regime the PTS and subsequently TS would hold two proficiency tests per year. Laboratories seeking designation must participate in a minimum of 3 out of 5 tests and must be successful in three consecutive tests.[298] Participating laboratories are given a performance rating from A to D to be considered for designation a laboratory must score AAA or two As and a B in consecutive tests. To maintain its designation a laboratory must participate, successfully, in at least one proficiency test per year.[299]

A sample removed for off-site analysis must be analysed by at least two different designated laboratories.[300] Ideally, such samples would be submitted to at least three laboratories to eliminate the potential problem of getting one positive and one negative result. Given the sensitivity likely to be attached to such samples it would be highly desirable for the laboratories to be located in different geographic or political regions. The requirement, therefore, was for a number of designated laboratories in each of the five UN regional groupings. The majority of the laboratories participating in the 'round robin' exercise were from WEOG. Only two were from Eastern Europe, Russia and the Czech Republic and one from Asia, China. There were no representatives from either Africa or Latin America. Clearly, in order to achieve a satisfactory balance a wider representation was required. It was essential, therefore, that the proficiency testing process should not only be a measure of performance but also designed to encourage laboratories to participate and gain the experience from doing so. The procedure eventually adopted by the Organisation, therefore, allowed those laboratories that wished to participate in the tests on a trial basis only, to do so. They received the same samples as those seeking to achieve or maintain designation and participated in the discussion of the results but were not formally rated by the Organisation. It was also essential that the requirements for designation should be worded in such a way that laboratories from different regions of the world, working to acceptable but different standards, should be able to qualify. The criteria for designation finally adopted by the Commission were as follows:

---

297 'Fourth International Inter-laboratory Comparison (Round-Robin) Test', PC-IV/B/WP.11, dated 27 September 1993.

298 Criteria for the Conduct of OPCW/PTS Proficiency Testing, 1st Conference of the States Parties, C1/DEC 65, 22 May 1997.

299 Designation of Laboratories, Note by the Director-General, S/86/1998, 17 November 1998.

300 CWC, Verification Annex, Part II, para. 57.

Such laboratories should:

(a) have established an internationally recognised quality assurance system;
(b) have obtained accreditation by an internationally recognised accreditation body for tasks for which they are seeking designation; and
(c) regularly participate and perform successfully in inter-laboratory proficiency tests. Analytical laboratories should obtain satisfactory results analysing control samples distributed by the Organisation.[301]

4.3 Transport of samples for off-site analysis

It is essential that any samples taken off-site for analysis reach the designated laboratories assigned to undertake their analysis in the same condition as when they left the site and that it be demonstrable that the integrity of the sample has not been compromised. The task of developing the appropriate procedures to achieve this aim was assigned to Working Group B and the Expert Groups working under it. In theory this should have been a relatively straightforward process, as the technical aspects of preparing samples and packing them for transport and establishing the necessary chain of custody to maintain their integrity were already well understood. The basic features of the protocol were, therefore, drafted quite early in the discussion of this topic.

The principal components of the proposed arrangement were as follows. The samples would be split into 6 to 8 aliquots at the inspection site in the presence of the inspected State Party. Each aliquot would be sealed with a numbered security seal. Two aliquots would be passed to the inspected site for their retention and the remainder packed for transport to the OPCW laboratory under a chain of custody procedure. On arrival at the OPCW laboratory the samples would be unpacked and the integrity of the seals checked. One aliquot of each sample would be retained by the Laboratory for future reference and the remainder packed for shipment to the three chosen designated laboratories along with a reference sample prepared by the OPCW laboratory and placed in an identical sealed and labelled sample tube. The samples would then be shipped to the designated laboratories under chain of custody procedures. On arrival at the designated laboratories the samples would be unpacked and their integrity confirmed prior to analysis by the Laboratory. After analysis the results would be reported to the Director-General for further action.

While the technical aspects of this proposed procedure were broadly acceptable to delegations and it eventually became the basis for the adopted procedure some delegations were concerned that it did not fully address the issue of confidentiality. Some of these delegations insisted that a representative of the State Party must be present at the OPCW laboratory during the unpacking and re-packing of the samples and at the designated laboratories during the unpacking and analysis of the samples. Other delegations pointed out that there was no provision in the CWC for this and that the associated delays likely to be incurred with adopting such a procedure would be unacceptable. Arranging for a representative of the inspected State Party to be present at

301 'Report of the Commission', PC-VI/22, dated 15 April 1994, para. 6.4.

the OPCW laboratory was the lesser problem, as the majority of States Parties either had representatives based in The Hague or in a nearby country and any associated delays were, therefore, likely to minimal. The far greater problem would be arranging for an inspected State Party representative to be present at each of the three designated laboratories receiving the samples. It proved impossible to resolve this issue during the life of the PrepCom and the issue remained unresolved at EIF.

To ensure the timely movement of samples to the OPCW laboratory and subsequently to the designated laboratories it was essential for them to be moved by air. The transport of hazardous chemicals by air is strictly governed by regulations issued by the International Air Transport Association (IATA). These regulations specify which chemicals can be transported by commercial aircraft, the maximum quantity that can be transported and how they must be packaged. Under these regulations some hazardous chemicals are banned from transport by passenger aircraft and some of the most hazardous cannot be flown on either passenger or cargo aircraft. By definition, samples taken during an inspection could contain highly toxic chemical warfare agents and, under the existing regulations, there was no provision for these materials to be transported by air. It was, therefore, essential for the Organisation to be able to demonstrate that these samples could be safely transported in commercial aircraft and to obtain the necessary approval for them to be transported by this means. Amendments to the IATA regulations are made on the recommendation of the International Civil Aviation Organisation (ICAO) and its Dangerous Goods Panel. Working Group B, therefore, instructed the Executive Secretary of the PTS to approach ICAO, as a matter of urgency and well in advance of the ICAO General Conference, with a view to seeking an early resolution of this problem.[302] Following discussions with the Chair of the Dangerous Goods Panel it was agreed that the PrepCom should seek approval for a new IATA hazardous goods category and associated packaging instruction for chemical samples being transported under the CWC. On 19 October 1993, in the presence of the Executive Secretary and the Director of Verification, the Dangerous Goods Panel considered and recommended that ICAO approve a new transport category headed 'Chemical Sample, toxic (liquid or solid)', a new special provision (A106) and associated packing instruction (623).

To comply with the new packaging instruction it was necessary for the samples to be packed in a specially designed container that would prevent the release of toxic material even under the most extreme circumstances, including a catastrophic failure of the aircraft. Two containers and associated packing, complying with packing instruction 623, were developed and tested, one by the US and one by the UK, during 1993-94. One container was subsequently flown, with samples, by a BA passenger aircraft from the UK to US in 1995 and a second by Lufthansa, from the Netherlands to South East Asia, again in 1995. Despite this early success it has proved difficult to get individual airlines to agree to accept the carriage of these samples. Irrespective of the fact that such samples, packed in the appropriate containers, are cleared for transport by passenger aircraft the final decision to accept such cargo remains with the individual airlines and their captains. Over the years the PTS and subsequently the TS

[302] 4th Report of Working Group B, para. 9.2, PC-IV/B/WP.12, 1 October 1993.

has expended considerable effort, with some limited success, to educate the airlines and their pilots to the minimal risks posed by these samples and the importance to the Organisation of being able to transport them rapidly by air. Despite these efforts, this issue remains a serious obstacle to the transport of samples for off-site analysis and also the movement of reference samples of schedule 1 chemicals between designated laboratories.

4.4 OPCW analytical database

The inspection equipment list includes two primary instruments for use in the chemical analysis of samples taken during an inspection. These are the GC/MS and the FTIR spectrometer. GC/MS would also be one of the principal tools used by designated laboratories for the off-site analysis of samples. Both these instruments produce a spectral fingerprint of the sample being analysed. By comparing these fingerprints with a library of fingerprints (reference spectra) of known compounds it is possible to identify the compounds present in the sample. The instrument's onboard computer can rapidly carry out such a comparison and provide a list of possible matches. An experienced analyst, undertaking a visual comparison of the unknown spectrum with that of the possible candidates identified by the computer, can then make a definitive decision on the identity of the unknown.

The key to the success of such a process is the library (database) of spectra of known compounds. A number of commercial databases containing reference spectra for many thousands of compounds were already available and one option was for the Organisation to acquire and use one of these. The adoption of this approach, however, posed two problems. Firstly, the chemical schedules annexed to the CWC contain many thousands of chemicals. Many of these compounds are not produced commercially and some may not even have been synthesised at all. Reference spectra for these compounds, therefore, were not likely to be routinely included in the available commercial databases. Secondly, and more importantly, the commercial databases, by their very nature, contained the spectra of thousands of commercially sensitive compounds that were not relevant to the CWC. The use of a commercial database was, therefore, unacceptable to delegations. The Government of Finland offered to make the database developed by its VERIFIN laboratory freely available to the Organisation.[303] While this database had been designed with the CWC in mind and therefore contained many of the relevant spectra, it was based on a software package that was incompatible with the commercial equipment being considered for use by the inspectorate. Delegations, therefore, decided that the most appropriate way forward was for the Organisation to develop and use its own analytical database.[304] It should be noted that, subsequently, the Government of Finland employed a consultant to convert the VERIFIN database to operate on the Microsoft Windows platform and donated it along with a GC/MS for use in the OPCW laboratory as a stand alone system.[305]

---

303 Finland, Database Offer, PC-IV/A/WP/8, 28 September 1993.

304 4th Report of Working Group B, para. 9.2(b), PC-IV/B/12, 1 October 1993.

305 'Report of the Commission', PC-VIII/18, dated 29 September 1994, para. 6.2.

A small taskforce of experts in the relevant fields, working initially under the auspices of the Expert Group on Equipment and subsequently under the Expert Group on Inspection Procedures, was established to undertake the task of developing the OPCW analytical database.[306] Signatory States were encouraged to submit spectra and supporting data on compounds of relevance to the CWC to the Taskforce for evaluation and validation.[307] In addition to evaluating and validating spectra provided by Signatory States for inclusion in the OPCW analytical database the taskforce also identified potential gaps in the database. Signatory States were encouraged to have their research laboratories provide reference spectra to fill these gaps. In many cases it was first necessary for them to synthesise the missing compound.

A major point of discussion was the question of which compounds should be included in the analytical database. Many delegations wanted the database limited to scheduled chemicals only. Analytical experts pointed out that this was not a practical option as, for example, some scheduled chemicals were insufficiently volatile to enable them to be analysed by GC/MS unless they were first converted to a more volatile derivative. It was, therefore, necessary for the spectra of these derivatives to be included in the database. In addition there were test mixtures used for calibration purposes that routinely did not contain scheduled chemicals and the spectra for these chemicals also needed to be present in the database. Even more contentious was the request to include degradation products of scheduled chemicals. In some samples, such as those collected during an investigation of alleged use, for example, any chemical agents originally present may have completely degraded and only their degradation products will be present in the sample. Analysis of these degradation products, however, can often be used to demonstrate that chemical agent was present at some point in the past. The analytical experts argued that, in order to be able to undertake such analysis, it was necessary for the database to include the spectra of the degradation products of the principal chemical agents. Despite the logic of the argument it proved extremely difficult to reach consensus on the inclusion of non-scheduled chemicals in the analytical database. Delegations argued that while the inclusion of non-scheduled chemicals in the database might be relevant for some circumstances or types of inspections they were not relevant for others. The compromise solution was to agree that rather than use the whole database for a given inspection a subset of the database, relevant to that particular type of inspection, would be selected by the Technical Secretariat in accordance with procedures agreed by States Parties. In addition the database and its contents would be made fully accessible to all States Parties.[308] With this understanding the inclusion of the spectra of a limited number of non-scheduled chemicals in the OPCW database was agreed. The addition of relevant spectra to the analytical database continued throughout the life of the PrepCom and the database has continued to be regularly updated since EIF.

---

306 'Report of the Commission', PC-V/12, dated 17 December 1993.

307 Note by the Executive Secretary, PC-IV/B/7, 20 August 1993.

308 Expert Group on Inspection Procedures, 'Eighth Report', PC-XI/B/WP.5, dated 19 June 1995.

4.5 **Operation of the GC/MS in the blinded mode**

Some delegations still had concerns about the use of the GC/MS, particularly at industrial sites. They argued, correctly, that a skilled operator could, by visual examination of the spectra produced from a given sample, potentially identify the presence of a particular compound irrespective of whether or not its spectrum was present in the spectral database. Access to the raw spectral data by the OPCW inspectors, therefore, could lead to a potential loss of confidential information. To eliminate this problem some delegations requested that the GC/MS be capable of being operated in a 'blinded mode'. This would require the computer software to be modified so that the on-board computer automatically compared the spectra from the sample with the reference spectra stored in the OPCW analytical database and only indicate the presence of chemicals relevant to the CWC. The operator would be prevented from seeing the raw spectral data and would have to rely solely on the analysis carried out by the instruments on-board computer. To carry out such an analysis, in a reliable and consistent manner, would require an extremely complex software package and, at the time, no such system was commercially available. The US National Institute of Standards and Technology (NIST), however, undertook to develop such a software package and make it freely available to everyone via the internet. A version of their AMDIS[309] programme specifically tailored for use by the CWC was developed and can be downloaded from the NIST website.[310] The two chosen suppliers of portable GC/MS instruments for use by the inspectorate were requested to modify their existing software to include the AMDIS package and enable the instruments to operate in the blinded mode.[311]

The major problem with the use of the GC/MS in the blinded mode is that automatic identification of compounds relevant to the CWC depends on their reference spectra being present in the OPCW analytical database. If the computer programme cannot make an exact match with a spectrum in the database then it will not make a positive identification. As discussed earlier there are many thousands of scheduled chemicals and the database is nowhere near complete and while the reference spectra of some of the more important compounds are included in the database many others are not. The success of the proposed blinded software approach will, therefore, be dependent on ensuring that reference spectra are available for the majority of the scheduled chemicals.

5. Inspection Procedures

The Expert Group on Inspection procedures was also responsible for dealing with a number of the more administrative issues relating to the conduct of inspections such as the use of non-scheduled aircraft, communications, point of entry and exit proce-

309 Automatic Mass Spectral Deconvolution and Identification Software.

310 <http://chemdata.nist.gov/mass-spc/amdis/explain.html>.

311 Expert Group on Inspection Procedures 'Thirteenth Report', PC-VIII/B/WP.2, dated 15 July 1994PC-XV/B/WP.9, dated 28 November 1996, para. 5(b).

dures POE, etc. A number of these issues are discussed in more detail in the following sections.

5.1 Specific types of equipment for specific types of inspection

One of the more contentious issues addressed by the Expert Group on inspection was the question of 'specific types of equipment for specific types of inspection'. The basis for this issue was the interpretation of the precise meaning of paragraphs 27 to 29 of Part II of the Verification Annex. Some delegations expressed the view that the language of these paragraphs placed no restriction on the Technical Secretariat's right to select any item of equipment from the approved list for use at any of the inspection sites covered by the CWC. While certain equipment items from the approved list might typically be selected for use at specific types of facilities, this did not preclude the possibility that any item of equipment from the approved list might be selected, should the Technical Secretariat consider it operationally practical to do so. Other delegations took the view that, in accordance with these same paragraphs, the Technical Secretariat shall select for any particular type of inspection only the equipment specifically designated for this type of inspection in the list of the approved equipment. Still other delegations expressed the view that the language 'to the extent possible' contained in paragraph 28 of Part II of the Verification Annex allowed for some flexibility in relation to the selection of approved equipment.[312] Despite many hours of discussion it proved impossible to reach a consensus on this issue and it remained unresolved at EIF. In order to facilitate the discussion the PTS produced a list of the equipment that it might routinely bring to each type of inspection.[313] While it had no formal status this list was used by the Technical Secretariat, after EIF, as the basis for the selection of equipment for a particular type of inspection.

5.2 Procedures for inspection equipment at the Point of Entry (POE)

At the point of entry, the inspected State Party has the right to inspect the equipment and confirm that it is an item from the approved list of equipment. This inspection process cannot be used as a means to delay the arrival of the inspection team at the inspection site beyond the 12 hour time limit specified in the CWC.[314] The State Party may reject an item of equipment if it is found not to match the approved specification for that particular item or any equipment for which incorrect documentation has been provided. It also has the right to reject an item of equipment if it believes that its use would be inappropriate for the particular type of inspection being undertaken.[315] Rejected equipment items will be stored at the POE under joint seal.

One of the tasks assigned to the PrepCom was to develop appropriate procedures for the inspection of equipment at the POE and this was one of the tasks delegated to

---

312 Expert Group on Inspection Procedures 'Third Report', PC-VIII/B/WP.2, dated 15 July 1994.

313 PTS Background Paper, 'Principles Governing the Selection of Equipment for Routine Inspections', dated 22 November 1996.

314 CWC, Verification Annex, Part II, para. 37.

315 CWC, Verification Annex, Part II, para. 29.

the Expert Group on Inspection Procedures. In drafting these procedures it was necessary to achieve a balance between the rights of the inspected State Party and those of the inspection team. For example, the inspected State Party may use non-destructive tests, such as x-ray, to examine the equipment but may not use any procedure that would interfere with the correct functioning of the item of equipment. The right to examine the equipment extends to both hardware and software. Any inspection of the software must not affect or change any data that is stored in the approved equipment and which is necessary for its proper performance. The examination of the equipment shall, at all times, be carried out in the presence of the inspection team. After considerable debate the Expert Group reached agreement on these procedures and these were forwarded to Working Group B and subsequently to the Commission.[316]

5.3 Measures relating to approved equipment at end of the inspection

A much more controversial issue was the drafting and reaching agreement on procedures for dealing with inspection equipment at the end of the inspection. While the CWC text provides guidance for dealing with inspection equipment at the point of entry/exit it provides no specific guidance on how to deal with inspection equipment before it leaves the inspection site. Basically, there were two main concerns. First, how to deal with contaminated equipment at the end of the inspection and secondly, how to ensure the removal of any confidential information not relevant to the CWC from the equipment. The following approach was taken to try and address these concerns.

In situations where contaminated inspection equipment cannot be readily decontaminated using approved health and safety procedures the inspection team and the inspected State Party will negotiate a solution to the problem. This may involve leaving the equipment behind for further decontamination by the State Party, followed by shipment back to the OPCW at a later date or, where it is the more economical solution, disposal either at the site or at an approved disposal facility. In principle any additional costs involved will be born by the side making the request.

Where the State Party has concerns that the inspection equipment may contain information not relevant to the CWC that cannot readily be removed at the site using agreed procedures three options would be available. Under option 1 the item of concern would be packed for transhipment and placed under joint seal. It would then be returned to the OPCW equipment store where, in the presence of a representative from the State Party, it would be unpacked and appropriate action taken to remove any potential confidential information remaining on the equipment. A second option, where practicable, would be for the State Party to request removal of the relevant parts, for retention at the site. For example, respirator filters or the sample inlet port and absorption column from the GC/MS. A State Party taking this option would be required to, immediately, replace any retained items with identical parts, that were acceptable to the Technical Secretariat and that would not result in any alteration to the operational

[316] Attachment 2 to the 3rd Report of the Expert Group on Inspection Procedures, PC-VIII/B/WP.2, 15 July 1994.

and technical capabilities of the approved equipment. Where immediate replacement is not feasible, the inspected State Party shall reimburse the inspection team for the cost of the retained parts before the team departs from the POE. In exceptional circumstances, where neither option 1 or 2 was acceptable, the State Party would have the option of retaining the item of equipment. In this situation the State Party would be required to reimburse the inspection team for the full replacement cost of the item, in a fully convertible currency, either before the team departs from the POE or in any case no later than seven days after its departure from the POE. The State Party would also be required to arrange for the disposal of the retained equipment or pieces of equipment, in the presence of the inspection team, before the team leaves the inspection site. In addition to the above options for dealing with potentially contaminated equipment it was agreed that the inspection team would, at the inspected State Party's request, provide it with copies of any electronic records or information collected at the site. The draft procedures developed by the Group were forwarded to Working Group B for approval in February 1995 and after a number of modifications by Working Group B forwarded to the Commission for adoption.[317, 318]

6. The Last Mile

The negotiation of the detailed procedures for inspections covered in this chapter were not easy and, on occasions, reaching consensus required considerable compromises by individual Signatory States. Once again, it is worth repeating that the CWC was not in force and no inspections were taking place. As a result, many delegations had no knowledge of what, in practical terms, an inspection might involve and how much actual risk there was to their national and commercial sensitive information from such inspections. It was inevitable, in such a situation, that those participating in the negotiations would err on the side of caution and this often made for slow and difficult progress. Despite these difficulties, by the time the 'trigger point' was reached and the 180 day countdown to EIF began many of the key decisions had been made. Even where there was not formal agreement on an issue, sufficient text had been developed to provide the Technical Secretariat with a basis on which to work.

For example, despite the failure to resolve the issue of 'specific types of equipment for specific types of inspection' there have been only a few instances, since EIF, of States Parties actually rejecting items of inspection equipment at the POE on the grounds that they consider them to be inappropriate for the particular inspection being undertaken. Where this has occurred it has mostly involved the GPS. A small number of States Parties have, as a matter of principle, blocked the use of the GPS at all inspections on their territory. It is important to note, however, that in every case alternative means of confirming the location of the inspected site have been made available to the inspection team. The rejection of an item of equipment at the POE has never, to date, prevented an inspection team from fulfilling its mandate.

---

317 Annex 1 to the 7th Report of the Expert Group on Inspection Procedures, PC-X/B/WP.9, 2 February 1995.

318 10th Report of Working Group B, PC-X/B/5, 6 April 1995.

Equally, concerns regarding the potential loss of confidential information during inspections – which were a major factor throughout the life of the PrepCom – proved to have been overstated and, in the ten years since EIF, more than a thousand inspections of industry sites have been completed without problems in this area.

Health and Safety has also not been an issue. The OPCW Health and Safety Policy and Regulations have been demonstrated to be highly effective. Problems that have arisen have been overcome using common sense rather than detailed guidelines. Indeed, in a paper submitted to the first CWC review conference, the Technical Secretariat stated: 'The OPCW has established an excellent safety record during its first five years of inspection activity'. In October 2000, the Organisation's inspectors completed 50,000 inspection days free of serious injuries or accidents causing lost time since the commencement of inspection activities.[319]

Once States Parties began to receive inspections under the CWC many of their concerns were eased and over the years since EIF the inspection process has been demonstrated to be both robust and effective while at the same time not overly intrusive for inspected States Parties.

---

319 Conference of the States Parties [first review conference], 'Technical Secretariat: Background paper on the conduct of inspections under the Chemical Weapons Convention and related issues', RC-1/S/1, dated 17 April 2003.

Chapter 8

PREPARING FOR DISARMAMENT: ARTICLES III, IV AND V

Ron G. Manley

1. INTRODUCTION

Each State Party to the Chemical Weapons Convention (CWC) undertakes to declare and destroy any chemical weapons and their associated production facilities owned or possessed by the State Party or that are located in any place under its jurisdiction or control.[320] The detailed requirements and timelines for this undertaking are set out in Articles III, IV and V of the Convention and in the associated Parts IV and V of the Verification Annex. Article III of the Convention sets out the declaration requirements for chemical weapons and their associated production facilities, while Article IV focuses on the requirements for the destruction and verification of these weapons. Article V deals with the actions required for the inactivation and subsequent destruction or, in exceptional cases, the conversion of chemical weapon production facilities for use for non-prohibited purposes and their verification. Negotiation of the CWC took many years and the contents of these three core articles were the subject of considerable debate throughout this period. A number of key issues needed to be addressed and resolved.

Of particular concern to a number of countries was the question of how to deal with historic chemical weapons left over from WWI and WWII. Over the years following both wars large numbers of these weapons had been abandoned or intentionally buried in many countries throughout the world. Even greater numbers had been disposed of by dumping at sea. While it was accepted that, in accordance with the proposed definition of a chemical weapon,[321] these were chemical weapons it was not acceptable to those countries faced with the problem, particularly were the weapons had been left on their territory by another state, that they should be subjected to same stringent declaration and destruction requirements as those to be applied to chemical weapons retained in military stockpiles. In order to overcome this problem it was agreed to define two sub classes of chemical weapons, namely, old chemical weapons and abandoned chemical weapons that, while still declarable and subject to destruction, would be subjected to a less stringent regime than that to be applied to stockpiled chemical weapons.

---

[320] CWC, Article I.

[321] CWC, Article II, para. 1.

2. Old Chemical Weapons

Accordingly, the definition of an old chemical weapon in Article II of the CWC recognises two specific sub classes of chemical weapon. The first are chemical weapons produced before 1925 and the second are chemical weapons produced between 1925 and 1946 that have deteriorated to such an extent that they can no longer be used as chemical weapons.[322] This qualification to the latter category of old chemical weapons became known as the 'usability criterion' and its precise definition was subsequently to become the subject of endless discussions throughout the life of the PrepCom.

The first category of old chemical weapons was targeted at the many chemical weapons left over from WWI and scattered across the various battlefields of Europe. The cut off date of 1925 was chosen to coincide with the signing of the Geneva Protocol for the prohibition for the use in war of asphyxiating, poisonous or other gases and of bacteriological methods of warfare.[323] Under Article III of the CWC these weapons, where recovered, must be declared and the required information, to the extent available, provided.[324] Once the Technical Secretariat of the OPCW has confirmed that the declared weapons meet the definition in Article II, paragraph 5(a) of the Convention the State Party shall treat them as toxic waste and destroy them in accordance with its national legislation.[325] Verification of the destruction of these weapons, by the Technical Secretariat, is not required.

Chemical weapons falling under the second part of the definition of old chemical weapons must also be declared. In this case it is the Technical Secretariat's task not only to verify the declaration but also to confirm that the weapons are no longer useable. A State Party is required to destroy this class of chemical weapon in accordance with Article IV and Part IV(A) of the Verification Annex.[326]

3. Abandoned Chemical Weapons

The definition of an abandoned chemical weapon applies to chemical weapons, including old chemical weapons, abandoned by a State, after 1925, on the territory of another State without its consent.[327] Declaration of chemical weapons falling into this class is required both from the territorial State Party and the abandoning State Party. It was recognised, even during the treaty negotiations, that, for both practical and technical reasons, this dual declaration requirement could not always be met. The major issue, however, was who should be responsible for the destruction of these weapons.

---

322 CWC, Article II, para. 5.

323 Thomas Stock, 'The CWC and old and abandoned CW', in T. Stock and K. Lohs (eds.), *The Challenge of Old Chemical Munitions and Toxic Armament Wastes* (Stockholm/Oxford, SIPRI/OUP 1997), p. 295.

324 CWC, Article III, para. 1(b).

325 CWC, Verification Annex, Part IV(B), para. 6.

326 CWC, Verification Annex, Part IV(B), para. 7.

327 CWC, Article II, para. 6.

Some countries argued that the original owner of the chemical weapons should be solely responsible for their removal and destruction. While other countries wished to place some limitation on the degree of responsibility of the abandoning State Party.

Discussions on this issue were greatly influenced by the dispute between China and Japan over Japanese chemical munitions abandoned in China between 1937 and 1943. China claimed that approximately 2 million abandoned chemical weapons had been discovered on its territory.[328] The final text of Article I of the CWC makes it clear that the abandoning State Party is responsible for the destruction of all chemical weapons that it abandoned on the territory of another State Party.[329] Such destruction is to be carried out in accordance with the provisions of the Convention.

The 1925 cut off date was chosen to exclude chemical weapons continuing to be recovered from the WWI battlefields. As a result these weapons will not be classed as abandoned chemical weapons and the responsibility for their destruction will rest with the Territorial State Party. In situations where the abandoning State Party cannot be identified or is not a State Party to the Convention the responsibility for the destruction of the chemical weapons also falls on the Territorial State Party. To ensure the timely destruction of these latter weapons, however, the State Party is entitled to request assistance from the OPCW and other States Parties. [330]

4. Buried and Sea Dumped Chemical Weapons

There remained the problem of what to do about chemical weapons that had been buried or dumped at sea. It was clearly not going to be practical for a State Party to declare and destroy chemical weapons buried on its territory if their location and condition were unknown. The situation with sea dumped munitions was even more complicated. While these buried or dumped weapons might well pose an environmental threat it was deemed unlikely that they would pose any military threat. It was, therefore, agreed that chemical weapons buried before a given date would not be covered by the Convention provided they remained buried. Where such weapons were subsequently recovered, however, they would have to be declared and destroyed in accordance with the requirements of the Convention. The key issue was the choice of a suitable cut-off date. The date finally chosen was 1 January 1977. Any chemical weapons buried after this date, by a State Party, must be recovered, declared and destroyed. It is reported that this cut off date was chosen to avoid embarrassing the Government of Austria.[331] Over the period 1974 to 1976, the Austrian Government had disposed of a large number of German chemical grenades left over from WWII by

328 Conference on Disarmament document CD/1127, 18 February 1992.

329 CWC, Article 1, para. 3.

330 CWC, Verification Annex, Part IV(B), para. 16.

331 Thomas Stock, 'The CWC and old and abandoned CW', in T. Stock and K. Lohs (eds.), *The Challenge of Old Chemical Munitions and Toxic Armament Wastes* (Stockholm/Oxford, SIPRI/OUP 1997), p. 297.

encasing them in concrete and burying them in a specially constructed, secure, underground store.[332] The adoption of an earlier date would have meant that the Austrian's would have had to recover and destroy these weapons. It was also agreed that chemical weapons dumped at sea before a given date would be excluded from the Convention. Reaching agreement on a cut off date in this case, however, proved to be more difficult and the matter was not finally settled until the closing days of the treaty negotiation. In the end the Chairman of the ad hoc Committee on Chemical Weapon, Ambassador von Wagner, asked those countries with an interest in this matter to submit to him, privately, the earliest cut-off date that was acceptable to them. Shortly after, the date of 1 January 1985 appeared in the Chairman's draft text of the Convention. While the country requesting this date has never been formally identified the Soviet Union/Russia, was considered to be a likely candidate.

5. Destruction Timelines

The CWC would require all its States Parties to declare and destroy any chemical weapons that they possessed. It was, therefore, also necessary to agree on a timetable for this destruction process. Those members of the Conference on Disarmament (CD) who did not possess chemical weapons considered that the destruction period should be as short as possible, thus removing the global threat from these weapons at the earliest opportunity. At one stage a period of 5 years from entry into force (EIF) of the CWC was being proposed. Given the size of their stockpiles, however, such a short timeframe was considered impractical by both superpowers.

Progress on this particular issue was further complicated by the stated desire of the US to retain part of its chemical weapons stockpile, as a deterrent, until all those states capable of producing chemical weapons had ratified the CWC. President George HW Bush summarised the US position on this issue in a speech to the General Assembly of the United Nations, in September 1989.[333] In this speech he stated that once the CWC had entered into force and the Soviet Union had become a State Party the US would destroy 98 percent of its chemical weapons within 8 years. He then went on to say that once all chemical weapons capable states had joined the CWC the US would destroy the remaining 2 percent, around 500 tonnes, within 2 years. While the US position was unacceptable to most members of the CD the French were prepared to endorse it on the understanding that all countries with chemical weapons would be allowed to retain a residual stockpile. Such an approach, which was reminiscent of the Nuclear Non-proliferation Treaty (NPT), was seen by many countries as once again creating a two class system where those who had chemical weapons would be allowed to keep them and those who did not would be prohibited from developing them. By its very nature it was also likely to encourage those countries that were

[332] Conference on Disarmament document CD/CW/WP.397, 5 May 1992.

[333] 'The President's chemical weapons initiative', The White House, Office of the Press Secretary, 25 September 1989.

capable of developing chemical weapons but currently did not have them to join the club by acquiring such weapons before the treaty came into force.

In May 1991, in order to push the treaty negotiations to conclusion, the US finally agreed to drop its plan to retain a security stockpile and accept the requirement for complete destruction of all chemical weapons within an agreed timeline. In his statement President Bush announced:

> … We are formally forswearing the use of chemical weapons for any reason, including retaliation, against any state, effective when the convention enters into force, and will propose that all states follow suit. Further, the United States unconditionally commits itself to the destruction of all our stocks of chemical weapons within 10 years of entry into force and will propose that all other states do likewise.

While many members of the CD would like to have seen a shorter deadline for the complete destruction of any declared chemical weapons stocks, the US proposal of 10 years, following entry into force of the CWC, was, in the end, accepted.[334] Provision, however, was made for the Conference of the States Parties, on the recommendation of the Executive Council, to grant an extension to this deadline if it deemed that the State Party's request for such an extension was justified.[335] Any such extension may not exceed a period of five years. It should be noted that the 10 year destruction period runs from entry into force and therefore, a State joining the Convention after this date will have less than 10 years to destroy any chemical weapons that it possesses. In order to ensure that those States Parties with chemical weapons are making progress towards meeting the 10 year deadline the CWC also imposes a number of intermediate deadlines. These require destruction of 1 percent of a State Party's stockpile of category 1 chemical weapons within 3 years, 20 percent within 5 years and 45 percent within 7 years.

The establishment of a deadline for the complete destruction of chemical weapons stockpiles was not only politically important but also necessary to ensure that those State Parties possessing such weapons were under pressure to destroy them as soon as possible. Nine years after entry into force of the Convention, however, it has become clear that the targets set were far too ambitious. For different reasons, both Russia and the United States will fail to meet the 10 year deadline.

6. Conversion of Chemical Weapons Production Facilities

The declaration, closure and inactivation of chemical weapons production facilities were seen as an essential requirement for a successful treaty. The majority view was that such facilities should also be completely destroyed and this is reflected in the final wording of the text of the CWC on this issue.

---

334 CWC, Article V, para. 6.

335 CWC, Verification Annex, Part IV(A), para. 26.

> Each State Party shall destroy all chemical weapons production facilities specified in paragraph 1 and related facilities and equipment, pursuant to the Verification Annex and.... [Article V, paragraph 8]

The destruction requirement is further amplified in Part V of the Verification Annex.

> A State Party shall destroy equipment and buildings covered by the definition of a chemical weapons production facility as follows:
>
> (a) All specialised equipment and standard equipment shall be physically destroyed;
> (b) All specialised buildings and standard buildings shall be physically destroyed. [VA, Part V, paragraph 26]

In effect this requires the total destruction of the chemical weapons production plant and all its associated buildings and support facilities.

This requirement posed a particular problem for the Soviet Union and its successor Russia. Unlike the US, whose chemical weapons production facilities were largely stand alone facilities, the Soviet facilities were incorporated within large, industrial, chemical industry complexes. While accepting the requirement for the destruction of specialised equipment and specialised features of buildings Russia argued that the requirement to destroy standard buildings and equipment, of a similar nature to that of other facilities in the industrial complex, could not be justified and would impose an unnecessary economic burden on the State Party concerned. While there was little support for this point of view, within the CD, it was eventually conceded that, in exceptional circumstances, a State Party should, subject to fulfilling certain conditions, be allowed to convert a chemical weapons production facility for use for purposes not prohibited by the Convention. A State Party seeking to take such action, however, would be required to submit a request, through the Executive Council of the proposed Organisation to its Conference of the States Parties, demonstrating the exceptional and compelling need to convert rather than destroy the facility. The final decision on the request would rest with the Conference of the States Parties, which, if it gave its approval, would also impose appropriate conditions.[336] While Russia saw this as the solution to its problem the United States and many other countries continued to take the view that total destruction was to be the normal approach and that 'conversion', if it occurred at all, would be an exceptional event. This difference in viewpoint was to prove a major stumbling block when the PrepCom took up the task of addressing the practicalities of 'conversion'.

7. Sampling at Chemical Weapons Storage Sites

The negotiating text of the CWC initially contained a provision allowing inspection teams to take samples from chemical weapons at chemical weapons storage sites in

[336] CWC, Article V, para. 13.

order to confirm the accuracy of the State Party's declaration. Very late on in the negotiations the United States realised that it might have a problem complying with this provision, as several of its states had passed environmental legislation preventing chemical weapons, stored within the state, from being opened other than during the destruction process at a chemical weapons destruction facility. As in this particular situation, State Law would have supremacy over any Federal obligations to an international treaty, such as the CWC, the US Federal Government would have had difficulty guaranteeing the international inspector's right to take samples during storage site inspections within these states. To resolve this problem the US negotiated a change to the final version of Part IV(A) of the Verification Annex allowing inspectors to select and tag munitions for sampling during storage site inspections. The State Party could then choose, either, to allow the munitions to be sampled at the storage site or to delay sampling until the tagged munitions had been transferred to a chemical weapons destruction facility.[337] As with many other issues, the practical aspects of how this tagging and subsequent sampling were to be undertaken was not addressed in the Convention text. The 'tagging issue', which arose out of this late change to the text, subsequently, became one of the many important practical issues that required further clarification after EIF.

8. Soviet Union/United States Bilateral Negotiations

The structure and content of Articles IV and V were of particular concern to the two known possessors of major stockpiles of chemical weapons the Soviet Union and the United States. In addition to their participation in the multilateral negotiations on the Convention at the CD, in Geneva, the two super powers also embarked on a series of bilateral negotiations. These bilateral negotiations, which began in 1976, initially made little progress and broke down in 1980 following the Soviet invasion of Afghanistan. In 1984 the US, Reagan Administration, decided to try and refocus the discussions, within the CD, by submitting a proposed draft for a chemical weapons convention. Shortly after, in November 1985, bilateral talks between the two superpowers, which had been largely stalled since 1980, resumed. At first little progress was made and it looked as if the negotiations would once again be stalled. In 1989, however, progress at last began to be made and regular, scheduled, bilateral sessions became a routine part of the negotiating process leading, in September 1989 to the signing, in Jackson Hole, Wyoming, of a memorandum of understanding between the US and Russia on chemical weapons.[338]

The Wyoming MOU, as it became known, provided for a number of actions to be undertaken in two separate phases. Phase 1, to be completed by February 1991, required the exchange of general data on each sides' chemical weapons capabilities and

[337] Verification Annex, Part IV(A), para. 49(b).

[338] Memorandum of Understanding between the Government of the Union of Soviet Socialist Republics and the Government of the United States of America Regarding a Bilateral Verification Experiment and Data Exchange Related to Prohibition of Chemical Weapons.

visits to relevant military and civil facilities to be chosen by the host country. Phase II, which was to begin not later than four months prior to the signing of the multilateral convention, specified that both sides would exchange more detailed data on chemical weapons' capabilities and carry out inspections to verify such data.

Following the success of the negotiations for the Wyoming MOU the two sides went on to negotiate a Bilateral Destruction Agreement (BDA).[339] Under the BDA, which was signed by both parties in June 1990, both states agreed to stop producing chemical weapons and to reduce their respective chemical weapons stockpiles to no more than 5000 agent tons by the end of 2002. Chemical weapons storage sites were to be subjected to on-site inspections and the destruction of the chemical weapons was to be verified by the continuous, on-site, presence of inspectors and monitoring instruments at the destruction facilities. Both sides also agreed to cooperate on establishing safe methods and technologies for destruction of their chemical weapons stockpiles. In accordance with the BDA, therefore, verification of the US and Soviet – and its successor, Russia – chemical weapon stockpiles and their subsequent destruction would be a bilateral arrangement. Russian inspectors would verify in the US and US inspectors in Russia. Under this arrangement the role of the OPCW, when it came into force, would, subject to the agreement of the Executive Council, be reduced to a simple monitoring or audit process.[340] The existence of the BDA was, subsequently, to have a major impact on the work of the PrepCom and on the future structure and size of the Technical Secretariat's Verification Division and Inspectorate.

The more immediate outcome of the bilateral discussions between the Soviet Union and the US was their impact on the final format and content of Articles IV and V of the CWC and the associated Parts IV and V of the Verification Annex. Having reached agreement between themselves on the key elements of these two Articles and the related parts of the Verification Annex the two superpowers were strongly opposed to any moves to make significant changes to them during the final multilateral discussions taking place within the CD. As a result these two core Articles of the Convention remained largely unchanged following the signing of the Wyoming Memorandum and the BDA.

9. Expert Groups

Those issues identified in the Paris Resolution, which were directly related to Articles III, IV and V are listed in Table 1 and Working Group B established a number of subsidiary Expert Groups to deal with these issues.[341] While membership of these Expert Groups was open-ended they were, in practice, much smaller bodies and in-

---

339 Agreement between the United States of America and the Union of Soviet Socialist Republics on Destruction and Non Production of Chemical Weapons and on Measures too Facilitate the Multilateral Convention on Banning Chemical Weapons. Available at <www.defenselink.mil/acq/acic/treaties/bda/text.htm>.

340 CWC, Article IV, paras. 13 and 14.

341 Paris Resolution, in L.W. Tabassi (ed.), *OPCW: The Legal Texts* (The Hague, TMC Asser Press 1999) p. 523-530.

cluded experts on the specific issues under discussion. Each Expert Group was assigned specific tasks from Table 1 and required to make recommendations on possible solutions to them. These recommendations were then considered by Working Group B and once agreed passed to the PrepCom for formal adoption by the Signatory States. As the work of the PrepCom proceeded a number of additional issues requiring elaboration were identified and those related to chemical weapons issues were once again assigned to Working Group B and delegated to the relevant Expert Group for consideration.

10. Developments in the Expert Group Structure

Working Group B initially established the Combined Group of Experts: Chemical Engineers to begin discussions of those verification issues involving chemical engineering expertise.[342] The Group met, for the first and only time, between 10 to 21 May 1993. While the Group was able to establish a list of general inspection activities for on-site verification it quickly realised that the differing requirements for inspections at different types of facilities were such that it was going to be necessary to address each of them as separate issues. In its report to Working Group B it also identified the following specific tasks that, in its view, would require resolution:

> Elaboration of model agreements for appropriate facilities to include, where necessary, provisions for adjusting a detailed facility agreement should the risk posed by a facility to the object and purpose of the Convention alter as a result of changes at the facility;
>
> Elaboration of formats for declarations and inspection reports;
>
> Additional discussion of criteria for determining the risk a Schedule 2 Facility poses to the object and purpose of the Convention and the development of procedures for the application of these criteria;
>
> Definition of the term 'reactor volume' in the context of the inspection at a Single Small-Scale Facility;
>
> Determination of how the definition of 'specialised equipment' could be applied in practice at Chemical Weapons Production Facilities.[343]

It also went on to recommend that Working Group B consider reorganising its approach to the resolution of these issues and those previously assigned to the Expert Group. During the next intersessional period a number of new Expert Groups were established to take forward the tasks originally assigned to the Combined Group of Experts: Chemical Engineers. Those relevant to Articles III, IV and V were Chemical Weapons Storage Facilities (CWSFs), Chemical Weapons Destruction Facilities

342 Report of Working Group B, PC-II/WGB/1, 20 April 1993.

343 Combined Group of Experts: Chemical Engineers, Initial Report, PC-III/B/WP.2, 21 May 1993.

(CWDFs), Chemical Weapons Production Facilities (CWPFs) and Old and Abandoned Chemical Weapons (OACW).

By mid 1994 it was clear that progress on the remaining outstanding issues had slowed to such an extent that a further change in approach was necessary. There were two principal reasons for this lack of progress. Firstly, the outstanding issues were the ones on which it was most difficult to achieve consensus and secondly, delays in Signatory States completing their ratification process meant that the CWC was not going to enter into force for some time.[344] Of particular concern were the difficulties being experienced by the Clinton Administration in getting the US ratification of the Convention through the US Congress. These delays meant that there was little pressure on delegations to make compromises and move towards consensus on many of the outstanding CW related issues. It is also worth noting that the work on CWSFs, CWPFs and CWDFs was heavily influenced by the widely held view, at that time, that the OPCW would limit verification at Russian and American chemical weapons sites to some form of complimentary monitoring regime, leaving primary responsibility for undertaking on-site verification to Russia and the US under the terms of the BDA.[345] In order to try and move things forward the Commission decided to combine the Expert Groups on CWSFs, CWPFs and CWDFs into a single Chemical Weapons Issues Group under the Chairmanship of Mr. Sylwin Gizowski of Poland. The Chairmen of the old groups were appointed to serve as Friends of the Chair on the outstanding issues relevant to their old group. It should also be noted, at this point, that the work of the Expert Groups on Equipment, Safety Procedures and Analytical Chemists, which is reported elsewhere in this book, also had a significant impact on the Article IV and V related issues.

During this period there was also a debate, among the delegations, as to whether Schedule 1 facilities should be treated as chemical weapon related or industry related. Some delegations took the view that, as these facilities were most likely to be military installations undertaking non-prohibited work on chemical weapons related materials for defensive purposes, they should, for verification purposes, be treated as Chemical Weapons related facilities. Other delegations argued that, while it was true that these facilities were undertaking work on Schedule 1 chemicals, this was a permitted activity and, as such, should be treated differently from those activities that were to be banned under the CWC. They further argued that as these facilities, were declarable under Article VI and not Article III, they should be treated, for verification purposes, as industrial facilities. This latter view prevailed and, following the July 1993 meeting of the Experts Group on Single Small-scale Facilities and Other Schedule 1 Production Facilities, issues related to Schedule 1 facilities were subsequently handled by the Expert Group dealing with Chemical Industry Facilities.[346]

---

344 In accordance with the CWC, entry into force would occur, automatically, 180 days after the deposit of the 65th ratification.

345 CWC, Article IV, para. 13.

346 Report of the Experts Group on Single Small-Scale Facilities and Other Schedule 1 Production Facilities, PC-IV/B/WP.4, 16 July 1993.

Para.	Task	Expert Group
a.	Guidelines on detailed procedures for verification and for the conduct of inspections, in accordance with, inter alia, Part II, paragraph 42, of the Verification Annex;	All CW Groups
e.	A list of approved equipment, in accordance with Part II, paragraph 27, of the Verification Annex;	Equipment
f.	Procedures for the inspection of equipment, in accordance with Part II, paragraph 29, of the Verification Annex;	Equipment
g.	Procedures concerning the implementation of safety requirements for activities of inspectors and inspection assistants, in accordance with Part II, paragraph 43, of the Verification Annex;	Safety Procedures
h.	Procedures for inclusion in the inspection manual concerning the security, integrity and preservation of samples and for ensuring the protection of the confidentiality of samples transferred for analysis off-site, in accordance with Part II, paragraph 56, of the Verification Annex;	Analytical Chemists
i.	Models for facility agreements in accordance with Part III, paragraph 8, of the Verification Annex;	All CW Groups and Model FA Group
j.	Appropriate detailed procedures to implement Part III, paragraph 11 and 12 of the Verification Annex, in accordance with paragraph 13 of that Part;	Chemical Engineers
k.	Deadlines for submission of the information specified in Part IV (A), paragraphs 30 to 32 of the Verification Annex, in accordance with paragraph 34 of that Part;	CWDF
l.	Recommendations for determining the frequency of systematic on-site inspections of storage facilities, in accordance with Part IV (A), paragraph 44, of the Verification Annex;	CWSF
m.	Recommendations for guidelines for transitional verification arrangements, in accordance with Part IV (A), paragraph 51, of the Verification Annex;	CWDF
n.	Guidelines to determine the usability of chemical weapons produced between 1925 and 1946, in accordance with Part IV (B), paragraph 5, of the Verification Annex;	Old and Abandoned
o.	Guidelines for determining the frequency of systematic on-site inspections of chemical weapons production facilities, in accordance with Part V, paragraph 54, of the Verification Annex;	CWPF
p.	Criteria for toxicity, corrosiveness and, if applicable, other technical factors, in accordance with Part V, paragraph 71 (b), of the Verification Annex;	CWPF

11. Common Issues

A number of the issues, such as declaration formats, inspection activities, model facility agreements and bilateral/multilateral verification arrangements were common to all Expert Groups dealing with verification of CW related facilities. Differences in the detailed requirements for each type of facility, however, were such that it was still necessary for them to be addressed separately by each of the individual groups.

11.1 Declaration formats

Reaching agreement on the formats for the declarations required under the CWC was a key task for all the Expert Groups dealing with this issue. The problem is that while the Verification Annex of the CWC provides detailed information on what is to be declared and when, it provides no guidance on how it should be provided. As written, the CWC leaves it up to each State Party to decide on the format and language[347] in which it will provide its declaration. The adoption of such an approach, however, would place an unnecessary burden on the Technical Secretariat of the OPCW who would be faced with the difficult task of processing and storing the large amounts of data to be provided. It was, therefore, important to reach agreement on standard formats to be used for each of the different declarations to be provided. It was also considered important that the agreed formats, to the extent practicable, should be designed to be machine-readable in order to speed up their processing. Another important factor was the need to be able to identify the confidentiality classification to be assigned to individual items or blocks of data. Accommodating all these requirements across the very different types of data to be declared was always going to be a difficult task and this proved to be the case. The issue was further complicated with respect to the declarations required for chemical weapons and their associated facilities by the existence of the Wyoming MOU and the BDA. Under these agreements, Russia and the United States had agreed to exchange data on their chemical weapons, etc., and had already developed appropriate formats for this purpose. Their preference, therefore, was for the OPCW to simply adopt these formats for all CW related declarations. While, at first glance, this appeared to be a sensible approach, experts from a number of delegations felt that the bilateral formats were not well designed, could not be readily made machine readable, did not take account of the need to assign confidentiality ratings to individual data items and did not take account of the fact that the declaration requirements under the bilateral agreements did not precisely match those of the CWC. In response Russia and the United States pointed out that, as – at that time – they were the only states to have admitted to the possession of chemical weapons and therefore likely to be affected by this issue, their preference should prevail.

The information to be submitted by States Parties with respect to CW destruction facilities is particularly complex. The Expert Group dealing with this particular aspect, therefore, decided that, before it could develop appropriate declaration formats, it was first necessary to clarify and agree on the precise information to be submitted under the relevant paragraphs relating to CW destruction. After discussing the issue it developed illustrative tables of the information requested, and to be supplied, for the General Plan for Destruction of Chemical Weapons, Detailed Annual Plans for Destruction and Annual Reports on Destruction.[348] Once these had been agreed it went on to develop appropriate declaration formats.

There were also extensive discussions on the declaration formats for old and abandoned chemical weapons. The primary problem in this case was that, due to their age and condition, detailed information on these weapons was, frequently, simply not available and the hazards associated with trying to obtain it were difficult to justify.

---

[347] While the CWC makes no stipulation on language for declarations a consensus gradually emerged, during the Preparatory Commission, that States would provide their declarations in one of the six official languages of the authentic texts of the Convention, namely, Arabic, Chinese, English, French, Russian and Spanish.

[348] Experts Group on Chemical Weapons Destruction Facilities, 'Initial Report', PC-IV/B/WP.1, dated 9 July 1993.

It, therefore, proved difficult to reach agreement on a standard format for their declaration.

After many hours of discussion a declaration handbook, containing formats for nearly all of the declaration requirements for chemical weapons and their associated facilities, was developed. Final agreement on the declaration requirements for CW production facilities, old CW and abandoned CW, however, could not be reached and, therefore, the handbook was never formally adopted by the CSP and States Parties were simply encouraged to use it when making their declarations. Despite this, virtually all States Parties used the forms and an updated but essentially unchanged version of the declaration handbook continues to be used.

This situation was to be repeated for a number of the issues that were formally listed as unresolved in the final report of the PrepCom. The Commission worked by consensus and so an objection by a single Signatory State was sufficient to block the adoption of any proposal. In many cases, therefore, while considerable progress had been made on a given issue, and much of the text developed was agreed, outstanding disagreements on a small number of points meant that the Commission was unable to formally adopt it. This work was rarely wasted, however, and it frequently formed the basis for the resolution of the issue after entry into force of the CWC.

11.2 **Inspection activities**

In accordance with the CWC it is the task of the Technical Secretariat to develop, taking into account guidelines approved by the CSP, an inspection manual setting out the procedures to be used by OPCW inspectors when undertaking on-site inspections and make it available to States Parties.[349] To facilitate this process Expert Groups were tasked to produce illustrative lists of activities to be undertaken for each type of inspection. This proved to be one of the easier issues to address and the relevant Expert Groups developed lists of inspection activities for each of the different types of CW related inspections. While consensus on the lists of inspection activities for CW storage facilities and CW destruction facilities was achieved, final agreement on those for CW production facilities and old and abandoned chemical weapons could not be reached. In the case of the latter, the problem was a fundamental lack of agreement on the actual level of verification to be applied to these weapons. This is discussed further under the section dealing with old and abandoned CW. Nevertheless, despite this failure to reach formal agreement on all of the illustrative lists, they, subsequently, formed the basis for the development of the OPCW inspection manual.

The training of the initial batch of OPCW inspectors was scheduled to begin approximately six months before entry into force of the CWC. Therefore, while the task of developing the inspection manual was formally the responsibility of the Technical Secretariat, it was necessary to have at least a draft version of the manual available before EIF and the establishment of the Technical Secretariat. A draft manual, for training purposes, was, therefore, developed by the Provisional Technical Secretariat. This draft manual in fact continued to be used by the OPCW for several years after

[349] CWC, Verification Annex, Part II, para. 42.

EIF for all on-site inspections. Based on the experience gained during those early years an extensively revised version was issued, by the Technical Secretariat, in 2001.

11.3 Model facility agreements

The CWC requires that routine inspections at CW related sites are governed by a facility agreement.[350] This legally binding agreement sets out the agreed, operational rules and procedures under which inspections at the facility, following the initial inspection, shall be undertaken. Its purpose is to provide some degree of predictability to both the inspected State Party and to the OPCW inspectors on how the on-site inspection will be carried out. For most CW related facilities the Convention requires that these agreements should be in place within 180 days of entry into force of the Convention for the State Party.[351] The one exception is for CW destruction facilities that are operational at EIF of the CWC or during the 12 months after EIF, which will, initially, be governed by transitional verification arrangements.

To ensure standardisation and equality of treatment the CWC requires these facility agreements to be based on model agreements adopted by the CSP. The task of developing the model facility agreements for each type of inspection was one of the tasks assigned to the PrepCom.[352] Development of these models was to prove to be a difficult and demanding task. A key problem was a fundamental difference of opinion between delegations on what was required. Some delegations took the view that the models should be largely illustrative, consisting primarily of a series of headings – identifying the principal areas and subjects to be covered – along with some explanatory text. Other delegations took the view that they should be fully detailed documents containing agreed text with blank spaces for the entry of data relevant to a particular facility. Despite this fundamental difference in approach work on these models continued and well developed and detailed drafts for each type of facility were prepared. It proved impossible, however, despite many hours of discussion – both within the individual Expert Groups dealing with CW related issues and in the Expert Group on Model Facility Agreements – to reach a final consensus on them. The development of model facility agreements for these facilities, therefore, remained one of the unresolved issues at EIF.

11.4 Bilateral/multilateral verification procedures

As discussed earlier the CWC provides for the option that States Parties may enter into bilateral arrangements to verify the destruction of their chemical weapons stockpiles and in such situations the Executive Council of the OPCW may decide to limit its verification activities to some form of complimentary monitoring. The CWC, however, provides no further guidance on what criteria should be used by the EC in reaching its decision or on how it should monitor its application. The relevant Expert Groups

---

350 CWC, Verification Annex, Part III, para. 3.
351 CWC, Verification Annex, Part III, para. 4.
352 Paris Resolution, para. 12(i).

were, therefore, tasked to address the issue and develop appropriate guidelines for this purpose. The following guidelines were developed by the Expert Group on Storage Facilities and subsequently adopted by the Commission:

> [T]he applicability of any bilateral or multilateral verification agreements [should] be assessed against the criteria of consistency, comprehensives, and effectiveness in accordance with the principles and provisions noted in the Chairman's Paper;[353]
>
> if complementary verification measures related to any bilateral/multilateral agreement have been implemented by the Executive Council, the Director-General should report to the Executive Council on the verification activities taken by the parties to the bilateral/ multilateral agreement and on the complementary measures. This should include an assessment of their effectiveness;
>
> should the Director-General have uncertainties at any time about the effectiveness of any bilateral/multilateral inspection regime he shall approach the States Parties concerned for clarification. If the uncertainties cannot be removed or if the facts established are of a nature to suggest that obligations undertaken under the Convention have not been met, the Director-General shall inform the Executive Council without delay; and
>
> if the Executive Council finds reason to doubt the effectiveness of any bilateral/multilateral agreement, it should consider directing the implementation of the Organisation's verification regime for the States Parties concerned. The Executive Council should take appropriate measures aimed at clarifying the issues prior to directing such action.[354]

A version of the above text, modified to take account of the specific requirements for a CW destruction facility, was also developed by the Expert Group on CW Destruction facilities and subsequently endorsed by the Commission.[355]

12. Chemical Weapon Storage Facilities

The Expert Group met for the first time from 5 to 9 July 1993. Its task was to initiate discussions on the verification procedures for Chemical Weapons Storage Facilities, concentrating on declarations, including declaration format content and guidelines for inspection procedures. The full list of tasks assigned to the Group is annexed to its initial report.[356] The Group met on a further two occasions, on 22- 26 November 1993 and 7-11 February 1994, to continue its work and made significant progress towards the resolution of a number of the issues assigned to it. Following the Group's third meeting, however, it was subsumed into the new Chemical Weapons Issues Group.

---

353 Expert Group on Chemical Weapons Storage Facilities, 'Second Interim Report', PC-VI/B/WP.9, 23 February 1994.

354 'Report of the Commission', PC-VI/22, dated 15 April 1994, para. 6.6.

355 PC-VI/22, para. 6.8.

356 Initial report of the Expert Group on Chemical Weapons Storage Facilities, PC-IV/B/WP.2, 9 July 1993.

The Group developed the guidelines for inspections procedures at CW storage facilities.[357] It also made a number of recommendations to Working Group B related to CW declarations for consideration and adoption by the PrepCom. Two important ones adopted by the Commission were as follows:

> the recommendation of Working Group B that the precision of the declarations of national aggregate quantities of toxic chemicals and their precursors defined as chemical weapons should be rounded up to the nearest one tonne and that the individual munitions and container items should be declared by nominal weight in kilograms;
>
> the understanding of Working Group B that simulant filled munitions intended for testing chemical weapons destruction procedures should be incorporated into national declarations;[358]

The need for this first recommendation arose because the CWC provides no guidance on the precision required for declarations of quantities of chemical agents and their precursors. The second part of the recommendation was particularly important as, in reality, chemical weapons are filled by volume and not by weight. The precise weight of toxic chemical in a chemical weapon or bulk container is, therefore, frequently, unknown. It was, therefore, accepted that declarations would have to be based on nominal weights and that during destruction this might possibly lead to some accounting problems.

The thinking behind the second recommendation was that, in order for these simulant munitions to serve the purpose for which they were designed, it was necessary for them to have the same dimensional and physical characteristics as real chemical weapons. The principal difference being that they were filled with a simulant rather than a toxic chemical. As a result inspectors visiting these facilities could face difficulties distinguishing these simulant munitions from the real ones and if one was declared and the other was not accounting problems could arise. Interestingly although adopted by the Commission the last recommendation was never adopted by the CSP of the OPCW. As a result those States Parties manufacturing simulant munitions for this purpose did not feel that they had to declare them and this did lead to complications after EIF.

12.1 CW storage locations

The Expert Group also considered the different types of locations where chemical weapons might be stored and made a number of recommendations, on how these should be declared and inspected, that were subsequently approved by the Commission. These recommendations were:

---

[357] Ibid.

[358] 'Report of the Preparatory Commission', PC-IV/23, dated 1 October 1993, para. 6.3.3.

in declaring chemical weapons, all locations must be specified. These locations include CW storage facilities, CW storage facilities at CW destruction facilities and temporary holding areas at CW destruction facilities;

declarations for each chemical weapons storage location and national aggregate declarations should each be submitted as complete documents containing appropriate chemical declaration forms as attachments;

temporary holding areas at chemical weapons destruction facilities be defined as locations within the declared perimeter of a chemical weapons destruction facility and that these holding areas should contain at any time no more than one week's amount of agent or material, based on the declared design capacity of the destruction facility;

CW stored in a temporary holding area at a CW destruction facility would not normally be subject to inspection by a CW storage facility inspection team. These verification activities would be the responsibility of a CW destruction facility inspection team;

CW stored in a CW storage facility at a CW destruction facility should be inspected by CW storage facility inspection teams. Subsequent inspections at these CW storage facilities could be done either by CW storage facility inspection teams or by CW destruction inspection teams as will be agreed in appropriate facility agreements; and

during the transitional period (Verification Annex Part IV (A), paras. 50 and 51), arrangements made between the OPCW and the States Parties for the inspection of CW at chemical weapons destruction facilities should be approved by the Executive Council.[359]

The need for these understandings arises from the fact that different verification regimes apply to CW storage facilities and CW destruction facilities. Once declared, chemical weapons may only be moved from the declared storage site for the purpose of destruction.[360] Unless weapons are being removed for destruction, therefore, the number stored at the site should remain unchanged. The storage sites will, however, still be subject to periodic re-inspection. CW destruction facilities, on the other hand, are subject to the continuous, on-site presence of inspectors during destruction operations.[361] Where the storage facility is at a different location from the destruction facility it is clear which inspection regime should be applied. In situations where they are collocated, however, further clarification was required. In particular it was important to clarify the status of temporary holding areas for chemical weapons at destruction facilities. It must be remembered that the purpose of these inspections was to provide confidence to all States Parties that these weapons were being accounted for and their destruction verified. It should also be noted that in accordance with the CWC the possessor State Party was responsible for the cost of these inspections.[362] It was important to both Russia and the United States to ensure that these costs were kept to a

[359] 'Report of the Commission', PC-V/12, dated 17 December 1993, para. 6.6.

[360] CWC, Article IV, para. 4.

[361] CWC, Verification Annex, Part IV(A), para. 59(b).

[362] CWC, Article IV, para. 16.

minimum. All parties to the discussion, therefore, had a vested interest in reaching a common understanding on these issues.

12.2 Frequency and duration of inspections

The CWC provides guidance on the maximum duration and frequency of inspections at chemical industry facilities. In the case of declared chemical weapons storage facilities, however, no such guidance is provided, other than that they should be subject to periodic re-inspection.[363] The frequency and duration of inspections at chemical weapons related facilities have significant implications for the possessor State Party, as it has to bear the cost of these inspections. The need for some clarification on this issue was recognised by the Signatory States and it was included in the tasks assigned to the Commission in the Paris Resolution. The Commission subsequently requested the CWSF Expert Group to address the issue.

Despite lengthy discussions, however, it proved difficult to reach consensus on this issue. Some delegations took the view that, as this issue was specifically identified in the Paris Resolution, a decision on this issue by the Commission was required. Other delegations held the view that the complexity and risks posed to the CWC by individual facilities might differ considerably and, therefore, it was not desirable to place predetermined limits on the frequency and duration of this type of inspection. Some felt that this was a matter that should be left to the Technical Secretariat who, in their view, would be best placed to assess the risk posed to the CWC by individual facilities.

The discussions were also, once again, complicated by the potential impact of the BDA and the general acceptance, by delegations, that verification by the OPCW would be limited to complimentary monitoring. Under this arrangement it was envisaged that the OPCW would not carry out separate inspections of Russian or US chemical weapons storage facilities but instead one or two OPCW inspectors would accompany the relevant Russian or American inspection team. The frequency and duration of such inspections would, therefore, to some extent, be determined by the partners to the BDA and not solely by the OPCW. There was, of course, the real possibility that another State Party would declare the possession of chemical weapons and this State Party would not be covered by a BDA. In the absence of any firm evidence that this would actually happen, however, it proved difficult to get Signatory States to pay other than lip service to this possibility. These factors not only influenced the discussions on this issue but also played a significant part in discussions on many issues related to the verification of chemical weapons related facilities.

In the end it was agreed to provide some broad guidelines on the frequency and duration of these inspections but leave the final decision on the frequency and duration of inspection to be applied to each site to the OPCW and its Technical Secretariat.

> Once facility declarations have been received by the OPCW, a determination should be made as to which facilities should be inspected first. Once all initial inspections are com-

[363] CWC, Verification Annex, Part IV(A), para. 42.

> plete and facility agreements finalised, the OPCW should then decide on the frequency of inspection of each facility. In determining the frequency of inspections at a particular CW storage facility, due regard should be given to any Executive Council decision to avoid duplication of adequate bilateral or multilateral verification regimes already applied to the facility. Possible criteria that could be used by the Technical Secretariat to determine the priority and frequency of inspection of a CW storage facility are at Appendix B. These criteria are purposely qualitative and do not represent an exhaustive listing. The Group, however, wished to include these criteria, which the Technical Secretariat may, on receipt of declarations and inspection reports, make more quantitative in nature.[364]

This proposal was finally put to the Commission for approval at its July 1994 meeting where it was adopted along with the following further clarification:

> The Commission *noted* that the following criteria used to determine the frequency of inspection of a chemical weapons storage facility (CWSF) should also be considered in deciding the duration of each inspection: agent weight, the number of items, the storage configuration, and the specific types and numbers of these specific types of chemical weapons as defined in Article II, paragraph 1 of the Chemical Weapons Convention (this is without prejudice to the elaboration of a clear understanding of what is considered to be a chemical weapon, in particular in relation to Article II, paragraph 1 (b) and (c)). The duration of the inspection will be facility dependant, negotiated, and included in each facility agreement after the initial inspection. As a general rule, the duration should be between 48 and 168 hours.[365]

The key point here is that the duration of repeat inspections at a given facility will be set down in the facility agreement for that facility. As such the duration will be subject to negotiation and agreement between the OPCW and the State Party concerned.

13. Chemical Weapon Destruction Facilities

The Expert Group on Chemical Weapon Destruction Facilities met for the first time, from 28 June to 2 July 1993, to initiate the discussion of issues relating to the destruction of declared chemical weapons. It met on two further occasions, 29 November to 3 December 1993 and 7 to 11 March 1994, before it was subsumed into the Expert Group on Chemical Weapons Issues. Among the tasks assigned to the Group by Working Group B were the common tasks, namely declaration formats, guideline for inspection activities and model facility agreements and bilateral/multilateral verification procedures. The outcome from the discussion of these tasks has been discussed previously.

In addition the Group was requested to address two further tasks identified in the Paris Resolution. Firstly, to establish deadlines for submission of the detailed facility information specified in Part IV(A), paragraphs 30 to 32 of the Verification Annex for

---

[364] Expert Group on CWSFs, first interim report, para. 9, PC-V/B/WP.13, 26 November 1993.

[365] 'Report of the Commission', PC-VII/8, dated 1 July 1994.

both existing and planned facilities. Secondly, to make recommendations for guidelines for transitional verification arrangements, in accordance with Part IV(A), paragraph 51, of the Verification Annex. Following its first meeting the Group also recommended that Working Group B add the issues identified in Table 2 to its list of tasks.[366]

13.1 Transitional verification arrangements

In order for the Technical Secretariat to be able to draft facility agreements governing on-site verification at CW related sites it will first be necessary for OPCW inspectors to carry out an initial inspection to gather the information necessary to compile the draft agreement. Once drafted, the facility agreement has to be formally agreed by both the State Party concerned and the OPCW. The CWC, therefore, allows a period of 180 days after EIF for the State Party, for the completion of this process.[367] It also recognises that the application of this deadline to CW destruction facilities operational at EIF or which are scheduled to begin operations within one year of EIF for the State Party would be impractical.[368] In this situation the CWC requires that transitional verification arrangements (TVAs) be developed and put in place.[369] Verification activities will then be governed by these arrangements until they are replaced by formal facility agreements. The Expert Group was tasked; first, to make recommendations on deadlines for the submission, by the State Party, of the information required to support the drafting of these TVAs; and secondly, to draw up appropriate guidelines for them.

	Identified Issues
a.	the meaning of 'completeness of destruction for chemicals' / 'destruction end-point'
b.	the precise requirements for the destruction of 'munitions and devices'
c.	the inventorying of chemical agent destroyed
d.	the problem of dèstruction processes that may produce Schedule 2 chemicals

A TVA is primarily meant to provide a provisional basis for the early presence of inspectors at the destruction facility. For original States Parties this transitional period could last for up to 330 days, however, for those States Parties ratifying after EIF it will be shorter. The Group concluded, therefore, given the time constraints, that the TVA should be negotiated from the very beginning in a manner that would enable its smooth transition into a permanent facility agreement within a relatively short period of time. They agreed on deadlines for the submission of the required information and developed appropriate guidelines for the TVAs, which were subsequently approved by the Commission.[370]

---

366 Experts Group on Chemical Weapons Destruction Facilities, 'Initial Report', PC-IV/B/WP.1, dated 9 July 1993.

367 CWC, Verification Annex, Part III, para. 4.

368 CWC, Verification Annex, Part III, para. 6.

369 CWC, Verification Annex, Part IV(A), para. 51.

370 PC-VI/22, 15 April 1994, para. 6.8.

13.2 Destruction criteria and methods

The CWC provides only limited guidance on how chemical weapons are to be destroyed. It simply states that, while it is up to each State Party to determine how it will destroy its chemical weapons, the following processes may not be used: dumping in any body of water, land burial or open pit burning. It also requires that the chemical weapons be destroyed at specifically designated and appropriately designed and equipped facilities.[371] It defines the destruction of a chemical weapon as:

> a process by which the chemicals are converted in an essentially irreversible way to a form unsuitable for the production of chemical weapons, and which in an irreversible manner renders munitions and other devices unusable as such.[372]

The text provides no further guidance on what is or is not an acceptable destruction method nor on what the term 'essentially irreversible' means. The two questions, therefore, were what should be understand by the term 'essentially irreversible' and at what point would the chemical weapon be considered as destroyed and no longer subject to verification – the destruction end-point.

Recognising that all destruction processes may ultimately be reversible, at least in theory, the Expert Group drew up the following qualitative criteria to determine the destruction end-point for toxic chemicals.

i. the reaction products cannot be easily separated; and
ii. the unseparated reaction products cannot be used in the final technological stage to produce chemical weapons; and
iii. the unseparated reaction products cannot be used effectively as a chemical weapon.[373]

The problem with using only qualitative criteria is that it still requires a subjective decision as to whether complete destruction has in fact been achieved. The Group, therefore, attempted to reach agreement on a quantitative figure for the destruction end-point. The difficulty here was that if the limit was set too low it might be impractical, in some plants or processes, to routinely confirm that the required end-point had been achieved. Setting a very low limit could also lead to a significant increase in the costs of destruction. Too high a limit, on the other hand, would have been seen as working against the aims of the Convention.

At that time, the United States had adopted incineration as the process for the destruction of its chemical weapons and was required, under national legislation, to meet destruction efficiency standards of at least 99.9999 percent. The US was, therefore, prepared to accept a maximum limit of one part per million (ppm) for the destruction end-point. There was considerable doubt among the experts present, however,

---

[371] CWC, Verification Annex, Part IV(A), para. 13.

[372] CWC, Verification Annex, Part IV(A), para. 12.

[373] Chairman's Paper, as annexed to the Experts Group on Chemical Weapons Destruction Facilities, 'Initial Report', PC-IV/B/WP.1, dated 9 July 1993, para. 9.

that other, well established, destruction processes, such as chemical neutralisation, could routinely meet such a low target. In addition a number of delegations considered that opting for such a low limit was unnecessary. Russia proposed a limit of 1 percent. They argued that residues containing less than this concentration of toxic chemical posed no military threat and, therefore, no threat to the CWC. They expressed the view that while it might be necessary to achieve lower concentrations to meet local environmental regulations this was a purely a national concern and not the responsibility of the OPCW. Neither of the proposed limits was acceptable to the majority of delegations. A compromise of 100 ppm was put forward but, despite many hours of discussion, consensus on a quantitative figure for the destruction end-point could not be achieved. Agreement was, therefore, limited to the qualitative criteria listed above and the question of deciding on a quantitative measure for the destruction end-point remained an unresolved issue.

For the destruction of munitions and devices the Group recommended that destruction be considered complete if they had been physically damaged (e.g., by being punched, drilled, cut into pieces, crushed or burned) to the extent that they could no longer be used for their designed application. In addition the damage to the munition or device should be readily visible to the inspectors and/or should be a function of a readily monitored process.

13.3 **Verifying the quantity of chemical weapons destroyed**

Determining the precise quantity of toxic chemical being destroyed, either by mass or by volume, during the destruction process could, in many instances, prove to be extremely difficult. In some processes, for example, the weapons may not be drained but simply opened and the chemical agent and munition processed together. Even where munitions are drained the amounts recovered will vary depending on the physical condition of the contents, e.g., agent quality and viscosity.[374] Equally during the actual destruction stage some material will be held up in the system and therefore an accurate mass balance (material balance) may not be achievable.

In accordance with the CWC OPCW inspectors are required to determine the specific type and quantity of chemical weapons being destroyed.[375] The text provides no further clarification as to what, in operational terms, this means. Once again it should be noted that the definition of a chemical weapon includes the toxic chemical, the munition and associated, specifically, designed equipment which may be being destroyed either together or separately. The question, therefore, was how were the OPCW inspectors to determine the quantities of individual components, particularly the toxic chemical, destroyed. While it might be practical for the inspectors to audit the destroyed hardware this approach was, for the reasons given above, not practical for the toxic chemical. Some experts expressed the view that by both monitoring the number

---

[374] R.G. Manley, 'Options for the Destruction of Chemical Weapons and Management of the Associated Risks', in M.A. Mehlman et al. (eds.), *Living in a Chemical World: Framing the Future in Light of the Past*, *Annals of the New York Academy of Science*, Vol. 1076, September 2006, pp. 540-548.

[375] CWC, Verification Annex, Part IV(A), para. 66(c).

of chemical weapons or containers entering the destruction process and the integrity of the destruction facility the spirit of the CWC could be met. The assumption here was that, provided the inspectors could satisfy themselves that once a chemical weapon entered the destruction process neither it nor its components could be removed from the facility without their knowledge, it would be sufficient to monitor the quantity and type of chemical weapons entering the system. It was considered that this should be feasible as, given the need to ensure containment of the toxic components during the destruction process, these facilities are, by there very nature, designed to have a high level of physical integrity. Whilst this approach was never formally adopted by the Commission it subsequently formed the basis for the Technical Secretariat's approach to the problem of verifying the type and quantity of chemical weapons destroyed at CW destruction facilities.

13.4 **Production of Schedule 2 chemicals as a by-product of destruction**

Another issue related to CW destruction and the determination of the destruction end-point was the problem of destruction processes that produced a Schedule 2 chemical as one of the reaction products. For example, the well established process of chemical neutralisation for the destruction of the nerve agent 'Sarin' while eliminating its toxicity does not result in the fracture of the carbon – phosphorus bond present in the molecule. By definition, therefore, the principal reaction product is a Schedule 2B chemical.[376] The key questions, therefore, were at what point is the chemical weapon considered to be destroyed and no longer subject to verification under Article IV and is the CW destruction facility to be considered a Schedule 2 production facility and, therefore, subject to declaration and verification under Article VI. Working Group B was requested to seek an opinion from its Legal Adviser on this issue and did so. The resulting legal opinion, while helping to clarify the matter further, did not provide a definitive solution to it.[377] The general consensus of the Expert Group was that, while under a strict interpretation of the CWC, the destruction facility would be a Schedule 2 production facility, subjecting it to two different verification regimes was difficult to justify. Providing the Schedule 2 chemical was not isolated and either subsequently destroyed or stored at the destruction facility it would pose no real threat to the object and purpose of the CWC and, therefore, only the Article IV verification regime should be applied. It was also considered that a second destruction step to treat the reaction products, including the Schedule 2 chemical, was desirable and likely, in many cases, to be necessary to meet National environmental standards. No consensus on the extent to which the verification regime under Article IV should apply to this second step, however, could be achieved. While, at the time, this lack of agreement was not seen to be a serious problem it did become a significant issue after EIF, when both Russia and the US decided to opt for this type of two stage destruction process for the disposal of some of their CW stockpile.

---

[376] Chemicals listed on Schedule 2B of the Annex on Chemicals to the CWC are considered to be potential precursors for the production of chemical weapons.

[377] Legal Opinion in Regard to Destruction of Chemical Weapons, PC-VI/B/6, 17 January 1994.

13.5 Simulant, training and museum exhibits

Given that an empty chemical munition still meets the CWC's definition of a chemical weapon, a question arose over the status of chemical munitions retained for training purposes and as museum exhibits. The Expert Group noted that, in the case of the former, there will be an ongoing requirement to train explosive ordinance personnel on how to deal with old or abandoned chemical weapons and potential terrorist devices for the foreseeable future. To be effective this training would need to be undertaken on real munitions and devices, albeit filled with a relatively harmless simulant.

The Expert Group concluded that:

> As there are no specific provisions within the text of the Convention covering the destruction of unfilled chemical munitions which a State Party may wish to retain for display or training purposes, it follows that the ordinary provisions for destruction shall apply.
>
> However, a State Party may wish to destroy unfilled chemical munitions using, on a case by case basis, a destruction process that meets the requirements of the Convention but does not preclude their use for either display or training purposes.[378]

In effect the munition or device must be either modified or destroyed to the extent that it no longer meets the definition of a chemical weapon. For a museum exhibit, for example, this could be achieved, without detracting from its value as an exhibit, by milling a slot down the back of the display piece to prevent it being refilled and used. In the case of training munitions the situation was more complex and it will be up to individual States Parties to demonstrate to OPCW inspectors that any such munitions and devices they retain for this purpose no longer meet the definition of a chemical weapon.

The problem of accounting for 'simulant' CW munitions has already been briefly discussed under the paragraphs dealing with the storage of chemical weapons. In order to test and commission new CW destruction plants there will be a need to manufacture large numbers of these munitions during the early years after EIF. In order to be fit for purpose these simulant munitions will need to closely match the physical and dimensional characteristics of a real chemical weapon. The question, therefore, was how could this be achieved without them also meeting the definition of a chemical weapon. Apart from the verification related problems there is the fact that the production of a chemical weapon by a State Party, after EIF, would, itself, be a breach of the CWC. The initial approach, adopted by the PrepCom, to the resolution of this problem was to recommend that they be included in national declarations as simulant munitions.[379] During subsequent discussions, however, those States Parties directly concerned with this issue, opposed their inclusion in national declarations. They took the view that the CWC contained no provision requiring the declaration of munitions

378 Appendix 4 of the Chairman's Paper annexed to the Third Report of the Expert Group on CW Destruction Facilities, PC-VI/B/WP.14, 11 March 1994.

379 'Report of the Preparatory Commission', PC-IV/23, dated 1 October 1993, para. 6.3.3.

that did not meet the definition of a chemical weapon. They argued, correctly, that if simulant munitions were to be classed as chemical weapons then not only would the facilities producing them need to be declared and destroyed but also their production itself would be in contravention of the CWC. Such an interpretation was, therefore, clearly not acceptable. Simulant munitions were, in their view, not chemical weapons and there was no requirement for them to be declared and verified. The issue remained unresolved and it was, once again, left to the States Parties concerned and the OPCW inspectors to sort out, during onsite inspections, after EIF. A decision on this issue was finally adopted, after EIF, at the 4th CSP in July 1999.[380]

13.6 Installed monitoring equipment

The CWC makes provision for the Technical Secretariat to be able to install monitoring equipment at CW destruction facilities for the purpose of assisting its verification activities.[381] The Expert Group was requested to make recommendations on appropriate items of equipment for this purpose for inclusion in the draft list of inspection equipment. This task was more complex than it might, at first, appear. The Group concluded that, while it might be practical to identify general types of equipment that would be suitable for this purpose it was impractical to identify and specify specific items of equipment. As the specific items of equipment needed will be dependent on many factors, including the design of the facility, the material being destroyed, the process being used and the parameters to be measured. The Group also drew attention to the fact that States Parties will, for their own purposes, be installing instrumentation in their destruction facilities and this may be capable of providing, with appropriate certification, much of the verification information required by the Technical Secretariat. Using existing installed equipment, where practicable, would also avoid the health and safety issues that might arise with the installation of OPCW purchased equipment in the facility. The most appropriate solution to the problem would be for the Technical Secretariat, where practicable, to negotiate with the State Party the inclusion of monitoring equipment to support its verification activities during the design and construction phase of a destruction facility.

In the view of the Expert Group the specification of installed monitoring equipment would have to be left until after EIF when the Technical Secretariat would be in a position to determine its actual need and also in a position to negotiate with the States Parties concerned for its installation. The Group, therefore, recommended and the Commission subsequently adopted it, that a line be maintained in the draft budget for the purchase of inspection equipment of this type.[382]

---

380 Simulation equipment, C-IV/DEC.15, 1 July 1999.

381 CWC, Verification Annex, Part III, para. 10.

382 PC-VI/22, dated 15 April 1994, para. 6.8.

14. Chemical Weapon Production Facilities

The Expert Group for CW Production Facilities met for the first time from 16 to 20 August 1993. It also met on two further occasions, from 11 to 15 October 1993 and from 17 to 28 January 1994, before being subsumed into the Expert Group on CW Issues. In addition to the common issues the Expert Group was specifically tasked to address the following two tasks from the Paris Resolution:

> Guidelines for determining the frequency of systematic on-site inspections of chemical weapons production facilities, in accordance with Part V, paragraph 54, of the Verification Annex; and
>
> Criteria for toxicity, corrosiveness and, if applicable, other technical factors, in accordance with Part V, paragraph 71 (b), of the Verification Annex;

In the report of its first meeting the Expert Group identified a number of other issues that, in its view, also needed to be addressed:

(a) Guidelines for closure and inactivation of CW production facilities, in accordance with paragraph 13 of part V;
(b) Permitted maintenance activities at a closed-down chemical weapons production facility;
(c) Risk assessment of the closed-down facility awaiting destruction;
(d) Production capacity as a measure of destruction and related issues such as the concept of levelling out and the agreed residual capacity level at the end of the eighth year after entry into force;
(e) Matters related to temporary conversion of CW production facilities for destruction of chemical weapons;
(f) Matters related to conversion of CW production facilities to purposes not prohibited;
(g) Formats for initial, interim and final inspection reports; and
(h) Inspection equipment and agreed equipment and devices to be installed at CW production facilities.[383]

When examining the work of this Expert Group it is important to note that the primary focus of the Russian/US BDA was the chemical weapon stockpiles and their destruction. Far less attention was paid, in this agreement, to the chemical weapons production facilities and their destruction. As a result the level of agreement between Russia and the United States on issues related to CW production facilities was less well developed and there were a number of areas where major differences between the two parties continued to exist. These differences had a major impact on all the issues under the purview of this Group and meant that it was difficult to achieve progress on many of them. As already discussed, under the section dealing with common issues, these differences resulted in a failure to even agree on a list of inspection activities for

---

[383] Initial Report of the Expert Group on CW Production Facilities, PC-IV/B/WP.9, 20 August 1993.

CW production facilities. A number of the issues considered by the Expert Group are examined in more detail in the following paragraphs.

14.1 Closure or inactivation

The CWC requires that those States Parties that possess CW production facilities shall take action to close them within 90 days of the Convention entering into force for the given State Party.[384] The purpose of this closure is to render the facility inactive. Paragraph 13 of Part V of the Verification Annex lists a number of measures that shall be taken to achieve this closure/inactivation. The Expert Group examined this list and developed appropriate guidelines to supplement it.[385] It also recommended that these should apply irrespective of whether the facility was to be destroyed, temporarily converted to a CW destruction facility or permanently converted for purposes not prohibited by the Convention. The Expert Group further recommended that, in order to ensure the safe conduct of on-site inspections, a State Party should be encouraged to complete the primary decontamination of the CWPF as part of its closure and inactivation measures. It was also understood that some limited decontamination capability might be required after closure and inactivation to ensure the safety of inspectors and personnel. A decontamination capability may also be required to provide safe conditions for dismantling and destroying the plant and to avoid potential environmental contamination. It was also noted that, in connection with these decontamination requirements, a limited amount of safety equipment would be required. The Commission subsequently adopted the above understandings at its Fifth Session.[386]

14.2 Permitted maintenance

Once closed and inactivated, maintenance activities at the production facility shall be limited to that necessary for the purpose of maintaining safety.[387] All planned maintenance activities shall be specified in a States Party's general and detailed plans for destruction and both these and unplanned maintenance activities will be subject to monitoring by the Technical Secretariat.[388] After discussion the Expert Group developed the following illustrative examples of what might be considered as allowable technical maintenance at a closed/inactivated CWPF:

(a) Replacement of light bulbs;
(b) Corrosion protection for structural members;
(c) Repairs to building structures for the safety of inspectors;
(d) Maintenance of communication systems;

---

[384] CWC, Article V, para. 7.

[385] Chart 1 of Appendix 1 of the Chairman's paper annexed to the Interim Report of the Expert Group on CW Production Facilities, PC-V/B/WP.6, 15 October 1993.

[386] 'Report of the Commission', PC-V/12, dated 17 December 1993.

[387] CWC, Verification Annex, Part V, para. 15.

[388] CWC, Verification Annex, Part V, paras. 16 and 17.

(e) Maintenance of safety equipment;
(f) Maintenance of first aid and medical equipment;
(g) Maintenance of heating, ventilation and air conditioning equipment not exclusively related to CW production;
(h) Repairs and maintenance to vessels containing residual CW agent after primary decontamination, waste materials or residual process chemicals necessary to prevent the release of these materials to the environment;
(i) Repairs to access roads; and
(j) Maintenance of utilities (e.g., electricity, potable water) not directly related to CW production.

The Expert Group also developed illustrative examples of non-allowable maintenance activities at a closed/inactivated CWPF:

(a) Repair of process equipment, except to prevent structural failure;
(b) Routine maintenance of process equipment;
(c) Routine maintenance of process equipment controllers;
(d) Upgrading of process equipment control software;
(e) Maintenance of heating, ventilation and air conditioning equipment directly related to CW production; and
(f) Repairs or maintenance to railways previously used to supply raw materials, unfilled CW hardware, etc.[389]

The last item on this second list posed a particular problem for Russia. Most of their CW production facilities were located in the middle of large industrial chemical production facilities containing large numbers of plants producing routine commercial chemicals. These sites often had complex railway systems for the transport of raw materials and products both within the site and to and from it. The closure of the railway line to the CW production facility or the placing of restrictions on its maintenance was, therefore, in some cases, not practicable. Russia, however, were prepared to accept sub-paragraph (f) providing the words '... except maintenance activity necessary for the performance of agreed activities' were added to this sub-paragraph. As, in their view, this would allow them to continue to use and maintain those railway lines necessary to serve the non-CW related production facilities at the site. The Russian proposal was not acceptable to the United States and, as a result, the Commission was unable to adopt the above illustrative lists. This illustrates the level of disagreement between these two states in relation to these facilities and the difficulties faced by them and the Group in reaching a consensus.

14.3 **Risk assessment**

The condition of CW production facilities at EIF will vary considerably and therefore the risk posed to the Convention by each of them will also differ. In general, the better

[389] Paras. 17 and 18 of the Chairman's paper annexed to the Interim Report of the Expert Group on CW Production Facilities, PC-V/B/WP.6, 15 October 1993.

the condition of a CW production facility, the higher the potential risk it will pose to the aims of the Convention. In order to determine which order to inspect the declared CW production facilities and the frequency of re-inspection the Technical Secretariat will need to carry out a risk assessment for each facility. The initial assessment will have to be based on the information provided by a State Party in its initial declaration and then re-evaluated following the initial inspection. To facilitate this process the Expert Group developed the following list of illustrative examples, placed in descending order of risk, of the possible status of declared CW production facilities:

(a) **Operational** – Is capable of start up with minimal time and effort;
(b) **Short Term Standby** – While the facility is not currently operating, it is being maintained for rapid restart. Can be restarted in a relatively short time (2 – 4 weeks) with minimal effort;
(c) **'Moth-balled'** – The facility is being maintained with preventative maintenance being performed. Can be restarted in 1 to 4 months with minimal effort;
(d) **'Closed'** – The facility has been closed with a minimum of maintenance, but is in sound condition. Can be restarted in 8 – 12 months with repairs and replacement of equipment needed;
(e) **Abandoned** – The facility has been abandoned, and is in poor condition. No maintenance work has been performed. Restarting will require major repairs and replacement of equipment. Time to restart will be at least 2 years. In many cases, it will take less time to replace than to repair the facility;
(f) **Converted** – The facility has already been converted for a non-prohibited use in accordance with the appropriate provisions of the Convention; and
(g) **Destroyed** – The facility has been completely destroyed and no longer exists (i.e. all specialised and standard equipment and specialised and standard buildings have been destroyed).[390]

A major factor in the re-assessment of the risk posed by a facility following the initial inspection will be the condition of the facility and the extent of the closure/inactivation measures taken by the State Party. The greater the degree of inactivation, the lower the potential risk of the CWPF to the aims of Convention and, correspondingly, the frequency of future inspection required. The Expert Group recommended that in undertaking the re-assessment the Technical Secretariat will need to take into account factors related to the practical possibility of resuming covert CW production at the CW Production facility without breaking the OPCW installed seals and blind flanges, the time in which such actions would be detected and the quantity and nature of CW that could be produced in the interim. The Group also went on to develop an extensive list of technical factors that might be used by the Technical Secretariat in making its risk assessment.[391]

---

[390] Para. 19 of the Chairman's paper annexed to the Interim Report of the Expert Group on CW Production Facilities, PC-V/B/WP.6, 15 October 1993.

[391] Appendix 3 to the Chairman's paper annexed to the Interim Report of the Expert Group on CW Production Facilities, PC-V/B/WP.6, 15 October 1993.

14.4 **Production capacity**

The CWC requires a State Party to destroy its CW production facilities within 10 years after EIF and that 'production capacity' shall be used as the means of measuring the progress of this destruction process. It also requires that the destruction be carried out at an agreed rate throughout this period to ensure a gradual 'levelling out' of CW production capability within the possessor States Parties.[392] For example, at the end of the eighth year after EIF the maximum permitted residual production capacity for Schedule 1 CWPFs would be 20 percent of the State Party's original declared capacity. The practical questions, therefore, were; what was meant by the term 'production capacity' and how should it be measured?

The Expert Group developed a series of understandings on this issue, including tables setting out the weighting factors to be associated with the destruction of groups of items subject to destruction in manufacturing and/or filling facilities. Weighting factors were provided for the following three types of facility:

a. manufacture and filling have taken place;
b. manufacture only has taken place; and
c. filling only has taken place.[393]

The Group also recommended that the Technical Secretariat should be responsible for verifying which of the items have been destroyed and that their destruction is complete. In situations where a State Party is unable to achieve the percentages set down in these understandings then the Director-General of the Technical Secretariat shall seek clarification from the State Party on this issue and, if appropriate, inform the Executive Council, without delay.[394]

14.5 **Conversion – temporary**

One approach to the destruction of chemical weapons is to convert a CW production facility to a CW destruction facility. There are a number of advantages in doing this as much of the supporting infrastructure necessary for the production of chemical weapons is also required for their safe destruction. Using the existing infrastructure means that the cost and timeframe necessary to convert such a facility can be significantly less than that required for building a new destruction facility. The CWC, therefore, includes provisions for a State Party to temporarily convert a CW production facility to a destruction facility for this purpose.[395] It also lays down a number of conditions, the most important being that the facility must be destroyed either at the end of the destruction process or within 10 years after EIF, whichever comes first.

---

392 CWC, Verification Annex, Part V, para. 30.

393 Destruction of CW Production Facilities, annexed to the Fifth Report of the Expert Group on CW Issues, PC-XIV/B/WP.2, 2 May 1996.

394 CWC, Verification Annex, Part II, paras. 64 and 65.

395 CWC, Article V, para. 12.

The Expert Group considered the issue of temporary conversion of a CW production facility to a CW destruction facility and developed a list of ten understandings.[396] It recommended and the Commission subsequently adopted that any temporary conversion of such a facility should be governed by these understandings. Within this list it specifically recommended that, in the absence of clear provisions within the Convention concerning the precise contents of a request for temporary conversion, the following information shall be provided by the State Party:

3.3.1 the name, address, and precise location of the facility;
3.3.2 a site diagram indicating all the structures and areas that will be involved in the destruction of chemical weapons and which also identifies all structures of the chemical weapons production facility that is to be temporarily converted;
3.3.3 the types of chemical weapons, and the type and quantity of chemical fill to be destroyed at the temporarily converted facility;
3.3.4 the destruction method(s);
3.3.5 a process flow diagram indicating which parts of the production process and which items of specialised equipment will be converted for the destruction of chemical weapons;
3.3.6 the seals and inspection equipment potentially affected by the conversion; and
3.3.7 a schedule identifying the time allocated to each of the following operations;
(a) process design,
(b) temporary conversion of the facility,
(c) installation of equipment,
(d) process commissioning,
(e) chemical weapon destruction operations,
(f) closure.

14.6 Conversion

The CWC normally requires that a State Party completely destroy its CW production facilities and all related facilities and equipment within the timeframes set down in the Convention.[397] In exceptional cases of compelling need, however, it also permits a State Party to seek permission to permanently convert a CW production facility for purposes not prohibited under the Convention.[398] The granting of permission to do this is not automatic and rests solely with the Conference of the States Parties who will determine each request on its own merit. It should be noted that the CWC provides no further clarification on what, in practical terms, is meant by the phrase '... exceptional cases of compelling need'.

Where a request for 'conversion' is granted the CWC stipulates that:

> The chemical weapons production facility shall be converted in such a manner that the converted facility is not more capable of being reconverted into a chemical weapons pro-

[396] Expert Group on Chemical Weapons and Associated Issues, 'Report', PC-VII/B/WP.9, dated 3 June 1994, paras. 3.2 to 3.11.

[397] CWC, Article V, para. 8.

[398] CWC, Article V, para. 13.

> duction facility than any other facility used for industrial, agricultural, research, medical, pharmaceutical or other peaceful purposes not involving chemicals listed in Schedule 1.[399]

In other words the converted facility shall pose no more risk to the CWC than a normal commercial chemical plant built to prevailing chemical industry standards. The immediate question is what standards, those of the State Party seeking 'conversion' or some other agreed international standard. This point was considered to be particular important as there were major differences in the levels of technology and sophistication being used by the chemical industries of the Signatory States. Additional guidance on the limitations on the use of a converted facility is provided in Part V of the Verification Annex:

> A converted facility shall not be used:
>
> (a) For any activity involving production, processing, or consumption of a Schedule 1 chemical or a Schedule 2 chemical; or
> (b) For the production of any highly toxic chemical, including any highly toxic organophosphorus chemical, or for any other activity that would require special equipment for handling highly toxic or highly corrosive chemicals, unless the Executive Council decides that such production or activity would pose no risk to the object and purpose of this Convention, taking into account criteria for toxicity, corrosiveness and, if applicable, other technical factors, to be considered and approved by the Conference pursuant to Article VIII, paragraph 21 (i).[400]

Once again the task of defining the criteria for toxicity, corrosiveness and, if applicable, other technical factors was left to the PrepCom to resolve and make recommendations to the first CSP. There are a number of further examples of where the practical aspects of dealing with the proposed permanent 'conversion' of CW production facility are by no means clear. For example, what buildings must be destroyed or at least modified and what could be retained. In the definition of specialised equipment what, precisely, was meant by the phrase:

> equipment specially designed, built or installed for the operation of the facility as a chemical weapons production facility, as distinct from a facility constructed according to prevailing commercial chemical industry standards for facilities not producing any chemical referred to in paragraph 8(a)(i) of Article II of the Convention, or for corrosive chemicals.[401]

The 'conversion' issue was, therefore, wide open to debate.

Another key factor in this debate was that the majority of those countries participating in the negotiation of the CWC and subsequently in its PrepCom saw destruction as being the norm with 'conversion' being an abnormal and exceptional event.

399 CWC, Article V, para. 14.
400 CWC, Verification Annex, Part V, para. 71.
401 CWC, Verification Annex, Part I, para. 5(a)(iii).

This, however, was not the view held by the Soviet Union or its successor Russia who saw 'conversion' of some or even all of its facilities as an economic necessity. The issue of 'conversion' therefore provoked considerable discussion both within the Expert Group and within the Commission itself.

Despite many hours of discussion within the Expert Group and the submission of papers on the subject by China, Iran, Russia, the United States and the Chairman of the Group, no agreement could be reached on the issue of 'conversion'. It was, therefore, passed forward, by the Commission, to the first CSP as one of the major unresolved issues. At its last meeting, during the closing days of the PrepCom, the Group, however, did manage to reach agreement on an understanding with respect to the issue of the 'development of criteria for toxicity, corrosiveness, etc. ...' and recommended this to the Commission for adoption.[402]

15. Old and Abandoned Chemical Weapons

The Expert Group on old and abandoned CW met for the first time from 22-26 November 1993 and continued to meet at regular intervals throughout the life of the PrepCom. In addition to the common issues addressed previously it mainly focused its attention on the following three issues; the verification regime to be applied to old chemical weapons (OCW), the verification regime to be applied to abandoned chemical weapons (ACW) and the question of 'usability'.

15.1 **Verification regime for old chemical weapons**

As stated previously, while OCW manufactured before 1925 must be declared and will be subject to an initial inspection by the Technical Secretariat to confirm the declaration, their subsequent destruction will not be subject to on-site verification. The CWC requires that a State Party shall treat these items as toxic waste and shall inform the Technical Secretariat of the steps taken to destroy them in accordance with its national legislation.[403] The issue for the Expert Group was the extent to which the verification requirements set out in Part IV(A) of the Verification Annex should be applied to chemical weapons manufactured between 1925 and 1946 and determined to be no longer usable as chemical weapons. The determining factor here was the interpretation to be placed on the following paragraph contained in Part IV(B) of the Verification Annex:

> Subject to paragraphs 3 to 5, a State Party shall destroy old chemical weapons that have been confirmed by the Technical Secretariat as meeting the definition in Article II, paragraph 5 (b), *in accordance with Article IV and Part IV (A) of this Annex.* Upon request of a State Party, the Executive Council may, however, modify the provisions on time-limit

[402] Annex 1 to the Second Report of the Expert Group 2 on Chemical Weapons Issues, PC-XVI/B/WP.5, 13 February 1997.

[403] CWC, Verification Annex, Part IV(B), para. 6.

> and order of destruction of these chemical weapons, if it determines that doing so would not pose a risk to the object and purpose of this Convention. The request shall contain specific proposals for modification of the provisions and a detailed explanation of the reasons for the proposed modification.[404] [emphasis added]

One interpretation of this phrase would require the application of not only the destruction obligations, but also the verification provisions under Part IV(A) to OCW produced between 1925 and 1946. Perhaps with some flexibility in regard to the number of inspectors participating in such inspections, as agreed between the inspected State Party and the Technical Secretariat. An alternative interpretation, however, foresaw a more flexible verification regime. One dependant on the risk assessment posed by the weapons that would neither apply, universally, the timing requirements for initial inspections as foreseen under Part IV(A) nor the requirement for the verification of destruction of OCW through continuous on-site monitoring with instruments and the physical presence of inspectors. The basis for this latter approach was that OCW were, by definition, no longer usable as chemical weapons and this implied that the drafters of the Convention recognised that they could be considered to pose a reduced risk to its object and purpose.

In the absence of any agreement on this issue the Expert Group sought a Legal Opinion on the interpretation of this paragraph. In summary the Legal Officer's opinion was as follows:

> Once the Technical Secretariat has determined that old chemical weapons produced between 1925-1946 can no longer be used as chemical weapons, it seems to the Legal Adviser that the general purpose criterion of not posing a risk to the object and purpose of the Convention would be satisfied if States Parties conferred on the OPCW enough flexibility to adapt the provisions under Part IV(A) to a variety of situations.[405]

This supported the view that the extent to which the verification requirements of Part IV(A) should be applied to OCW should be based on the assessed risk that they posed to the CWC. The Legal Opinion, however, was not universally accepted and discussion on this issue continued until the end of the PrepCom. While the Commission was never able to reach consensus on this issue the Legal Opinion did become the basis for the approach to the verification of OCW adopted by the Technical Secretariat after EIF.

15.2 Verification regime for abandoned CW

The principal protagonists in the debate on this occasion were of course China and Japan. As explained earlier these two countries had a major influence on the drafting of this part of the CWC. Once again the debate was over the extent to which the verification requirements of Part IV(A) should be applied to ACW. The issue here,

---

404 CWC, Verification Annex, Part IV(B), para. 7.

405 Legal Opinion in regard to the scope of para. 7, Part IV(B) of the Annex on Implementation and Verification concerning old chemical weapons, PC-VI/B/1, 14 January 1994.

however, was complicated by the fact that, in accordance with the CWC's definition, ACW may include either OCW manufactured between 1925 and 1946 or more modern chemical weapons.[406] Whilst, at first sight, it might be assumed that abandoned chemical weapons would be subject to the full destruction and verification requirements of Part IV(A) and the destruction of abandoned OCW treated in the same manner as that to be applied to OCW, consensus on adopting this approach could not be achieved within the Expert Group.

The situation was further complicated by the fact that, in this case, two State Parties are involved, namely, the Territorial State Party (TSP) and the Abandoning State Party (ASP). The CWC requires both these parties to agree on a plan for the destruction of the ACW. The ASP shall provide all necessary financial, technical expertise as well as other resources and the TSP shall provide appropriate cooperation.[407] Where the two State Parties have concluded an agreement for the destruction of the ACW the Executive Council may, in certain circumstances, decide that this agreement take precedence over the provisions of Part IV(B).[408] The issue of the verification regime to be applied and who would be primarily responsible for its application was, therefore, by no means straightforward and, despite many hours of discussion, the PrepCom could reach no agreement on this issue.

15.3 **Usability**

An even more difficult issue was determining the criteria to be used to decide that a chemical weapon produced between 1925 and 1946 was no longer usable as a chemical weapon.[409] The definition of a chemical weapon in the CWC, itself, added to the problems associated with resolution of this issue. The definition is made up of three parts, the toxic chemical, the munition or device used to deliver it and any equipment specifically designed for use with these munitions and devices. It further states that any of these parts, whether taken together or separately, constitute a chemical weapon.[410] What this means, in effect, is that when deciding whether a chemical weapon is no longer useable it is necessary to take into consideration the condition of both the munition and its chemical fill.

While it was relatively easy to draw up a list of characteristics that would enable OPCW inspectors to determine whether a munition was useable or not the situation with respect to the chemical fill was much more complex. Even assuming that agreement could be reached on what constituted an 'unuseable' chemical fill the practical difficulties and hazards involved in determining the status of the fill in a chemical weapon of this age are such that its application would, more often and than not, prove impractical. In many cases the current state of chemical weapons manufactured between 1925 and 1946 is such the even the identity of the chemical fill, let alone its condition, is unknown.

406 CWC, Article II, para. 6.
407 CWC, Verification Annex, Part IV(B), para. 15.
408 CWC, Verification Annex, Part IV(B), para. 18.
409 CWC, Article II, para. 5.
410 CWC, Article II, para. 1.

Despite numerous attempts to reach agreement on appropriate criteria for determining the 'useability' of chemical weapons produced between 1925 and 1946 no consensus could be reached and this situation remains the same almost ten years after EIF. In practice States Parties have used their own judgement when declaring chemical weapons as meeting the definition of OCW. OPCW inspectors, in their turn, have used the criteria set down in the inspection manual, which are based on the discussions of the Expert Group, coupled with their experience to assess these declarations. To date States Parties have tacitly accepted this approach.

16. Article IV and V Verification Costs

In accordance with the CWC each State Party is required to bear the cost of destroying any chemical weapons and CW production facilities that it owns or possesses and, unless the Executive Council decides otherwise, the costs of the verification of the storage and destruction of these weapons and production facilities.[411, 412] The CWC, however, makes no attempt to define what is or is not a verification cost. The Expert Group on Chemical Weapons Issues was, therefore, tasked to make recommendations on this issue.

Some members of the Group took the view that these verification costs should be limited to those inspection costs listed in paragraph 26 of Part II of the Verification Annex for which, in other circumstances, the State Party could seek reimbursement. For example, in-country transportation, lodging, meals, medical care, etc. Most delegations, however, took the view that this was far too narrow an interpretation and that, in addition to the in-country costs, other costs such as international travel, inspectors salaries and a proportion of the relevant overhead costs of the Verification Division and the Inspectorate should be included. In order to facilitate the discussion the Technical Secretariat produced a list of all possible verification costs and members of the Group were invited to divide them into two columns those to be paid for by the State Party and those to be born by the Organisation. While there was general agreement that all in-country costs and the cost of international travel should be born by the State Party no agreement on who should cover the relevant proportion of the inspectors salaries and overhead costs could be achieved.

It is also important to note that, at this time, the expectation was that, due to the existence of the BDA, verification by the Technical Secretariat of Russian and US chemical weapons and associated production facilities would be limited to complimentary monitoring. The significance of this was that the CWC also states that where the Executive Council opts for complimentary monitoring the relevant costs of this monitoring shall be born by the Organisation.[413] The assumption at the time, therefore, was that any decision on verification costs would not apply to either Russia or the United States but only to some, hypothetical, third party or parties. Therefore,

---

[411] CWC, Article IV, para. 16.

[412] CWC, Article V, para. 19.

[413] CWC, Article IV, para. 16.

despite the fact that the Commission had flagged this as an important issue the pressure to achieve consensus within the Group was largely absent. This situation was to change dramatically after EIF when, due to changing circumstances, there was an urgent need to resolve this issue. Even with this increased pressure, however, agreement was not finally reached until the 3rd CSP, which took place in November 1998.[414]

There was also some debate as to whether the requirement to bear the cost of verification also applied to old and abandoned chemical weapons and the issue was briefly discussed by the Expert Group on Old and Abandoned CW. A number of the delegations faced with the problem of dealing with these weapons took the view that, in accordance with the first paragraph of Article IV of the CWC, as reproduced below, these weapons were exempt from the impact of paragraph 16 of Article IV and, therefore, any verification costs should be born by the Organisation.

> The provisions of this Article and the detailed procedures for its implementation shall apply to all chemical weapons owned or possessed by a State Party, or that are located in any place under its jurisdiction or control, except old chemical weapons and abandoned chemical weapons to which Part IV (B) of the Verification Annex applies.[415]

A number of delegations, however, did not agree with this interpretation and so the issue remained unresolved and open for discussion for a number of years after EIF.

17. The End Game

On the 31 October 1996 Hungary became the 65th State to deposit its ratification of the CWC thereby automatically triggering entry into force of the CWC 180 days later on the 29 April 1997. The passing the trigger point dramatically increased the pressure on the PrepCom to complete its work and discussion on all the outstanding issues intensified. In theory this should have led to significant progress being made on the unresolved issues related to Articles III, IV and V. In reality this simply did not happen. The primary reason for this was that neither of the two known 'possessor states' – Russia and the United States – had ratified the Convention at this point and it was not at all clear that either of them would do so before EIF. As a result there was little willingness among the delegations to compromise and virtually no progress was made on the unresolved issues relating to the Articles during this last six months in the life of the PrepCom.

In its final report the Commission listed those Article III, IV and V related issues that had been resolved and recommended them to the first CSP for adoption.[416] In this report it also provided the CSP with a list of unresolved issues. While this latter list

[414] Costs of Verification under Articles IV and V, C-III/DEC.8, 17 November 1998.

[415] CWC, Article IV, para. 1.

[416] 'Final Report of the Preparatory Commission for the Organisation for the Prohibition of Chemical Weapons to the First Session of the Conference of the States Parties of the Organisation for the Prohibition of Chemical Weapons and to the First Meeting of the Executive Council of the Organisation for the Prohibition of Chemical Weapons', PC-XVI/37, dated 15 April 1997.

was extensive it should be noted that many of them, such as the model facility agreements for CW related facilities, for example, were in fact well developed and close to resolution. A number of them were simply being held hostage by individual delegations or small groups of delegations in order to put pressure on other delegations to agree to unresolved issues which were of particular concern to them. In order to facilitate the future work of the OPCW on these outstanding issues the PrepCom also provided the CSP with an extensive list of those national papers and non-papers related to the unresolved issues.[417]

It should also be remembered that discussions during the PrepCom were held in a somewhat sterile environment. The CWC was not in force, there was no OPCW and no declarations were being made or inspections taking place. Also many Member States had no experience of on-site inspections and, therefore, no knowledge of what, in practical terms, an inspection would involve. In respect to Article III, IV and V issues the situation was further complicated by the fact that only a few Member States had any hands on experience of dealing with chemical weapons and their associated production facilities. In the absence of such knowledge and experience it was often extremely difficult for them to join consensus on the, often, highly technical issues related to the implementation of Articles III, IV and V.

Therefore, whilst it is true that the PrepCom failed to fully resolve a number of the Article III, IV and V issues identified in the Paris Resolution much was, nevertheless, achieved. A considerable amount of groundwork was put in place and this, subsequently, formed the basis for the successful development of the Organisation after EIF.

18. Post EIF Realism

Entry into Force of the CWC on 29 April 1997 was marked by a number of important events. In respect to Articles III, IV and V four were of particular significance. The first was the ratification of the CWC by the United States, on the 25 April 1997, four days before EIF. The second was the failure of Russia to ratify the CWC by EIF. Russia did not deposit its ratification until 5 November 1997, around six months after EIF. The third issue, linked to this, was a decision by Russia not to ratify the BDA but instead to opt, after ratification of the CWC, for verification of its chemical weapons and related facilities by the OPCW. The last issue was the declaration by two States Parties – India and one other, who opted not to be named publicly – that they also possessed chemical weapons stockpiles and associated facilities. This meant that with the United States there were three CW possessor states at EIF.

It should be remembered that the assumption, throughout the life of the PrepCom, was that only Russia, the United States and, a token one other State would declare as 'possessor states'. More important was the further assumption that verification of Russia and United States stockpiles and their associated facilities would be under-

[417] List of Associated Papers to Unresolved Issues, PC-XVI/39, 5 May 1997 and Addendum 1, 14 May 1997 and Addendum 2, 21 May 1997.

taken in accordance with the BDA and that verification by the OPCW would be limited to complimentary monitoring. The situation faced by the OPCW immediately after EIF was, therefore, very different from that envisaged by the PrepCom and this had a major impact on the work of the OPCW and in particular its Technical Secretariat during the first year after EIF. Details of this impact are discussed elsewhere in this book but for completeness it is perhaps worth looking at one specific issue, the question of 'Conversion'.

As discussed previously it was not possible to reach consensus on the practical aspects of dealing with requests to permanently convert a CW production facility for purposes not prohibited by this Convention. In particular it was not possible to agree on what was precisely meant by the phrase 'in exceptional cases of compelling need'. This was a classic example of the problems that arose in the PrepCom with trying to reach consensus on issues for which there were no practical examples on which delegations could base their judgement. After EIF of course the situation was very different and, much to everyone's surprise, the United States submitted the first request for 'conversion' of a CW production facility, as part of its initial declaration, 30 days after EIF.

The request related to its Marquardt facility, located in Van Nuys, California. In its request the US stated that between February 1992 and February 1994, it had undertaken the elimination of the chemical weapons production capability from this facility. All specialised equipment and specialised building features used for the delivery and filling of binary components, as well as all specialised equipment used for chemical weapons production, had been inactivated and removed. A number of buildings, however, remained at the site and were now used for commercial purposes unrelated to the CWC, for example, the production of commercial aircraft parts, the production of motion pictures and television programmes, and warehousing. In order to avoid having to destroy these building the US sought formal approval for the 'conversion' of this facility in accordance with the provisions of the CWC.

In the view of many delegations the US request was clearly based solely on economic grounds and, therefore, in agreeing to it they were accepting that the phrase 'in exceptional cases of compelling need' included purely economic reasons. This view was endorsed by the second request for 'conversion' of a CW production facility, which was submitted by the United Kingdom on the 10 October 1997.

The UK stated, in its request, that all specialised buildings and equipment at its CW production facility at Nancekuke in Cornwall had been destroyed in 1980. The remaining nine standard buildings – some predating the site's role as a CWPF – had been retained and refurbished to support the use of the site by its new occupants, the Royal Air Force, as a radar station. In the words of the UK request 'there were strong economic considerations to retain the buildings due to their accommodations, basic wiring, plumbing and heating systems'.[418]

The approval of these two requests opened the way for Russia to, subsequently, seek and gain approval to convert a number of its CW production facilities on primarily economic grounds. Without the earlier requests it would have had great difficulty

---

[418] Report by the Director-General, EC-VI/DG.6*, dated 29 October 1997.

justifying its position that phrase 'in exceptional cases of compelling need' included economic reasons.

Many of the other unresolved Article IV and V issues from the PrepCom were either resolved or, in some cases, simply went away once practical examples of their potential impact on the CWC and its implementation became available and States Parties were better able to understand the implications of their decisions.

Chapter 9

KEEPING PEACEFUL USES PEACEFUL: ARTICLE VI

Daniel Feakes

1. INTRODUCTION

As a former OPCW Director of Verification notes: 'The concept of verifying the civilian chemical industry, and in particular of allowing teams of international inspectors to carry out on-site inspections of civilian chemical industrial facilities of the States Parties was quite unprecedented'.[419] However, this is necessary because the CWC addresses a problem of which one of the key aspects is the dual-use nature of the materials and equipment covered; they have legitimate peaceful purposes, but they can also be used for the illicit production of chemical weapons. For example, chlorine was used as a chemical weapon during the First World War but it is also widely used in modern day chemical industry. Similarly, thiodiglycol is a precursor for mustard gas but is also used in felt tip pen ink. Many of the processes used in the production of a large number of legitimate commercial chemicals, such as esterification, condensation, chlorination and fluorination, are the same processes required to produce chemical warfare agents.[420]

In addition, parts of the chemical industry have historically played a major role in producing chemical weapons. Indeed the massive use of chemical weapons during the First World War was only possible due to the rapid growth of the chemical industry in Europe in the late 19th and early 20th centuries. Most chemical which can be used as weapons have their origins not within the military establishment, but within civilian industry. Even in the 1980s, chemical industry was supplying precursor chemicals, either wittingly or unwittingly, to chemical weapons programmes in the USA, the USSR and Iraq. In a paper submitted to the OPCW Conference of the States Parties in 1999, Australia used recent examples to demonstrate why verification of the chemical industry was relevant to preventing chemical proliferation:

> In considering the risk to the object and purpose of the Convention posed by the various types of industry facilities, it is useful to consider recent trends in chemical weapons

[419] Ron Manley, 'Declaration and verification of the global chemical industry', *OPCW Synthesis* (Autumn/November 2000), pp. 19-21, p. 19.

[420] Robert Mathews, 'Verification of chemical industry under the Chemical Weapons Convention', in JB Poole and R Guthrie (eds.), *Verification 1993: Arms Control, Peacekeeping and the Environment* (London, VERTIC/Brassey's 1993), pp. 41-54 at p. 41.

(CW) proliferation. When Iraq began its CW production program, it was able to obtain some chemicals, including Schedule 2 precursor chemicals such as thiodiglycol and dimethyl methylphosphonate, on the international chemical market. However, Iraq also purchased DOC production facilities (typically pesticide production plants) and used these for domestic production of CW agents. In the late 1980s, when it became more difficult for Iraq to import chemicals relevant to CW production, Iraq started developing Schedule 3 facilities (producing, inter alia, thionyl chloride, phosphorus trichloride and trimethyl phosphite) to supply the precursors required for its weapons program. We understand that other countries of CW proliferation concern have followed a similar pattern, developing apparently legitimate Schedule 3 and DOC production facilities and then diverting the output to CW programs.[421]

2. The Involvement of the Chemical Industry in the CWC Negotiations

2.1 **Why did industry get involved?**

The involvement of the chemical industry has been recognised as a key factor in the successful negotiation of the CWC. While the actual discussions and negotiations in Geneva were conducted by diplomats and government scientific advisers, representatives of the chemical industry had significant input into the process, both nationally in capitals and internationally in Geneva. But the constructive involvement of the chemical industry was not a given. Relations between government and the chemical industry were antagonistic in many countries during the 1970s and 1980s as governments imposed increasingly stringent safety and environmental regulations on the industry, notably following the release of dangerous chemicals in Seveso and Bhopal. In addition, chemical weapons were seen as a 'niche' problem largely unconnected to the chemical industry and one to which it had few resources to direct. However, this situation changed during the 1980s with the growing realisation that governments were committed to negotiating a comprehensive convention against chemical weapons which would impact on the chemical industry and the confirmation that chemical weapons were a real security threat through their use by Iraq against Iran and attempts at their acquisition by Libya.[422]

The Iraq and Libya cases had a profound effect on the chemical industry's attitude towards the negotiations because, contrary to initial media reporting that Iraq's chemical weapons had been supplied by the USSR,[423] it turned out that a significant proportion of the precursor chemicals and production equipment had been supplied from open commercial sources. Western industry and Japan were keen to take measures to pre-

[421] Australia, 'Non-paper. Chemical Weapons Convention (CWC) industry verification: Inspections of Schedule 3 and Discrete Organic Chemical (DOC) facilities', C-IV/NAT.7, dated 24 June 1999.

[422] Kenneth Timmerman, *The Death Lobby: How the West Armed Iraq* (London, Fourth Estate 1992); Thomas Wiegele, *The Clandestine Building of Libya's Chemical Weapons Factory. A Study in International Collusion* (Carbondale and Edwardsville, Southern Illinois University Press 1992).

[423] Derek Wood, *Jane's Defence Weekly*, 31 March 1984, 'Gulf chemicals could be Soviet'; Christopher Walker (from Aqaba), *The Times* (London), 4 April 1984, pp. 1 and 30, 'Russians pour in Iraqi war supplies'.

clude a public relations disaster and portray chemical industry in a better light. During this time frame surveys in the US showed that the image of the chemical industry ranked below that of the tobacco industry and it not only wanted to preclude a PR black eye, but wanted to show the US population that it was proactive in relation to a noble cause. This factor was apparent from a very early stage; in 1984 a US State Department official testified to Congress that chemical companies 'do not want a situation where the whole industry is given a black eye because of the use of chemical weapons. So they have an interest in stopping this practice and stopping any possibility that their good profession and good name is tarnished'.[424] While the chemical industry was already supportive of a chemical weapons convention before these events, they served to increase its desire to become involved in the negotiations and to declare its strong support for a total ban on chemical weapons. As the verification of the chemical industry became a major issue in Geneva in the mid-1980s, so chemical industry involvement increased. Whereas earlier government-industry interaction had been largely passive with governments seeking technical advice from industry, during the 1980s industry adopted a more proactive role actually lobbying the negotiators and tabling its own proposals at a national and at an international level.

2.2 The mechanics of interaction

On a national level, chemical industries had frequent contacts with their own governments. One of the earliest national chemical industries to turn its attention to the chemical weapons negotiations was the American. Representatives of the US Manufacturing Chemists Association (MCA, later renamed the Chemical Manufacturers' Association (CMA), now the American Chemistry Council (ACC)) and the Arms Control and Disarmament Agency (ACDA) first met to discuss the CWC in 1978 and an informal dialogue was initiated the following year.[425] From the mid-1980s the Chemical Manufacturers Association set up a Chemical Weapons Disarmament Workgroup which met every month and included a session with government officials. Similarly in the UK, government and the chemical industry came together from the mid-1980s onwards to discuss the projected CWC in the Government-Industry Working Group. Writing about the US, one industry participant in the process noted 'this informal private-public partnership is unparalleled in US arms-control experience'.[426] Similar

[424] Ambassador Adelman, Joint Hearing before the Committee on Foreign Relations and the Subcommittee on Energy, Nuclear Proliferation and Government Processes of the Committee on Governmental Affairs, US Senate [98th Congress, 2nd session], 28 June 1984, *Chemical Warfare: Arms Control and Nonproliferation*, S. HRG. 98-1044.

[425] This dialogue benefited from an amazing continuity in that the CMA and ACDA were represented by the same two individuals (Will Carpenter and Robert Mikulak respectively) throughout this entire period. Indeed, on 8 February 1992 the American Association for the Advancement of Science recognised their efforts by jointly awarding them the Hilliard Roderick Prize in Science, Arms Control and International Security for 'their tireless efforts to overcome the technical and diplomatic obstacles to international agreements on chemical weapons'.

[426] Kyle Olson, 'Disarmament and the chemical industry', in Brad Roberts (ed.), *Chemical Disarmament and US Security* (Washington, DC, Center for Strategic and International Studies/Westview Press 1992), pp. 97-105, p. 98.

government-industry consultative mechanisms were set up in many other countries to the mutual advantage of both sides. Governments received technical advice from industry and a deeper understanding of its concerns, while industry gained a better appreciation of the limitations imposed on governments by the consensual nature of multilateral diplomacy. In addition, some of the national and international chemical industry associations conferred periodically. Prominent among these were the Chemical Industry Association (CIA) in the UK, CEFIC, the Western European association representing EU members, CMA from the US, the Canadian Chemical Producers Association (CCPA) and the Japan Chemical Industry Association (JCIA). A practical outcome of these contacts was the various national trial inspections which many states conducted in their chemical industries, following earlier trials by Australia[427] and the Netherlands[428] in 1986 and a SIPRI-Pugwash conference on the subject in 1985.[429] Altogether over 60 of these national (and some multinational) trial inspections were conducted between 1988 and 1992, the majority of which were trial routine inspections under the draft treaty's regime for Schedule 2 chemicals.[430] One of the first seminars organised in The Hague after the CWC was opened for signature focused on the national and multinational trial inspections and acted as a forum to apply the lessons learned and share experiences of past trial inspections.[431]

At the international level, the chemical industry focused its attention on Geneva as the location of the CWC negotiations. In July 1987, some 60 chemical industry representatives from 32 countries met in Geneva, firstly among themselves, then informally with CWC negotiators. Such meetings became regular occurrences in Geneva as the negotiations progressed. Indeed, the chemical industry formed an international coalition the more effectively to get its message across in Geneva. The main participants in this coalition were the chemical industries of Western Europe (organised under the umbrella of CEFIC, the European Chemical Industry Council), Japan (the Japan Chemical Industry Association), Canada (the Canadian Chemical Producers Association), Australia (the Australian Chemical Industry Council), and the US (the Chemical Manufacturers Association). The industry associations also operated together through the International Council of Chemical Associations. It took the chemical industry time to learn how to interact constructively with the Geneva negotiations. For example, a letter from CEFIC in December 1987 which expressed the association's 'strong reservations' about the draft schedules of chemicals and stated that proposals for a 'Schedule 4' were 'not only unacceptable but also unworkable', was not well

---

427 Australia, 'Verification of non-production of chemical weapons and their precursors by the civilian chemical industry: Trial inspection of an Australian chemical facility', CD/698, dated 4 June 1986.

428 Netherlands, 'Verification of non-production of chemical weapons', CD/706, dated 20 June 1986.

429 SIPRI, *The Chemical Industry and the Projected Chemical Weapons Convention: Proceedings of a SIPRI/Pugwash Conference*, SIPRI Chemical and Biological Warfare Studies Nos. 4 and 5 (Oxford, Oxford University Press 1986).

430 Ralf Trapp, *Verification Under the Chemical Weapons Convention: On-Site Inspection in Chemical Industry Facilities*, SIPRI Chemical and Biological Warfare Studies No. 14 (Oxford, Oxford University Press 1993), pp. 110-111.

431 Provisional Technical Secretariat, Occasional Paper No. 1, 'Seminar on national trial inspections, 2 October 1993, The Hague, Summary of Proceedings'.

received by CD delegates.[432] During meetings in New York in October 1988, industry put forward proposals that failed to acknowledge the linkages between various provisions within the rolling text and which were misinterpreted as obstructionist by delegates.[433] However, things improved and large meetings between chemical industry representatives and CD delegates were held in Geneva in July 1987 and July 1988. This interaction culminated in the 1989 Government-Industry Conference Against Chemical Weapons in Canberra at which about 95 percent of the world's chemical production capacity was estimated to have been represented. Further meetings between industry representatives and CD delegates were held in Geneva in 1990 and 1991. The interaction was a two-way process as well, with some countries using their chemical industry associations to get more pragmatic provisions inserted into the draft text. From being passive providers of technical advice to national delegations in the beginning, by 1988 the chemical industry had become a key contributor to their eventual successful conclusion.

In Canberra from 19 to 22 September 1989, 375 delegates from 66 countries and four international organizations participated in the Government-Industry Conference against Chemical Weapons (GICCW). About half of the delegations included representatives of national chemical industries, these accounting for about 20 percent of the participation; and many delegations also included representatives of trades unions and of industrial and trade departments of government. It is said that about 95 percent of the world's chemical production capacity was represented.

The industry participants adopted a collective statement in which, among other things, they expressed their 'willingness to work actively with governments to achieve a global ban on chemical weapons, and their willingness to contribute additional momentum to the Geneva negotiating process' and stated their 'willingness to continue their dialogue with governments to prepare for the entry into force of an effective Chemical Weapons Convention which protects the free and non-discriminatory exchange of chemicals and transfer of technology for economic development and the welfare of all people'. They also agreed to establish an International Chemical Industry Forum, meeting in Geneva, as a focal point for industry input into the treaty negotiations.

A key factor in the successful involvement of the chemical industry in the CWC negotiations was the facilitation of such interaction by non-governmental organisations, particularly the Stockholm International Peace Research Institute (SIPRI) and the Pugwash Conferences on Science and World Affairs. Both organisations had also undertaken earlier detailed studies related to the verification of chemical industry and realised the importance of industry involvement.[434] For example, in 1970 and 1971,

---

[432] One diplomat said the letter 'managed to offend everybody without having any influence'. However, it should also be pointed out that the chemical industry was not united in its opposition to Schedule 4, for example some national associations were not opposed. *Chemical and Engineering News*, 'Chemical industry helps Geneva negotiators draft balanced, effective chemical weapons control and disarmament treaty', 28 March 1988, p. 15.

[433] *The Arms Control Reporter*, '17-18 October: Chemical manufacturers met in Washington and New York to try to find a consensus on ways of furthering the talks', 704.B.321-322.

[434] SIPRI, *Chemical Disarmament: Some Problems of Verification* (Stockholm, Almqvist and Wiksell International 1973).

SIPRI hosted symposia as part of a project on the verification of non-production of organophosphorus chemical warfare agents, results from which were later published.[435] During the workshops of the Pugwash Chemical Warfare Study Group in 1977, 1978 and 1979 participants visited industrial facilities in West Germany, the US and Sweden respectively.[436] Building on these studies once actual negotiation of a chemical weapons convention had begun but before the diplomats had addressed the issue of verifying non-production of chemical weapons in a concerted fashion SIPRI and Pugwash returned to the subject by convening a conference on the chemical industry and the projected chemical weapons convention in 1985 in Stockholm. Once again, the proceedings of the conference were published by SIPRI.[437] Three years later, SIPRI undertook another study, this time on the non-production by industry of chemical-warfare agents and technical verification under a CWC.[438] During this study, its coordinator noticed that

> a prominent aspect of the contributions from the representatives of the chemical industry is the constructive approach and willingness of the chemical industry to address problems which even, at the best, will create still new burdens of compliance with national and international verification regulations.[439]

Also, chemical industry representatives were frequently invited to Pugwash workshops, which one participant describes as a 'valuable addition' to the other, more formal meetings.[440] Writing about such meetings, the same author says: 'NGOs have been able to bring key government and industry officials together in a forum where candid dialogue has occurred on major technical and operational issues'.[441] Between 1988 and 1991, SIPRI and Pugwash collaborated again on a project which addressed the practical problems liable to be encountered during the implementation of the CWC verification provisions in their application to 'dual-use' chemicals, with the mustard-gas precursor thiodiglycol being chosen for case-study.[442]

---

435 SIPRI, *The Problem of Chemical and Biological Warfare. Volume VI: Technical Aspects of Early Warning and Verification* (Stockholm, Almqvist and Wiksell International and New York, Humanities Press 1975).

436 SIPRI, *The Chemical Industry and the Projected Chemical Weapons Convention: Proceedings of a SIPRI/Pugwash Conference*, SIPRI Chemical and Biological Warfare Studies No. 4 (Oxford, Oxford University Press 1986), p. x.

437 Ibid.

438 Johan Lundin (ed.), *Non-Production of Chemical-Warfare Agents: Technical Verification under a Chemical Weapons Convention*, SIPRI Chemical and Biological Warfare Studies No. 9 (Oxford, Oxford University Press 1988).

439 Ibid., p. 189.

440 Will Carpenter and Michael Moodie, 'Industry and arms control', in Raymond Zilinskas (ed.), *Biological Warfare: Modern Offense and Defense* (Boulder, Lynne Rienner 2000), pp. 177-191, p. 182.

441 Will Carpenter, 'The perspective of the Western chemical industry', in Benoit Morel and Kyle Olson (eds.), *Shadows and Substance: The Chemical Weapons Convention*, Ridgeway Series in International Security Studies (Boulder, Westview Press 1993), pp. 115-126, p. 116.

442 Johan Lundin, *Verification of Dual-Use Chemicals under the Chemical Weapons Convention: The Case of Thiodiglycol*, SIPRI Chemical and Biological Warfare Studies No. 13 (Oxford, Oxford University Press 1991).

2.3 **Industry concerns**

At a meeting in Zurich in January 1988 chemical industry representatives from CEFIC, CMA and JCIA identified a number of priority areas for the chemical industry in the CWC negotiations: the protection of confidential business information; protocols for inspections; data reporting methodologies for commercial chemicals of interest to the treaty; the technical requirements for an international inspectorate; the scope of materials to be covered by the treaty; and monitoring devices and techniques. Having conceded that in order to be effective, a chemical weapons convention would necessarily require inspection of the chemical industry, representatives of industry were keen to keep intrusions to a minimum, hence the focus on confidentiality and inspection protocols. At a meeting in 1985, Will Carpenter of CMA said: 'Industry would not object to on-site inspections and to scrutiny of records. But we are concerned that there be safeguards to protect intellectual property'.[443] Industry was also concerned about the public relations impact if it became widely known that facilities were being inspected by 'chemical weapons' inspectors. They were therefore keen that facility-specific information such as names and locations would be protected. However, it was not until 1989 that the CWC negotiators paid sufficient attention to confidentiality issues following pressure from chemical industry representatives who pointed out that the current rolling text devoted less than one page to confidentiality and that the *ad hoc* committee had not addressed the topic since 1987.[444] One spur to the progress on confidentiality in 1989 was the national trial inspections in which industry had been participating since 1988, as the chairman of the Industry Forum at the GICCW told participants: 'These trials have shown that intrusive inspection procedures need not compromise industry's legitimate right to maintain confidentiality of sensitive commercial information'.[445] With procedures for routine chemical weapons inspections largely agreed, pressure from the chemical industry was a major factor in the drafting of the CWC Confidentiality Annex.

3. Industry-Related Provisions of the CWC

Writing in 1994, three observers of the CWC negotiations commented that 'verification of activities not prohibited by the Convention will be a very complex mix of science, technology, commerce and politics'.[446] The verification regime which was finally agreed to in Geneva represents a very delicate balance between a number of

---

[443] Quoted in: Lois Ember, 'Chemists work with arms control agency toward chemical arms ban', *Chemical and Engineering News*, 5 May 1986, pp. 18-19.

[444] Kyle Olson, 'The proposed chemical weapons convention: An industry perspective', *Chemical Weapons Convention Bulletin*, No. 2 (Autumn 1988), pp. 1-3.

[445] Government-Industry Conference Against Chemical Weapons, 'Industry Forum: Report of the chairman, Mr Tom Reynolds, President of the Chemical Confederation of Australia'.

[446] Julian Perry Robinson, Thomas Stock and Ronald Sutherland, 'The Chemical Weapons Convention: the success of chemical disarmament negotiations', *SIPRI Yearbook 1993: World Armaments and Disarmament* (Oxford, Oxford University Press 1993), pp. 705-734.

competing interests, not least between the requirement to provide enough information to assure States Parties that their counterparts are complying with their obligations, while at the same time ensuring that confidential business information not related to CWC compliance is not released. A participant in the CWC negotiations has noted that 'the development of the verification provisions for chemical industry has been one of the most complex aspects of the CWC, and has involved long and often tedious negotiations, particularly since 1987'.[447] Reflecting this complexity, provisions relating to verification of the chemical industry are found throughout the Convention, including its annexes. Article II provides key definitions, Article VI sets out the verification regime, the Annex on Chemicals identifies certain chemicals 'for the application of verification measures', the Verification Annex contains detailed provisions on declaration and inspection procedures and the Confidentiality Annex outlines provisions for the protection of confidential information.

3.1 Article II: Definitions

Article II is an integral part of the Convention as it provides the definitions for key terms found within the treaty. For example, part of the Article II definition of a chemical weapon is 'toxic chemicals and their precursors, except where intended for purposes not prohibited under this Convention, as long as the types and quantities are consistent with such purposes'. This represents what is known as the 'general purpose criterion'.[448] It means that any toxic chemical, irrespective of whether or not it is listed in the Annex on Chemicals, is a chemical weapon unless it is being produced for purposes not prohibited under the Convention. The definition of a chemical weapon is therefore not based on any tangible characteristics of particular chemicals, but on the intent of the producer and on the types and quantities of chemicals produced. Article II then goes on to define what falls under its definition of a 'toxic chemical':

> Any chemical which through its chemical action on life processes can cause death, temporary incapacitation or permanent harm to humans or animals. This includes all such chemicals, regardless of their origin or of their method of production, and regardless of whether they are produced in facilities, in munitions or elsewhere.

Here Article II includes an important qualifier with respect to the lists of chemicals included in the CWC stating that these 'schedules' (see below) contain 'toxic chemicals which have been identified for the application of verification measures', in other words the scope of the CWC does not apply only to chemicals listed in the schedules. Article II next defines what is meant by 'peaceful purposes' which includes 'industrial, agricultural, research, medical, pharmaceutical or other peaceful purposes'.

---

[447] Robert Mathews, 'Verification of chemical industry under the Chemical Weapons Convention', in JB Poole and R Guthrie (eds.), *Verification 1993: Arms Control, Peacekeeping and the Environment* (London, VERTIC/Brassey's 1993), pp. 41-54 at p. 41.

[448] For more on the 'general purpose criterion' see UK, Department of Trade and Industry, *Annual Report 2004: Operation of the Chemical Weapons Act 1996*, section 8, 'The general purpose criterion', pp. 26-28.

Finally, Article II contains a number of definitions specifically relating to industry verification, namely 'production', 'processing' and 'consumption'.[449]

3.2 Article VI: Activities not prohibited under the Convention

Article VI is linked directly to Article II as it relates to 'activities not prohibited' under the CWC. According to Krutzsch and Trapp:

> Article VI is thus a consequence of the comprehensive scope of the Convention on the one hand, and of the intricacies created by the very nature of chemical weapons, for example the existence of 'dual-use' chemicals, on the other.[450]

Article VI establishes the right of States Parties to 'develop, produce, otherwise acquire, retain, transfer and use toxic chemicals and their precursors for purposes not prohibited' under the CWC. In addition, Article VI also creates the legal basis for 'data monitoring and on-site verification' related to such chemicals, facilities and activities. The detail of these regimes is laid out in the Verification Annex. Three of these regimes relate to the 'schedules' contained in the Annex on Chemicals, while the fourth relates to discrete organic chemicals and the facilities producing them.

The regime for Schedule 1 chemicals as detailed in Part VI of the Verification Annex allows States Parties to produce and use such chemicals for research, medical, pharmaceutical or protective purposes as long as the types and quantities are justifiable for such purposes. The aggregate amount of such chemicals that a State Party can possess at any given time must not exceed one tonne. The types of facilities that are allowed to produce Schedule 1 chemicals are defined in the CWC. They are required to make annual declarations of past and anticipated activities, and are subject to international monitoring. The CWC also imposes transfer restrictions on Schedule 1 chemicals whereby they can only be exported to other States Parties for research, medical, pharmaceutical or protective purposes. They cannot be exported to non-States Parties or retransferred to a third state. Although included in Article VI, the Schedule 1 provisions are primarily aimed at government facilities such as chemical defence laboratories rather than industrial sites. Indeed, few of the chemicals on Schedule 1 are produced or traded commercially. One exception is saxitoxin, used in marine toxin detection kits, that was the subject of a long-running debate soon after the CWC entered into force. In the end, a technical change was made to the Verification Annex to allow the transfers of small amounts of saxitoxin between States Parties without a 30 day prior notification, but requiring that notification should be made by the time of transfer.[451]

---

[449] '(a) "Production" of a chemical means its formation through chemical reaction; (b) "Processing" of a chemical means a physical process, such as formulation, extraction and purification, in which a chemical is not converted into another chemical; (c) "Consumption" of a chemical means its conversion into another chemical via a chemical reaction.'

[450] Walter Krutzsch and Ralf Trapp, *A Commentary on the Chemical Weapons Convention* (Dordrecht, Martinus Nijhoff Publishers 1994), p. 97.

[451] This represented the first change to the text of the CWC since its adoption in 1992. The change was in the form of a new paragraph in Section B of Part VI of the Verification Annex, paragraph 5bis, which reads: 'For quantities of 5 milligrams or less, the Schedule 1 chemical saxitoxin shall not be subject

Few commercial Schedule 1 facilities have been declared, most are Government owned and operated. Thus, it is the regimes for Schedule 2 and 3 chemicals and for 'other chemical production facilities' that are most relevant to the chemical industry. With regard to Schedule 2, Part VII of the Verification Annex specifies that a State Party shall declare to the OPCW each facility on its territory producing, processing or consuming any Schedule 2 chemicals above the declaration threshold (one tonne per year for most Schedule 2 chemicals). Any such facility producing, processing or consuming Schedule 2 chemicals above the inspection threshold (10 tonnes per year for most Schedule 2 chemicals) is additionally subject to on-site inspection. One of the requirements of the initial inspection is to gather the information necessary to enable an assessment of the potential risk posed by the site to the object and purpose of the CWC. This risk assessment, which is made by the Technical Secretariat, is used as the basis for determining the frequency and intensity of subsequent inspection of the facility. An inspection cannot last for longer than 96 hours, unless both the State Party and the inspectors agree to an extension and no plant site can receive more than two inspections per year. As of November 2006, 467 Schedule 2 sites had been declared and 223 had been inspected. In addition, since 2000, States Parties have been banned from exporting Schedule 2 chemicals to non-States Parties except for those products packaged for individual use and in mixtures below specified concentration limits.

For plants producing Schedule 3 chemicals Part VIII of the Verification Annex specifies that the declaration threshold is 30 tonnes per year, while the inspection threshold is 200 tonnes per year. As of November 2006, 504 Schedule 3 facilities have been declared of which 179 have so far been inspected. Although exports of Schedule 3 chemicals are still permitted from States Parties to non-States Parties, end use certificates are required stating, *inter alia*, that the chemicals will only be used for peaceful purposes and will not be retransferred. With respect to 'other chemical production facilities', Part IX of the Verification Annex requires that States Parties have to declare all plant sites that have produced over 200 tonnes of unscheduled 'discrete organic chemicals' (OCPFs) or over 30 tonnes of unscheduled 'discrete organic chemicals' that contain the elements phosphorus, sulphur or fluorine. Since 29 April 2000, plants producing over 200 tonnes of unscheduled discrete organic chemicals have also been subject to inspection. As of November 2006, 5,206 OCPFs have been declared and 375 have so far been inspected. The regime for OCPFs was one of the final elements of the CWC verification regime to be agreed in the endgame of the negotiations. It is fully consistent with the June 1991 proposals from the chemical industry for 'free access' to all chemical production facilities.

3.3 Article IX: Consultations, cooperation and fact-finding

The provisions of Article IX (see also Chapter 11) can be applied to any facility or location within a State Party, whether declared or not. This means that the provisions

to the notification period in paragraph 5 if the transfer is for medical/diagnostic purposes. In such cases, the notification shall be made by the time of transfer'. See *United Nations Treaty Collection*, C.N.916.1999 TREATIES-7, dated 8 October 1999.

of Article IX also apply to chemical industry. During the negotiations, a number of states conducted practice challenge inspections at their own civil chemical facilities which demonstrated

> that a mandatory anywhere, any time challenge inspection scheme at short notice can be effectively implemented without unduly compromising confidential or secret data, information, features and the like, so long as appropriate procedures and methodologies are followed.[452]

Confidential business information could be protected, even during a challenge inspection. While supportive of the concept of challenge inspections, the chemical industry was also keenly aware of the disruption which a challenge inspection could cause to the operation of an industrial plant. Although challenge inspections were thought to likely be rare events anyway, the chemical industry was keen to lessen the likelihood of a challenge inspection at an industrial facility. This partly explains industry support for the OCPF regime and 'free access' to chemical production facilities; the broader the scope of routine inspections under Article VI, the less the likelihood of a challenge inspection. To date, no challenge inspections have been requested, but the OPCW has carried out a number of challenge inspection exercises, including one at an industrial facility in Brazil in October 1999. After this exercise, senior staff of the facility wrote to the OPCW to share their experiences. They stated that 'Finally, we would like to emphasise that none of our regular work routines were affected by the exercise. Our factory continued working as usual during the inspection week and we suffered no delays to our production routines'.[453]

3.4 Annex on Chemicals

The concept of lists or 'schedules' of chemicals was first introduced during the US-USSR bilaterals in the early 1980s and later taken up by the CD, with the negotiations initially focusing on five categories of chemicals: super-toxic lethal chemicals; other lethal chemicals; other harmful chemicals; key precursors including key components of binary or multi-component weapons; and other precursors. Facilities to be included in the systematic verification regime were to be identified by their producing, processing or consuming, above certain thresholds, one or more of the chemicals listed on a schedule. The contents of the schedules were the result of what one expert described as 'difficult and prolonged negotiations'.[454] The US draft of 1984 contained four schedules, three containing toxic chemicals and key precursors (A, B and C) and

---

452 Ralf Trapp, *Verification Under the Chemical Weapons Convention: On-Site Inspection in Chemical Industry Facilities*, SIPRI Chemical and Biological Warfare Studies No. 14 (Oxford, Oxford University Press 1993), p. 75.

453 OPCW, Technical Secretariat, 'Note by the Technical Secretariat: Formil Quimica Ltda, Brazil', S/165/00, dated 10 February 2000.

454 Ralf Trapp, *Verification Under the Chemical Weapons Convention: On-Site Inspection in Chemical Industry Facilities*, SIPRI Chemical and Biological Warfare Studies No. 14 (Oxford, Oxford University Press 1993), p. 7.

one (D) containing 'agreed methods for measuring lethal toxicity'.[455] However, three was always a popular number for categories of chemicals; in 1985 Sweden proposed three schedules based on progressively more stringent regimes along with a combination of the general purpose criterion and an assessment of the risk each chemical posed to the Convention.[456] This combination became the foundation of the routine verification regime, but it was not until the chairman's drafts of 1992 that the 'toxicity' criterion became merely one criterion among many in determining the positioning of a chemical in the schedules. The schedules are thus 'negotiated lists of chemicals which have been identified for the application of verification measures'.[457] Indeed, the Annex on Chemicals emphasises that 'these Schedules do not constitute a definition of chemical weapons'.

Agreement was reached in Geneva on the types of chemicals that should be contained within each of the three schedules. Schedule 1 contains toxic chemicals and precursors that have been produced or used as chemical weapons (or which contribute to the production of chemical weapons in the case of precursors), that are deemed to pose a high risk to the object and purposes of the CWC and that have little or no use for peaceful purposes. Therefore, Schedule 1 includes toxic chemicals including nerve agents such as sarin, tabun, VX and their homologues, blister agents, two toxins and precursors including methylphosphonyl difluoride (DF) and O-ethyl O-2-diisopropylaminoethyl methylphosphonite (QL). Schedule 2 contains toxic chemicals and precursors that pose a significant risk to the CWC by virtue of high toxicity or other properties, as well as those which are either precursors to chemicals in Schedule 1 or are important in the production of a Schedule 1 chemical and that are not produced in large commercial quantities for peaceful purposes. So, Schedule 2 contains chemicals like Amiton which was developed as an insecticide but proved too toxic for agricultural activities and dimethyl methylphosphonate which is used in the production of flame retardants but can be used as a precursor for the production of sarin. Finally Schedule 3 contains toxic chemicals and precursors which have been produced or used as chemical weapons, that pose a risk to the CWC due to their toxicity or other properties, that are important in the production of Schedule 1 or 2 chemicals and that are produced in large commercial quantities for peaceful purposes. Schedule 3 therefore includes dual use chemicals such as phosgene that was used as a chemical weapon in the First World War but which now has large commercial applications in the production of plastics, pesticides and so on, and trimethyl phosphite which is a precursor for permitted production of insecticides and flame retardants but can be used as a precursor for nerve agents.

While it was very clear which schedule some chemicals should be placed on, agreement in Geneva on the placement of others was 'agonizingly slow and tedious',

455 USA, 'Draft convention on the prohibition of chemical weapons', CD/500, dated 18 April 1984.

456 Sweden, 'A comprehensive approach for elaborating regimes for chemicals in a future chemical weapons convention', CD/632, dated 20 August 1985.

457 Ralf Trapp, *Verification Under the Chemical Weapons Convention: On-Site Inspection in Chemical Industry Facilities*, SIPRI Chemical and Biological Warfare Studies No. 14 (Oxford, Oxford University Press 1993), p. 8.

according to one participant.[458] The negotiators had to balance the risk to the CWC with the quantities produced, processed or consumed by the chemical industry. The schedules as finally agreed in Geneva form part of the text of the CWC. Acknowledging the major political influence on the negotiation over the schedules, the fact that the lists may need to be updated as technology and industrial practice advanced and taking into account early experience in the implementation of Article VI, the negotiators also included in Article XV of the CWC a mechanism for administrative and technical changes to the schedules which avoided the potentially lengthy process of seeking a formal amendment to the CWC. Instead, changes to the schedules (and non-substantive changes to most parts of the Confidentiality and Verification Annexes) can be adopted by recommendation of the Executive Council and acceptance by all States Parties.[459] So far, no changes have been made to the schedules. However, the First CWC Review Conference in 2003 requested the Executive Council to consider developments in relation to new chemicals and assess whether they should be considered in the context of the Schedules.[460]

4. Industry Interaction with the Preparatory Commission

Given its significant role in the CWC negotiations, it was only to be expected that the chemical industry would be keen to have a role in the PrepCom too. As at the CD in Geneva, industry's formal role was limited by the rules of procedure of the PrepCom which stated that 'plenary meetings of the Commission shall be held in private unless the Commission decides otherwise'. A number of states, such as Germany, Italy and Switzerland, for example, overcame this problem by adding industry representatives to their delegations. The United States while not including representatives from industry as part of its delegation, often invited the industry people to act as advisors in The Hague. This situation led to the chemical industry voicing concerns during early 1993 about 'the limited opportunities for the chemical industry to follow and take part in the work of the Expert Groups'.[461] In response, the PrepCom decided to host annual combined meetings between chemical industry representatives and its expert group on chemical industry facilities in order to re-establish the dialogue which had existed before. The first such meeting took place in October 1993 and was attended by 132 people from 40 countries and one international organisation, including industry

[458] Robert Mathews, 'Verification of chemical industry under the Chemical Weapons Convention', in JB Poole and R Guthrie (eds.), *Verification 1993: Arms Control, Peacekeeping and the Environment* (London, VERTIC/Brassey's 1993), pp. 41-54 at p. 46.

[459] To date, this simplified process has been used twice to change the text of the Verification Annex; once in 2000 with regard to transfers of the Schedule 1 chemical saxitoxin and once in 2005 with regard to the timelines for conversion of former chemical weapons production facilities.

[460] Conference of the States Parties [first review conference], 'Report of the first special session of the Conference of the States Parties to review the operation of the Chemical Weapons Convention [first review conference] 28 April – 9 May 2003', RC-1/5, dated 9 May 2003.

[461] Thomas Stock, 'The Chemical Weapons Convention: Institutionalization and preparation for entry into force', *SIPRI Yearbook 1994: World Armaments and Disarmament* (Oxford, Oxford University Press 1994), pp. 685-711, p. 709.

or trade-association executives from Austria, Brazil, Cuba, Finland, France, Germany, India, Israel, Japan, the Netherlands, Russia, South Africa, South Korea, Ukraine, the UK and the USA.[462] At its fifth plenary meeting in December 1993, the PrepCom instructed the PTS to hold regular briefings for industry in The Hague and to designate specific staff members as points of contact for industry. A second meeting took place in April 1994 attended by representatives of the chemical industries of Algeria, Bulgaria, China, France, Germany, India, Italy, Japan, The Netherlands, Poland, Russia, Sweden, the UK and the USA, as well as delegations from 34 Member States and CEFIC.[463] A third such meeting took place in June 1995 attended by delegations from 22 chemical industry associations or bodies and from 34 Member States.[464] These meetings served as an opportunity for dialogue between PrepCom delegates and chemical industry representatives and continued the constructive involvement of the industry in the evolution of the CWC that had begun in Geneva. However, the involvement was at a less frequent and lower level as industry representatives realised that some discussions in The Hague were repeats or re-openings of those which had already taken place in Geneva. Others also felt that the chemical industry had 'done its bit' during the negotiations.

5. Major Industry and Related Issues for the Preparatory Commission

Once the institutional machinery was established, work on substantive issues could begin in the expert groups. From March 1993 onwards, the various subsidiary bodies of the PrepCom were in virtually continuous session in The Hague. Many were on issues relating to administrative and budgetary matters and on chemical weapons issues, but as described above there were also groups on chemical industry issues mandated to work on those issues in the Paris Resolution which related to the chemical industry. The Paris Resolution only makes specific mention of two issues relating to the chemical industry:[465] 'Guidelines for provisions regarding scheduled chemicals in low concentrations, including in mixtures, in accordance with Part VII, paragraph 5, and Part VIII, paragraph 5, of the Verification Annex'. However, most of the issues

[462] 'Combined experts group on chemical industry facilities and industry representatives. Panel discussions: Effect on the chemical industry of the Chemical Weapons Convention. 6-7 October 1993: Report', PC-V/B/WP.1, dated 8 October 1993.

[463] 'Second Combined Meeting of the Expert Group on Chemical Industry Issues and Industry Representatives', *Information Series B* (Chemical Industry), No. 2, May 1994.

[464] Working Group B, 'Expert group on chemical industry issues: Chairman's summary of the combined meeting with chemical industry, PC-XI/B/WP.10 of 27 June 1995; and 'Third combined meeting of the expert group on chemical industry issues with industry representatives', *Information Series B* (Chemical Industry) No. 4, July 1995.

[465] Although virtually all Schedule 1 facilities were anticipated to be military or government-owned (as proved to be the case) it was decided, after considerable debate, that because these are permitted activities under the Convention and their verification regime falls under Article VI to include them under chemical industry issues. In reality, due to their very nature, the verification of Schedule 1 chemicals was very different to the others.

listed in the Paris Resolution were cross-cutting issues which related to both chemical weapons and chemical industry verification; for example all of the issues relating to the general rules and provisions relating to the conduct of inspections under Parts II and III of the Verification Annex and the issues relating to the Confidentiality Annex. In addition, as already described many issues considered within expert groups moved between groups in a circular fashion rather than being considered continuously by the same group. Sometimes this was done to unbundle contentious issues or to avoid blockages, but it was also done to encourage progress by changing the environment, for example by changing the chairman or the secretary. Therefore, the following description of the major industry related issues arising during the PrepCom proceeds in a thematic fashion rather than by expert group.

5.1 Declarations and inspections

The submission of national declarations forms the baseline for the CWC verification regime. A principal aim of on-site inspections is to verify the accuracy of the declarations submitted to the OPCW. Therefore, the design of the declaration system was an important element of the CWC negotiation and its elaboration occupied much of the PrepCom's time. While the development of guidelines on low concentrations of Schedule 2 and 3 chemicals in mixtures was the only specific chemical industry issue mandated to the PrepCom by the Paris Resolution, many other issues, such as the declaration formats to be used, would need to be agreed and other issues were likely to emerge along the way. The expert group on industrial declarations first met in June 1993 and immediately began addressing many of these issues. In early 1994, an expert group on inspection procedures was established bringing under one roof most of the issues related to the actual conduct of routine inspections (another group dealt specifically with challenge inspections). Many of the issues that it discussed had to do with finding the balance between the rights of the inspection team to fulfil the inspection mandate and the rights of the inspected State Party to protect its confidential information. For some delegations, this was the crucial struggle which could significantly affect the effectiveness of the CWC verification regime as designed by the CWC negotiators in Geneva. Chapter 8 deals with preparations to conduct inspections.

As described earlier, the CWC requires States Parties to declare facilities producing, processing, consuming, importing or exporting Schedule 2 chemicals and facilities producing, importing or exporting Schedule 3 chemicals. However, it also states that declarations 'are generally not required for mixtures containing a low concentration' of a Schedule 2 or 3 and defers the development of guidelines to the PrepCom. In addition, the CWC requires States Parties to submit 'declarations of aggregate national data' (AND) for the previous year of quantities of Schedule 2 chemicals produced, processed, consumed, imported or exported and of Schedule 3 chemicals produced, imported or exported. Agreement on guidelines for scheduled chemicals in mixtures was important as it would affect the numbers of facilities declared and also have implications for reporting on transfers of scheduled chemicals. If states operated different national low concentration limits, then one state would declare facilities which in another state would not be declared. The chemical industry was particularly keen that the low concentrations issue be resolved as soon as possible in order to ensure a 'level playing field' for chemical companies and to avoid multinational companies having to deal with differing national regulations. 'Captive use' referred to the production and consumption of a scheduled chemical within the same facility. Some delegations argued that the scheduled chemical produced should be declared, while others argued that as it was consumed within a relatively short time, it did not need to be declared.

Despite pressure from the chemical industry, neither of these issues was resolved by the PrepCom and they were passed on to the OPCW. So was a further declaration-related issue regarding the declaration of aggregate national data. The lack of agreement on low concentrations caused discrepancies between national declarations and remained unresolved a long time after entry into force. These issues have been resolved in a gradual manner and with the benefit of implementation experience in the years since 1997: Issues relating to the transfer of Schedule 2 chemicals and the declaration of Schedule 2B and 3 chemicals were resolved by decision of the fifth session of the CSP in May 2000;[466] issues relating to the transfer of Schedule 3 chemicals were resolved at the sixth CSP a year later.[467] At its seventh session in 2002, the CSP agreed to apply these low concentration limits to AND declarations for production, processing, consumption, import and export of Schedule 2 chemicals and the import and export of Schedule 3 chemicals.[468] At its ninth session in 2004, the CSP decided that Schedule 2 or 3 chemicals produced in a 'captive use' situation do need to be declared even if they are chemically stable and exist for a sufficient time to make isolation possible.[469] While political discussions took place in the expert groups, the PTS proceeded as best it could, in the absence of certain agreements, with the development of the Declaration Handbook. The Declaration Handbook was never formally adopted by the PrepCom (although Signatory States did submit many comments on it). Indeed, the PTS, supported by some States Parties, pushed to leave the Declarations Handbook as a living document that would be expected to be modified by the TS based on experience built up after entry into force. Even in a draft form it ensured that the PTS and Signatory States had enough information to be able to fulfil their obligations upon entry into force of the CWC.

The actual procedures to be used by inspectors and the methods by which they were to conduct inspections, occupied a great deal of time (and are described in more

466 Conference of the States Parties [fifth session], 'Decision: Implementation of restrictions on transfers of Schedule 2 and Schedule 3 chemicals to and from states not party to the Convention', C-V/DEC.16, dated 17 May 2000; and 'Decision: Guidelines regarding low concentration limits for declarations of Schedule 2 and 3 chemicals', C-V/DEC.19, dated 19 May 2000. Although low concentration limits for Schedule 2A and 2A* are still under discussion.

467 Conference of the States Parties [sixth session], 'Decision: Provisions on transfers of Schedule 3 chemicals to states not party to the Convention', C-VI/DEC.10, dated 17 May 2001.

468 Conference of the States Parties [seventh session], 'Decision: Guidelines regarding declarations of aggregate national data for Schedule 2 chemical production, processing, consumption, import and export and Schedule 3 import and export', C-7/DEC.14, dated 10 October 2002.

469 Conference of the States Parties [ninth session], 'Decision: Understanding of the concept of 'captive use' in connection with declarations of production and consumption under Parts VII and VIII of the Verification Annex to the Chemical Weapons Convention', C-9/DEC.6, dated 30 November 2004.

detail in Chapters 7 and 8). While the negotiators in Geneva had agreed broad principles, there was still much detail to be elaborated. An additional factor was that, to a large extent, the PrepCom was operating in a vacuum; there was little experience of the kind of international, intrusive verification regime for which the PrepCom was trying to lay the groundwork. The relevant experience which did exist, for example from UN and national investigations of alleged use between 1982-92, the national trial inspections conducted between 1988-92, the IAEA and from UNSCOM, was incorporated where appropriate, but the experts in The Hague were largely starting from scratch. As the Technical Secretariat pointed out in a report to the first CWC review conference in 2003: 'Many Member States had little past experience with on-site inspections in their territories; even more lacked experience in relation to the international inspection of privately owned facilities. Article VI was clearly a step into the unknown. Six years later, the OPCW can state that it has mastered the challenge of establishing a well-functioning system of declarations and inspections in the chemical industry of the States Parties'.[470]

Among the first issues to be addressed was the question of the size and composition of inspection teams. This of course had a bearing upon the size and structure of the PTS as a whole as well as on the qualities of individuals to be recruited, and so was a fairly urgent issue, especially given the need to prepare a budget for the following year. The expert group on inspection team composition only met once, in May 1993, and devised illustrative examples of inspection team size. For initial inspections of industrial facilities the maximum team size was estimated to be 12, and 10 was the estimated maximum for a routine industrial inspection.[471] These figures went on to be incorporated into the PrepCom's budgets and became fixed, although they had been intended to be indicative.[472] A subsequent expert group on inspectorate planning met in July 1993 and agreed that the basis of the inspectorate would be full-time rather than temporary inspectors and that regional offices could be established, if needed. The group also recommended dealing with the expected intense workload soon after entry into force through the use of sequential inspections. Many of the major issues relating to inspection procedures are described in the thematic sections that follow, but it was clear by the end of 1997 that during the PrepCom the PTS had amassed enough information and developed adequate procedures that it could effectively carry out inspections in industrial facilities around the world.

In order to lay down more facility-specific rules for inspections, the CWC provides for facility agreements to be agreed between the Technical Secretariat and the inspected States Parties. Such agreements are required for Schedule and 2 facilities and can be requested by the inspected State Party for Schedule 3 facilities and OCPFs. Various expert groups under Working Group B, including one on declarations and model facility agreements, spent much time developing model facility agreements for

---

470 OPCW, Conference of the States Parties [first review conference] 'Note by the Director-General to the first review conference', RC-1/DG.1, dated 17 April 2003, p. 10.

471 'Combined group of experts: Inspection team composition: Report', PC-III/B/WP.3, dated 28 May 1993.

472 In fact, the maximum team sizes were never used from entry into force onwards, as the technical requirements of the inspections coupled with manpower availability served to reduce the team sizes.

chemical industry facilities. A major source of disagreement related to the nature of model facility agreements for industrial facilities. Some delegations argued that such agreements should be as 'loose' as possible, while others argued that they should be fairly binding and detailed thus leaving little room for negotiation during the initial inspection. In addition, the development of model facility agreements was another area into which concerns about confidentiality encroached. In fact, for some delegations the whole point of facility agreements was to serve as another tool in controlling access by the inspectors to confidential information. The concept of facility agreements was largely taken from the verification system operated by the IAEA for nuclear facilities with the expectation that it would also be required for chemical facilities. However, in practice since entry into force some States Parties have argued that for industry inspections facility agreements are not effective and due to the ever changing plant and plant site configurations will be obsolete and will require revision before they can be approved by the Executive Council. Thus, while many have been drafted for Schedule 2 facilities, relatively few have actually been approved by the Executive Council and no State Party has requested a facility agreement for a Schedule 3 facility or an OCPF.

5.2 Confidentiality

As already discussed, the protection of confidential business information was among the main concerns of the chemical industry from the days of the CWC negotiations onwards. It soon became apparent, especially by late 1993, that confidentiality was going to be a – perhaps the – biggest obstacle to progress during the PrepCom: 'It is apparent that the balance between confidentiality and the effectiveness of verification will be one of the most difficult to strike in the implementation of the CWC'.[473] The fairly broad provisions agreed during the CWC negotiations in Geneva required a lot of further elaboration by the PrepCom and in that elaboration there was scope for the balance between the rights of the inspection team and the inspected State Party to be titled in the latter's favour. Given the numerous points within the verification regime at which concerns about confidentiality arose, the issue was a perennial one in multiple expert groups, for example data systems and inspections procedures: 'Concerns about confidentiality have led to some of the most protracted debates and resulted in an apparent lack of progress on a wide range of issues'.[474] This reflected the concerns of industry and delegations with the protection of confidential information during on-site inspections and the Organisation's procedures for protecting confidential information submitted to, or acquired by it.

In terms of the tasks mandated by the Paris Resolution (guidelines for procedures on the release of classified information by the Organisation; a classification system

[473] Robert Mathews and Antony Taubman, 'Preparing for implementation of the Chemical Weapons Convention: Progress during 1994', in JB Poole and R Guthrie (eds.), *Verification 1995: Arms Control, Peacekeeping and the Environment* (London/Boulder, VERTIC/Westview 1995), pp. 161-179 at p. 169.

[474] Robert Mathews, 'Preparing for implementation of the Chemical Weapons Convention: Progress during 1995', in JB Poole and R Guthrie (eds.), *Verification 1996: Arms Control, Peacekeeping and the Environment*, (London/Boulder, VERTIC/Westview 1996), pp. 125-150 at p. 135.

for levels of sensitivity of confidential data and documents; and recommendations for procedures to be followed in case of breaches or alleged breaches of confidentiality), these were assigned to an expert group on confidentiality which began meeting in January 1994 under the chairmanship of Antony Taubman of Australia. In its first report, the group acknowledged that its work would have to take into account 'the need for concern about confidentiality to be balanced against the requirement for overall transparency and suitable intrusiveness in verification activities.'[475] The group set out by developing a draft OPCW policy on confidentiality setting out basic policy guidelines on confidentiality. After numerous meetings, the group finished its work and the eleventh plenary of the PrepCom approved it in July 1995. At the group's second session in March 1994, it recommended a classification system for confidential information based on three categories: OPCW Restricted; OPCW Protected; and OPCW Highly Protected, which was also incorporated into the draft OPCW policy on confidentiality.[476] The PrepCom's sixth plenary in April 1994 approved this classification system and adopted it as the classification system of the PrepCom as well.[477]

A related area was the design and establishment of the Information Management System (IMS) on which confidential information would be processed and stored. While the basic design of the IMS was established fairly early on, work on the installation of the system was stalled due to a dispute between delegations on the level of security of the system. Some delegations insisted upon a high standard of computer security but were then unwilling to provide the PTS with the additional funding to purchase and implement such a system. Within the PTS a huge amount of work was done in relation to the practicalities of implementing the policy on confidentiality and the classification system. It was realised relatively early that OPCW staff could not be vetted to any meaningful degree before being given access to confidential information. All had to sign 'secrecy agreements' and confidential information was only to be accessible on a 'need to know' basis but at the end of the day staff needed access to information in order to carry out their work. The emphasis within the system that was developed, was on document control and tracking, creating an audit trail so that, if information was misused, it should be possible to find out who had misused it. This meant that systems for logging access to and copying and printing of documents had to be designed. By entry into force, an extremely elaborate system had been developed but it was hampered by the fact that while delegations had agreed to the storage of declarations in electronic form, they had not agreed to those same declarations being electronically searchable. As a result, immediately after EIF all declarations were stored, processed and handled in hardcopy form. It took a further 2 years to convince delegations that the Organisation's IT system and protocols were of a standard that their declarations could be safely scanned and stored electronically. When submitting their initial national declarations after entry into force, most States Parties unsurprisingly

[475] Working Group B, 'Expert Group on Confidentiality: First interim report', PC-VI/B/WP.1, dated 14 January 1994.

[476] Working Group B, 'Expert Group on Confidentiality: Second report', PC-VI/B/WP.15, dated 18 March 1994.

[477] 'Report of the Commission', PC-VI/22, dated 15 April 1994.

chose to use the highest (OPCW Highly Protected) classification category. For example, the Director-General reported to the fifth session of the CSP in 2000 that, between entry into force and the end of 1999, a total of 34,185 or 73 percent of the pages submitted had been classified by the Member States as OPCW Highly Protected or OPCW Protected.[478] Given the elaborate procedures within the Technical Secretariat and the absence of electronic processing, this put an immense strain on the Technical Secretariat staff.

An issue which related to confidentiality but which arose in other expert groups, particularly on equipment and inspection procedures, was clandestine sampling. This referred to the hypothesis that an inspector might deliberately set out to pick up samples when in a facility for later analysis or sale to a company's rivals. There was also the worry that contamination from one facility might be transferred on an inspector's clothing or equipment to another facility, and then be used to raise concerns about the latter facility's compliance. Although an extremely unlikely scenario (inspectors, like all OPCW staff, signed secrecy agreements when they began working, Member States have the right to refuse entry to individual inspectors, a rogue inspector would basically need a lot of luck to ensure that he was selected to be on the inspection team that went to the plant in which he was interested, that he would be able to take a sample, get it out without being noticed and get it analysed) it was one which several delegations took very seriously to the extent of preventing agreement on seemingly trivial issues, like the addition of 'reusable boots' to the list of approved inspection equipment. Some delegations were so worried about such scenarios that they tried to insist that inspection teams would only use equipment provided by the inspected State Party rather than their own equipment. In fact using provisions of the Health and Safety Policy some States Parties have managed to ensure that inspection teams use State Party supplied boots, uniforms, hard hats and so on.

During the PrepCom, many delegations were very concerned about 'rumour damage'; the concept that visits to facilities by 'chemical weapons' inspectors would be very damaging in public relations terms. This was a problem about which industry had already raised concerns and was one which exercised several delegations during the PrepCom. As described earlier, the CWC Confidentiality Annex has a general prohibition on the release of information by the OPCW. Noting the practice in Iraq of UNSCOM inspectors being 'doorstepped' by the media upon completing inspections, some delegations were almost paranoid about the potential for attracting bad publicity in the local population. Accordingly, much time was spent developing a media and public affairs policy, which was eventually adopted by the tenth PrepCom plenary in April 1995.[479] Confidentiality concerns had been incorporated into the policy, which stated: 'Members of the inspection teams shall neither initiate contacts with, nor comment on, any aspect of a specific inspection activity in a State Party for the benefit of the news media or the general public'.

---

[478] Conference of the States Parties [fifth session], 'Report by the Director-General: Status of implementation of the regime governing the handling of confidential information by the Technical Secretariat in 1999', C-V/DG.5, dated 8 May 2000.

[479] 'Report of the Commission', PC-X/23, dated 7 April 1995.

In the event, these concerns turned out to be overstated. After entry into force there was very little press interest in the conduct of OPCW inspections and, where media interest was registered it was at the instigation of the inspected State Party. For example, Switzerland took to issuing a press release at the conclusion of every industrial inspection, something which there was no intention of doing in the beginning.[480] After the chemical industry had gained experience in hosting OPCW inspections, its concerns about 'rumour damage' lessened once facility operators reported that the inspectors were competent people and that their inspections were no more noticeable than those by health and safety officials or maintenance workers. According to the OPCW's Director of Verification in 2000:

> [T]he widespread apprehension that industry facilities receiving inspections from 'chemical weapons' inspectors under the 'chemical weapons convention' might be damaged by adverse publicity, has proved to be groundless in practice. OPCW inspectors routinely arrive at industry sites, inspect them, and depart virtually unnoticed.[481]

In a report to the first CWC review conference in 2003, the Technical Secretariat noted that:

> The performance of the [inspection teams] during the conduct of inspections has been recognised as being technically proficient and highly professional, with the [inspection teams] strictly following the inspection mandate and the provisions of the Convention. No incident of breach of confidentiality has ever occurred during an on-site inspection.[482]

5.3 Other issues

The CWC assigns an important role to sampling and analysis as a tool to be used by inspection teams during on-site verification. In the part of the Verification Annex relating to Schedule 2 inspections, the Convention states that 'sampling and analysis *shall* be undertaken to check for the absence of undeclared scheduled chemicals'. For Schedule 3 and OCPF inspections, the Convention states that 'sampling and analysis *may* be undertaken to check for the absence of undeclared scheduled chemicals. In cases of unresolved ambiguities, samples may be analysed in a designated off-site laboratory, subject to the inspected State Party's agreement'. During the CWC negotiations in Geneva, it was expected that sampling and analysis would be a frequent occurrence during chemical weapons and chemical industry inspections. Accordingly, much time was spent during the PrepCom on developing procedures for on-site (and off-site) sampling and analysis and on the contents of the central analytical database

[480] AFP from Bern, 1 December 1997; Beat Soltermann, 'Säurefabrik wird auf Chemiewaffen inspiziert'.

[481] Ron Manley, 'Declaration and verification of the global chemical industry', *OPCW Synthesis* (Autumn/November 2000), pp. 19-21, p. 20.

[482] OPCW, Conference of the States Parties [first review conference], 'Technical Secretariat: Background paper on the conduct of inspections under the Chemical Weapons Convention and related issues', RC-1/S/1, dated 17 April 2003.

against which samples would be analysed. These discussions are covered in more detail in Chapter 7.

Despite the provisions of the CWC and the expectations of the negotiators, the use of sampling and chemical analysis has proved to be 'the rare exception rather than the norm'.[483] On occasion the analytical capabilities of the inspected State Party have been employed during inspections.[484] And, in fact, it was only in 2001 that an OPCW inspection team first used its own equipment to take a sample at a industry facility (at a Schedule 2 facility in the UK[485]), The reasons for this are complex, but the two main ones are the practicalities of shipping the inspectors' GC/MS (gas chromatograph/ mass spectrometer) and its supporting equipment from The Hague to the inspection site (it weighs between 300 and 1500kg depending on how much peripheral equipment is taken, and has a bulk of about 1 cubic metre or greater) and the concerns of the chemical industry about the intrusiveness of the GC/MS equipment.[486] In a report to the First CWC Review Conference, the OPCW Director-General stated: 'The frequency with which on-site analysis has been used in chemical industry inspections does not, however, currently reflect the role that the Convention assigns to this inspection tool. The Secretariat continues to study and to discuss with interested States Parties how best to use sampling and on-site analysis in chemical industry inspections'.[487]

Another example of a cross-cutting issue related to the scope of chemicals relevant to the CWC. As mentioned above, the CWC prohibits the development, production, stockpiling and use of *all* toxic chemicals and precursors 'except where intended for purposes not prohibited under this Convention, as long as the types and quantities are consistent with such purposes'. However, the Convention also includes three schedules of toxic chemicals and precursors which have been 'identified for the application of verification measures'. During the PrepCom, some delegations attempted to argue that this latter provision meant that verification under the CWC should focus only on scheduled chemicals. Such assertions came up most often in relation to equipment for sampling and analysis where it was argued that equipment or software should be configured so as to only identify scheduled chemicals. For example, in July 1995, India argued:

---

483 Ron Manley, 'Verification under the Chemical Weapons Convention: A reflective review', *Pure and Applied Chemistry*, Vol. 74, No. 12 (2002), pp. 2235-2240 at p. 2239.

484 OPCW, Conference of the States Parties [first review conference], 'Technical Secretariat: Background paper on the conduct of inspections under the Chemical Weapons Convention and related issues', RC-1/S/1, dated 17 April 2003.

485 UK, Department of Trade and Industry, *Annual Report for 2001 on the Operation of the Chemical Weapons Act 1996*: 'This development was welcomed as the UK had urged the OPCW to begin sampling and analysis during routine inspections in accordance with the CWC. ... It is important for the wider integrity and effectiveness of the Convention's verification regime that the OPCW is able to conduct sampling and analysis during routine inspections', p. 7.

486 Ron Manley, 'Verification under the Chemical Weapons Convention: A reflective review', *Pure and Applied Chemistry*, Vol. 74, No. 12 (2002), pp. 2235-2240 at p. 2239.

487 OPCW, Conference of the States Parties [first review conference], 'Note by the Director-General: Report of the Scientific Advisory Board on developments in science and technology', RC-1/DG.2, dated 23 April 2003, p. 3.

> [A]s it is, the implementation of the Convention would be a very challenging task with the scheduled chemicals; so we should not widen the scope of the Convention by including other chemicals which are not scheduled chemicals, because the list of these other chemicals is endless. I would like to emphasise the importance of restricting ourselves to only those chemicals which are included in the Convention.[488]

Such an interpretation would have the effect of restricting the scope of the CWC's verification regime to the scheduled chemicals which themselves largely reflect the technology of the 1970s. The CWC would therefore not prohibit the use of newly discovered toxic chemicals as weapons, or the use of chlorine, a traditional chemical warfare agent which could not be listed in any of the schedules because of its massive use in chemical industry. This line of argumentation was strongly countered by a number of delegations, among them Australia:

> [A] restrictive interpretation of the CWC, paring all effective prohibitions and verification activities down to scheduled chemicals alone, would establish loopholes grave enough to defeat the purpose of the CWC, and would condone historical incidents of chemical warfare.[489]

None the less, the GC/MS equipment is equipped with software that allows varying levels of access to the retention time and mass-spectrometric information. More detail on the GC/MS can be found in Chapter 7.

5.4 Entry into force

Due to the CWC-stipulated focus on chemical weapons inspections in the first few months after entry into force, the first industrial inspection did not take place until December 1997 at a Schedule 2 facility in Switzerland.[490] In contrast to the short deadlines imposed for chemical weapons and Schedule 1 facilities, the CWC states that Schedule 2 facilities should receive their initial inspection 'as soon as possible but preferably not later than three years after entry into force'. No timelines were imposed on the conduct of Schedule 3 inspections and the CWC clearly stated that OCPF inspections could not start until the beginning of the fourth year after entry into force. Once conducting industry inspections, the Technical Secretariat discovered quite quickly that many States Parties had not expected it to get off the ground so quickly. Indeed, it appears that some States Parties had not anticipated how successful the PrepCom had been in creating the infrastructure to support inspections. Many States Parties had not provided inspection-related information to the OPCW, for example the location of the point of entry, and many inspection teams that conducted initial

---

[488] 'Statement by the alternate representative of India at the eleventh session of the Preparatory Commission for the Organisation for the Prohibition of Chemical Weapons', PC-XI/18, dated 25 July 1995.

[489] Australia. 'The 'scope' of the Chemical Weapons Convention and the role of its Schedules', PC-XI/B/WP.13, dated 25 July 1995.

[490] AFP from Bern, 1 December 1997; Beat Soltermann, 'Säurefabrik wird auf Chemiewaffen inspiziert'.

Schedule 2 inspections had to spend time on the first day explaining to facility personnel what the CWC was and why they were being inspected, something which the inspected States Parties should really have already done. In fact some States Parties had no implementing regulations and no National Authority, agency in each State Party that is responsible for verification matters.

Writing in 2000, the OPCW Director of Verification said:

> In the period since [entry into force] the Secretariat has undertaken more than 300 inspections under Article VI at chemical industry sites in 43 States Parties. Despite the anxieties on both sides these inspections have proceeded without incident.[491]

This is not just the opinion of the Technical Secretariat either, chemical industry has also echoed it:

> To date, the management of CWC treaty implementation has been exceptional. ... I'm very pleased to note that facilities inspected in the United States have had only favourable reports of their interaction with inspectors from the OPCW Secretariat.[492]

This success was all the more remarkable given the fact that a great many issues were still listed as being 'unresolved'. However, it served to illustrate that many of the concerns had been primarily political and that with common sense and improvisation the verification regime could be made to work. Writing later about the frantic nature of the months immediately following entry into force, the now-retired Director of Verification said:

> With hindsight, the chaos of those early months actually made a significant contribution to the formation of the Secretariat's culture. The sheer volume of work that had to be completed forced staff rapidly to establish working relationships and to trust and depend upon each other. People simply had to be prepared to compromise. Gradually, many came to realise that the breadth of experience available in working with people from different cultures and backgrounds was a distinct advantage. There was no shortage of new ideas and different approaches to solving the many problems that arose.[493]

6. Conclusions

The implementation of the CWC since 1997 has demonstrated that many of the concerns expressed during the negotiations and during the PrepCom itself have proved to be unfounded. Perhaps the most significant relates to the protection of confidential business information which was a major issue in Geneva and, as described above, was

---

491 Ron Manley, 'Declaration and verification of the global chemical industry', *OPCW Synthesis* (Autumn/November 2000), pp. 19-21, p. 20.

492 Frederick Webber, 'A US industry perspective on the implementation of the Chemical Weapons Convention', *OPCW Synthesis* (Autumn/November 2000), pp. 16-18, p. 16.

493 Ron Manley, 'Building an international organization', in Rosemary Bechler (ed.), *Intercultural Dialogue*, British Council Birthday Counterpoints (London, British Council 2004), pp. 32-47, p. 42.

probably the biggest issue in the PrepCom too. However, experience since entry into force demonstrates that the OPCW has been able to protect the information entrusted to it. In 2000, the US General Accounting Office reported to Congress:

> We found that chemical companies believe that they have been able to protect their proprietary information, in part because of provisions within the Convention and U.S. law and through extra measures taken by companies before and during inspections. ... US companies we spoke with have indicated that there has been no adverse publicity related to the inspections under the Chemical Weapons Convention.[494]

Perhaps the clearest statement of this fact comes from the then president of the American Chemistry Council, Frederick Webber:

> We have been very encouraged by the demonstrated effectiveness of protection for confidential business information implemented under the CWC. The Council is not aware of any failure with or problems in protecting this information during industry CWC inspections. More to the point, I'm not aware that any proceedings to remedy the wrongful disclosure of confidential information have been initiated under the CWC's Confidentiality Annex. Put simply – confidential information is staying that way.[495]

Considering the near paranoia in some industry statements about confidentiality, this is praise indeed.

Finally, it must be emphasised that this success and the continuing support of the chemical industry for the CWC is dependent upon its close involvement in the process, from the beginning of the negotiations in the 1980s, through the preparatory phase in the 1990s, to the implementation of the CWC in the late 1990s and to the present day. This was recognised by the Director-General of CEFIC in 2000: 'An important lesson learned from the Convention is that the involvement of industry is essential, not merely during the negotiations, but also during the implementation process'.[496] As chemical weapons stockpiles are gradually destroyed and more resources become available for the prevention of chemical *re*armament, the chemical industry will find itself more not less involved in the implementation of the CWC. The OPCW Director-General recognised the synergistic relationship between the CWC and the chemical industry in a report to the first CWC review conference:

> The Convention and the OPCW cannot function properly without the support and engagement of the chemical industry. This partnership reflects not only the long involvement of the chemical industry in the negotiations of the Convention, and the industry's involvement in its implementation, but also the nature of that involvement. Declarations and inspections under Article VI, as well as the enforcement of export controls for sched-

---

494 USA, General Accounting Office, 'Arms control: Experience of US industry with Chemical Weapons Convention inspections', 13 September 2000, GAO/T-NSIAD-00-249, p. 4.

495 Frederick Webber, 'A US Perspective on the implementation of the Chemical Weapons Convention', *OPCW Synthesis* (Autumn/November 2000), pp. 16-18.

496 Alain Perroy, 'The contribution of the chemical industry to the Chemical Weapons Convention', *OPCW Synthesis* (Autumn/November 2000), pp. 4-5, p. 5.

> uled chemicals, require a true partnership between the OPCW, the National Authorities, and the chemical industry. This will be even more important in the future, given the high pace of technological and organisational change in the industry. … The dialogue between the OPCW and chemical industry associations worldwide will continue and intensify in the future.[497]

The second CWC Review Conference in 2008 will provide an ideal opportunity to review the operation of the CWC industry verification regime and to make adjustments to equip it for the future.

[497] OPCW, Conference of the States Parties [first review conference], 'Note by the Director-General to the First Review Conference', RC-1/DG.1, dated 17 April 2003, p. 22.

Chapter 10

National Implementation: Article VII

Lisa Tabassi

1. Introduction

The fundamental mandate of the Preparatory Commission for the Organisation for the Prohibition of Chemical Weapons (PrepCom for the OPCW) was to carry out the necessary preparations for the effective implementation of the Chemical Weapons Convention (CWC).[498] That is the explicit overall purpose[499] for which the PrepCom was established by the Paris Resolution.[500] 'Effective implementation' would encompass the competent functioning of all players involved: the OPCW itself as an international organisation, each of its organs and subsidiary organs, and most importantly, each State Party to the Convention and its agents.

It is the State's agents who must initiate and carry out the incorporation of the Convention's norms into the national legal system and subsequently to enforce those norms as national law. To this end, one of the PrepCom's principal explicit tasks was to 'facilitate the exchange of information between Signatory States concerning legal and administrative measures for the implementation of the Convention and, if requested, give advice to Signatory States on these matters…'.[501]

The Convention's Article VII, entitled 'National Implementation Measures' requires each State Party to:

> Designate or establish a National Authority to serve as national focal point for effective liaison with the OPCW and other States Parties;
>
> Adopt, in accordance with its constitutional processes, the necessary measures to implement its obligations under the Convention, including penal measures in respect of activities prohibited by the Convention, extended extraterritorially to its nationals;

[498] 1993 Convention on the Prohibition of the Development, Production, Stockpiling and Use of Chemical Weapons and on Their Destruction, corrected and amended text available at <www.opcw.org>.

[499] Para. 1 of the Text on the Establishment of a Preparatory Commission, annex to the Resolution Establishing the Preparatory Commission for the Organisation for the Prohibition of Chemical Weapons, adopted in Paris during the Signing Ceremony of the CWC, 13-15 January 1993. This text is discussed in Chapter 4.

[500] Resolution Establishing the Preparatory Commission for the Organisation for the Prohibition of Chemical Weapons.

[501] Subpara. 14(a) of the Text on the Establishment of a Preparatory Commission, annex to the Paris Resolution.

I.R. Kenyon and D. Feakes, The Creation of the OPCW

Inform the OPCW of the legislative and administrative measures taken to implement the Convention;

Not permit in any place under its control any activity prohibited by the Convention;

Cooperate with other States Parties and afford appropriate forms of legal assistance;

Assign the highest priority to ensuring the safety of people and to protecting the environment, in implementing the Convention;

Treat as confidential and afford special handling to information and data received in confidence from the OPCW; and

Cooperate with the OPCW and assist the OPCW's Technical Secretariat.

No deadlines are set for any of those obligations by the Convention except to notify the OPCW at entry into force of the Convention who the National Authority is. Ideally, the necessary measures would be in place when the Convention enters into force for the State in order for the State to be in a position to enforce the Convention nationally from the outset. Since some of the Convention's obligations must be met immediately or soon after entry into force, any delay in adopting the necessary measures could mean that the State would not be able to comply with its obligations on time. The failure to designate or establish the National Authority would be a serious matter since the OPCW would lack the formal interlocutor with which to liaise on implementation.

The tasks explicitly set by Article VII enumerated above, as well as the tasks implicit in enforcing the legislation, fall across the complete spectrum of government activity. In practice, to carry out those tasks, action would be required variously by: parliament, enforcement agencies (customs and police), the judiciary, a number of ministries (including foreign affairs, defence, industry, agriculture, environment and health) and other agencies (national security). In practice, states would find that the National Authority must be an inter-ministerial or interagency body, at least to some extent.

The breadth of activity was foreseen during the negotiations of the Convention and addressed by the PrepCom in its activities during the preparatory phase. Even so, the complexity of the matter and the extent of support most States Parties would need for national implementation exceeded those expectations.

2. 'Necessary Measures'

The term 'necessary measures' is not defined or amplified by Article VII or elsewhere in the Convention. The term also appears in Article VI, paragraph 2, which requires that each State Party

> adopt the necessary measures to ensure that toxic chemicals and their precursors are only developed, produced, otherwise acquired, retained, transferred, or used within its territory or in any other place under its jurisdiction or control for purposes not prohibited under [the] Convention.

Implied in that term (and later seen in practice) are legislation adopted by parliament or promulgated by the executive together with the administrative structure and systems to enforce that legislation, including import/export controls.

The core principle of treaty law, as codified in the 1969 Vienna Convention on the Law of Treaties,[502] is the principle of *pacta sunt servanda*: treaties will be performed by the parties in good faith. Another customary rule codified by the Vienna Convention establishes that a party may not invoke the provisions of its internal law as justification for its failure to perform a treaty.[503] Reading those two rules together, the assumption is that each State Party will ensure on the national level that the treaty's provisions are respected and that its national laws are consistent with its treaty obligations.

Article VII of the Convention only specifies that necessary measures will be adopted, penal legislation will be enacted and the National Authority will be designated or established. The requirements under Article VI, aimed at non-proliferation, could be very far-reaching. It is left entirely to the State's discretion what form and content those measures will take nationally. Since the creation of national law, the enforcement of it and the structure and administration of government are all sovereign acts reserved exclusively for states, it is not surprising that the Convention is so vague on the critical matter of national implementation. Furthermore, Article VII is totally silent on other aspects of national implementation, such as the obligation to prepare national declarations to the OPCW and to destroy chemical weapons stockpiles. Implicit in Article VII is the link to every other article in the Convention since it is states which are the members of the OPCW and it is states which govern the territories where the treaty is performed and regulate how it is performed. The results reviewed by the OPCW ultimately are *all* results of national implementation, one way or another.

3. National Implementation as Envisaged during the Treaty Negotiations 1984-1991

The scope of activities which would be necessary for national implementation was already being contemplated by the states which were actively participating in the negotiations of the Convention's text in the Conference on Disarmament in Geneva. Among the *travaux préparatoires* are national papers submitted by a few states in which their views were formalised. Non-governmental organisations (NGOs) active in the field were also studying the matter closely as the end game approached.

502 Article 27.

503 Article 28.

In 1984, Yugoslavia tabled a working paper in which it proposed that verification be based on a combination of complementary and supplementary international measures to monitor the production of super-toxic lethal chemicals and national measures to monitor production of less lethal toxic chemicals. In addition the National Authority would assist the international authority and would also be obliged to prevent activities violating the Convention. Even though administrative and economic systems of States Parties are disparate, the structure, composition and functioning of national authorities should be agreed and monitoring systems would be standardised. Each National Authority would have as a member a representative of another State Party nominated by the international authority.[504]

In 1985, the German Democratic Republic tabled a working paper in which it drew on working papers tabled earlier and proposed the elements which eventually appeared in the text of Article VII, paragraph 1. Additionally, it foresaw that each State Party would need to establish a national system for implementation of the Convention, comprising: law and other regulations constituting the legal structure of supervision and control; a national authority; and organisation and operational elements at the facility level. It also enumerated a list of functions, rights and duties of the National Authority domestically and internationally which in practice has proven to be an accurate reflection of what effective National Authorities do. It also proposed the elements of a national system for accounting and control of chemicals, national inspections and a national inspectorate which have also played out in practice.[505]

In 1991, Australia tabled a working paper on its strategy for preparing for the implementation of the Convention in Australia by developing: the legislative and administrative framework; documentation enabling declarations; modifications to the Harmonised System codes to identify declarable imports and exports; broad agreement between government agencies, industry and unions on the powers and functions of the National Authority and the scope of national implementing legislation; preparations for inspections; a register of national experts; a register of relevant production facilities; national verification measures; and information to disseminate to key players and the public.[506] In introducing the paper to the Conference on Disarmament, the Ambassador O'Sullivan of Australia indicated that Australia was finding the task of putting into place the necessary administrative structure for implementation of the Convention to be no simple task. He warned that there was a big gap in understanding the complexity of the treaty between the states negotiating it and familiar with its details and the busy government official in other countries who were not present in Geneva but who nevertheless would be required to undertake the considerable administrative and commercial requirements that the Convention would impose.[507]

Scholarly research also commenced in the NGO community. The Federation of American Scientists Fund in 1988 began publishing the quarterly *Chemical Weapons*

---

[504] Conference on Disarmament documents CD/482, dated 26 March 1984, and CD/PV.255, dated 3 April 1984, pp. 21-22.

[505] Conference on Disarmament document CD/620, dated 23 July 1985.

[506] Conference on Disarmament document CD/1055, dated 5 February 1991.

[507] Conference on Disarmament document CD/PV.582, dated 14 February 1991, pp. 10-14 at 12-13.

Convention Bulletin of the Harvard Sussex Program on CBW Armament and Arms Limitation (HSP taking over the publishing in 1990), to disseminate news, background and commentary relevant to chemical arms control. The Stockholm International Peace Research Institute (SIPRI) compiled a study on national implementation of the Convention in 1990[508] and VERTIC's Yearbook included a chapter on national implementation of the Convention in 1992.[509]

4. Activities to Support Preparations for National Implementation 1993-1997

Recognising that effective implementation would rest on a network of National Authorities functioning successfully, implementation support during the preparatory phase centred on the study of, and sensitization to, the role of the National Authority and the development of national implementing legislation. Both these aspects – the role of the National Authority and the legal framework for national implementation – were addressed positively throughout the preparatory phase. The PrepCom's Provisional Technical Secretariat (PTS) and Signatory States worked jointly and separately on this subject during 1993-1997 as did NGOs active in the field, scholars and academia.

The subject of national implementation was first raised in the Preparatory Commission by Working Group B's Group of Experts on Technical Cooperation and Assistance in August 1993. The Expert Group recommended that:

> the Provisional Technical Secretariat solicit, as appropriate, the planned or enacted national legislation and associated implementing documentation of the Member States and make them available to the Members, upon request, in order to facilitate the national implementation.[510]

The Executive Secretary of the PTS responded by requesting Member States of the PrepCom to provide preliminary information on, *inter alia,* progress on the establishment of the National Authority and 'the approach concerning the relevant implementing legislation (if required by national procedure) – whether implementing legislation will be adopted before or after actual ratification'.[511] Working Group B endorsed the Expert Group's recommendation and noted the Executive Secretary's action.[512] Repeat requests by the Executive Secretariat for information on the status of prepara-

---

[508] T. Stock and R. Sutherland (eds.), *National Implementation of the Future Chemical Weapons Convention*, SIPRI Chemical and Biological Warfare Studies No. 11 (Oxford, Oxford University Press 1990).

[509] H. Fox and R. Mathews, 'The Future Chemical Weapons Convention and Its National Implementation', in J.B. Poole and R. Guthrie (eds.), *Verification Report 1992: Yearbook on Arms Control and Environmental Agreements* (London, VERTIC 1992), pp. 173-187.

[510] PC-IV/B/WP.6, dated 9 August 1993.

[511] PC-IV/3, dated 19 August 1993.

[512] Subpara. 8.5 of PC-IV/B/12, dated 1 October 1993.

tions were made and did not yield significant results.[513] Status reports were primarily received orally in sessions of the PrepCom or in the course of seminars.

Forging ahead proactively, the first initiatives to examine and promote preparations for national implementation commenced in 1993 and were developed further throughout the preparatory phase.

5. Manual for National Implementation

Sponsored by the Parliamentarians for Global Action, a Committee of Legal Experts was invited to a meeting in the Peace Palace in The Hague 1-4 December 1993 to discuss national implementation. The Committee's 22 members were drawn from all regions[514] in a collaborative effort between DePaul University College of Law in Chicago and the Legal Division of the PTS. The Committee's task was to examine and comment on the draft *Manual for National Implementation of the Chemical Weapons Convention*, prepared by Professor Barry Kellman of DePaul University and Messrs. Edward A. Tanzman, David S. Gualtieri and S. William Grimes of the Argonne National Laboratory in Illinois. The Manual was published in December 1993.[515] It identified 11 tasks which all States Parties would need to accomplish to implement the Convention and an additional task for possessor states:

Giving the Convention force and effect nationally;
Designation or establishment of the National Authority;
Restrictions on production and transfer of certain chemicals;
Enactment of penal legislation;
Responsibility and method for gathering declarable data;
Responsibility and procedure for inspections;
Protection of confidential information;
Protection of public safety and the environment;
Remedies for contravention of private rights and property;
Enabling legal assistance;
Respect for privileges and immunities; and
Implementation of destruction obligations (for States possessing chemical weapons).

6. Model National Implementing Legislation, National Examples and Assistance with Legislative Drafting

Almost immediately in 1993, Australia submitted model legislation as a national paper entitled the *Illustrative Model Legislation for the Incorporation of the Chemical*

513 PC-VI/8, dated 22 March 1994.

514 Argentina, Australia, Bangladesh, Cameroon, Costa Rica, Ethiopia, France, Germany, India, Islamic Republic of Iran, Israel, Italy, Japan, Kenya, Morocco, Peru, Poland, Russian Federation, Sweden, United States of America.

515 A second revised version was published in February 1998: B. Kellman and E. Tanzman, *Manual for National Implementation of the Chemical Weapons Convention* (Chicago, International Criminal Justice and Weapons Control Center 1998).

Weapons Convention into Domestic Law.[516] It had been initially prepared and disseminated by Australia's Chemical Weapons Regional Initiative which had been founded in 1988 to familiarise states in southeast Asia and the South Pacific region with the Convention and the legal, administrative and technical actions necessary to prepare for national implementation of it. The model was presented as an example of a possible approach to implementing legislation and was accompanied by extensive commentary.

The impetus for assisting states with implementing legislation gained further momentum in 1994 when it was identified that in a number of countries the delay in ratification was due to technical obstacles – the need to prepare draft legislation or collect data on declarable activities – before the ratification bill could be tabled in parliament.[517]

Rather late in the process, the Legal Division of the PTS prepared model national implementing legislation. Initially it was considered that models were of little utility (a still valid view) since legislation must be tailored to fit the State's particular legal system and its factual situation as well (a significant chemical industry declarable under the Convention, possession of chemical weapons or not, import/export activity in scheduled chemicals). However, a frequent starting point for legislative drafters is the study of a model or examples from states having a similar legal system. The demand by states for a model led to the preparation and dissemination in 1996 of the *Model National Implementing Legislation*, including a brief commentary.[518] The model was aimed to assist states possessing no chemical weapons and little or no declarable chemical industry – presumably the category of states with the least justification to allocate priority and resources to the preparation of implementing legislation for the Convention. The only state which based its legislation closely on the model was Peru. Others presumably used it as a point of reference.

As time went on, national examples of parliamentary bills were made available by Signatory States and were widely distributed by the PTS. Early examples included those of Australia, Canada (in English and French), Finland, Germany (which provided translations in English, Russian and Spanish as well), South Africa, Sweden, and Switzerland.

The national approaches to legislation varied considerably. Australia and Canada were preparing single parliamentary acts devoted to implementing the Convention. Germany had existing penal legislation to implement the Geneva Protocol in its War Weapons Control Act 1961 and was supplementing it with a new law covering definitions and the Convention's requirements for declarations, inspections, protection of confidential information and restrictions on transfers of scheduled chemicals. Sweden was amending a series of laws: its Penal Code, the Act and Ordinance concerning Military Equipment, the Act prohibiting the export of products which can be used for

516 PC-IV/A/WP.10, dated 28 September 1993.

517 R.J. Smith/HSP, 'A Preliminary Survey of the Status of National Preparations to Ratify and Implement the Chemical Weapons Convention', paper delivered at the Seminar on National Implementation, The Hague, 30 September 1994, PTS Occasional Papers, No. 6, pp. 12-20 at 20.

518 PC-XI/7/Rev.1, dated 31 May 1996.

mass destruction purposes, the Act on chemical products, the Act on Immunity and Privileges in Certain Cases and its new draft Secrecy Act. In addition, it was supplementing those with a new law on CWC inspections. Switzerland was pursuing a twin approach of amending its Federal Law on War Materiél and preparing a new Federal Law on the Control of Dual-Use Goods. South Africa was adding a new law under its umbrella Weapons of Mass Destruction Act. The European Union initiated the process to harmonise Convention-related reporting procedures, criminal codes and import-export regulations among its Member States.[519]

Japan was the first to enact legislation and bring it into force even before the Convention itself did. In 1995 Japan enacted its implementing legislation early as an immediate response by parliament to the sarin gas attacks on the town of Matsumoto and the Tokyo subway by the terrorist group Aum Shinrikyo. Japan considered that the legislation in force at the time of the attack needed improvement to enable police to prevent future instances and to allow investigators and prosecutors to fully address the full scope of the acts.[520]

Workshops on drafting national implementing legislation were conducted by the Legal Division of the PTS in cooperation with the Harvard Sussex Program in Brussels in 1995[521] and 1996.[522] The workshops were organised with the assistance of the ACP House (a venue for meetings of a grouping of the African, Caribbean and Pacific countries in Brussels) and were oriented towards Member States with no chemical weapons and a small to medium chemical industry.

Finally, as a matter of urgency, the Legal Adviser addressed letters to the representatives of ratifying states in November 1996 and February 1997, reminding them of their country's impending obligation to submit information on their implementing legislation and inquiring whether assistance was needed.

7. Regional Seminars on National Implementation

The first regional seminars on national implementation commenced in 1993. The first one was conducted jointly by the Government of Chile and the PTS and was held in Santiago on 9-10 September 1993. Participants from states in the Latin American and Caribbean region, NGOs and academia gathered to discuss national legislation, national authorities and the transfer of dual use chemicals and technology. At the request of Working Group B,[523] these seminars continued in a series organised jointly by the PTS with governments throughout the preparatory phase to disseminate and exchange information on legal and implementation issues.

---

519 *Chemical Weapons Convention Bulletin* (March 1994) 5.

520 See further, L. Tabassi and R. Silvers, 'Enforcing the CWC: Actual Investigations and Prosecutions of Offenders' (2004) Vol. 2, issue 4, *Chemical Disarmament*, pp. 18-25 and Y. Seto, 'Forensic Investigation of the Sarin Gas Attacks in Japan', in R. Yepes and L. Tabassi, *Treaty Enforcement and International Cooperation in Criminal Matters* (The Hague, TMC Asser Press 2002), pp. 301-307.

521 *Chemical Weapons Convention Bulletin* (December 1995) 6.

522 *Chemical Weapons Convention Bulletin* (March 1996) 5.

523 Subpara. 8.5(c) of PC-IV/B/12, dated 1 October 1993.

The second one was conducted jointly by the Government of Poland and the PTS in Warsaw, 7-8 December 1993.[524] The workshop comprised three working sessions: practical national implementation for entry into force (discussing outreach to industry, declarations and inspections); national legislation; and national authorities. At that time, there were two schools of thought regarding the organisation of a National Authority. One approach had the National Authority functioning as a coordinator for channelling information between governmental agencies responsible for Convention implementation and the OPCW. The second approach would empower the National Authority as a single agency with enough competence to implement a compulsory national monitoring system.[525]

A Trust Fund was established in 1994 and voluntary contributions were made by Signatory States to finance the regional seminars.[526] In total, 17 regional seminars were conducted during the preparatory phase. The proceedings were published by the PTS in the Occasional Papers Series and summaries were reported to the PrepCom: Bangkok, Thailand (8-10 May 1994);[527] Brno, Czech Republic (1-2 June 1994);[528] Lima, Peru (1-3 September 1994);[529] Pretoria, South Africa (12-14 September 1994);[530] Jakarta, Indonesia (28-30 November 1994);[531] Minsk, Belarus (25-27 January 1995);[532] Yaounde, Cameroon (13-15 February 1995);[533] Havana, Cuba (14-16 March 1995);[534] Yamoussoukro, Côte d'Ivoire (8-11 May 1995);[535] Seoul, Republic of South Korea (7-9 June 1995);[536] Addis Ababa, Ethiopia (27-29 November 1995);[537] Wiener Neustadt, Austria (6-8 March 1996);[538] Gozo, Malta (12-14 June 1996);[539] Tehran, Iran (22-25 June 1996);[540] and Makuhari, Japan (16-17 October 1996).[541]

8. Seminars on National Implementation

The first Seminar on National Implementation was convened in The Hague by the PTS as a on 18 December 1993, following the close of the Fifth Session of the Pre-

524 PC-V/A/WP.9, dated 15 December 1993 and PTS Occasional Papers, No. 3.

525 F. Calderón, 'Possible Activities Signatory States Should Avoid in Order to Facilitate their Compliance with the Convention', paper presented at the Regional Seminar on National Authority and National Implementation Measures for the Chemical Weapons Convention, Warsaw, 7-8 December 1993, PTS Occasional Papers No. 3.

526 PC-IX/2, dated 18 November 1994.

527 PC-VII/B/WP.14, dated 29 June 1994; and PTS Occasional Papers No. 4.

528 PC-VII/B/WP.13, dated 28 June 1994; and PTS Occasional Papers No. 5.

529 PC-VIII/8, dated 22 September 1994; and PTS Occasional Papers No. 8.

530 PC-VIII/B/WP.13, dated 27 September 1994; and PTS Occasional Papers No. 7.

531 Subpara. 5.5 of PC-IX/6, dated 1 December 1994; and PTS Occasional Papers No. 9.

532 PC-X/B/WP.17, dated 3 April 1995; and PTS Occasional Papers No. 15.

533 PC-X/B/WP.20, dated 7 April 1995; and PTS Occasional Papers No. 10.

534 PC-X/B/WP.19, dated 6 April 1995; and PTS Occasional Papers No. 12.

535 PTS Occasional Papers No. 11.

536 PTS Occasional Papers No. 13.

537 PC-XII/B/WP.10, dated 13 December 1995; and PTS Occasional Papers No. 14.

538 PTS Occasional Papers No. 16.

539 PC-XIV/B/WP.10, dated 19 July 1996; and PTS Occasional Papers No. 18.

540 PC-XVI/B/WP.11, dated 22 July 1996; and PTS Occasional Papers No. 17.

541 PTS Occasional Papers No. 19.

paratory Commission. The programme focused on progress in national implementation, industry requirements, legislative issues, and practical tasks ahead. The Seminar was attended by 133 participants from 56 countries, research institutes and NGOs. Similar seminars were again organised either as single events[542] or to follow sessions of the PrepCom. They were designed to enable Signatory States to exchange views, information and practical experience on implementation issues and to enable the PrepCom to become aware of current problems faced in implementation or ratification efforts.[543]

As entry into force of the Convention drew nearer, national seminars organised by the newly designated or established National Authorities began to be conducted to disseminate information on the Convention and the OPCW as outreach to the stakeholders.[544]

Another means of disseminating information on the Convention and implementation was the internet. The PTS set up an experimental website in 1995 to assist National Authorities and a study was undertaken to assess its viability as a permanent site. A background paper was prepared for consideration by the Group of Experts on Technical Cooperation and Assistance which concluded that its utility had been demonstrated.[545]

9. Training Courses for National Authorities

Also at the request of Working Group B,[546] courses for the personnel of National Authorities were developed. In May 1994 the Expert Group on Technical Cooperation and Assistance reviewed the proposed content of a basic course for personnel of National Authorities and encouraged Member States to offer courses in various regions and in different languages to enable the largest number of National Authorities to benefit.[547] In cooperation with the PTS, the first two courses were arranged during July and August by the Netherlands. The courses were attended by a total of 74 participants from 43 Signatory States,[548] all but five from developing countries. Following this experience, the Expert Group revised the curriculum into a 115-hour course which was approved by the PrepCom in December 1994.[549]

---

542 Seminar on National Implementation, The Hague, 30 September 1994 (PTS Occasional Papers No. 6).

543 At the close of the Eighth Session (30 September 1994); at the close of the Fourteenth Session (27 July 1996).

544 Algeria, 3 March 1996 (*Chemical Weapons Convention Bulletin* (June 1996) 11; Italy, 23-24 January 1997 and Spain, 24 February 1997 (*Chemical Weapons Convention Bulletin* (March 1997) 7.

545 Subparas. 1.3 and 3.1-3.2 of PC-XII/B/WP.4, dated 19 October 1995.

546 Subpara. 8.5(b) of PC-IV/B/12, dated 1 October 1993.

547 Subpara. 2.3 of PC-VII/B/WP.6, dated 20 May 1994.

548 Subpara. 1.32 of PC-IX/6, dated 1 December 1994.

549 Subpara. 7.4 of PC-IX/11, dated 9 December 1994, approving the revised curriculum as contained in the annex to PC-IX/B/WP.4. The Expert Group later proposed curricula for one- and five-day courses as well (PC-XII/B/WP.4, dated 19 October 1995).

General
History of chemical warfare
The Chemical Weapons Convention
The OPCW

National implementation
Legal rights and obligations
Setting up and running a National Authority
Data handling and confidentiality
Communication with the OPCW
Identification of declarable activities and facilities
Export and import data
Operational tasks relating to declarations
Communication with the OPCW
Operational tasks relating to international cooperation, trade and assistance
Dissemination of information on the CWC

Verification
Receiving inspections
The inspection process
Article IX (clarification procedures and challenge inspection)
Investigations of alleged use
Verification scenarios involving National Authority
Introduction to chemical weapons and chemical defence
Introduction to chemical hazards and chemical weapons agents
Introduction to monitoring, sampling and analysis
Personal protection and medical countermeasures
Introduction to decontamination and contamination control

In 1995, a Trust Fund for Courses for Personnel of National Authorities was established. to assist in funding the costs of courses.[550] Six subsequent courses were arranged by the PTS in facilities provided by the Netherlands government in 1995,[551] 1996,[552] and 1997,[553] and by the governments of India and Tanzania in 1996.[554] A fee of approx. US$500 was charged to participants to cover full board, medical insurance, instructional materials and in-country transportation for the courses (except the shorter courses in Curacao and the final one in Woensdrecht for which the fees were less). Within the limits of voluntary contributions received, the PTS was able to sponsor participants from developing countries.

---

550 PC-X/7, dated 22 March 1995.

551 Woensdrecht, 11-29 September 1995 (PC-XI/B/2, dated 12 April 1995).

552 Ypenburg, 19-27 September 1996 (PC-XIV/B/5, dated 22 July 1996 and Corr.1, dated 23 July 1996) and Willemstad, Curacao, Netherlands Antilles 28 October-1 November 1996 (PC-XV/5, dated 13 September 1996).

553 Ypenburg 10-28 February 1997 (PC-XV/B/12, dated 11 December 1996); Woensdrecht 10-28 February 1997 (PC-XVI/B/1, dated 3 February 1997), and shortened to five days (18-24 March 1997) due to the imminent entry into force of the Convention (PC-XVI/B/4, dated 19 February 1997).

554 Gwalior, India 15 April-3 May 1996 (*Chemical Weapons Convention Bulletin* (March 1996) 5 and (June 1996) 10); Arusha, Tanzania 18 November-6 December 1996 (PC-XV/B/4, dated 11 September 1996).

During the ramp-up phase prior to entry into force, France conducted a training course for French-speaking National Authorities in November-December 1996.[555]

10. National Papers on Implementation

Initially a group of states (Austria, Republic of Korea, South Africa and Turkey) prepared a quick reference guide to the basic rights and obligations of a State Party to the Convention.[556]

As time went on, to assist other states with the process of preparing for national implementation, a number of Signatory States submitted national papers on their experiences: Australia,[557] Belarus,[558] Canada,[559] Cuba,[560] Czech Republic,[561] The Netherlands,[562] Romania,[563] Sweden,[564] Switzerland.[565]

11. NGO Collaboration

In 1993 the PTS initiated an International Information Project on Implementation of the Chemical Weapons Convention in cooperation with the Harvard Sussex Program on CBW Armament and Arms Limitation (HSP). A Conceptualisation Conference was held in The Hague in November at which there was agreement that HSP would produce information on specific topics for the PTS to meet the needs of officials and others developing national policies regarding the Convention and its implementation. It was intended that the materials would eventually be aggregated into a Guide to the Chemical Weapons Convention, but this was superseded by alternative projects.[566] Subsequently, in 1995, the PTS agreed to accept a Researcher funded by HSP. The Researcher would assist in work intended to promote entry into force and implementation of the Convention and serve as liaison between the PTS and HSP to assist with HSP's production of public information materials on the Convention. A principal record of the activities during the preparatory phase are the sections entitled, 'Progress in The Hague: Building the Organization for the Prohibition of Chemical Weapons', in HSP's quarterly *Chemical Weapons Convention Bulletin*.[567] Representatives of HSP

555 *Chemical Weapons Convention Bulletin* (March 1997) 7.
556 Prepcom/II/WP.3, dated 22 April 1993.
557 PC-IV/A/WP.10, dated 28 September 1993.
558 PC-X/B/WP.16, dated 3 April 1995.
559 PC-VIII/17, dated 29 September 1994.
560 PC-V/A/WP.1, 6 October 1993.
561 PC-V/B/WP.9, dated 5 November 1993.
562 PC-VI/A/WP.6, dated 24 February 1994.
563 PC-IX/B/WP.12, dated 7 December 1994.
564 PC-IV/A/WP.9, dated 28 September 1993.
565 PC-IX/B/WP.14, dated 9 December 1994.
566 PC-IX/B/WP.13, dated 8 December 1994.
567 *The Chemical Weapons Convention Bulletin* (*The CBW Conventions Bulletin* from September 1997) is available via <http://www.sussex.ac.uk/spru/hsp>.

regularly presented papers or served as lecturers in seminars and courses organised by the PTS.

SIPRI's Chemical and Biological Warfare (CBW) Project continued to monitor and to annually document progress on the Convention and national implementation efforts in the *SIPRI Yearbook* chapters. Representatives of SIPRI frequently participated in regional seminars and workshops on implementation organised by the PTS.

The Hague Academy of International Law organised a colloquium on 24-26 November 1994 at the Peace Palace. Leading experts in international law gathered to study the Convention as a breakthrough in multilateral disarmament. The progress achieved on the Paris Resolution tasks was analysed in depth by the PrepCom's Legal Adviser.[568] The second part of the colloquium was devoted to implementation by States Parties, with studies of implementation and legislation presented by legal experts from Belgium, Greece, India, United Kingdom, and the United States.[569] Other legal aspects affecting national implementation were also examined: the relations between the Convention and other relevant international norms; the protection of the environment; the transfers regime and constraints on the freedom of trade; the regulation of private activities and the conflict of laws; and disputes between the inspected State Party and the inspection team.

The SIPRI-Saskatchewan-Frankfurt Group convened a conference on the Effective Implementation of the Chemical Weapons Convention in Bad Homburg, Germany, on 8-10 September 1995. It was the final stage of a 14-month research project sponsored by the Germany Volkswagen Foundation. During the course of the project the Group identified legal, technical and administrative issues for the implementation process, monitored and analysed the work of the PrepCom, and participated in the seminars organised by the PTS. Participants were requested in advance to identify any problems being encountered in preparing legislation, setting up national authorities, collecting information from industry and preparing for inspections and any legal problems in national implementation. The Conference focused on declarations requirements, inspection requirements and Article XI issues related to trade and export control. During the Conference, a number of participating states delivered status reports on their preparations for implementation and establishment of a National Authority.[570] In its summary, the Group noted 'that two and a half years after the Signing

568 F. Calderón, 'The Preparatory Commission for the Organization for the Prohibition of Chemical Weapons', in D. Bardonnet (ed.), *The Convention on the Prohibition and Elimination of Chemical Weapons; A Breakthrough in Multilateral Disarmament* (Dordrecht, Martinus Nijhoff Publishers 1995), pp. 27-150.

569 See E. Roucounas, 'L'Autorité Nationale, pp. 243-256; B. Kellman, 'Adaptation of National Legislation to Implement the Chemical Weapons Convention', pp. 257-266; J. Verhoeven, 'La mise en œuvre de la Convention sur l'interdiction et l'élimination des armes chimiques; problèmes et prospectives', pp. 267-284; N. Sims, 'Adaptation of National Legislation to the Implementation Requirements of the Chemical Weapons Convention: Common Law Systems', pp. 285-300; and S. Rama Rao, 'National Measures for the Implementation of the Chemical Weapons Convention: Certain Legal Aspects', pp. 301-314, in D. Bardonnet (ed.), *The Convention on the Prohibition and Elimination of Chemical Weapons; A Breakthrough in Multilateral Disarmament* (Dordrecht, Martinus Nijhoff Publishers 1995).

570 Argentina, Australia, Austria, Brazil, Canada, Denmark, Finland, Italy, Japan, The Netherlands, Norway, Romania, Russian Federation, Switzerland, Sweden, United Kingdom, United States. See 'Country

Ceremony of the Convention, most of the 44 ratifying countries were not seriously advancing in national preparations since they did not anticipate that the Convention would enter into force any time soon'. However, the countries with significant chemical industry of relevance to the Convention, which would need a detailed implementation process, had completed their legislation and designated their National Authority. Preparations were underway for collection of declarable data.[571]

In 1995 the American Bar Association's Section of Natural Resources, Energy and Environmental Law organised a conference on Implementing the Chemical Weapons Convention: the Nuts and Bolts of Compliance in Washington, D.C., on 7 February 1995. Continuing with the concerns over protection of confidential business information which had been an issue for the United States during the negotiations of the Convention, the conference focused on potential loss of confidential information and remedies, preventive measures for industry, the right to privacy in the United States, international claims and dispute resolution and the US draft implementing legislation.[572]

Meanwhile, the Pugwash Conferences on Science and World Affairs, which had been engaged with issues of chemical and biological weapons since the 1950s, had decided, in conjunction with the Harvard Sussex Program, to reconstitute its long standing study-group on those issues into the Pugwash Study Group on Implementation of the Chemical and Biological Weapons Conventions.[573] This new group first met in May 1993. It specializes in private twice-yearly international workshops that bring together officials from capitals, diplomats and governmental and non-governmental scientists to discuss questions of implementation.

12. The Result: Status at Entry into Force and Progress in the First Decade

Just weeks before entry into force, the Executive Secretary published a warning:

> … an additional word of caution: ratification without effective implementation at the national level is fraught with danger. The nature of the Convention's regime is such that national implementation is crucial to ensure its efficacy. As Executive Secretary, I have serious concerns that many countries, which have either ratified the Convention or are close to doing so, have not invested enough in their processes of national implementation. If national procedures are not in place in time, states parties could actually find

Reports on the Implementation of the CWC and the Establishment of the National Authority', in T. Kurzidem, Y. von Lersner, P. Radler, T. Stock, R. Sutherland (eds.), *Conference Proceedings, Bad Homburg 8-10 September 1995*, pp. 18-26.

[571] Kurzidem et al. (eds.), *Conference Proceedings, Bad Homburg 8-10 September 1995*, pp. 4-5.

[572] American Bar Association Section of Natural Resources, Energy and Environmental Law, *Implementing the Chemical Weapons Convention: The Nuts and Bolts of Compliance* (Washington, D.C., Sonreel Seminar Series), 7 February 1995.

[573] J P Perry Robinson, 'The impact of Pugwash on the debates over chemical and biological weapons', in Allison L de Cerreño and Alexander Keynan (eds.), *Scientific Cooperation, State Conflict: The Role of Scientists in Mitigating International Discord*, Annals of the New York Academy of Sciences, Vol. 866 (1998) pp. 224-252.

> themselves in advertent breach of provisions of the Convention. This situation could erode confidence in the Convention, unnecessarily complicate political relations as well as committing already scarce resources to deal with unintentional non-compliance...[574]

In the first six months after entry into force of the Convention, out of 101 States Parties, 59 had notified the OPCW of their National Authorities and 20 had submitted information on their implementing legislation: Argentina, Australia, Austria, Belarus, Brazil, Czech Republic, Finland, Germany, Italy, Kenya, Malta, The Netherlands, New Zealand, Norway, Oman, Peru, Republic of Korea, South Africa, Sweden, and the United Kingdom of Great Britain and Northern Ireland.[575]

Historically, improvements in establishing the legal framework have been incremental:

Status at:	No. of States Parties	No. (and percentage) of States Parties that had made Article VII(5) submissions	Legislation covers areas key to enforcement of the CWC	Draft legislation proposed or commented on by the Secretariat, upon request
C-I: May 1997	87	0 (0%)	Not available	0
C-II: Dec. 1997	103	24 (23%)	Not available	0
C-III: Nov. 1998	120	40 (33%)	Not available	0
C-IV: July 1999	125	43 (34%)	Not available	0
C-V: May 2000	133	48 (36%)	Not available	6
C-VI: May 2001	143	53 (38%)	Not available	8
C-7: Oct. 2002	145	70 (48%)	39 (27%)	16
C-8: Oct. 2003	154	94 (61%)	51 (33%)	36
(Action Plan adopted)				
C-9: Nov. 2004	166	96 (58%)[576]	52 (31%)	66
C-10: Nov. 2005 (Action Plan ended)	174	106 (61%)	59 (34%)	156
20 June 2006 (Action Plan Follow-up)	178	109 (61%)	64 (36%)	198[577]

By the time of the OPCW First Review Conference in 2003, the slow pace in creating the national administrative and legal framework to implement the Convention was seen to be a problem affecting the operation of the Convention. The Review Conference called upon the OPCW Executive Council (EC) to recommend, and the OPCW Conference of the States Parties (CSP) to develop and adopt, a plan of action regarding the implementation of Article VII obligations, with the objective of fostering the full and effective implementation of the Convention by all States Parties.[578] The even-

574 I.R. Kenyon, 'Entry into Force: the Test of our Preparations', *Chemical Weapons Convention Bulletin* (March 1997) pp. 1-3 at 3.

575 Annex 3 to C-II/2*, dated 31 October 1997.

576 The percentage shown is the proportion of States Parties at that date, therefore while numbers of submissions are increasing the total number of States Parties sometimes rises faster.

577 One-hundred and ninety-eight drafts have been submitted by 99 States Parties. In some cases, States Parties have requested advice on drafts several times during their governmental consultative process. Most of the drafts commented on are still going through the process of parliamentary approval.

578 Subpara. 7.83(h) of the 'Report of the First Special Session of the Conference of the States Parties to Review the Operation of the Chemical Weapons Convention (First Review Conference) 28 April-9 May 2003', OPCW document RC-1/5, 9 May 2003.

tual decision creating the Action Plan was adopted by the Conference in October 2003.[579]

The Action Plan set a time frame of November 2005 by which time all States Parties which had not yet done so were expected to have: (a) designated or established a National Authority; (b) enacted the legislation, including penal legislation, and/or adopted the administrative measures necessary to implement the Convention; and (c) provided to the OPCW Technical Secretariat (TS) with the full text of the legislation and information on specific measures taken. Under the Action Plan, States Parties were requested, *inter alia*, to set their own realistic target dates for the steps they needed to take to meet the deadline and to inform the Secretariat of any assistance needed to meet their national implementation obligations. States Parties were encouraged to lend advice to each other, upon request, to meet the Action Plan objectives and to inform the Secretariat of what assistance they could offer.

At the conclusion of the Action Plan in November 2005, results were nominal: out of 174 States Parties 148 (85 percent) had a National Authority and 106 (61 percent) had adopted legislation, although only 59 (34 percent) considered their legislation to be comprehensive.[580] The primary achievement under the Action Plan was the momentum it generated among States Parties: assistance towards meeting the Action Plan objectives had been requested by, and provided to, 107 States Parties by the Secretariat and/or States Parties and the number of States Parties that sought advice on draft legislation more than tripled. The actual number of States Parties that made progress on their legislative processes increased from approximately 100 in October 2003 to approximately 150 by November 2005.

Since it was clear that progress had been achieved but that additional time would be required for the draft legislation to be adopted by parliaments, the Conference decided upon a follow-up period which would conclude in December 2006.[581]

A simple reliance on the numbers of submissions, however, is misleading. By means of a legislation questionnaire issued in 2002,[582] States Parties assessed whether their implementing legislation was comprehensive enough to fully enforce the Convention's provisions. Although one-third of States Parties reporting implementing legislation indicated that their legislation is comprehensive, in most cases it is the parliamentary act being reported. In many cases the parliamentary act needs regulations in order to be implemented and enforced. Most States Parties have not yet done their regulations.

Furthermore, even when regulations have been done, States Parties are not collecting data in the same ways. As indicated above, the Convention is silent on this matter. The result is that, even as increasing numbers of legislation are being adopted by parliaments, discrepancies in declarations of imports and exports of scheduled chemicals remain at 75 percent. The mechanism by which States Parties would be able to ascertain that there is no diversion of scheduled chemicals is not working. At some

---

579 Conference decision C-8/DEC.16, dated 24 October 2003.

580 Note by the Director-General: Report on the Plan of Action Regarding the Implementation of Article VII Obligations (EC-42/DG.8 C-10/DG.4 and Corr.1, respectively, dated 7 and 26 September 2005; EC-M-25/DG.1 C-10/DG.4/Rev.1, Add.1 and Corr.1, respectively, dated 2, 8 and 10 November 2005).

581 Conference decision C-10/DEC.16, dated 11 November 2005.

582 S/317/2002, dated 18 September 2002.

point, consensus to harmonise must be reached if States Parties wish to see the Convention operate in the manner in which it was intended.

13. Conclusion

Neither during negotiations of the Convention nor during the initiation of implementation support during the preparatory phase 1993-1997, was it ever imagined the duration or depth of support that would be needed by states for effective national implementation. As the OPCW Director-General emphasized in his final report on the Action Plan in 2005, national implementation of the Convention is a process that will need continuing support.[583]

Even when the explicit obligations of Article VII have been met by all States Parties, it will form only the foundation for full and effective implementation at the national level. States Parties will continue to need to devote resources to enable a vital National Authority and the vigilant application and enforcement of the legislation and administrative measures they have adopted. The development and maintenance of the capacity for effective national implementation is an ongoing need. Experience has shown – both during the time of the PrepCom and in the OPCW today – the sharing of experiences amongst States Parties is the key component in identifying and promoting best practices in national implementation. A partnership between the Secretariat and States Parties leads to effective implementation support and effective implementation as well.

Beyond the institutional and legal framework, if the Convention is to operate in the manner in which it was agreed, further work by States Parties may be needed in order to collect data in a way in which the problem of discrepancies in declarations of transfers of scheduled chemicals will be resolved. Only then can there be confidence that no diversion of scheduled chemicals is taking place and the Convention's non-proliferation objectives are being met. Further technical and cooperation may also be needed to ensure that the Convention's destruction deadlines can be met by the possessor States Parties. In the matter of national implementation complete reliance on the principle of *pacta sunt servanda* may not be enough. The Westphalian notion of the sanctity of sovereignty may need to be eroded slightly further. States may have considered in 1992 that agreeing to the concept of intrusive verification and challenge inspection was the maximum impingement upon their sovereignty which they could accept. In reviewing the results of their collective national implementation in 2006, in good conscience and good faith it could be recognised that consensus to some degree on *how* the treaty will be implemented nationally is needed in order to ensure that the object and purpose of the Convention are met.

---

583 C-10/DG.4/Rev.1 EC-M-25/DG.1, dated 2 November 2005, p. 3, para. 12.

Chapter 11

Maintaining Honesty: Article IX

Ralf Trapp

1. Introduction

Reaching agreement on Article IX – entitled 'Consultation, Co-operation and Fact-finding' – was a major effort in the negotiations in the Geneva Conference on Disarmament (CD). It consumed a fair share of negotiation time, much at ambassadorial level (with the Chairman of the Ad Hoc Committee on Chemical Weapons personally conducting these negotiations), and remained on the agenda until the very end of the negotiation process. When the CD negotiations were concluded in 1992, challenge inspection – the key element of Article IX – was heralded by some negotiators as a breakthrough of fundamental importance, the beginning of a journey into uncharted waters of international relations.

Article IX deals with consultation, cooperation and fact-finding–in plain English, it deals with how to resolve concerns about possible non-compliance. Despite the generally-accepted legal doctrine of *pacta sunt servanda* (treaty obligations will be honoured), negotiators recognised early on that a treaty that was to abolish an entire category of weaponry, in particular one that had been used in the past as a weapon of mass destruction, needed to provide safeguards against treaty failure, including mechanisms to resolve concerns about cheating. There was historical precedent for nations that had assumed obligations not to arm with chemical weapons and that nevertheless managed to develop, manufacture and stockpile chemical weapons. Violations of the Geneva Protocol had only recently been verified by the United Nations. And, in any event, the level of mistrust between the East and the West was such that neither was prepared to exclude the possibility of a violation by the other side. The routine verification regime of the Convention provided under Articles III, IV, and V of the Convention, together with the corresponding Parts of the Verification Annex, created mechanisms to verify declarations as well as destruction activities.[584] The verification provisions under Article VI enhance confidence in legitimate chemical activities of the States Parties and provide deterrence against cheating at declared industrial facilities as long as the inspection regime remains both sufficiently stringent and unpredictable. However, these routine inspection mechanisms lack the capability to verify

[584] Routine inspections of industry are covered in Chapter 10 and other aspects of inspections are covered in Chapters 7 and 8.

I.R. Kenyon and D. Feakes, The Creation of the OPCW

undeclared facilities or activities. Given the relative easy with which chemical weapons can be made by nations that have a developed chemical industry, there was doubt as to whether a routine verification system based on declarations, on its own, could provide sufficient assurance of treaty compliance.

But the approaches for how to provide that extra assurance (and deterrence) varied considerably between the alliances as well as individual countries, with some favoring traditional diplomatic mechanisms of bilateral or multilateral consultation whilst others insisting on on-site access to verify the situation at a suspect facility.

Article IX provisions on bilateral and multilateral consultative mechanisms had been agreed in the 1980s, the latter involving the Executive Council as well as the good offices of the Director-General. They build on traditional means used in international relations, recall well-established mechanisms normally applied in the relations between nation states, and give the CWC treaty organisation (the OPCW) and its statutory organs, in particular the Director-General and Executive Council, roles as fact-finders and, in the case of the Council, arbiter. The Conference of the States Parties is there as the ultimate decision maker on all treaty-related matters, within the broad powers and functions given to it by the Convention.

But challenge inspection was a different matter. The concept of challenge inspection, originally proposed in the 1970s as a means of challenging allegations of treaty non-compliance, formally entered the negotiations when the United States tabled its draft Chemical Weapons Convention in 1984.[585] Although the 'special inspections' that the US proposed in that draft where not exactly the sort of challenge inspection that was finally agreed, the US proposal, after elaboration and discussion in the Conference on Disarmament, established the principles of 'anytime, anywhere, without right of refusal' as the key features of the mechanism. To no surprise at the time, it was rejected by the Soviet Union and the other members of the Warsaw Treaty Organization. In 1987, however, then Soviet Foreign Minister Edward Shevardnadze, elaborating on a previous statement by Michael Gorbachev, accepted challenge inspection as a means of treaty verification, in principle.[586] Some observers in the West saw this simply as a calling of a US bluff, but it nevertheless opened the way for serious negotiations of the challenge inspection mechanism.

But these were no easy negotiations. After all, the principles established for challenge inspection meant that even the most secret installations (military, intelligence) as well as private facilities could be inspected without a possibility for the challenged site to refuse the inspection. This concept went far beyond the kinds of on-site inspection concepts so far accepted and applied in practice.[587] There was, at least in theory, the possibility that highly-sensitive facilities such as nuclear military installations could be exposed by the mechanism. There was a fear, which remains even today, that the mechanism might be abused by some States either to gather intelligence, or to harass

---

585 USA, 'Draft convention on the prohibition of chemical weapons', CD/500, dated 18 April 1984.

586 Conference on Disarmament document CD/PV.428, 6 August 1987, pp. 10-11; Conference on Disarmament document CD/PV.429, 11 August 1987, pp. 2-7.

587 These include the Intermediate-range Nuclear Forces (INF) Treaty and the Conventional Armed Forces in Europe (CFE) Treaty, both of which had limited inspection rights, predominantly at military bases in Europe and North America. States in other regions of the globe had no such experience.

another State. For some countries, there also was the problem of how to bring the mechanism in line with constitutional protections of private enterprise.

The sensitivities were such that both Article IX and Part X of the Verification Annex remained among the last elements if the CWC to be agreed. Differences on key issues remained until the very end of the negotiations – the resolution finally proposed by the Ad Hoc Committee Chairman in his revised draft Chemical Weapons Convention[588] became part of a final take-it-or-leave-it package, as described in Chapter 1.

When he introduced the draft Chemical Weapons Convention to the First Committee of the United Nations General Assembly, the Chairman of the CD Ad-Hoc Committee on Chemical Weapons, Adolf Ritter von Wagner of Germany, described this final compromise as follows:

> Article IX provides for consultative clarification procedures and, in conjunction with part X of the Verification Annex, for short-notice challenge inspections. A State party may request a challenge inspection of any facility or location in the territory of another State party for the purpose of clarifying and resolving any questions concerning possible non-compliance. The request will then be 'multilateralised' and the inspected State party must permit the technical secretariat to conduct the inspection and is obliged to grant the organization's inspection team access. However, there are a number of measures available to the inspected State party to protect those activities and installations from undue intrusion it considers unrelated to the inspection request.[589]

He went on to state:

> [t]he challenge inspection regime constitutes a novelty in the verification of a universally applicable arms-control and disarmament treaty. Furthermore, it constitutes a politically sensitive concept which balances carefully the verification interests of a State party and of the international community and the interests of the inspected State party to protect sensitive information not related to the chemical weapons Convention. It also balances national sovereign rights and the rights of the community of States parties as represented by the executive council and executed by the technical secretariat.[590]

2. Key Provisions of Article IX

Paragraphs 1 and 2 of Article IX confirm the rights of States Parties to resolve any matters involving compliance concerns amongst themselves, using arrangements that the parties concerned can agree on. Although the treaty introduces an element of ur-

---

[588] Chairman of the Ad Hoc Committee on Chemical Weapons, 'Draft Convention on the Prohibition of the Development, Production, Stockpiling and Use of Chemical Weapons and on their Destruction', CD/CW/WP.400/Rev.2, dated 10 August 1992.

[589] Official Records of the United Nations General Assembly, Forty-seventh Session, Verbatim Record of the 4th meeting of the First Committee held on Tuesday, 13 October 1992 at 10 a.m., New York, document A/C.1/PV.4, p. 63.

[590] Ibid., p. 63.

gency, by making reference to a ten-day response period for responses to such inquiries, it leaves the details of how to resolve such concerns to the parties involved. The mechanism is essentially private and does not involve the institutional framework of the OPCW.

Paragraphs 3 through 7 deal with a variety of mechanisms to resolve non-compliance concerns through the OPCW Executive Council, as appropriate with the assistance of the Director-General. If called to do so, the Director-General will convene a panel of experts to assess information provided in the case. The Council acts as mediator and arbiter in the case. But all these provisions relate to information exchanges (part of which may, of course be arrangements for on-site visits depending on the circumstances), not to an actual on-site inspection. All States Parties, as well as the Conference of the States Parties, will be informed about these endeavours and can take whatever measures they deem necessary (or, in the case of the Conference, agree on).

Under paragraph 8, each State Party has the right to request a challenge inspection in any facility or location of another State Party in order to resolve a non-compliance concern. This right is without prejudice to the State Party having made other attempts to clarify the situation (i.e., it can file request even if it has not previously tried to clarify the situation with the other State Party concerned). The right is conditioned in several ways (it has to be within the scope of the Convention, based on a non-compliance concern which is to be specified in the request, and it must avoid frivolous or abusive requests). The Executive Council has a mandate to assess requests, and may decide within 12 hours after receiving a request and with three-quarters majority against the execution of the inspection if these conditions were not met. Otherwise, however, the inspection will be executed, and the inspected State Party is under the obligation to provide access to the requested site within prescribed time frames, and to make all reasonable efforts to demonstrate its treaty compliance. It can 'manage' access in order to protect sensitive activities and installations unrelated to chemical weapons. It cannot, however, deny access altogether or otherwise obstruct the inspection and prevent the inspection team from implementing its inspection mandate.

The balancing act between protecting the right of the inspected State Party to protect confidential information unrelated to chemical weapons and ensuring that it will meet its obligation to demonstrate treaty compliance is achieved by a concept which the Convention calls 'managed access'. This concept was developed by the United Kingdom in the late 1980s and early 1990s, based on a series of national trial inspections at sensitive facilities.[591] The objective of these trials was to demonstrate that a challenge inspection could be conducted even at the most secret facilities in the land. The trials were used to develop procedures to manage inspections at such sites in such a way that the inspection mandate could be implemented without compromising national security and secrecy.

---

[591] John R. Walker, 'Chemical Weapons Verification: the UK's Practice Challenge Inspection Programme at Gevremnet Facilities', in J.B. Poole (ed.), *Verification Report 1991: Yearbook on Arms Control and Environmental Agreements* (London, VERTIC 1991), pp. 97-104.

The principle of managed access is often compared to peeling off layers from an onion to gradually reveal more of its content (in the inspection: until sufficient information has been revealed to answer the compliance question whilst essential information that was to be kept secret had not been exposed). Techniques developed to manage access included, for example, the shrouding of equipment and other items (and the partial removal of the shrouding on request by the inspection team if there was a need to establish the general nature of a shrouded item), the switching-off of computer displays, the removal of displays such as maps and plans, the masking of sensitive information in documents, or certain restrictions on access to specific buildings or structures (e.g., a limitation on the number of identical buildings that could be accessed, or of the time allowed for inspecting them, or of the number of individuals allowed to access them). At the bottom of all of these techniques was the principle that access was neither full and comprehensive, nor denied altogether, but that the degree of access was the subject of negotiations between the inspection team and the inspected State Party. Whilst the inspected State Party had the right to control access and to prevent the disclosure of confidential information unrelated to chemical weapons, it remained under an obligation to provide sufficient access so that the inspection team could satisfy itself (and subsequently the Executive Council) that no treaty violation had occurred. The inspection team, in turn, was under an obligation to keep its intrusion to the absolute necessary, but had to collect sufficient data so it could implement its inspection mandate.

All in all, the procedure for challenge inspection is the most elaborate and detailed inspection procedure in the Convention, with 17 paragraphs in Article IX and 61 paragraphs in Part X of the Verification Annex detailing every step in the process, from the submission of a request to the conduct of the inspection to the consideration of the final inspection report. Consequently, when the PrepCom returned to the issue of challenge inspection (which was the only aspect of Article IX implementation it ever addressed), one of the first question was what these talks were about. Was this a continuation (perhaps a revision) of the negotiations of the challenge inspection mechanism? Was it an extension of these negotiations so as to complete the procedural framework for challenge inspection? Or was it an attempt to make practical preparations for the implementation of the mechanism?

3. Start of Work on Challenge Inspection by the Preparatory Commission

The PrepCom took up the issue of challenge inspection in August 1993. This followed previous Expert Group discussions on the composition of inspection teams[592] and informal discussions in July 1993[593] about the objectives and content of the negotiations on challenge inspection.

---

[592] Combined Group of Experts: Inspection Team Composition, PC-III/B/WP.3, dated 28 May 1993.

[593] 'Note by the Executive Secretary: Consultations on Challenge Inspection', PC-IV/B/6, dated 19 August 1993.

The Combined Group of Experts[594] dealing with inspection team composition had already touched upon challenge inspection as one of several inspection types, and addressed team size and composition as well as the skills make-up of the team required for each such inspection type. As the basis for its estimates, the expert group had used a variety of sources, which included:

- the provisions of the Chemical Weapons Convention;
- experiences from the national trial inspections carried out during 1988-1992, *inter alia,* as contained in various documents from the CD and its subsidiary bodies;
- experiences from various United Nations and national investigations of alleged use of chemical weapons during 1982-1992;
- experiences from the United Nations Special Commission (UNSCOM) inspections in Iraq during 1991-1993;
- informal working papers submitted by the delegations of France, the Russian Federation, South Africa, the United Kingdom and the USA;
- other relevant material including working papers presented to the Preparatory Commission.

This expert group did not, however, go into the details of how such inspections ought to be conducted. It provided examples for the possible team make-up for two different challenge inspection scenarios: one a military depot suspected of stockpiling chemical weapons, the other a suspected CW production/weaponisation facility. The report showed that the experts anticipated a broad range of requirements, depending on the scenario and the characteristics of the facility to be inspected, and that team composition and size would have to be adapted in accordance with these parameters.

Based on subsequent informal consultations, the Executive Secretary then confirmed a list of issues that delegations had agreed they would take up in a new Expert Group on Challenge Inspection, and informed delegations that at the initial meeting of that group, the focus of the work would be on activities in the period from the initiation of a challenge inspection to the arrival of the inspection team at the point of entry (POE). Subsequent activities would be taken up in a later meeting. There were early indications that more than 2 expert group meetings might be required to cover the issue.[595]

The issues agreed for the initial meeting ranged from the format and content of the different types of notifications required in challenge inspection to guidelines for States

---

594 The reference to 'combined' expert groups was only used in the early days of the Preparatory Commission; it was to indicate that this was an expert group that brought together more than one kind of technical expertise. In practice, members of expert groups of the Preparatory Commission were often delegates resident in The Hague, sometime supported by technical experts sent from capitals, and the concept of expert groups being made up predominantly of specialists from one particular field of expertise or training (chemical engineers, equipment specialists, medical doctors, weapons designers, etc.) was only followed in a few cases (such as in the development of the draft OPCW health and safety policy).

595 'Note by the Executive Secretary: Consultations on Challenge Inspection', PC-IV/B/6, dated 19 August 1993, p. 1.

Parties, as well as the Technical Secretariat, regarding such issues as the content of an inspection request or the key elements of an preliminary inspection plan or checklist for inspection planning based upon whether the facility or location is declared or undeclared, the type and size of the facility or location to be inspected and the inspection mandate (e.g., team composition, equipment required for the inspection, etc.). Other issues that had previously been identified for this expert group included, *inter alia*, the development of guidelines for the conduct of challenge inspection, health and safety procedures, issues related to inspection equipment, and formats and guidelines for inspection reports.[596]

4. Discussions of the Practical Aspects of Challenge Inspection

Challenge inspection comprises a set of procedures that the negotiators in Geneva had left without loose ends – or so many people thought. Every aspect of how to request, prepare, conduct and report on such an inspection had been the subject of extended negotiations, and the set of procedures developed in the Convention was seen by many as exhaustive. In addition to the provisions contained in Article IX and Part X of the Verification Annex, additional provisions can be found in other Parts of the Verification Annex as well as the Confidentiality Annex. Different from other types of inspection, the negotiators had avoided passing any specific task regarding challenge inspection to the PrepCom. Also, they had made provisions, in Part I of the Verification Annex, for exempting certain provisions on challenge inspection from future attempts to make modifications under a simplified amendment procedure which the Convention calls 'change' and which is otherwise reserved for the adaptation, as may be necessary, of administrative and technical provisions in the Convention's Annexes.[597]

Any attempt to add to this procedural framework could have exposed divergent treaty interpretations, re-opened the negotiations and undermined the consensus that was reached in Geneva. There was therefore the question what the expert group could do without running the risk of unraveling previous agreements. The group, guided by its Chairman Andrea Perugini of Italy, decided to focus on a number of practical guidelines and understandings, starting with the development of notification formats. It also discussed certain other issues (inspector selection, inspection mandate, confidentiality and equipment), without however reaching the same degree of agreement as it did with the formats.[598]

The formats for the different types of notification required in challenge inspection came with a set of common understandings regarding both content and timing of the notifications. These formats and agreed understandings further clarified the proce-

---

[596] Meetings of Expert Groups under Working Groups A and B, Illustrative Weekly Schedule for July to September 1993, PC-III.9, dated 30 June 1993, p. 6.

[597] This procedure is contained in paras. 4 and 5 of Article XV. However, para. 4 explicitly exempts the challenge-inspection related definitions in Part I of the Verification Annex from the change procedure.

[598] Expert Group on Challenge Inspection, Initial Report, PC-IV/B/WP.10, dated 27 August 1992.

dural framework of challenge inspection, and provided operational guidance for its initiation. They were not formally adopted by the PrepCom at this early stage, but the Commission came back to them later on when it had become clear which issues regarding challenge inspection the future States Parties could agree on, and where there remained different views.

In subsequent meetings, the Expert Group on Challenge Inspection covered essentially all procedural steps associated with challenge inspection, from the submission of an inspection request to the consideration of the final inspection report by the Executive Council. It also reviewed material previously developed. Essentially, the group had embarked on developing a 'package' that would provide understandings and technical guidance on all aspects of challenge inspection. It therefore avoided bringing specific draft decisions or understanding to the Commission for formal approval, and restricted itself to informing the Commission about the progress it was making with elaborating its material.

In November 1993, the Group started discussing issues directly related to the conduct of challenge inspection, including the issues of securing the site, managed access and sampling and analysis. It also continued reviewing the issues it had previously taken up, thereby adding further technical explanations to the procedural framework of challenge inspection that clarified certain provisions of Part X of the Verification Annex. Important issues that were discussed at this stage, and that would later turn rather more complicated and contentious, included the use of inspection equipment. In 1993, the Expert Group was actually able to agree that in challenge inspection, all equipment drawn from a list approved by the Technical Secretariat and the Conference of the States Parties is available for challenge inspections.[599] It developed a number of planning guidelines for the preparation, deployment and use of inspection equipment in challenge inspection, and agreed on certain operational aspects regarding the use of location-finding equipment, photographic and communications equipment which would later be taken up again by the Expert Group on Inspection Procedures when it addressed the operational requirements, technical specifications and acceptance criteria of inspection equipment in general.

In February and March 1994, the expert group developed further the technical guidance on how to conduct a challenge inspection, developed illustrative lists of activities as well as elements to be included in the different reports due in a challenge inspection (preliminary findings, provisional report and final report), and continued its work on operational requirements for inspection equipment in challenge inspection.[600]

Other issues that the expert group took up at this stage included an understanding that in challenge inspections, there was no place for any 'temporary inspectors' given the Convention's provisions on the designation of inspectors for challenge inspection,[601] a concern that the use of languages in inspection conduct needed to be re-

---

[599] Expert Group on Challenge Inspection, First Interim Report, dated 19 November 1993, Annex (Chairman's Paper), para. 10.

[600] PC-VI/B/WO.13, dated 4 March 1994.

[601] The OPCW actually uses such a concept today for routine inspections of chemical weapons facilities – inspectors are contracted on the basis of a Special Service Agreement and can be called on short

solved, and provisions for the inspected State Party to inspect the team's inspection equipment after it had been used, for confidentiality reasons. This issue would later be taken up by the Expert Group on Inspection Procedures, which would develop a whole set of procedures for the inspection of inspection equipment after completion of inspection activities.[602] Confidentiality concerns would also surface during the negotiations of the OPCW health and safety policy.

However, as would become ever more obvious in subsequent Expert Group sessions, whilst the group was able to agree on many of the technical procedures, guidelines and understandings that related to the initial phase of a challenge inspection (from the submission of the request to the pre-inspection briefing and the preparation of an inspection plan) or its tail end (from the out-briefing at the inspection site to the submission of the inspection report to the Executive Council), it encountered major difficulties when addressing the actual inspection conduct (including the application of the Convention's concept of 'managed access'[603]). Even more difficult was it for the Expert Group to come to grips with the decision-making functions of the Executive Council both upon receipt of a challenge inspection request, and with regard to the procedure that follows the submission of the inspection report to the Council. With two exceptions, the list of issues that the Expert Group had drawn up in March 1994 for future consideration looked remarkably similar to the list of items which, three years later, the PrepCom would have to include in its final report as unresolved issues concerning challenge inspection.

The work of the Expert Group on Challenge Inspection slowed down considerably after March 1994. In April 1995, the PrepCom reviewed the issue again at its Tenth Session. It received an oral report for the Expert Group Chairman, but no further progress was reported at the time, and no draft decisions came forward.[604] In July 1995, the group met again to review its package, and to begin developing illustrative examples of the type of information which might be included under 'all appropriate information on the basis of which the concern (of possible non-compliance) has arisen', in the context of a challenge inspection request. But the meeting did not move beyond discussions of a series of Chairman's Non-papers (regarding the above-mentioned examples for information to be included in a challenge inspection request, a proposed format for a challenge inspection mandate, and a non-paper on the question of abuse of the right to request a challenge inspection). No results were recorded and no decisions forwarded to the Commission.

The Expert Group on Challenge Inspection had almost run out of steam – many of the technical issues it had initially taken on had been moved into the framework of other Expert Groups (Confidentiality, Inspection Procedures, Health and Safety) and what was left were largely issues in the 'too-difficult-to-resolve' category.

---

notice to take part in such routine inspections. The concept is not applied to inspections under Article VI of the Convention, nor to challenge inspection.

[602] These procedures were adopted by the First Session of the Conference of the States Parties: Decision 'Measures in relation to approved equipment following completion of inspection activities', C-I/DEC.51, dated 16 May 1997.

[603] Chemical Weapons Convention, paras. 46 through 52 of Part X of the Verification Annex.

[604] PC-X/B.5, dated 6 April 1995, para. 6.

In October 1995, the group met again (Ian Mundell of Canada chaired the meeting in the absence of the Chairman, Andrea Perugini of Italy). It managed to reach agreement on 'Illustrative examples of the type of information which might be included under "All appropriate information on the basis of which the concern (of possible non-compliance) has arisen", in the context of Format 1', and finalised work on the 'Format of an Inspection Mandate for the Conduct of a Challenge Inspection'. These, together with the notification formats originally developed, were sent to the Commission for approval,[605] and the Commission followed that recommendation.[606]

These practical results had been achieved despite the fact that the more difficult and essentially political issues related to the concept of challenge inspection had been looming all along. The adoption of illustrative examples of the type of information which might be included under 'All appropriate information on the basis of which the concern (of possible non-compliance) has arisen' was a first step into this more controversial domain. It dealt with certain practical aspects of how to implement the challenge inspection mechanisms, but at the same time raised concerns in some Member States that viewed any such additional clarifications as attempts to create conditions that could be used to obstruct the mechanism in the future. At the same time, it became clear that other Member States (who saw challenge inspection as a measure of last resort, almost an admission that the treaty had failed, and considered it to be highly confrontational) needed reassurances that the mechanism would be handled with care, and that its abuse would be avoided.

5. The Question of Abuse

When the group met again in February 1996, it returned to the abuse issue, based on a Chairman's discussion paper. It also received national non-papers on the issue from the delegations of China, Israel and the Russian Federation. These discussions, first of all, made a helpful and necessary distinction between abuse (by a State Party requesting a challenge inspection) and misconduct (by one or more of the members of the inspection team). Whilst the latter is addressed in the context of the OPCW's staff regulations and rules, the former is a matter that would concern the Executive Council. The Council deals with possible abuse on two occasions: when it receives a request for a challenge inspection and has to consider, in accordance with paragraph 17 of Article IX, whether to decide to abandon it, and again when the inspection has been conducted and the Council considers the inspection report under paragraph 22 of Article IX. Under that provision, the Council considers whether non-compliance has occurred, as well as whether the right to request a challenge inspection has been abused (and if so, whether the requesting State Party shall bear all or part of the cost of the challenge inspection).

---

605 PC-XII/B/WP.3, dated 17 October 1995, para. 3.

606 PC-XII/17, dated 14 December 1995, para. 8.2.

The Convention does not define 'abuse', but it qualifies the right to request a challenge inspection in several ways. Such requests must be based on a non-compliance concern,[607] and the requesting State Party is to keep:

> the inspection request within the scope of this Convention and to provide in the inspection request all appropriate information on the basis of which a concern has arisen regarding possible non-compliance with this Convention as specified in the Verification Annex. Each State Party shall refrain from unfounded inspection requests, care being taken to avoid abuse.[608]

The Commission had already adopted a decision that clarified what 'all appropriate information' encompasses, but there was a strong desire by many Member States to go further, and to make future considerations by the Council of what was abusive more predictable. On the other side of the political spectrum, there were Member States that feared that such further clarification could have an inhibitive effect on challenge inspection. In particular, these Member States had concerns that the fact that an inspection did not find evidence of non-compliance was not to be seen as an indicator of abuse.

The Expert Group on Challenge Inspection managed to agree on a number of illustrative indicators of abuse, which the Commission endorsed at its 13th Plenary Session in March 2006.[609] These indicators fall into two broad categories: information available to the Executive Council *before* the challenge inspection was conducted (whether the request had been within the Convention's scope; the results of any previous clarification attempts; information submitted on the site to be inspected including assessments of its authenticity and reliability; and whether the a challenge inspection request had previously been made by the same State Party *vis-à-vis* the same inspection site, and if so, their number and frequency), and information that *resulted* from the inspection (whether information contained in the request had been shown to be false; and whether the requesting State Party's observer had given raise to concern, including on matters relating to confidentiality (e.g., as reflected or assessed in any comments in the preliminary or final inspection report)).

The Expert Group on Challenge Inspection continued discussing issues related to possible abuse and in particular the cost aspects of abuse (a next meeting was held in April 2006), as well as the other issues that remained on its agenda (operational requirements for inspection equipment in challenge inspection, list of activities and illustrative elements of inspection reports in challenge inspection, and the timing of notification of a challenge inspection), but was no longer able to develop agreements on any of the still-open issues. Many of the practical aspects of inspection conduct had been absorbed in the work of the Expert Group on Inspection Procedures. Other issues had been resolved in previous work of other expert groups (for example, in the context of the development of the OPCW's Health and Safety as well as Confidentiality Policies).

---

607 Chemical Weapons Convention, Article IX, para. 8.

608 Ibid., para. 9.

609 PC-XIII/B/WP.4, dated 15 February 1996.

6. The Confidentiality Issue

Although negotiators in the Expert Group on Challenge Inspection had always been aware of the special needs in challenge inspection concerning the protection of confidentiality, much of the procedural and technical framework that could be used to those ends was in fact not developed by that expert group, but by others. One could argue that rather than resolving all challenge-inspection related issues in one expert group, some delegations favoured an approach whereby such issues would 'infiltrate' many other negotiation areas unrelated to (or not exclusively related to) challenge inspection. This may have been a reflection of the complexities involved, it may have been a response to concerns of some Member States that the protections afforded under Part X of the Verification Annex with regard to the protection of sensitive installations might be insufficient unless they were reinforced by complementary procedural and technical regulations elsewhere (in particular with regard to industry inspections – note that Parts VII to IX of the Verification Annex make explicit reference to the possibility for the inspected State Party to invoke managed access procedures with regard to access into structures or buildings at the declared plant site that are outside the declared plant),[610] or it may have been the result of the relatively small number of meetings which the Expert Group on Challenge Inspection held (if compared to the number of meetings held, for example, by the Expert Group on Inspection Procedures). Also, it was the result of having a dedicated expert group for the development of confidentiality procedures.

The result of this 'infiltration' process was that capability limitations on verification methods and equipment which the Convention clearly envisaged as protections under challenge inspection, to protect information that was unrelated to chemical weapons, became intrinsic features of inspection methods and equipment across the verification spectrum.

Examples for this trend can be found in the health and safety procedures applicable during inspections (where the provision of health and safety information by the inspected State Party, or the ability of an inspection team to collect its own health and safety monitoring data on-site, are conditioned by measures to protect confidential information), the adoption of procedures regarding check of inspection equipment after the cessation of inspection activities (procedures that were not foreseen by the Convention), or the requirement that certain inspection instruments can be 'blinded'. These issues have already been discussed elsewhere in this book (Chapter 7). Another example for how after the entry into force, such restrictions were imposed in addition to the protections already provided by the CWC, was the adoption of procedures to make inspector notebooks transparent to the inspected State Party:

The PrepCom did not adopt any explicit decision on how to treat inspector notebooks. But one consequence of its treatment of confidentiality issues was that upon the start of inspection operations, the Technical Secretariat was instructed by the Executive Council to adopt a standard operating procedure (SOP) that would open-up the notebooks used by inspectors during inspection conduct to the inspected State

---

610 CWC, Verification Annex, Part VII, para. 25; Part VIII, para. 20; and Part IX, para. 17.

Party. Under this procedure, if an inspected State Party so requested, inspection teams would, upon completion of their inspection activities, review their notes and eliminate any information not related to the inspection, and, thereafter and if so requested, they would surrender copies of their notes to the inspected State Party.

This issue has been discussed in some detail in the literature, and characterised as a misinterpretation of the provisions of the Convention. This discussion will not be repeated here.[611] What should be noted, however, is that although the SOP applies to all types of inspections, it is particularly problematic in a challenge inspection. If a challenge inspection would take place at a facility that had in fact violated the Convention, the SOP would almost certainly prevent inspection team members from recording information that could demonstrate the non-compliance act (alternatively, inspectors who would be recording such data and then surrender copies of their notes to the inspected State Party would betaking considerable personal risks). The SOP, if implemented in a challenge inspection, has the potential of undermining the very purpose of the inspection.

7. Other Challenge Inspection Issues

Additional understandings and procedures developed in expert groups (other than the Expert Group on Challenge Inspection) regarding challenge inspection relate to the observer, as well as to the procedural overlap between investigations of alleged use of chemical weapons (which can be initiated under either Article IX or X) and challenge inspection.

7.1 Provisions regarding the observer in challenge inspection

The observer is a feature unique to challenge inspection. He or she is a representative of the State Party requesting the challenge inspection who, upon acceptance by the inspected State Party, is entitled to come to the inspection site and observe the inspection. The observer will be briefed about the progress made in the inspection by the inspection team leader, and can make proposals for inspection activities or objects to be scrutinized. He or she has the right to stay in regular contact with the embassy of the requesting State Party. The observer, however, is not a member of the inspection team and the inspected State Party has the right to control his/her access at the inspection site.

Issues regarding the observer had already been taken up when the Expert Group on Challenge Inspection developed the notification procedures and formats. But issues related to the observer also came up in other expert groups.

The health and safety regulations included a whole section regarding health and safety considerations for the observer.[612] Essentially, this section recognises that both

---

611 Walter Krutzsch and Ralf Trapp, *Verification Practice Under the Chemical Weapons Convention – A Commentary* (The Hague, London and Boston, Kluwer Law International 1999), pp. 19-21.

612 Ibid., para. 5.2.2

the OPCW and the inspected State Party lack control over the observer's health and safety background. The onus to provide information on that background is on the requesting State Party, and the inspected State Party has the right to receive that information. At the same time, it is clear that the observer is under an obligation to respect the safety regulations that apply at the inspection site, be they OPCW or local/national safety regulations.

In a wider sense, the role of the observer is taken up in the OPCW Confidentiality Policy, under its Part IV dealing with basic responsibilities. The policy makes a useful clarification, namely that as a representative of the requesting State Party, the observer is bound not only by the provisions in Article IX and Part X of the Verification Annex, but also of Article VII, paragraph 6 (dealing with the special handling procedures that a State Party shall afford to confidential information it receives from the OPCW). As a consequence,

> the requesting State Party shall be fully responsible for and shall take all necessary measures to ensure that the observer complies with and is individually bound by all relevant provisions of this Policy, as well as to ensure that effective legal remedies and penalties are available in the event of the observer breaching confidentiality, comparable to the measures taken in the event of an official of that State Party breaching confidentiality. … [f]or his part, the observer is to adhere to and be bound by all provisions of this Policy relating to the protection of confidential information, and shall not take any unauthorised action in this regard.[613]

7.2 Challenge inspections conducted to investigate allegations of chemical weapons use

An investigation of the alleged use of chemical weapons (IAU) can either be initiated under Article X, or Article IX. In the latter case, it is a challenge inspection.

That firstly means that the work done by the Commission on future investigations of alleged use will also be relevant to challenge inspections if the request is based on an allegation that chemical weapons may have been used by a State Party. Two specific decisions on IAUs were prepared by the Commission:

- an understanding on the status of 'qualified experts' in IAU, which clarifies that such experts are members of the inspection team and therefore under the same obligations (e.g., with regard to confidentiality or the need to sign a secrecy agreement with the OPCW) as OPCW inspectors; and that they may only use OPCW approved equipment (if they bring their own equipment, it can only be brought onto the inspection site and used with the express consent of the inspected State Party);[614]
- a decision on sampling and analysis in IAU, which provides practical technical guidance on the time requirements for sampling and analysis after the alleged use of chemical weapons, on the selection of samples, sample preservation and

613 Ibid., Part IV, para. 2.2.2

614 Conference of the States Parties, First Session, Decision C-I/Dec.46, dated 16 May 1997.

transportation, sample preparation and splitting, and chemical analysis off-site.[615]

Secondly, there was the question of how the procedural framework of Part XI of the Verification Annex, dealing with IAUs, applies if the investigation was a challenge inspection. For example: how would the provisions on managed access in challenge inspection apply when Part XI of the Verification Annex stipulates that inspection teams shall have access to any and all areas which could be affected by the alleged use of chemical weapons (including, but not limited to, hospitals, refugee camps and other locations it deems relevant to the effective investigation of the alleged use of chemical weapons)?[616]

This relationship between Parts X and XI of the Verification Annex came up in the Expert Group on Inspection Procedures in 1994. To help resolving the issue, Working Group B requested a legal opinion on the matter, which was provided by the Commission's Legal Adviser in December 1994.[617] That legal opinion essentially clarified that the provisions of both Parts apply side by side (those of Part XI being 'additional provisions [that] address specific procedures required in cases of alleged use of chemical weapons'[618]). It went on to state that 'the inspectors will not be limited by a specific perimeter, but will be able to go to any and all affected areas',[619] and that '[p]aragraph 15 has no bearing on the issue of managed access. Under paragraph 47 of Part X the inspected State Party may designate only the points of entry or exit to the perimeter, but not the places to which the inspection team should go or the places within the perimeter to which inspectors may have access.'[620] It also addressed issued related to the collection and analysis of samples.

The Commission was unable to reach agreement, however, on this legal opinion, and the issue was set aside.

8. Article IX – The Implementation

Ten years after the entry into force of the Convention, the OPCW has yet to conduct a challenge inspection. Also, not a single compliance issue has been brought before the Executive Council for consideration and resolution. At the First Review Conference, the States Parties noted that bilateral consultations to clarify issues had been used, and that this mechanism was valuable in ensuring compliance with the provisions of the Convention, and in clarifying and resolving concerns. The First Review Conference

615 Conference of the States Parties, First Session, Decision C-I/Dec.47, dated 16 May 1997.

616 Chemical Weapons Convention, Part XI of the Verification Annex, para. 15.

617 Note by the Executive Secretary *Legal Opinion on the relationship between Parts X and XI of the Verification Annex if an investigation of alleged use of chemical weapons were initiated pursuant to Article IX*, PC-X/B.1, dated 21 December 1994.

618 Chemical Weapons Convention, Part XI of the Verification Annex, para. 2.

619 Ibid., para. 9.

620 Ibid., para. 12.

encouraged the States Parties to make full use of this bilateral-consultation mechanism.[621]

At the same time, the Review Conference recognised that the Secretariat, with the support of interested States Parties, had been working hard towards establishing an operational capability to mount a challenge inspection should it be called to do so. Exercises have been conducted that tested that OPCW capacity, and it is fair to say that today, the Technical Secretariat of the OPWC can respond effectively to any request for a challenge inspection should a State Party decide to file such a request. In the absence of such requests so far, the assumption has to be that other compliance assurance mechanisms by and large have been working to the satisfaction of the parties, and that all States Parties continue to be aware of the concerns of a possible abuse of the challenge inspection mechanism and consequently have been handling this delicate tool with much consideration and care.

[621] Report of the First Review Conference, document RC-1/5, dated 9 May 2003, para. 7.86.

Chapter 12

HELPING THOSE THREATENED: ARTICLE X

Ian R. Kenyon & Hassan Mashadi

The most significant use of chemical weapons on the battlefield in modern times occurred in the Iran/Iraq War where extensive use of both mustard gas and nerve agents by Iraq caused massive casualties among the inadequately protected Iranians. The use of these weapons directly influenced the outcome of the war resulting in acceptance of a UN Security Council brokered ceasefire on the original borders. Political considerations, inadequate export controls among industrialised states and the geo-political situation around the Iran/Iraq War had assisted Iraq in obtaining the equipment and raw materials needed for the production of the weapons. The subsequent formation of the 'Australia Group' to coordinate common tightening of these controls made it impossible for Iran to build up a retaliatory chemical weapon production capability or to purchase respirators and other essential protective equipment for their forces. The rationale for controls on protective equipment was that the first essential in building up an offensive chemical weapons capability is to provide your own troops with the ability to operate effectively in a chemical environment.

Partly in consequence of the above, the topic of assistance to States attacked with chemical weapons was one of the most controversial issues throughout the negotiations in Geneva, continued as such through the PrepCom period and persists as a problem during the implementation of the Chemical Weapons Convention.

1. THE POLITICAL DEBATE

The negotiations for the elements of the CWC dealing with assistance for this purpose drew lessons from what had, or had not, been achieved in earlier arms control agreements concluded in Geneva.

The 1972 Biological Weapons Convention contains a short article providing for action to be taken in cases where a Party suffers from the results of violation of the convention by another Party.

> Article VII
>
> Each State Party to this Convention undertakes to provide or support assistance, in accordance with the United Nations Charter, to any Party to the Convention which so requests,

I.R. Kenyon and D. Feakes, The Creation of the OPCW

> if the Security Council decides that such Party has been exposed to danger as a result of violation of the Convention.

The text of the corresponding provisions of the 1977 ENMOD Convention[622] reads as follows:

> Article V, paragraph 5
>
> Each State Party to this Convention undertakes to provide or support assistance, in accordance with the provisions of the Charter of the United Nations, to any State Party which so requests, if the Security Council decides that such Party has been harmed or is likely to be harmed as a result of violations of the Convention.

Provision of assistance also featured in the drafts for the chemical weapons convention from the early days of negotiations in Geneva. References to assistance were contained in the numerous submissions relating to the text of the Convention to the Conference on Disarmament (CD) and its predecessor bodies.[623]

1.1 Areas of disagreement

The simple formulation used in the BWC was not going to command consensus during the negotiations for a variety of reasons. There were a number of areas of disagreement between the Non-Aligned Group members (NAM) of the CD and the industrialized countries.

The NAM believed that assistance provisions would play a pivotal role in universality of the Convention. In their view States Parties would assume obligations throughout the treaty and only Articles X (on assistance) and XI (on technical cooperation) would bring them something in return. Other members of the CD pointed out that the primary benefit received by *all* States Parties is the security derived from chemical weapon disarmament. It was pointed out that:

> As long as countries with a CW capability remain outside the Convention, those which have abjured these weapons would continue to feel threatened and the chemical weapons prohibition regime would remain incomplete, if not fragile… A State Party which feels threatened in either of these situations might find itself compelled to acquire a deterrent chemical weapons capability of its own and therefore to withdraw from the Convention. Such an act could trigger a chain reaction leading to the withdrawal of other states parties and quite possibly to a collapse of the CW prohibition regime. If appropriate provisions are contained in the Convention, the incentives for States to adhere to the Convention

---

[622] 1977 Convention on the Prohibition of Military or Any Other Hostile Use of Environmental Modification Techniques, for text see *Arms Control*, Josef Goldblat, 2nd edn. (London, Sage Publications 2002) (enclosed CD ROM).

[623] These include: CCD/361 of 1972 (Bulgaria, Byelorussian Soviet Socialist Republic, Czechoslovakia, Hungary, Mongolia, Poland, Romania, the Ukrainian Soviet Socialist Republic and the Union of Soviet Socialist Republics); CCD/420 of 1974 (Japan); CD/294 of 1982 (Union of Soviet Socialist Republics); CD/500 of 1984 (United States); CD/752 of 1987 (Pakistan); CD/809 of 1988 (Argentina); CD/1024 of 1990 (Peru).

> could be enhanced and the pressures upon a State Party to withdraw could be considerably reduced.[624]

The developing countries were of the view that assistance should be automatic, speedy and obligatory and there should be no political filter which could prevent or delay the delivery of assistance.[625] Their arguments included:

- It is essential to guarantee the security of those who renounce the CW option in order to ensure universality of the CWC;
- Effective assistance will deter possible violations because CW use will become less effective;
- To ensure the automaticity the Executive Council should have under its control a stockpile of protective equipment which could be placed at the disposal of the threatened State.[626]

The industrialised countries advanced a more voluntary concept of assistance arguing:

- How can assistance be delivered if the requesting party is a violator of the CWC? The voluntary aspect should be given importance and priority otherwise the matter will become politicized.[627]
- Automaticity may lead to the abuse of the right.[628]
- If assistance becomes mandatory it will require a lot of technical capabilities of States Parties. Can they afford to provide it?[629]

In examining the relationship between Article X and Article XI[630] in assisting States Parties to develop protection industries or protective capabilities, the NAM maintained that the Convention should provide for international cooperation and assistance in the development of a protective capability by States whose security might be threatened by the retention or acquisition of a chemical weapons capability by an adversary. They stressed that:

> the Convention should contain provisions for the widest possible dissemination of scientific and technical knowledge on protective measures and equipment.[631]

---

[624] Proposal on Article X (Assistance) of the Draft Convention on Chemical Weapons. Paper presented by Pakistan to the Conference on Disarmament (CD/752) 23 April 1987.

[625] Chairman's paper, 'Article X: Assistance and Protection against Chemical Weapons', CD/CW/WP.324, dated 10 January 1991.

[626] Paper presented by Pakistan, CD/CW//WP.165 (CD/752), dated 23 April 1987.

[627] Presentation by the United States in Working Group of Ad Hoc Committee, dated 23 February 1988.

[628] Presentation by the French delegation in Open-Ended Consultations on Assistance, dated 29 March 1990.

[629] Presentation by the UK delegation in Working Group B, dated 23 February 1988.

[630] Article XI – Economic and Technological Development – is discussed in Chapter 14.

[631] Paper by Pakistan mentioned above, CD/752, dated 23 April 1987.

In their view:

> a wider dissemination of technical knowledge on protective equipment measures and wider use of such measures could increase the incentives for States which potentially fear the use of such weapons.

The counter-argument put forward was that this is a commercial transaction which can be implemented bilaterally with no need of involvement of the OPCW.

The role of the UN Security Council (UNSC) was also divisive with the majority of NAM members supporting the need for provisions in the CWC on effective collective sanctions against a State Party which acted in violation of the Convention and against any other State whose activities posed a threat to its objectives. Believing that there had been a lack of a proper response by the UNSC *vis-à-vis* the extensive use of chemical weapons by Iraq against Iranian troops and civilians and also against the Iraqi people, they were reluctant to leave violations to be established by the UNSC. Conversely, the industrialised countries preferred a greater role for both the UNSC and the Executive Council of the OPCW.

Further topics of disagreement included: recognition of technical dimensions of assistance and preparations of relevant lists for possible inclusion as an annex to Article X; clarification and discussion of various time frames and operations of the provisions; provision of assistance in destruction of chemical weapons and chemical weapons production facilities; and assistance in preservation of the environment against chemical hazards.

1.2 An attempt to find common ground

The issue of Article X was debated in Group A of the CD's Ad Hoc Committee on Chemical Weapons. The Chairman of this group circulated a paper proposing a compromise solution.[632]

The chairman noted that there seemed to be two kinds of assistance: one in the form of speedy, obligatory and automatic by the CWC organisation, and another, after necessary inspection and on a voluntary basis, based on the capability and the wishes of States Parties. In his view, this can be carried out in the following ways:

- In cases where a State Party claims to have been subjected to chemical attack, emergency assistance will be delivered within 24 hours. This emergency assistance will be obligatory and automatic and will be carried out under the supervision of the Director-General of the Technical Secretariat. He will also in parallel dispatch a team for evaluation of the situation;
- In case a State Party claims to have come under chemical threat, measures to investigate the situation and a report of the situation passed to the Executive Council. If the claim is substantiated, as decided by a majority vote in the Executive Council, the 'emergency assistance' which is obligatory and automatic will be

632 Chairman's discussion paper, Article X, Group A/5, dated 28 May 1991.

delivered under the supervision of the Director-General of the Technical Secretariat; and
- Other forms of assistance could include 'humanitarian' and 'supplementary' assistance which after necessary study and decision-making will be provided voluntarily (by the States Parties or from the voluntary fund).

2. The Adopted Text

The developments relating to the Iran-Iraq War, while having some positive effects on the negotiations, politicised negotiations of Article X and prevented negotiators from deliberating the technical aspects of implementation of the Article and operationalisation of its provisions. In the view of the NAM this resulted in some shortcomings in the Article and its corresponding section (Part XI) in the Verification Annex.

Article X, paragraph 1 defines the protection to be provided as:

> For the purposes of this Article, 'Assistance' means the coordination and delivery to States Parties of protection against chemical weapons, including, inter alia, the following: detection equipment and alarm systems; protective equipment; decontamination equipment and decontaminants; medical antidotes and treatments; and advice on any of these protective measures.

Throughout the preparatory phase and to date during the implementation of the Convention, the old debate of the role of OPCW in assistance lingers on. The meaning of the terms 'coordination' and 'delivery' has not been discussed and their operationalisation not been completed. Lack of consensus in this area has affected the operation of the whole Article. There remains a need for consensus on the definition of coordination (whether the TS will coordinate the assistance operation or just coordinate the communications and contacts between the offering States Parties and the requesting State Party). The issue of delivery is even more controversial. One group of States Parties stress that the Technical Secretariat neither has the capacity nor the mandate to deliver assistance and paragraph 1 referring to the 'Organisation' means 'States Parties'. This ambiguity which has immense operational implication emanates from the following provisions of Article X:

- 'Each State Party undertakes to provide assistance through the Organization' [paragraph 7];
- 'The Executive Council … shall take a decision … whether to instruct the Technical Secretariat to provide supplementary assistance', 'When so decided by the Executive Council, the Director-General shall provide assistance immediately', and 'The States Parties shall make the fullest possible efforts to provide assistance' [paragraph 10]; and
- 'the Director-General shall notify all States Parties and shall take emergency measures of assistance' [paragraph 11].

The article continues by reaffirming the right to acquire protection, either by domestic production or by external acquisition.

3. The Preparatory Commission

The PrepCom delegated work on Article X issues to its Working Group B which, in turn passed them to an Expert Group entitled 'Technical Cooperation and Assistance', which also considered issues relating to Article XI and general questions of cooperation in operation of the Convention. The agreements between the organisation and individual Member States, required under Article X, paragraph 7b proved straightforward. The working group simply mandated the legal department of the Provisional Technical Secretariat to produce a suitable draft and this was adopted at the seventh session of the commission in July 1994.[633]

The group also recommended that a separate expert group be established to address the issue of transparency in national protection programs and to agree how these should be reported, even though this fell within their remit as part of Article X. In fact this remained one of those unresolved issues passed to the new organisation after entry into force.

Article X, paragraph 4 requires each State Party to provide annually to the Technical Secretariat information on its national protection program for the purposes of transparency. The PrepCom was unable to agree on reporting procedures and referred the issue to the Conference of States Parties. Their efforts were aimed mainly at striking a balance between transparency and intrusion into national security; the degree of detail in reporting; and to whom the information could be made available. After EIF, many delegations took the view that, in the absence of an agreement on the information to be provided and the format for its provision, they were not able to make a declaration under this provision. It was only in November 2004 that the OPCW adopted a format for submission of national protection programmes.

The issue of the databank of information on assistance to be held by the Technical Secretariat was also handled by asking the PTS to make the necessary preparations, although the Commission did assist by endorsing the list of data types provided in a chairman's paper,[634] by requesting Member States to provide the databank with documents and requesting the Executive Secretary, *within the budget*, to begin an active search for documents on protection against chemical weapons.[635]

Article X, paragraph 5 requires the Technical Secretariat to maintain a data bank of 'freely available information' on protection and to provide 'expert advice' to States Parties. (Article X, paragraph 6 notes that States can act bilaterally outside the procedures of the Convention.) The PrepCom succeeded in achieving its objective in this

633 Draft Model Bilateral Agreement Concerning the Procurement of Assistance, Annex A, PC-VII/B/WP. 6.

634 Expert Group on Technical Cooperation and Assistance, 'Second Interim Report', PC-V/B/WP.16, dated 3 December 1991, Appendix 4.

635 Expert Group on Technical Cooperation and Assistance, 'Second Interim Report', PC-V/B/WP.16, dated 3 December 1991.

area and recommended that the data bank on protection against chemical weapons, to be established in accordance with Article X, paragraph 5 of the Convention, be part of a library in the Technical Secretariat, and that this repository of information be indexed by a database which should be a standard commercially or otherwise available bibliographical programme allowing for the inclusion of data types such as those listed in Appendix 4.[636] The corresponding decision of the Conference of States Parties[637] has so far been only partially implemented due to lack of adequate resources and to practical issues (responsibility for the content, liability, availability, whether to use primary or secondary sources).

As indicated in the first section of this chapter, the real nub of the Article is in the next three sections, Article X, paragraph 7 which sets out the undertaking to provide assistance; paragraph 8 on the right to request assistance; and the remaining paragraphs 9, 10 and 11 which set out the procedures for investigations by the Director-General and related actions by the Executive Council. It is worthwhile to quote paragraphs 7 and 8 in full:

> 7. Each State Party undertakes to provide assistance through the Organization and to this end to elect to take one or more of the following measures:
> a) To contribute to the voluntary fund for assistance to be established by the Conference at its first session;
> b) To conclude, if possible not later than 180 days after this Convention enters into force for it, agreements with the Organization concerning the procurement, upon demand, of assistance;
> c) To declare, not later than 180 days after this Convention enters into force for it, the kind of assistance it might provide in response to an appeal by the Organization.
>
> If, however, a State Party subsequently is unable to provide the assistance envisaged in its declaration, it is still under the obligation to provide assistance in accordance with this paragraph.
>
> 8. Each State Party has the right to request and, subject to the procedures set forth in paragraphs 9, 10 and 11, to receive assistance and protection against the use or threat of use of chemical weapons if it considers that:
> a) Chemical weapons have been used against it;
> b) Riot control agents have been used against it as a method of warfare; or
> c) It is threatened by actions or activities of any State that are prohibited for States Parties by Article I.

Regarding implementation of these two paragraphs, the Commission adopted three documents:

- Establishment of a Voluntary Fund;[638] that the administration of Fund shall be in accordance with the applicable OPCW Financial Regulations. The group successfully reduced its workload by recommending that the procedures for operat-

636 'Report of the Commission', PC-V/12, dated 17 December 1993, para. 6.7(b).
637 C-I/DEC.53.
638 PC-XIII/A/2.

ing the voluntary fund for assistance should be developed by an expert group on financial matters and that the necessary software for operating the databank should be selected by the Expert Group on Data Systems. The CSP consequently adopted the detail procedure for its implementation;[639]

- Understanding on the status of 'Qualified Experts' in the context of Investigation of Alleged Use of Chemical Weapons;[640] and
- List of Items to be Stockpiled for Emergency and Humanitarian Assistance in Accordance with Article VIII(39)(B);[641] One partial success of the expert group related to the requirement that they should develop lists of items to be stockpiled for emergency and humanitarian assistance. They failed to do anything so prescriptive but, on the recommendation of the Group, the Commission adopted the 'indicative lists of *categories of information on assistance* that could be made available by States Parties'.[642] [emphasis added]

It will be seen that, by contrast with the Biological Weapons Convention quoted at the beginning of this chapter, the CWC allows the State Party itself to decide that it has been the subject of chemical weapons use (or threat of use) and this immediately triggers the mechanism under this Article. It is worthy of note, given the current concerns over terrorism, that only 8(c) mentions a State as the perpetrator – 8(a) would clearly include use by non-state actors.

The Convention lays particular duties on the Technical Secretariat relating to Article X. These are in Article VIII:

> 39. The Technical Secretariat shall:
> [...]
> (b) Not later than 180 days after entry into force of this Convention, coordinate the establishment and maintenance of permanent stockpiles of emergency and humanitarian assistance by States Parties in accordance with Article X, paragraphs 7 (b) and (c). The Technical Secretariat may inspect the items maintained for serviceability. Lists of items to be stockpiled shall be considered and approved by the Conference pursuant to paragraph 21 (i) above;
> (c) Administer the voluntary fund referred to in Article X, compile declarations made by the States Parties and register, when requested, bilateral agreements concluded between States Parties or between a State Party and the Organization for the purposes of Article X.

This in turn led to the requirements in the Paris Resolution, paragraph 12 that:

> The Commission shall develop, inter alia, [...] for consideration and approval by the Conference of States Parties [...]:
> a. [...]

639 C-I/DEC.52.
640 PC-XII/17, subpara. 8.6(b), then C-I/DEC.46.
641 PC-VII/8 then C-I/DEC.12.
642 Annex B to PC-VII/B/WP.6.

b. Lists of items to be stockpiled for emergency and humanitarian assistance in accordance with Article VIII, paragraph 39 (b);
c. [...]
d. Procedures for the provision of information by States parties on their programmes related to protective purposes, in accordance with Article X, paragraph 4.

4. Article X: Unfinished Business?

As was mentioned before, the politicisation of Article X and lack of sufficient time during the endgame prevented the CD negotiators from elaborating the detailed procedure for its implementation as had been done in the case of Article VI. According to Article X each State Party has the right to request and to receive assistance and protection (subject to procedures) against the use or threat of use of chemical weapons if it considers that:

(a) Chemical weapons have been used against it;
(b) Riot control agents have been used against it as a method of warfare; or
(c) It is threatened by actions or activities or any State that are prohibited for States Parties by Article I.

There were calls for detailed procedures for each case mentioned in Article X. However, the Convention in Part XI of the Verification Annex only refers to Investigation in cases of use of Chemical Weapons. Procedures for assessment of threat and provision of assistance do not figure in the Convention primarily because there were last minute objections to the inclusion of reference to threat.

> Threat of use: threat of use of course contains two components-the existence of chemical weapons which pose a threat and which can be judged objectively, and the intent to use those weapons if they exist which of course can only be subjective assessment. It is difficult to see how the Organisation will be able to make evaluations of such threat in a consistent manner.
> ... but threat also depends on the likely intent of the state possessing the means to threaten and, as with (b) above, this would require subjective evaluation.[643]

Similarly there exists no procedure or mechanism in case of use of riot control agents as a method of warfare. Paragraph 1 of Part XI of the Verification Annex states:

> Investigations of alleged use of chemical weapons, or of alleged use of riot control agents as a method of warfare, initiated pursuant to Articles IX or X, shall be conducted in accordance with this Annex and detailed procedures to be established by the Director-General.

[643] Informal Non-Paper by United Kingdom of Great Britain and Northern Ireland, dated 25 January 1989 (paras. b and c, p. 2).

The following paragraph 2, however, says 'The following additional provisions address specific procedures required in cases of alleged use of chemical weapons.' In other words there is a need to develop procedures for both assessment of threat and investigation of use of riot control agents.

5. Conclusion

In the fourteen years since the CWC was opened for signature there has been no case of use of chemical weapons in interstate warfare, although it was considered necessary to make provision to protect the troops against the possibility of such use during the 2003 invasion of Iraq, as it had been in 1991. The situation in civil war situations has been less clear cut with, for example, allegations of use in Bosnia.[644] Meanwhile, the use of Sarin by Aum Shinrikyo, first in Matsumoto, Japan in 1994 and then in the Tokyo subway system in 1995 opened a new aspect in the problem for governments in protecting their people against chemical weapons. The Aum precedent, coupled with the demonstration on 11 September 2001 of the willingness of terrorist groups in the 21st century to cause very high levels of civilian casualties has needed new laws and expensive equipment and training for forces of law and order and emergency responders. Whilst the large industrialised countries can cope with these demands from their own resources and expertise, the vast majority of countries are going to need help if they find themselves targeted. It would seem appropriate for OPCW, perhaps in the context of the Second Review Conference of the CWC, to consider whether it is time to put more resources and political effort into improving the implementation of Article X.

[644] Thomas Stock, Maria Haug, Patricia Radler, 'Chemical and biological weapon developments and arms control', *SIPRI Yearbook 1996* (Stockholm/Oxford, SIPRI/OUP 1996), pp. 661-708 at p. 662.

Chapter 13

Cooperation in Peaceful Uses: Article XI

Ian R. Kenyon & Sergei Kisselev

The major dilemma of those attempting to negotiate regimes to control weapons of mass destruction has been the problem of the dual use to which the necessary technologies can be put – to produce such weapons or for non-warlike purposes of great benefit to mankind. The issue is addressed in the 1968 Nuclear Non-Proliferation Treaty (NPT) in its Article IV. In its first paragraph it sets out the principle of the right of all states to peaceful use of the technology:

> 1. Nothing in this Treaty shall be interpreted as affecting the inalienable right of all the Parties to the Treaty to develop research, production and use of nuclear energy for peaceful purposes without discrimination and in conformity with Articles I and II of this Treaty.

It then goes on to require an undertaking of the parties to cooperate in such peaceful use:

> 2. All the Parties to the Treaty undertake to facilitate, and have the right to participate in, the fullest possible exchange of equipment, materials and scientific and technological information for the peaceful uses of nuclear energy. Parties to the Treaty in a position to do so shall also co-operate in contributing alone or together with other States or international organizations to the further development of the applications of nuclear energy for peaceful purposes, especially in the territories of non-nuclear-weapon States Party to the Treaty, with due consideration for the needs of the developing areas of the world.

This apparently liberal regime is however constrained by the previous Article III which requires that:

> 2. Each State Party to the Treaty undertakes not to provide: *(a)* source or special fissionable material, or *(b)* equipment or material especially designed or prepared for the processing, use or production of special fissionable material, to any non-nuclear weapon State for peaceful purposes, unless the source or special fissionable material shall be subject to the safeguards required by this Article.

The 'safeguards' to which this article refers are applied by the International Atomic Energy Agency (IAEA). Each state acquiring source or special fissionable material declares the amount and its location to the Agency which then sends inspectors to confirm the declaration. The inspections continue at regular intervals to assure the international community, and in particular the supplier state, that the material has not been diverted to improper uses.

This arrangement has not been sufficient to satisfy the principal owners of the technology that their overriding need to prevent diversion of materials to nuclear weapons purposes can be met. They have, therefore, formed the Nuclear Suppliers Group (NSG), through which they coordinate their export control policies and share information about attempts to acquire the most sensitive technologies. They routinely refuse to provide uranium enrichment plants, offering instead supplies of enriched fuel. They similarly refuse to cooperate in construction of plants for the reprocessing of spent fuel for the recovery of plutonium, advocating instead the so-called 'once through' fuel cycle. These activities have been a matter of dispute between the members and non-members of the NSG at the successive five yearly review conferences of the NPT.

Another factor in the politics of peaceful use of dual use technologies is the long-standing agreement within the IAEA that the safeguards budget should be balanced by an equivalent financial commitment to technical assistance in the peaceful use of nuclear energy for developing countries.

The Biological Weapons Convention (BWC), opened for signature four years after the NPT, also contains an article on peaceful uses (Article X). This takes a slightly different approach, starting with a paragraph virtually identical with the second paragraph in Article IV of the NPT:

> 1. The States Parties to this Convention undertake to facilitate, and have the right to participate in, the fullest possible exchange of equipment, materials and scientific and technological information for the use of bacteriological (biological) agents and toxins for peaceful purposes. Parties to the Convention in a position to do so shall also cooperate in contributing individually or together with other States or international organizations to the further development and application of scientific discoveries in the field of bacteriology (biology) for prevention of disease, or for other peaceful purposes.

and continuing with a paragraph which, rather than talking of 'inalienable rights', insists on implementation in a manner not likely to damage the economic interest of developing states:

> 2. This Convention shall be implemented in a manner designed to avoid hampering the economic or technological development of States Parties to the Convention or international cooperation in the field of peaceful bacteriological (biological) activities, including the international exchange of bacteriological (biological) agents and toxins and equipment for the processing, use or production of bacteriological (biological) agents and toxins for peaceful purposes in accordance with the provisions of the Convention.

The BWC contains no provisions for verification involving international inspection and so there is no equivalent in its Article X to the link between Articles III and IV in the NPT described above.

The 20 years which passed between the opening for signature of the BWC and of the CWC saw a further worsening of relations between developed countries and some of the developing countries with regard to the problem of transfer of dual use technologies. In particular, developed countries had found it necessary to set up an export control regime (known as the 'Australia Group') to coordinate control of the export of materials and equipment relevant to the production of chemical and biological weapons. The developing countries which had been most affected by the activities of this group wished to ensure that the new Chemical Weapons Convention regime would obviate the need for the Australia Group's regulation of sensitive chemicals and chemical technologies and that the States Parties to the CWC would not suffer any restriction in imports of such items for peaceful purposes.

The CWC as finally negotiated contains two paragraphs in its Article XI 'economic and technological development'. The first of these paragraphs is almost identical to the second paragraph in Article X of the BWC:

> 1. The provisions of this Convention shall be implemented in a manner which avoids hampering the economic or technological development of States Parties, and international cooperation in the field of chemical activities for purposes not prohibited under this Convention including the international exchange of scientific and technical information and chemicals and equipment for the production, processing or use of chemicals for purposes not prohibited under this Convention.

The second paragraph is more elaborate. It opens with two subparagraphs which are in substance similar to material in the NPT and BWC:

> 2. Subject to the provisions of this Convention and without prejudice to the principles and applicable rules of international law, the States Parties shall:
>
> (a) Have the right, individually or collectively, to conduct research with, to develop, produce, acquire, retain, transfer, and use chemicals;
> (b) Undertake to facilitate, and have the right to participate in, the fullest possible exchange of chemicals, equipment and scientific and technical information relating to the development and application of chemistry for purposes not prohibited under this Convention;

It continues, however, with text which is clearly designed to inhibit the activities of the Australia Group:

> (c) Not maintain among themselves any restrictions, including those in any international agreements, incompatible with the obligations undertaken under this Convention, which would restrict or impede trade and the development and promotion of scientific and technological knowledge in the field of chemistry for industrial, agricultural, research, medical, pharmaceutical or other peaceful purposes;
> (d) Not use this Convention as grounds for applying any measures other than those provided for, or permitted, under this Convention nor use any other international agreement for pursuing an objective inconsistent with this Convention;

(e) Undertake to review their existing national regulations in the field of trade in chemicals in order to render them consistent with the object and purpose of this Convention.

Even this strong text was not sufficient for all the members of the non-aligned group (the Group of 21) within the Conference on Disarmament (CD) to agree, at the end of the 1992 session, to the closure of the drafting process on the CWC and its transmission to the United Nations General Assembly. They insisted on a statement of policy on behalf of the Australia Group. A statement was made in August 1992 by the representative of Australia on the behalf of the 22 participants of the group.[645]

In the statement, the 22 participants 'undertake to be original signatories' of the CWC and 'fully to comply' with Article XI which, they say:

> aims at facilitating the fullest possible exchanges in the field of chemical activities for purposes not prohibited under the convention so as to promote the harmonious economic or technological development of all States parties.

Further:

> They undertake to review, in the light of the implementation of the convention, the measures that they take to prevent the spread of chemical substances and equipment for purposes contrary to the objectives of the convention, with the aim of removing such measures for the benefit of States parties to the convention acting in full compliance with their obligations under the convention. They intend thus to contribute actively to an increase in commercial and technological exchanges between States and to the universal and full implementation of the convention on the prohibition of chemical weapons.

This essentially broke the deadlock and after some more days of debate the CWC was indeed adopted by consensus by the CD and forwarded to the UNGA which commended it to its Member States for signature and ratification. However, the problem of export controls did not go away and formed the background to the debate on technical assistance issues throughout the life of the PrepCom.

To assist in the fulfilment of its mandate, the PrepCom established a range of expert groups under the supervision of its two Working Groups. Working Group B established a single Group of Experts on Technical Cooperation and Assistance with a wide remit. After its first working session in May/June 1993 the expert group considered the terms 'technical cooperation' and 'assistance' as they are used in the Convention and observed that:

- the multifaceted terms technical cooperation and assistance among States Parties and between States Parties and the Organisation apply in their general meanings to many provisions of the Convention;

---

645 Statement made on behalf of the 'Australia Group' by the Representative of Australia, Ambassador Paul O'Sullivan, at the 629th Plenary Meeting of the Conference on Disarmament, CD/1164, dated 7 August 1992.

- technical cooperation and assistance run throughout the Convention as common threads and serve as a lubricant for the smooth meshing of its gears;
- the terms should be interpreted in the broad sense of process – permitting the Convention to operate successfully – rather than in the restricted sense of giver and receiver;
- all parts of the Convention are inter-related and are to be implemented as a whole.[646]

Several provisions in the Convention pertain to the multifaceted meanings of technical cooperation and assistance. Perhaps the most general in scope appears in Article VIII, paragraph 21(g) requires the Conference of the States Parties to 'foster international cooperation for peaceful purposes in the field of chemical activities'.

From the outset, the Group's work was overshadowed by the disagreement between developed and developing Signatory States on whether national and international export control regimes, including the Australia Group, and the restrictions which they might apply on trade among future States Parties to the CWC, should or in fact could exist, without violating the undertaking of free trade in Article XI. The discussion was complicated by the lack of a single view of this issue among developing countries. This was not surprising, in view of the different status enjoyed by individual developing countries *vis-à-vis* the Australia Group and in the light of varying bilateral relationships between individual developed and developing countries.

The Australia Group members were of the opinion that export licensing measures were fully consistent with and entirely supportive of the undertaking under Article XI. They also stressed that Article XI obligations cannot be taken out of context and should be seen as complementary to Article I. They argued that the trade restrictions set out in the Verification Annex of the Convention are not the only ones which are legitimate and that if those trade restrictions were adopted as the standard for all States Parties they would seriously undermine the effectiveness of the CWC as the barrier to the spread of chemical weapons. They also held that the Convention does not establish any specific period within which national reviews under Article XI, paragraph 2(e) should take place. The Australia Group members therefore argued in favour of taking a more practical approach aimed at developing specific technical cooperation programmes for the OPCW.

While developing countries, in general, held the view that the maintenance of parallel export control regimes would be incompatible with a State Party's obligations under the CWC and would lead to the creation of two separate categories of States Parties – those enjoying free trade and those subjected by the former to discriminatory export controls – there were different degrees of opinion as to when such parallel regimes should cease to exist and what shape international cooperation should take under Article XI.

The Asian Group seemed to be the one most divided. As a common denominator, it held the view that all parallel regimes regulating trade in chemicals would be in contravention with the letter and spirit of the Convention and should cease to exist.

646 PC-III/B/WP.4.

Some delegations in this group took a much more specific view, seeking adequate assurances that existing restrictions on trade would be reviewed once the Convention was in force and that the provisions of Article XI should be duly implemented at EIF. They also sought a clarification on this matter by the Australia Group.[647] At the same time, there were obvious disagreements as to the role of the application of end-use certificates among States Parties as a possible alternative to export control measures unrelated to the CWC.[648]

Members of the African and the Latin American groups, while not disputing the argument of the incompatibility of CWC transfer restrictions and parallel export control regimes, took a more pragmatic view that, in order to facilitate the fullest possible exchange of chemicals, equipment and technical information for purposes not prohibited under the Convention, it was necessary for the PTS to strengthen the outreach and support activities to different regions through the holding of technical meetings, seminars and courses. They also saw this as a means to promote the ratification of the CWC.[649] One member of the Latin American group stressed, however, the urgency of obtaining guarantees of removal of any restrictions on trade[650] and insisted that such guarantees should be obtained before EIF.

One related issue which made the whole discussion more complicated was whether the scope of the CWC verification regime included unscheduled chemicals, whether such unscheduled chemicals may be considered of dual-use nature and whether trade in them may at all be restricted by the non-proliferation regime of the Convention. Some developing countries held the view that unscheduled chemicals, and specifically toxic chemicals among them, can only be controlled if added to one of the Schedules.[651]

The Australia Group, on the contrary, held that keeping unscheduled chemicals outside the scope of CWC verification would be contrary to Article I obligations never to assist in any way the manufacture of chemical weapons, since some of these unscheduled chemicals, if diverted, may be used as CW precursors. Members of this group argued, in this context, that national export licensing policies were focused solely on preventing assistance to activities banned under the CWC and therefore represented a means of fulfilling the Article I obligations. Moreover, they indicated that national export control measures are fully supportive of the undertaking under Article XI, which are complementary to Article I.[652] One member of the Australia Group stressed that it could not and would not agree to any reduction or limitation of these effective and essential measures.

Despite all the technical nuances of positions held by various members of the PrepCom, the bottom line of the discussion around the implementation of Article XI was CWC compliance. Some members of the PrepCom believed that the Convention

647 PC-XII/16.

648 PC-XV/10, PC-XV/B/WP.6.

649 PC-XII/13, PC-XVI/26.

650 PC-XIII/11.

651 PC-XII/B/WP.9.

652 PC-XII/B/WP.11.

possesses the adequate and the only vehicle to investigate suspicions of non-compliance through its consideration by the Executive Council and the Conference of the States Parties, including through the mechanism of Article IX, and that therefore a suspicion of non-compliance by an importing State Party should not be treated as a trade issue warranting unilateral action, but as an issue affecting security interests of all States Parties to the Convention. According to this view, in case there are no sound reasons for suspicion of non-compliance by the importing State Party, the exporting State Party cannot impose any restrictions other than those in the export control regime of the Convention.

On a somewhat conciliatory note, some of the proponents of this approach believed that parallel export control groupings are thus not necessarily contrary to the Convention, provided that their members are States Parties to the Convention and that their export control legislation that surpasses or is incompatible with the Convention is not applied to transfers among States Parties. Conversely, parallel export control regimes with schedules and scope exceeding those of the Convention were only applicable to States not party. In other words, political arrangements among States Parties can play a non-proliferation role but, insofar as there are international verifiable legal instruments with similar purposes, they must evolve in order not to contradict the letter and spirit of those international treaties.[653]

The opposite view held that individual States Parties retain the ultimate authority to judge compliance or non-compliance by others and, therefore, the right to adopt unilateral measures under Article I, including by refusing transfers of sensitive chemicals or technologies.[654]

The stalemate in the discussion of the issue of export controls produced a dual effect. On the one hand, both sides made more carefully argued, albeit more diametrically opposed, elaboration of their views. Concrete proposals were put forward by some developing countries to establish multilateral CWC control mechanisms which could substitute parallel export control regimes from the date of entry into force of the Convention.[655] All this, however, did not produce any substantive forward movement. The Expert Group on Technical Cooperation and Assistance found itself gradually unable to agree on meaningful official reports of its activities (its last, Eleventh, Report was adopted in June 1996, with ten months remaining until the EIF).[656] The PrepCom likewise was unable to make any recommendations on Article XI issues in its Final Report to the First Session of the CSP.[657] On the other hand, other, more

[653] PC-XIII/12.

[654] This view was expected by many observers to be driven, during the preparatory period, by the untested nature of the Article IX procedures. Nevertheless, even after a few years into the CWC implementation, including after numerous recourses to the procedures of bilateral consultation and clarification under Article IX, at least one State Party formally reconfirmed this view on compliance judgment.

[655] PC-XV/B/WP.6.

[656] PC-XIV/B/WP.6.

[657] 'Final Report of the Preparatory Commission for the Organisation for the Prohibition of Chemical Weapons to the First Session of the Conference of the States Parties of the Organisation for the Prohibition of Chemical Weapons and to the First Meeting of the Executive Council of the Organisation for the Prohibition of Chemical Weapons', PC-XVI/37, dated 15 April 1997.

modest ideas pursuing the objective of facilitating developing countries' access to modern technical information and technologies proved to be more successful.

Following its meeting in July 1993 the Group of Experts on Technical Cooperation and Assistance reiterated the urgent need for cooperation in assisting Signatory States to prepare for the entry into force of the Convention by mutually and collectively supporting efforts to harmonise legislation and implementation systems with the requirements of the CWC.[658] The Group put a considerable amount of effort during its succeeding meetings into helping the Secretariat to organise a series of courses and seminars related to national implementation. This exercise is described in Chapter X.

The Group also discussed issues relating to the provision of Assistance under Article X, including, *inter alia*, the Voluntary Fund, types of assistance, stockpiling of equipment and material for assistance and measures for protection. All of this work is described in Chapter 12.

In February 1994:

> the Group explored, on a preliminary basis, various issues arising out of its mandate regarding the implementation of Article XI. It agreed that the scope of that mandate encompassed the suggestion of practical ways and means for the promotion of free trade and international cooperation in the field of chemicals for purposes not prohibited under the Convention and the definition of the role of the Conference of the States Parties (CSP), the Executive Council (EC) and the Technical Secretariat in the implementation of such measures.
>
> The Group agreed that the CWC is a disarmament treaty and that it also represents an opportunity for the enhancement of the economic and technological development of all States Parties through, *inter alia*, the facilitation of free trade in chemicals for purposes not prohibited under the Convention. The Group discussed various practical measures for the effective implementation of the provisions of Article XI. There was some divergence of views on effective means of implementation of the Article. It was therefore agreed that these matters require further consideration.
>
> The Group agreed that the fullest possible use should be made of the mechanisms of consultation and cooperation that will be established by the entry into force of the Convention in order to resolve any concerns that might be raised by a State Party or any organ of the OPCW about the compliance of another State Party with the Convention. When a State Party felt that its rights under Article XI were being infringed or that a State Party was not fulfilling its obligations under Article XI the matter could be brought to the attention of the CSP and the EC by the aggrieved State Party for resolution according to the relevant provisions of the Convention.
>
> The Group attempted to identify obstacles, incompatible with CWC obligations, which impede or restrict international cooperation in the field of trade in chemicals, or in the scientific and technical exchange of information amongst States Parties in relation to chemical activities not prohibited under the Convention. There were diverse opinions as to the identity and nature of these obstacles. Again it was agreed that these matters require further consideration.

[658] PC-IV/B/WP.6.

> Regarding the role of the organs of the OPCW in promoting the implementation of Article XI, the Group discussed whether the Technical Secretariat should compile and maintain an inventory of relevant national regulations in the field of trade in chemicals. It was also discussed that such information could be available to States Parties, if necessary, in preparing their own regulations and could also provide relevant information in case of any concern about the consistency of the regulations of another State Party with the object and purpose of the CWC. There was a discussion, but no consensus on the Technical Secretariat's role in identifying obstacles and subsequently urging States Parties to render them consistent with the object and purpose of the CWC. It was agreed that this matter requires further consideration.[659]

Unfortunately, the phrase 'these matters require further consideration' occurs only too frequently in this and subsequent reports of the group. It is also evident from this report that the issue of the Australia group had not gone away.

The lack not only of consensus but even of focus on the object of the debate is clearly demonstrated by the following extract from a report of the group in mid-1994:

> During the present meeting there was a divergence of opinions on some basic principles. While some delegations held that more results could be achieved in the short-term if measures for practical implementation were discussed and finalised first, others considered it impossible to debate practice before establishing principles. These matters will therefore need further consideration.
>
> There was a divergence of opinions on whether all national preparations for implementation of obligations under Article XI, particularly measures to review national regulations in the field of trade in chemicals, should be finalised before or after entry into force of the Convention for a State Party. Some delegations stressed that it would be unacceptable to have two ways of preparing for implementation of the Convention before entry into force. Others emphasised the view that overall effective implementation of the Convention will steadily enhance confidence in ways which will substantially boost the kinds of cooperation foreseen under Article XI. The view was expressed that it was not in the mandate of the Preparatory Commission to devise implementation procedures going beyond treaty-mandated obligations and the mandate of the Paris Resolution. Some delegations expressed the view that individual Member States should be encouraged to begin or continue, as appropriate, the review required under Article XI at the earliest opportunity. It was announced by certain delegations that their national reviews in this context had already commenced.[660]

At a meeting towards the end of 1994 the group finally got down to discussing some practical steps that could be taken to implement Article XI and related provisions.

These included, *inter alia*, the issue of a possible establishment of a database to facilitate the exchange of information relating to economic and technological development in the field of chemicals, and other measures that could be taken by the OPCW to foster international cooperation for peaceful purposes in the field of chemical activities.

---

659 PC-VI/B/WP.8.

660 PC-VII/B/WP.6 and Corr.1.

> 3.3 The possible content and structure of a database to facilitate the exchange of information relating to economic and technological development in the field of chemicals were discussed to provide a better basis for the Secretariat's study of such a database. The Group concluded that the establishment of a database would be most useful, that it would need to be developed over a period of time and that it should facilitate and enhance the access of States Parties to information relevant to the Convention without prejudice to confidentiality, copyright or commercial obligations.[661]

The group went on to provide guidance on precisely how the database should be set up. This discussion was continued at a further meeting in early 1995.

> The Expert Group discussed the use of databases to meet Article XI requirements. It felt that the establishment of a library, consisting, *inter alia*, of databases containing information relevant to the facilitation of the exchange of information relating to economic and technological development in the field of chemistry, would be most useful. The library should, if possible, be available at entry into force of the Convention.[662]

The group on this occasion, in addition to instruction on how the database should be operated, also gave guidance on its content.

Towards the end of 1995 the group arranged for an end user survey of information requirements to facilitate information exchange in relation to Article XI.

> The Group concluded that it would be worthwhile to begin, on an experimental basis for the duration of 1996, an information service (library) as outlined in subparagraph 4.10 of the Annex to PC-XI/A/WP.5. The information service would cover fields such as 'Dangerous properties of chemicals', 'Producers and suppliers of chemicals', and 'Producers and suppliers of technology and/or equipment for the production, processing and handling of chemicals'.
>
> The information service should be within resources as specified in subparagraphs 4.10 and 7.6.5(b) of the Annex to PC-XI/A/WP.5. The costs of the experimental information service should not exceed Dfl. 80,000, and may not include any financial commitments beyond the end of 1996. The manpower requirement is estimated to be less than six person-months. An evaluation of the utility of the service should take place not later than the end of 1996.
>
> The information should be drawn from commercial and other publicly available data sources, subject to copyright regulations. Requests for information should be sent directly to the Secretariat, whenever possible. Responses to requests could be either information on the subject available to the Secretariat or referral to an outside information source.[663]

The Group also agreed guidelines for the Secretariat website, which until that time had been run on an experimental and informal basis. Unfortunately this was the last

[661] PC-IX/B/WP.4.
[662] PC-X/B/WP.13.
[663] PC-XIII/B/WP.3.

substantive achievement of the Group, which for the rest of the time of the existence of the PrepCom failed even to agree the content of reports of its sessions.

All of this was serviced by the Technical Cooperation and Assistance Division of the Provisional Technical Secretariat (PTS). However the division did not simply write down the disagreements of the working group with regard to the possibilities for technical cooperation in accordance with Article XI but performed some serious work of its own in identifying such possibilities to be offered to the Organisation after entry into force of the Convention. Most of the work of the Division as agreed by the Commission in its successive programmes of work relates to either training National Authorities or preparations for implementation of Article X but there is a small amount relating to Article XI:

Programme for 1996

(j) contribute to the development and finalisation of the design of the database for the IMS/OPCW on national and multilateral measures governing trade and cooperation among future States Parties in the chemical field;

New activities

(l) in cooperation with the Information Systems Branch, assemble and determine the organisation of books and other documents and materials, that will constitute the data bank related to Articles X and XI, which will require a greater effort due to the paucity of contributions to date;
(m) [...];
(n) identify measures to promote international cooperation in the chemical field;
(o) [...]; and
(p) support the participation of laboratories from developing countries in the inter-laboratory comparison tests.[664]

Programme for 1997
Identify measures for promoting international cooperation in the chemical field;

Support the participation of laboratories from developing countries in the inter-laboratory comparison tests;

Operate an information service, to facilitate the exchange of information relating to economic and technological development in the field of chemistry; and

Operate the permanent Secretariat Internet Website.[665]

That they were reasonably successful is shown by the current activities of the International Cooperation and Assistance Division of OPCW which are described on the website at the end of 2006 as follows:

[664] PC-VIII/A/WP.7, Annex, p. 129.
[665] PC-XV/A/WP.2, p. 129.

While the CWC seeks to ban chemical weapons, it also provides for international cooperation among States Parties in the pursuit of chemistry for peaceful purposes.

International cooperation is provided in many areas: from sponsoring chemical research and improving laboratory capacity to specialised internships and training in the implementation of the Chemical Weapons Convention and safe chemical management.

The provisions of the CWC have to be effectively and stringently implemented to ensure that a global chemical weapons ban is achieved. Support programmes, funded by the Member States, enhance the Organisation's ability to hinder prohibited activity and to extend the benefits of peaceful uses of chemistry to all.

The OPCW Associate and Internship Support programmes provide specialised training in modern industrial practices and skills development to chemists and engineers from Member States where economies are either developing or are in transition. Industrial internships and project work provide insight into best practice methodology in the safe management of chemicals and in the implementation of the Convention.

The OPCW supports the exchange of scientific and technical information among Member States to promote the peaceful uses of chemistry. A variety of research projects in developing countries are also funded in part by the OPCW. Research in any of the following areas may be considered for financial support: environmentally sound technologies for the destruction of hazardous chemicals, analytical methods relating to toxic chemicals, safer alternatives to Scheduled chemicals, medical treatment for accidental exposure to hazardous chemicals, and practical applications of chemistry in industrial, agricultural, medical, pharmaceutical or other peaceful purposes.[666]

[666] <http://www.opcw.org>.

Chapter 14

The First Ten Years

Ralf Trapp

1. Introduction

As the Chemical Weapons Convention (CWC), and with it the OPCW, approach their 10th anniversary, it is opportune to reflect on what the Preparatory Commission (PrepCom) actually achieved, and to what extent it succeeded in preparing the OPCW, its Technical Secretariat and its Member States for a successful implementation of the CWC. Had the preparations with regard to institution building, recruitment, acquisition of hardware and adoption of procedures been adequate for the OPCW to tackle its mandate successfully? Alternatively, had the package of unresolved issues come in the way of implementing the provisions of the Convention? How solid were the foundations laid by the PrepCom, and how successful would the new organisation be in steering its course into unfamiliar territory, avoiding obstacles resulting from a lack of agreement on key issues in the PrepCom as much as from unexpected encounters in the implementation process itself?

2. The First Session of the Conference of the States Parties

The First Session of the Conference of the States Parties (CSP) opened on 6 May and closed on 23 May 1997. It received the Final Report of the PrepCom and endorsed the draft decisions it had prepared, thereby formalising the results of four years of PrepCom work and making them part of the legal fabric of the emerging OPCW. This included decisions on the regulations that would govern the work of the OPCW in future.[667] Numerous decisions were taken by the CSP to regulate the future inspection conduct of the OPCW, to guide States Parties in their national implementation (including their submission of initial and annual declarations), and to authorise the Technical Secretariat to implement the mandates given to it by the Convention, including such areas as the conduct of inspections and the provision of assistance and protection against

[667] Whilst the financial regulations and the host country agreement were adopted in their final form, subject to future amendments, the staff regulations remained interim regulations. The tenancy agreement between the OPCW and the Netherlands and related Understandings and Supplementary Understandings on the Approval of the Sale of the OPCW Building also remained preliminary at this stage.

chemical weapons. The CSP also appointed the first Director-General (José Mauricio Bustani of Brazil) and elected the initial members of the Executive Council of the OPCW.

This institutional and procedural framework remained somewhat incomplete. The many issues that the PrepCom had been unable to resolve were, of course, not resolved during those 17 days. The First Session of the CSP managed to resolve a small number of them, focusing on issues that were absolutely essential for the successful start of OPCW operations. These included the programme and budget for the first year and the list of approved inspection equipment. Without the former, the OPCW would not have been able to properly finance its operations in 1997. Without the latter, OPCW inspection teams would have been in a difficult and vulnerable position in the initial inspections, including with regard to whether they could actually use their health and safety equipment, communications equipment, location finding equipment and computers. That could have significantly compromised the conduct of inspections from the very outset. As it was, the decision on the list of approved equipment was adopted by the CSP at its First Session, albeit together with a number of caveats that could be used by inspected States Parties, at their discretion, to limit the use of certain types of equipment by inspectors. A number of States Parties placed reservations on record with regard to specific items of equipment, and the Technical Secretariat in turn took formal notice of these reservations.

There remained the question of what to do about the 'unresolved issues' after the First Session of the CSP. Simply brushing them under the carpet was not an option. But neither was there an easy way of resolving them in a short time. The Convention, of course, provides for mechanisms to deal with issues that affect the implementation process: the Executive Council would normally be the statutory organ of the OPCW to discuss and resolve such issues, and as necessary it would bring them to the attention of the Conference of the States Parties for decision-making. At that early point in time after the entry into force of the Convention (EIF), there were two problems with such an approach: firstly, the 'unresolved issues' had a constituency that was much broader than the Executive Council and there was a fear that by tasking the EC with their resolution, the negotiation process might not be inclusive. Secondly, the mechanism had to be capable of involving Signatory States in an appropriate way. This was necessary so as to ensure that decisions developed by the OPCW would not create problems that would make it more difficult for these Signatories eventually to join the Convention and become States Parties. Important States such as Russia, Pakistan and Iran were all experiencing delays in their ratification proceedings and would only join the Convention several months after EIF – there was no point in pursuing a mechanism of problem resolution that would exclude these States altogether. At the same time, the mechanism had to respect to new situation, with the treaty actually being in force and the PrepCom no longer in existence: it needed to respect the different status of States Parties and Signatory States.

As a consequence, the First Session of the CSP adopted a mechanism for dealing with the unresolved issues which was rather unique: it mandated the Chairman of the Committee of the Whole of the CSP (a Conference organ that normally only works whilst the conference is actually in session) to manage an intersessional negotiation process based on appointed 'facilitators' that were to try and resolve specific issues assigned to them. The facilitators were to make proposals to the Committee of the Whole at the next Session of the CSP. Each proposal was to be accompanied by a report issued by the facilitator in his or her name, describing the consultation process and the rationale for the proposal submitted. In addition, the decision recognised that issues could be brought to the Executive Council, both by States Parties and by the Director-General, when the implementation of the Convention required their immediate resolution or urgent action. The facilitators were to make every reasonable effort to ensure that all States Parties had an opportunity to participate in the resolution of the issues. Signatory States were to be given a reasonable opportunity to express their views during the facilitators' consultation process.[668]

This mechanism was to be an interim measure, only to be used for one intersessional period. As it turned out, the OPCW used it for several years before the remaining unresolved issues were finally included in the EC work programme. Only in July 1999 did the CSP decide to move the remaining issues into a working group under the EC. That working group was to be open to all States Parties. Facilitators that had already started working on the resolution of issues were invited to continue their work in the new procedural context.[669]

Even today, there remain issues on the EC work programme which the PrepCom had failed to resolve. Other issues that required decision-making by the EC or the CSP were to be added to the list over the years, and the current work programme of the EC contains a total of 60 issues (some made up of multiple sub-issues) that remain to be resolved. Some of them are issues which belong to the routine agenda of the EC, such as regular reviews of progress made in Chemical Weapon destruction. But a majority of items on the list originates from the list of unresolved issues submitted to the OPCW by the PrepCom. The need to deal with this legacy was recognised by the First Review Conference in 2003. Its report makes reference in several places to the need to speed-up the work towards resolving them.[670] Since 2003, some further progress has been made, albeit in an incremental manner.

But did the fact that so many issues still remain unresolved significantly affect the implementation process of the Convention? Or was the impact largely marginal? To answer this question, and in any event to see how the process of CWC implementation has been progressing since the Convention's entry into force, it is useful to analyse how the OPCW itself has assessed the initial years of CWC implementation. In a comprehensive manner, this was done by the First Review Conference of the CWC. The following sections look at key implementation areas and review the status of

---

668 Conference of the States Parties, Decision 'Procedure for Addressing Unresolved Issues during the First Intersessional Period', First Session of the Conference of the States Parties, document C-I/DEC.70, dated 22 May 1997.

669 Conference of the States Parties, Decision 'Procedure for Addressing Unresolved Issues during the Fourth Intersessional Period', Fourth Session of the Conference of the States Parties, document C-IV/DEC.18, dated 2 July 1999.

670 Report of the First Special Session of the Conference of the States Parties to Review the Operation of the Chemical Weapons Convention ('First Review Conference'), document R-1/5, dated 9 May 2003.

CWC implementation and OPCW evolution, taking into account the findings of the First Review Conference as well as developments that have taken place since then.

3. Institution Building

The PrepCom had given the OPCW a good head-start. Most essential mechanisms and procedures were in place, the construction of the OPCW headquarters building was well under way (the Organisation had secured adequate interim accommodation that could support its operations in the early days of CWC implementation), equipment had been purchased, the laboratory and equipment store in Rijswijk were ready to go into operation, and inspector candidates had been recruited and trained in what was hoped would be adequate numbers.

In fact, to create the procedural systems and logistical infrastructure, acquire the necessary hardware, and most importantly identify, select, hire and train several hundreds of highly-qualified staff members from a broad geographical range of future States Parties had been a major accomplishment of the PrepCom. The OPCW was well-prepared to start implementing the provisions of the Convention in most programme delivery areas.

One key procedure, however, had not been fully agreed – namely the procedure for implementing the Convention's requirement that the possessor States Parties (with reference to Article IV as well as V) were to pay for the verification of their chemical weapon stockpiles and production and storage facilities as well as their destruction. Throughout its proceedings, the PrepCom had kept to the planning assumption that there would be a bilateral agreement between the USA and Russia, which would limit the OPCW's verification measures to an auditing of the bilateral verification measures. This assumption was maintained despite the clear warnings to the contrary by Russia, following the Russian government decision not to submit the previously negotiated bilateral agreement for parliamentary approval. As the matter turned out, Russia was not among the initial States Parties, and the bilateral agreement did not enter into force. Also, there were more than the three possessor States Parties assumed for planning purposes during the preparatory phase. In short, a decision on the mechanism for how possessor States Parties were to pay for the international verification of their stockpiles and facilities had not been agreed, and was now urgently needed.

At the First Session of the CSP, this issue was addressed through an interim approach agreed as part the decision on the programme and budget for the remainder of 1997. This first OPCW budget included reimbursement criteria for Article IV and V inspections which ensured that the OPCW would be reimbursed for certain expenses directly related to the inspection (costs of the actual on-site inspection, amenities during the in-country period, as well as transportation costs from and back to The Hague). However, reimbursement of costs associated with other inspection-related activities such as inspection planning, sample analysis, the preparation of inspection reports, the negotiation of facility agreements and the processing of site-related declarations remained under evaluation. The same applied to equipment-related costs (purchase and replenishment costs for equipment and spares, servicing and calibration costs, storage costs, costs for the OPCW laboratory and depreciation of durable OPCW equipment for time spent in-country) as well as costs for the recruitment and training of inspectors.[671]

When the CSP at its Third Session in 1998 eventually took its decision on the reimbursement mechanism, only the costs for the involvement of members of an inspection team in inspection planning before and in inspection report generation after an inspection were included in the reimbursement formula, all other cost elements were not considered any further. At the same time, the Conference agreed that in future, the use of on-site monitoring instruments could be considered at CW facilities, in particular in destruction facilities (CWDFs), to reduce the costs of verification (an issue that would be taken up again in a decision of the First Review Conference on optimisation of verification measures at CWDFs).[672] The decision did not address the cost of verification of old and abandoned weapons – the former was resolved in 1999, the latter remains unresolved as of date.

The decision on the reimbursement of verification costs under Article IV and V, together with planning assumptions that the OPCW made in its early budgeting processes, would in a few years have severe effects on the financial stability of the Organisation. On the budget side, States Parties found it difficult to accept predictions of CW destruction activity that fell clearly short of CWC requirements. That inflated the projected verification activity, and as a result the anticipated 'income' from Article IV and V verification reimbursements. On the reimbursement side, invoicing by the Secretariat was slow in early years of OPCW operations; payment by the inspected States Parties was even slower. Under the OPCW's financial regulations, any moneys received after 31 December of a given budget year cannot be used to finance activities of that year and will be treated as surplus funding and, therefore, returnable to the States Parties. In other words, the verification activities under Article IV and V were financed from the regular budget on the assumption that the reimbursements would eventually replenish that expense, but if some of these reimbursements arrived in the following year, that money was lost.

In the first years of OPCW operations, this inherent flaw in the adopted financial mechanisms did not become apparent. Owing to the inevitable time lag in reaching a fully operational status, the early OPCW budgets had sufficient 'buffer' to compensate for the cash-flow shortage caused by the mechanism. However, as the OPCW became fully operational, budgets became tighter and budget forecasts more reliable, the system finally failed. Exaggerated by weaknesses in its financial controls, the OPCW found itself in a financial crisis at the end of 2000, which forced the then Director-General, José Bustani, to impose austerity measures and to drastically cut programme delivery across the board.

This and other disputes between the DG and a number of States Parties on key policy, managerial and implementation issues resulted in a deterioration of the rela-

---

[671] Conference of the States Parties, First Session, Decision 'Programme of Work and Budget and Working Capital Fund', document C-I/DEC.74*, dated 23 May 1997, Annex, pp. 59-61.

[672] Conference of the States Parties, Third Session, Decision 'Costs of Verification under Articles IV and V', document C-III/DEC.8, dated 17 November 1998.

tionship between him and certain States Parties, leading to calls for his resignation and eventually his dismissal by a Special Session of the CSP in 2002 one year into his second four-year term of office.[673] It should be noted that Bustani took the OPCW before the ILO Administrative Tribunal. He won his case, based on the tribunal's consideration that

> [in] accordance with the established case law of all international administrative tribunals, the Tribunal reaffirms that the independence of international civil servants is an essential guarantee, not only for the civil servants themselves, but also for the proper functioning of international organisations. [674]

The tribunal set aside the decision taken by the CSP and instructed the OPCW to pay compensation as well as damages to Mr Bustani.

A new Director-General (Rogelio Pfirter of Argentina) was voted into office in July 2002.[675] In terms of institutional stability, this appointment was a turning point for the OPCW. It had barely survived a political as well as financial crisis of significant magnitude. The trust within the organisation had suffered considerable damage, between groups of States Parties as well as between the Secretariat and the policy-making organs. There was an urgent need for consolidation and restoration, for the reestablishment of a common sense of purpose in the OPCW.

A first indication that this was succeeding came with the First CWC Review Conference (FRC) in April and May 2003. Not only did that review conference manage to adopt a political declaration wherein the States Parties stated their common positions on all aspects of the implementation of the CWC.[676] It was able also to adopt a detailed assessment of the past operation of the Convention and agree on numerous recommendations for its future implementation. These were contained in the final report of the First Review Conference.[677]

With regard to institution building, the First Review Conference confirmed that the OPCW 'has at its disposal qualified and trained staff, and equipment and procedures fit for the tasks to be fulfilled under the Convention'.[678] It reviewed the budgetary and financial mechanisms of the OPCW and underlined the need for the Council, with the support of the Secretariat, to continue monitoring and improving the imple-

---

[673] Conference of the States Parties, First Special Session, Decision under item three of the agenda of the First Special Session of the Conference of the States Parties, document C-SS-1/DEC.1, dated 22 April 2002.

[674] International Labour Organisation, Administrative Tribunal, Ninety-Fifth Session, Judgment 2232 in Geneva on 16 July 2003.

[675] Conference of the States Parties, First Special Session, Decision 'Appointment of the Director-General', document C-SS-1/DEC.3, dated 25 July 2002.

[676] Political Declaration of the First Special Session of the Conference of the States Parties to Review the Operation of the Chemical Weapons Convention (First Review Conference), document RC-1/3, dated 9 May 2003.

[677] Report of the First Special Session of the Conference of the States Parties to Review the Operation of the Chemical Weapons Convention (First Review Conference), document RC-1/5, dated 9 May 2003.

[678] Ibid., para. 7.125.

mentation of these mechanisms. It encouraged the Director-General to move ahead with the stepwise introduction of results-based budgeting, and called for the finalisation of the OPCW Financial Regulations.[679] The Review Conference also addressed the functioning of the policy-making organs (CSP and EC) as well as of the OPCW's advisory bodies (Scientific Advisory Board (SAB), Confidentiality Commission (CC), and Advisory Board for Administrative and Financial Matters (ABAF)) and made recommendations on how they could further improve their work. Other recommendations related to the effective use of information technology, the possible implementation of the ISO-17799 information-security management standard for the future handling of confidential information as well as other measures to improve the system for handling confidential information, and the future development of the relations between the OPCW and the host country – relations which the FRC characterised as excellent.

One further issue of the OPCW's institutional framework that had yet to be agreed was how to implement the principle of a 'non-career organisation' – a concept implicit in the Convention, but formally established by the CSP in a Staff Regulation in 1999.[680] At a Special Session of the CSP convened alongside the First Review Conference, the CSP adopted a decision that reaffirmed an earlier decision limiting the tenure of internationally-recruited as well as all professional Secretariat staff to seven years (with certain exceptions at the discretion of the Director-General). The decision stipulated the immediate implementation of the tenure policy in 2003, and the application of an effective starting date for its application of 2 July 1999. At the same time, it gave the Director-General discretion to continue, on an exceptional basis, employing staff past the seven years of service, subject to certain conditions and in any case not leading to any such staff being employed by the OPCW after 31 December 2009.[681] Part of this decision was that the Director-General was

> to report fully to the Council at least annually on the implementation of the decisions of the Council and of the Conference with respect to tenure, including on the criteria applied to effect the turnover of staff.[682]

Some Secretariat staff members who were immediately affected by the application of this decision appealed to the ILO Administrative Tribunal, but lost their case. In its judgment, the ILOAT recognised that the policy, as it had been adopted by the highest policy-making organ of the OPCW, had to be implemented as stated. To quote the words of the judgment:

> If … all the persons in the pool of those whose contracts are coming to an end have exemplary performance records and are in positions which must continue to be filled if the

679 Ibid., para. 7.127.

680 Conference of the States Parties, Fourth Session, Decision 'OPCW Staff Regulations', regulation 4.4, document C-IV/DEC.25, dated 2 July 1999.

681 Conference of the States Parties, Second Special Session, Decision 'Tenure Policy of the OPCW', document C-S-II/Dec.1, dated 30 April 2003.

682 Executive Council, Twenty-Second Meeting, Decision 'Tenure Policy of the OPCW', document EC-M-22/DEC.1, dated 28 March 2003.

> Organisation is to function properly, there is no objective, consistent or strictly rational basis on which the administration can decide who is to stay and who is to go. It is the classic case of the exercise of discretion'.[683]

Inevitably, there was an immediate impact on staff morale. At the same time, preserving institutional memory as well as technical competence in areas where there is limited supply of new (replacement) expertise from States Parties (such as persons with detailed knowledge of the design or manufacturing of chemical weapons) became an issue that the OPCW had to address with urgency.

In 2006, it became clear that the Director-General needed to request an extension of his discretion to renew contracts beyond seven years of service, and more importantly to continue employing certain staff members from the 'original' lot beyond 2009. He therefore requested that the CSP extend his discretion to 2012 – the new CW destruction deadline agreed by the CSP for the two major possessors. While it is obvious that the tenure scheme adopted by the OPCW had a significant effect upon the integrity and long-term competence of the Technical Secretariat it remains to be seen whether alternative tenure schemes such as those used by the International Atomic Energy Agency (IAEA) or the Comprehensive Nuclear-Test-Ban Treaty Organisation (CTBTO) Preparatory Commission should have been opted for instead.[684] Be that as it may, the issue of tenure will remain under close scrutiny as the OPCW approaches the review of its programme objectives at the expiration of the Convention deadline for the completion of the elimination of CW stockpiles.

In sum, then, the OPCW has emerged over the past ten years as a modern, still-evolving and ever-learning international institution that has all the ingredients it needs to face future challenges. It certainly has not reached the point of seniority, but it has managed to circumnavigate major obstacles and mature to a point where its Member States are confident that they can rely on its services. The organisation has sorted out most of its internal issues, and dealt with external challenges successfully. It has shown growing leadership, competence and professionalism. This has enabled it to implement its mandate under the Convention so far, as will be explained in the following sections of this chapter.

4. Elimination of Chemical Weapons Stockpiles and Production Facilities

A first adjustment that was needed after the entry into force was the number of CW possessor States Parties the OPCW would have to deal with: the PrepCom had (for planning purposes) assumed there would be three – Russia and the USA as the two States that had gone on public record before the EIF confirming their possessor status,

---

683 ILOAT judgment 2407, Considerations, para. 20.

684 Under the IAEA's staff regulations, a small percentage of staff members can be kept on long-term contract upon completion of their seven-year tenure if that was in the interest of the agency. Also, former staff members can be re-appointed after 12 months of separation from the agency.

and one more to take care of any surprises. When the CWC entered into force, that one additional possessor State became two (India and one other State Party whose identity the OPCW maintains confidential at its request). Russia, on the other hand, was not among the original States Parties and only joined the Convention in November 1997, some 6 months after the EIF.

Later on, the number of possessor States Parties increased again: Albania, one of the original States Parties, notified the OPCW in November 2002 that it had discovered certain amounts of chemical weapons.[685] In February 2004, Libya joined the CWC as the sixth possessor State Party.

As at the end of 2005, all six possessor States Parties had declared a total of 69,551.217 metric tons of category 1 chemical weapons (measured in agent tons), or 71,000 agent tons of category 1 and 2 chemical weapons (i.e., chemical weapons in the form of either filled munitions/devices or bulk agent). This overall stockpile included about 15,000 tons of Sarin, 9,200 tons of Soman, 2,300 tons of Tabun, 19,600 tons of V agents, 17,400 tons of mustard gas, 6,700 tons of Lewisite, and smaller amounts of a variety of other agents or agent mixtures.

The other planning assumption that needed revision after EIF was the number of States Parties that would declare CW production facilities. As opposed to CW stockpiles, where only those that actually exist when the Convention enters into force for a State Party need to be declared, all CW production facilities that have existed since 1 January 1946 must be declared, even if they have already been destroyed or converted to other purposes. The number of States Parties declaring CWPFs was therefore to be expected to exceed the number of States Parties with current stockpiles, but how many of them would still require inspection, destruction and/or conversion was uncertain. By the end of 2005, 12 States Parties have declared a total of 64 former CW production facilities to the OPCW. 38 of them had been destroyed by that date, 15 converted for legitimate purposes (they remain under OPCW verification for a minimum of ten years). Of the remaining 11, 4 had yet to be destroyed, while the conversion of the remaining 7 had yet to be completed.[686]

But whilst the progress in the elimination of CW production capacity has been more or less in accordance with the targets set by the CWC, the destruction of the CW stockpiles has experienced significant delays. The initial concern was the late start of CW destruction by Russia. But over the years, all possessor States Parties have experienced delays at times, caused by such factors as technological difficulties, legal hurdles, safety issues that needed to be resolved, or financial and managerial problems that needed to be addressed.

In December 2006, the Eleventh Session of the CSP addressed a series of requests for extensions of the CW destruction deadlines, and authorised the following new final CW destruction deadlines: India – 28 April 2009; the Libyan Arab Jamahiriya –

---

685 Report of the OPCW on the Implementation of the Convention on the Prohibition of the Development, Production Stockpiling and Use of Chemical Weapons and on their Destruction in 2002, document C-8/5, dated 22 October 2003, para. 3.

686 Ibid., para. 1.20.

31 December 2010; Russia – 29 April 2012; the United States of America – 29 April 2012; and one further, unnamed State Party – 31 December 2008.[687]

These new destruction timelines for chemical weapons stockpiles modify the CWC's disarmament timeframe significantly. This eventuality had been foreseen by the drafters of the Convention, and mechanisms are provided by the Convention to deal with such necessities. Yet, there is no mechanism in the Convention that would allow for a further extension beyond 2012. As the OPCW approaches its Second Review Conference, there have been indications that even this new deadline may not be met by all possessor States Parties. How the OPCW will deal with such a situation, should it indeed materialise, remains to be seen.

Despite these delays, the assessment of the First Review Conference in 2003 that '[t]he possessor States Parties are fully committed to meeting their destruction obligations … as required by the Convention'[688] remains the consensus view of the CWC States Parties. Although chemical weapons disarmament is progressing at a pace considerably slower than anticipated by the CWC, the OPCW has provided both the transparency through verification that has created reassurances of the determination of the possessor States Parties to meet their obligation to eliminate their CW stockpiles, and the political mechanisms to deal with any problems that are being encountered on the road to the complete elimination of all declared chemical weapons.

5. Verification

The differences between PrepCom planning assumptions and post-EIF realities had a significant impact on the evolving OPCW verification system. The Inspectorate and Verification Divisions had been designed – in staff size as well as skill composition – against a set of assumptions, some of which needed significant modification after EIF. Most importantly, by the end of 1997, there were more than 3 possessors of CW stockpiles, but there was no bilateral verification agreement between Russia and the United States. The OPCW had to mount full international verification at all declared CW facilities. At the same time, Russia was not among the initial States Parties, and inspections of the Russian CW facilities did not commence until the beginning of 1998.

The delay in the ratification by Russia created some space in the initial inspection campaign which was otherwise driven by tight and front-loaded deadlines in the CWC, which all link to the entry into force of the CWC for a State Party. That spacing-out, and the introduction (with the consent of the States Parties involved) of sequential inspections of CW facilities during the initial inspection campaign, made it possible for the OPCW to actually inspect all declared CW facilities within the time frames required by the CWC.

---

687 OPCW Press Release 'Annual Chemical Weapons Convention Conference Concludes; Final Stockpile Destruction Deadlines Extended to 2012' , The Hague, 11 December 2006, <http://www.opcw.org/pressreleases/2006/PR94_2006.html>.

688 Ibid., para. 7.40.

It was not possible, however, also to comply with the CWC requirement to agree for each of these (as well as certain other) facilities a facility agreement that would govern future inspection conduct. Part III of the CWC's Verification Annex requires that all CW and Schedule 1 facilities be equipped with such an agreement, and that all these agreements be concluded within 180 days after the CWC enters into force for a State Party. The facility agreements, so the CWC assumed, would be prepared on the basis of model agreements which the CSP would have adopted at its First Session. But this had not been possible. Instead, the verification of these facilities would continue on the basis of the CWC's provisions, a series of CSP decisions on specific verification issues pertaining to CW facilities, and tentative agreements that would be incorporated into draft facility agreements and that would be applied by the OPCW and the State Party concerned for as long as the draft facility agreement remained pending in the Executive Council. In parallel, the OPCW intensified its efforts to complete the models for facility agreements of Schedule 1 facilities as well as for Schedule 2 facilities where inspections had not yet started. (Schedule 3 and other chemical production facility plant sites may have facility agreements if requested by the inspected State Party. This has not occurred in the first 10 years and no model agreements for these types of facilities have been developed.)

This initial inspection campaign after the EIF went surprisingly smoothly, despite some inevitable problems. In a very short period of time, the OPCW Inspectorate and Verification Divisions gathered a vast amount of practical experience in the planning and conduct of inspections. Equally important, a significant number of States Parties that never before 1997 had acquired any practical experience with the receipt and escorting of international on-site inspections had moved into this new world of international verification, embraced it and shown their readiness to work together with the OPCW on the effective and honest implementation of the CWC's verification system. By the end of 1997, the OPCW had concluded 5 temporary verification agreements with the United States, covering the CW destruction facilities already in operation at the time, and was providing systematic verification coverage for all ongoing CW destruction operations. It had completed its campaign of initial inspections of all declared CW storage and production facilities and initiated work on a number of facility agreements. It had also completed its campaign of initial inspections at Schedule 1 facilities and submitted the first two daft facility agreements to the EC for consideration and adoption.[689]

Also in 1997, the OPCW initiated the inspection of industrial facilities, beginning with the initial inspection of five Schedule 2 plant sites. The Convention allows for a period of three years after EIF for the initial inspection of these plant sites – a goal that was met by the OPCW. In 1998, the OPCW initiated the inspection of Schedule 3 plant sites. As of May 2000, the OPCW began inspecting other chemical production facilities (OCPFs) producing discrete organic chemicals. This was in accordance with paragraph 22 of Part IX of the Verification Annex, which stipulates that this should

689 Report of the OPCW on the Implementation of the Convention (29 April-28 October 1997), document C-II/2/Rev.2, dated 5 December 1997, paras. 2.19-2.24.

take place unless the CSP at its regular Session in the third year after EIF decided otherwise (which it did not do).

When the OPCW initiated industry inspections in 1997, the United States of America was still lacking its implementing legislation and had therefore not submitted a full declaration under Article VI. None of its private-sector Article VI facilities had been declared, and the initial burden of industry inspections fell on other States Parties, mostly located in Europe and Asia. This caused significant irritation in States Parties that had declared their chemical industry facilities and opened them up for OPCW inspection. One of the principles that the world's chemical industry had emphasised all through the negotiation and PrepCom processes, namely that the industry verification system had to be created on a level playing field, could not be met during the early years of CWC implementation. This resulted in restrictions on the numbers of Schedule inspections that could be planned pending receipt of the US initial declaration.

This issue was finally resolved when, in the year 2000, the United States finally submitted their full Article VI declaration. By that time, the OPCW had already conducted a significant number of Article VI inspections: 28 in 1997, 94 in 1998, and 80 in 1999. With the US Article VI declaration finally on file, this number jumped to 140 in the year 2000.[690]

By that time, the OPCW had developed its operational concept for how to conduct Article VI inspections, based on practical experience gathered in almost 200 inspections in close to 40 States Parties. But the commencement of industry inspections in the United States exposed a number of issues where the Technical Secretariat and some States Parties had taken different views on how certain provisions of the CWC needed to be implemented. And this was reflected in twelve inspections recording uncertainties. To some extent, these issues were the result of changes that had taken place in the chemical industry over the past 5-10 years; changes which called for a review of how certain definitions (for example the definitions of plant versus plant site) could be applied. That in turn affected the specific access rights that OPCW inspection teams would have, both in terms of physical access to certain areas at an industrial facility and to records kept by the facility. Also, some of the remaining unresolved issues (for example the continuing lack of agreement on the low-concentration guidelines for mixtures containing scheduled chemicals) had affected the situation. As a result, the list of unresolved issues in the industry verification area that was before the EC increased considerably. It took some time and effort to resolve most of these differences. Generally-accepted pragmatic solutions in certain key areas of inspection conduct at Article VI facilities were only just reached when the OPCW moved into the preparatory phase for its First Review Conference.

When the First Review Conference addressed the functioning of the CWC verification system, it concluded that

---

690 Report of the OPCW on the Implementation of the Convention on the Prohibition of the Development, Production Stockpiling and Use of Chemical Weapons and on their Destruction in 2000, document C-VI/5, dated 17 May 2001, para. 11.

> the OPCW has established a verification system that meets the requirements of the Convention. The OPCW has at its disposal a well-trained inspectorate, approved equipment and other technical capabilities, procedures to plan and conduct on-site inspections as required under the Convention, and a network of designated laboratories for off-site chemical analysis. There is, however, room for increased efficiency. The First Review Conference also noted that a number of procedures and guidelines that the Convention requires remain to be finalised and adopted. The Council has already included these in its work programme, and should resolve them as soon as possible.[691]

The system was working well, despite some shortcomings such as the lack of implementation by a good number of States Parties of the standing arrangements for inspection conduct which the CWC requires.[692] The main conclusion of the First Review Conference was that the system needed to be further optimised – not only to save costs but also to avoid an increase in the size of the Inspectorate in the light of emerging requirements in the CW destruction area. It had become clear

> that a large part of the OPCW's verification resources have in the past been spent on the verification of chemical weapons destruction operations. The planned increase in chemical weapons destruction in coming years and any resource constraints will require a thorough review of the current verification methodology used for chemical weapons destruction verification, as part of the effort to optimise the verification regime of the Convention.[693]

Since 2003, the OPCW Secretariat and States Parties have made significant efforts further to optimise the CWC verification system. Progress has been made with regard to all types of inspections, but of particular importance were the savings achieved at CW destruction sites. In a recent OPCW paper on developments since the First Review Conference, prepared in support of the preparatory work for the Second Review Conference of the CWC in 2008, the OPCW Secretariat stated that the optimisation measures had included an increase in the use of sequential inspections, reductions in the size of inspection teams, streamlining of reporting and other verification procedures, and more extensive use of recording devices at CW destruction facilities. In addition, the OPCW now uses an on-call inspector scheme to beef up its capacity to inspect CW facilities, CW destruction sites in particular. In its latest medium-term plan, the OPCW stated that

> [t]he increasing inspection workload will ... place a premium on continuing efforts to optimise verification (in particular with respect to Articles IV and V). The scheme for on-call inspectors, whereby inspectors work under a special-service agreement, needs to be maintained if the Secretariat is to accommodate the demand for inspections while keeping to realistic resource levels. The optimisation of verification activities, in particu-

---

691 Ibid., para. 7.27.
692 Ibid., para. 7.35.
693 Ibid., para. 7.36.

> lar at CWDFs, has led to savings equivalent to more than 40 additional inspector posts.[694]

Should there be further delays in destruction operations, additional pressure on the required Inspectorate resources would be the result.

All in all, it is fair to state that the OPCW has established a reliable, robust and effective international verification system that has proven its aptness in more than 2000 routine on-site inspections at military as well as private-sector facilities in over 70 States Parties. This outstanding achievement is testimony to the fact that the hard work of the PrepCom, both Secretariat and Member States, is paying dividends.

There are two verification measures which in its first ten years, the OPCW has not been called upon to execute: investigations of alleged use of CW, and challenge inspections. This is not to say that there were no compliance concerns that might have led to such verification requests. In practice, OPCW States Parties preferred instead to use other clarification mechanisms, either on a bilateral basis or through the good offices of the OPCW. The First Review Conference, in fact, encouraged States Parties to 'make full use of this bilateral-consultation mechanism'. It also

> noted that no challenge inspection had been requested since the entry into force of the Convention, … [and] expressed its confidence that the States Parties will continue to uphold the value of the challenge inspection mechanism for compliance and compliance assurance, and at the same time keep any challenge inspection request within the scope of the Convention, and refrain from requests that are unfounded or abusive.[695]

With regard to investigations of alleged use of CW, the First Review Conference

> stressed the importance of investigations of alleged use or threat of use of chemical weapons. For such situations, the OPCW must have the capacity, and be ready at all times, to investigate the need for follow-on action by the OPCW and by individual Member States, and to facilitate the delivery of assistance. The First Review Conference noted that the Secretariat had established the Assistance Coordination and Assessment Team (ACAT), the overall function of which had yet to be defined.[696]

The OPCW's capacity to investigate allegations of CW use has in the meanwhile been further developed, a recent example being a joint OPCW-NATO-UN OCHA exercise held in 2005 in the Ukraine. Some shortfalls remain, albeit more with regard to the delivery and coordination of assistance than the investigation conduct itself (for detail see further below).

The maintenance of a stand-by capability to successfully implement challenge inspections and investigations of alleged use of chemical weapons presents a strong challenge to the OPCW. It puts extra pressures on an already resource-stretched in-

[694] Medium-term Plan for the Period from 2007-2009, OPCW document C-11/S/1 EC-46/S/4, dated 3 July 2006, para. 29.

[695] Ibid., paras. 7.86-7.89.

[696] Ibid., para. 7.100.

spectorate that will in coming years have to struggle with both an increase in CW destruction activity and a steady staff-turnover resulting from the application of the OPCW's tenure policy. Both types of special inspections require certain skills which are rarely used in routine inspections. Such skills require extra efforts to develop and maintain. And finally, maintaining this capability requires constant political and financial support by the States Parties, some of which may question the wisdom of spending money on a verification tool that has never been used. Despite all these constraints, the OPCW has demonstrated that it can effectively implement a challenge inspection and is well on the way to being prepared to execute investigations of alleged CW use, should it be requested to do so.

Whilst the inspection system of the OPCW has been functioning rather well over the past ten years, the basis for its routine elements – the declarations by States Parties – remained a concern for a long time. A large number of States Parties had not prepared and submitted their initial declarations within the time frames required by the CWC. These are due within 30 days of the Convention entering into force for a State Party. Although by the end of 1999, a total of 94 States Parties had submitted their initial declaration (which included all of the declared chemical weapons possessor States Parties and, with the exception of the United States of America, all States Parties with a sizeable chemical industry), a third of all States Parties had failed to file their initial declaration.[697] As with certain other requirements in the area of national implementation, this was an indication that many States Parties had failed to take the measures they needed to fully comply with the requirements of the CWC. To remedy the situation, the OPCW initiated in 2000 a dedicated project to assist States Parties with the preparation and submission of their initial declarations. This included Director-General's demarches to the Foreign Ministers of the States Parties that needed to take action, concerted lobbying and technical assistance by the Technical Secretariat and Director-level visits to the capitals of seven of the above States Parties. This campaign was coordinated with the activities of a number of States Parties that had indicated their readiness to help with demarches and the conduct of these visits.

The result of this concerted campaign was that by the end of 2000, all but the five (new) States Parties had submitted their initial declarations to the Organisation. In subsequent years, the OPCW continued to assist new States Parties, if so requested by them, in the preparation of their initial declaration. A high compliance standard is maintained by the OPCW with regard to the submission of initial declarations.

The success of the initial declarations project also demonstrated that dedicated support should also be provided to States Parties with regard to other key aspects of the security regime foreseen in the Convention, dependent on full and effective national implementation. At the end of 2000, a separate implementation support programme was established in the Technical Secretariat in order to assess the progress with national implementation and coordinate assistance (national implementation is discussed in more details below). The situation when the verification of CW-related facilities was well under way and the initial verification of Schedule 1 and 2 facilities

[697] Conference of the States Parties, Report of the Organisation on the Implementation of the Convention (1 January-31 December 1999), document C-V/5, dated 15 May 2000, para. 5.

has been completed was also helpful by allowing to provide better focus on national implementation and to commit more resources to helping to improve it.

Two substantive issues remained of particular concern. The completeness of Article VI declarations remained uncertain as many States Parties had failed to identify some or all of their declarable industry facilities, in particular in the category of 'other chemical production facilities'. Secondly, there were considerable, and disturbing, discrepancies between the declarations submitted by States Parties regarding their exports and imports of scheduled chemicals. These discrepancies were of such a level and nature that it became quite clear that the system of transfer notifications and declarations was not working properly.

To rectify the first problem, the OPCW has provided, since 2001, assistance to States Parties in the identification of declarable industry facilities, based on open-literature and Internet searches and evaluations (the so-called Article VI Project). Whilst there was some initial resistance on the part of some States Parties, who considered that such Secretariat activities resembled a kind of 'investigation' and might trespass into territory that was their own domain (namely their own national implementation), the success of the project in terms of increasing the number of States Parties that submitted facility declarations and subsequently received inspections soon silenced these concerns. Since 2003, the project has been integrated into the OPCW's wider assistance package for national implementation support, including the 2003-2005 OPCW Action Plan on the Implementation of Article VII Obligations and the follow-up measures taken in subsequent years.

The second issue – discrepancies between export and import declarations regarding transfers of scheduled chemicals between States Parties – was approached as a harmonisation issue. It had become clear that States Parties were using different definitions and criteria in the monitoring and calculation of their exports and imports of scheduled chemicals. Many States Parties relied on customs data for the identification of such transfers, but their statistical systems (which are in many States based on the Harmonised Commodity Description and Coding System of the World Customs Organisation) did not allow them to identify transfers related to specific scheduled chemicals. Before entry into force, the PrepCom had worked with the World Customs Organisation on a non-binding recommendation that would enable States Parties to break-out in their national statistical nomenclatures individual scheduled chemicals they traded, so they could make better use of their customs statistics for CWC declaration purposes. This recommendation has been updated twice since the entry into force of the CWC.[698] However its wider implementation by a larger number of States Parties remains yet to be achieved. Also, the recommendation only addresses transfers of neat chemicals and a few mixtures, but many scheduled chemicals that are traded in formulations or mixtures cannot so be identified. Another source for the

698 Recommendation of the Customs Co-Operation Council* on the Insertion in National Statistical Nomenclatures of Subheadings for Substances Controlled Under the Convention on the Prohibition of the Development, Production, Stockpiling and Use of Chemical Weapons and on their Destruction, adopted 18 June 1996, amended 25 June 1999 and 1 July, 2006. <http://www.wcoomd.org/ie/En/Recommendations/recommendations.html>.

discrepancies was that different States Parties had taken different national decisions on issues that remained unresolved in the OPCW. Decisions on rounding rules, on how to aggregate national aggregate data, and on low concentration guidelines for mixtures containing scheduled chemicals all affected the way in which national statistical data were calculated by States Parties, and harmonisation of their different methodologies remains an urgent matter. Finally, it had become quite apparent that many States Parties simply lacked the legislative and administrative basis to enforce an effective export/import control system for scheduled chemicals – many of the discrepancies were in fact situations where only one of the two States Parties involved in a transfer of a scheduled chemical submitted a declaration. This lack of national implementation, and the measures taken by the OPCW to rectify the situation, are discussed below.

To sum this up, the declaration system of the CWC was a weak point in the initial years of CWC implementation, with delays in the submission of initial declarations, gaps in the declaration of Article VI facilities, and persistent discrepancies between transfer declarations of different States Parties. Much has been improved over the years, and the confidence in the accuracy and completeness of declarations submitted by the States Parties has increased. But this will remain an issue to which the OPCW will need to pay attention in the future, and continuing assistance to States Parties in their enactment and enforcement of national implementation measures will remain important if there is to be full confidence in the declarations submitted by all States Parties.

Another issue that caused difficulties in the implementation of the declaration system was the delay in the setting-up of the OPCW verification information system (VIS) – the industry declaration module of that system is finally coming into production as this paper is being written. That database management system was to process, evaluate and store declaration data and assist with inspection planning. However, as a result of disagreements and consequential delays during the PrepCom, the VIS was not ready at EIF. (It should be noted that both the United States and Finland had provided to the PrepCom prototype systems that for one reason or another proved not suitable.) The OPCW Secretariat decided instead to employ an electronic document management system, residing on a secure network, which enabled it to manage the submitted paper-copy declarations in an electronic work environment. This was far short of the relational database management system that had been assumed would be supporting operations, but it at least enabled the use of standard information technology in a secure network configuration (certain evaluation functions remained for a long time outside the network, and were performed on specifically-controlled stand-alone machines), and to automate some of the verification processes over time. In 1997, even that secure electronic network environment still had to be fully developed and audited to a point where all States Parties were ready to accept that their declaration data be placed on it. Some States Parties insisted that their declaration data must be handled as hard-copy only until such time when they were reassured that the OPCW system for electronic handling of declaration data was secure and reliable.

Ten years after EIF, the verification information system is finally nearing completion. In its Medium-Term Plan submitted in 2006, covering the period from 2007 to 2009, the Secretariat envisaged

> the completion, during the period covered by this MTP, of the Verification Information System (VIS), which will support all verification activities under Articles III, IV, V, and VI. The VIS will comprise an industry component, a chemical weapons component, and a variety of analytical tools.[699]

More detail was provided in a Secretariat background paper prepared for the open-ended working group for the preparation of the Second Review Conference, and key parts of the industry component of the VIS were finally to go into operation at the end of 2006.

6. National Implementation

When the First Review Conference addressed the comprehensiveness and quality of national implementation measures adopted by the States Parties, it recorded in its Final Report that 'national implementation is one of the essential conditions for the functioning of the Convention and for its full, effective, and non-discriminatory implementation'.[700] Furthermore,

> [n]ational implementation is also important in relation to the ability of the Convention to respond to changes in the security environment or in science and technology that may affect the Convention. It contributes to meeting new challenges, including the possible use of toxic materials by non-state actors such as terrorists.[701]

However, despite the efforts made by the PrepCom, and subsequently by the OPCW, to encourage States Parties to establish well-functioning and fully authorised National Authorities and to enact effective implementing legislation, including penal legislation, a large number of Sates Parties had failed to comply with these CWC requirements.

In 2003, the Secretariat informed the CSP that by September of that year, only 123 of the 153 States Parties (80%) had notified the OPCW of their National Authorities. Ninety-three States Parties (61%) had submitted information on their implementing legislation, however only 51 (33%) had reported that their national implementing legislation covers all key areas of enforcement.[702]

This depressing situation prompted the First Review Conference to call for an Action Plan to improve the situation with regard to the implementation of Article VII

---

[699] Ibid., para. 34.

[700] Ibid., para. 7.74.

[701] Ibid., para. 7.75.

[702] Note by the Director-General 'Report on National Implementation Measures', document C-8/DG.5, dated 18 September 2003, para. 3(b).

obligations. This Action Plan was subsequently prepared by the EC, and adopted by the CSP at its 8th Session in the autumn of 2003.[703]

The adoption of an Action Plan was a novelty in the OPCW – only one other Action Plan (on universality) has been adopted, also in 2003. It was clear from the nature of the plan that this was not simply a statement of determination to change the situation. The Action Plan created a conceptual structure and procedural framework for *joint* action by the Secretariat, the EC and the States Parties. A core aspect of it was the development and implementation of an assistance programme for States Parties lacking capacity – an assistance programme that *combined and coordinated* support measures undertaken by States Parties in their respective outreach programmes with implementation support projects pursued by the Technical Secretariat. By setting firm targets for a range of national implementation measures to be implemented within the two-year time frame of the Action Plan, it also made clear that the responsibility to establish full national implementation was with the States Parties that had failed to take action in the past. Although not (at that stage) cast in language that would suggest that this was a non-compliance matter, the adoption of an Action Plan created significant pressure on States Parties that had not adopted their national implementation measures, as well as on the Secretariat that was to deliver an assistance package that by far exceeded any of its past efforts. Also, the emphasis in the OPCW assistance concept shifted from its traditional regional and sub-regional seminars towards tailored on-site missions to individual States Parties that needed specific support. This, in a sense, was a repeat of the campaign that the OPCW had undertaken in 2000, when it resolved the situation with regard to the submission of initial declarations. But this time, the goal was not to persuade governments in a one-off effort to complete a declaration form. It was instead to help governments create favourable conditions, political support and effective participation in a multi-stakeholder effort to create national laws and regulations, and to establish administrative structures to enforce them – something that cannot be achieved with a single visit of a few days. Sustained and well-coordinated (as well as well-resourced) assistance over a longer time period was needed to swing the situation around.

It is worth highlighting what the Technical Secretariat recorded when, at the end of the Action Plan in 2005, it analysed the reasons that had led to so many States Parties falling behind with adopting their national implementation measures. It concluded that

> [t]here were a variety of reasons why some States Parties were not able to fully meet the objectives of the plan of action. Many of them had to raise awareness of and generate domestic support for the plan, and engage and educate stakeholders, before they could begin drafting legislation and setting up a functioning National Authority. It was also important that the stakeholders fully understood the complexities of the Convention, how it applied to their particular situations, and what was required for its implementation. … In other cases, either the States Parties did not have drafters with sufficient experience to

[703] Conference of the States Parties, Decision 'Plan of Action Regarding the Implementation of Article VII Obligations', document C-8/Dec.16, dated 24 October 2003.

> draft implementing legislation, or the experienced drafters they had did not have time. Finally, internal economic and political factors or external events (including conflicts and wars) in some cases hindered States Parties from making initial preparations for full national implementation. Once the drafting of legislation was underway and practical measures to set up a functioning and fully empowered National Authority were being taken, limits on human and financial resources caused delays in a number of States Parties. Events unrelated to the implementation of the Convention interfered in some cases with the process of completing various steps under the plan of action. For example, changes in government or elections delayed this process or caused setbacks, and draft legislation had to be resubmitted or redrafted. Once submitted to parliament, implementing legislation for the Convention competed with other draft legislation for inclusion in the parliamentary calendar and for parliamentary time.[704]

Two years, of course, were not enough to fully remedy the situation. Also, the number of States Parties had been steadily increasing and new States Parties often faced start-up problems similar to those of the older States Parties. Consequently, the CSP decided a set of follow-up measures, effectively extending the Action Plan by one year (and again by one more year in 2006). But significant progress has now been made: at the time of writing, 95 percent of all States Parties have established or designated their National Authority. Progress in enacting legislation has been less impressive, and assistance to those States Parties that still need to complete their action under Article VII continues. What has changed is that almost all States Parties that still lag behind have actually started working on their legislation. Most of them share their drafts with the OPCW and invite advice and comments. This enables the Secretariat to provide advice on how to ensure the full and comprehensive coverage of all requirements by these draft bills.[705]

As the OPCW approaches the 10th Anniversary of the entry into force of the CWC and the Second Review Conference, it can conclude that finally, the situation with regard to national implementation is improving. This will in particular strengthen the implementation of the CWC's non-proliferation provisions, both with respect to international verification under Article VI (it will ensure that the declaratory basis for industry inspections will become more accurate and complete) and with regard to national controls of the manufacturing, use and trade (including exports and imports) or CWC-relevant chemicals. In this way, the OPCW will also increasingly be in a position to make a tangible contribution to international efforts to prevent the misuse of toxic chemicals by criminal and terrorist organisations.

---

[704] Note by the Director-General 'Report on the Plan of Action Regarding the Implementation of Article VII Obligations', document C-10/DG/4/Rev.1 EC-M-25/DG.1, dated 2 November 2005, Annex, paras. 5 and 6.

[705] Details, both in overall statistical terms and for each State Party of the CWC, have been published in: Note by the Director-General 'Report to the Conference of the States Parties at its Eleventh Session on the Status of Implementation of Article VII of the Chemical Weapons Convention as at 1 November 2006', document C-11/DG.6, dated 23 November 2006.

7. Assistance and Protection

Assistance and protection was an area where the PrepCom had not been able to complete the preparations for a smooth entry into force in all aspects. Whilst it had prepared a decision on a lists of items to be stockpiled for emergency and humanitarian assistance,[706] established the Voluntary Fund for Assistance,[707] provided some guidance on the establishment of the OPCW databank on protection,[708] and adopted a model that the OPCW and interested States Parties were to use in the conclusion of bilateral procurement agreements for the delivery of assistance and protection (one of the response mechanisms of the OPCW to provide assistance after incidents when chemical weapons have been used against a State Party),[709] there was no agreement on the exact nature and scale of the OPCW's response mechanism to requests for assistance. Such questions as the desired size of the Voluntary Fund, and of the stockpile for emergency and humanitarian assistance, had not been resolved. Except for certain aspects of how to conduct an investigation of alleged use, there was no operational concept of how the OPCW would respond to a request for assistance, and there were no tested mechanisms for alerting States Parties to the need to provide assistance, for the assessment of what types of assistance were actually needed, and for the coordination of international assistance that would arrive in the field in response to an OPCW appeal.

There also was no agreed set of procedures for the submission by States Parties of information on their national protective programmes.

As a consequence of these outstanding decisions, as well as of differences in views between States Parties about what exactly OPCW's role with regard to a response to CW incidents should be, implementation of Article X started slowly. The number of States Parties that made the required pledges under paragraph 7 of Article X regarding how they will respond to an appeal from the OPCW for assistance remained small, the amounts paid into the Voluntary Fund for Assistance stayed well below the PrepCom estimates of what a single emergency response operation was likely to cost, and the submission by States Parties of information on their protective programmes was more than hesitant.

Five years after the entry into force, for example, the Voluntary Fund for Assistance had received fewer than 1.1 million Euros. Only 32 States Parties had made a pledge for their response to an appeal for assistance by the OPCW (many of which lacked the precision that would be needed for proper advance planning), only one

---

706 Conference of the States Parties, Decision: Lists of Items to be Stockpiled for Emergency and Humanitarian Assistance in Accordance with Article VIII(39)(B) (Paris Resolution, Subpara. 12(B), document C-I/Dec.12, dated 16 May 1997.

707 Conference of the States Parties, Decision: Voluntary Fund for Assistance, document C-I/Dec.52, dated 16 May 1997.

708 Conference of the States Parties, Decision: Data Bank on Protection against Chemical Weapons to be Established in Accordance with Article X(5) of the Convention, document C-I/Dec.53, dated 16 May 1997.

709 Conference of the States Parties, Decision: Model Bilateral Agreement Concerning the Procurement of Assistance, document C-I/Dec.54, dated 16 May 1997.

State Party had entered into a procurement agreement for the delivery of assistance, and the number of State Party submissions on national protective programmes stood at a meagre 22.[710]

Nevertheless, the OPCW was able to develop over the years one area of programme delivery that is little emphasised by the CWC itself but has turned out as rather an important programme delivery area in practice: the provision of expert advice to States Parties on how they could improve their protective capacity against chemical weapons. This started with some States Parties offering training for technical experts from other States Parties in the use of their protective equipment (as part of their pledges under paragraph 7 of Article X), or in analytical procedures (early examples included Finland, Switzerland and Sweden). Over time, other States Parties joined this process by offering their expertise, and an OPCW protection network was set up that helped develop the OPCW concept of assistance further. At the same time, members of the network were available as trainers and instructors for protection courses in other States Parties, or for regional such courses. It should be noted that this shift of emphasis from developing an operational concept for an international assistance response after the use of chemical weapons against a State Party, towards a stronger focus on developing the indigenous protective capacity of States Parties, makes good sense for most scenarios of how chemical weapons might be used. Different from biological and nuclear weapons, the response times after a chemical attack measure in hours. Unless there is a high probability of follow-on chemical attacks (as would be the case in a fully-fledged chemical war), an international assistance response will in most cases arrive well after it was needed on the ground, no matter how well-developed the international mechanism was. Strengthening indigenous capabilities was therefore a much more effective way of preparing for the possibility that chemical weapons might one day be used against a State Party.

In parallel to developing this capacity building concept, the OPCW Secretariat continued to work on its operational concept for the delivery of assistance. These measures were coordinated with relevant UN organisations that had experience in international response mechanisms, notably the UN Office for the Coordination of Humanitarian Affairs (OCHA). The evolving OPCW concept included the use of an Assistance Coordination and Assessment Team that would be made up of OPCW and State Party experts, including inspectors, CW specialists from the Verification Division and staff of the International Cooperation and Assistance Division. The concept was presented to the EC, but never approved. The Secretariat worked on its implementation within the tight constraints of the approved budget, which allowed it to test some of the investigation and response mechanisms. But clearly, a full operational capability for the OPCW to mount an effective and well-coordinated response to a chemical attack on a Sates Party was not achieved.

When the First Review Conference assessed the situation, it noted with concern the implementation gaps with regard to Article X, and called upon States Parties to

---

[710] Report of the OPCW on the Implementation of the Convention on the Prohibition of the Development, Production, Stockpiling, and Use of Chemical Weapons and on their Destruction in 2002, document C-8/5, dated 22 October 2003.

resolve their differences and put the required procedures into place. Furthermore, in its report, it stated that

> [i]n relation to the provision of expert advice by the Secretariat to States Parties that wish to further develop and improve their protective capacity, the First Review Conference noted the work of the OPCW protection network. The First Review Conference also noted that the number of requests for such expert advice received from States Parties recently exceeded the capacity of the Secretariat. The First Review Conference reiterated that the Secretariat must respond to such requests in an effective manner, within the limits on the resources available to it. Furthermore, States Parties should, on a voluntary basis, provide support to the OPCW so it can respond more effectively to requests for expert advice.[711]

As for the international assistance mechanism foreseen by Article X, the First Review Conference

> stressed the importance of investigations of alleged use or threat of use of chemical weapons. For such situations, the OPCW must have the capacity, and be ready at all times, to investigate the need for follow-on action by the OPCW and by individual Member States, and to facilitate the delivery of assistance. The First Review Conference noted that the Secretariat had established the Assistance Coordination and Assessment Team (ACAT), the overall function of which had yet to be defined. This was an important and urgent matter. ACAT has been tested in assessment mode in exercises. The First Review Conference requested the Council to take up the possible function of the OPCW in facilitating the efficient delivery of assistance. In this context, the need was stressed for the OPCW to coordinate its activities in an assistance operation with other international agencies involved in an emergency response, in particular the UN Office for the Coordination of Humanitarian Affairs.[712]

In subsequent years, the situation has incrementally improved. The issue of submission by States Parties of information on their protective programmes became one of the indicators of the comprehensiveness of national implementation measures adopted by States Parties, and was assessed as part of the progress made with the Action Plan on Article VII. In 2004, the EC was finally ready to adopt the missing guidelines and formats for these submissions.[713] EC and CSP continued to remind States Parties of their obligation to make their assistance pledge and clarify how they would respond to a call by the OPCW for assistance after a CW use against another State Party; by 2005, the number of States Parties that had responded had risen to 66. The number of States Parties that had submitted information on their protective programmes had risen to 54. The Voluntary Fund for Assistance stood at Euro 1.2 million – still far short of

---

711 Ibid., para. 7.96.

712 Ibid., para. 7.100.

713 Conference of the States Parties, Decision: Submission of Information Regarding National Programmes Related to Protective Purposes, Pursuant to Article X, para. 4 of the Convention, document C-9/Dec.10, dated 30 November 2004.

the original estimates of what would be needed. And the data bank of protection was on the way of being populated.[714]

In 2005, the OPCW successfully tested its capacity to investigate allegations of the use of chemical weapons against a State Party, and to assess the needs for and coordinate the delivery of an international emergency response after a State Party's request for assistance under Article X, in an exercise jointly conducted with NATO's Euro-Atlantic Disaster Response Coordination Centre (EADRCC) and hosted by the Ukraine. The exercise simulated a terrorist use of chemical weapons. OPCW conducted an investigation of alleged use of chemical weapons, and participated in the coordination of an international assistance response that involved teams that had been mobilised under both NATO and OPCW emergency response mechanisms. An on-site operations-and-coordination centre (OSOCC) was set up by the United Nations Office for the Coordination of Humanitarian Affairs, and the OPCW took a lead role in coordinating the operations of the international emergency responders.

When the OPCW Secretariat evaluated the results of this joint exercise, it concluded that

> Joint Assistance 2005 provided the OPCW with an invaluable opportunity to test its procedures and capabilities in a complex and challenging environment. The exercise required the Secretariat to coordinate its activities with international consequence-management personnel from OPCW Member States, international organisations, and regional organisations. It served as a further reminder to the international community that the OPCW can contribute valuable specialised resources to respond to the use of chemical weapons. More generally, the exercise helped to raise the profile of the OPCW and increase understanding of its activities. The connections and contacts made during the exercise with other organisations will provide a foundation for future cooperation in areas of mutual interest.[715]

Ten years after the EIF, the OPCW is finally on the way towards full and effective implementation of the provisions of Article X of the Convention. There is no question that more work needs to be done to fully develop the role of OPCW in capacity building and responding to assistance requests with regard to protection against chemical weapons. But the concept of how the OPCW would respond to a call for assistance seems finally to become agreeable to all States Parties.

8. International Cooperation in the Peaceful Uses of Chemistry

The way in which Article XI of the CWC was to be implemented was probably the single most controversial issue of CWC implementation after the EIF. The PrepCom

---

[714] Report of the OPCW on the Implementation of the Convention on the Prohibition of the Development, production, Stockpiling and Use of Chemical Weapons and on their Destruction in 2005, document C-11/4, dated 6 December 2006.

[715] Note by the Director-General 'Report on Joint Assistance 2005, Lviv Ukraine, 9-13 October 2005', document S/554/2005, dated 8 March 2006, para. 29.

had not been able to prepare a single draft decision on the matter. Its expert group on international cooperation and assistance (ICA) had managed to draw up an illustrative list of possible OPCW projects in the area, and there was a degree of acceptance among States Parties that that list might be used by the Secretariat to implement projects on an experimental basis. So that is what the Secretariat actually did – using the list of potential international cooperation projects as a starting point and developing an ICA portfolio for the OPCW based on experience gathered, feedback about their usefulness from States Parties, and comments received in every year's programme and budget negotiations.

The initial layout of the ICA programme was a mixture of outreach and support activities for National Authorities and other national agencies (for example, national laboratories) that were involved in the CWC implementation, information gathering on what other international agencies were already doing with regard to promoting international cooperation in the chemical field, and some new projects that were to promote international cooperation through internships, scientific exchanges including the facilitation of participation of scientists from developing countries at scientific conferences of relevance to the CWC, exchanges of equipment and expertise between scientific and research institutions including laboratories, and support for small-scale research projects in relevant areas.[716] Much of this was meant to be 'seed money' that would promote promising scientific individuals or projects in developing and transition countries, but require little investment from the OPCW. No project money could be spent on equipment purchase or investment into other hardware, constructions and the like.

As the OPCW gathered experience with implementing IC programmes, some of these programmes were formalised and rules and criteria for their implementation adopted. The conference support programme and the programme for support of small-scale research projects (the latter in part implemented in cooperation with the Stockholm-based International Foundation for Science, a non-governmental organisation which assists capacity-building in developing countries in sciences related to natural resources) were among the more successful projects and continue to attract requests for support that now exceeds the funding available through the OPCW.

Projects more directly related to capacity-building in States Parties for the implementation of the CWC, such as training programmes for personnel of national authorities, regional and sub-regional outreach programmes to key stakeholder communities, or thematic workshops directly related to CWC implementation (for example, declaration workshops, the use of electronic tools for the preparation of declarations, or the involvement of customs authorities in CWC implementation) were moved to a new, separate implementation support programme of the ICA Division in 2000 (see the discussion above with regard to verification and national implementation support).

By the end of 1999, the concept of a new programme (the OPCW Associate Programme) had been developed with the support of experts from States Parties and

---

[716] Conference of the States Parties, Annotations to the 1997 OPCW Budget, document C-I/Dec.74 (Annotations), dated 23 May 1997.

the chemical industry. This programme would soon become one of the flagship programmes of the OPCW in the international cooperation field.[717] It was designed to combine efforts in the field of international cooperation in the manufacturing of chemicals (including the spreading of expertise in modern industry operations and in chemical safety) with the requirements of implementing the CWC in the chemical industry. It soon found the support of the chemical industry, which participates by making its facilities available for internships (attachments) under the programme,[718] and is an example for how international cooperation and transfer of information and expertise in the peaceful uses of chemistry can be suitably combined with non-proliferation objectives of the OPCW.

But all along, the OPCW failed to reach a formal agreement on how to implement the requirements of Article XI. While the organisation allocated certain amounts of money every year to these projects (somewhere between 6 and 7% of the annual budget are spent on ICA activities), it failed for many years to reach agreement on the content the IC programmes on a long-term basis. Several attempts to develop a decision of the CSP to settle the matter failed; to no less degree caused by the continuing disagreement between States Parties on certain trade issues (in particular the continuation of Australia Group expert control measures *vis-à-vis* CWC States Parties). This kept hostage a more pragmatic decision on the nature, scope and size of OPCW international cooperation programmes for many years. When the First Review Conference reviewed the implementation of these provisions of the CWC, all it could do, by and large, was to reaffirm the provisions of the CWC. The Report of the First Review Conference did, however, recognise the need to resolve the situation, and it underlined the importance of the OPCW international cooperation programmes and the 'valuable contribution to the promotion of the Convention as a whole, including its universality'[719] that they make.

In subsequent years, the OPCW worked hard towards reaching an agreement on the matter. In November 2005, the CSP finally adopted a decision on the full implementation of Article XI.[720] Finally, a Conference decision provided strategic guidance to the OPCW Secretariat and Member States on what to do with Article XI. It committed the OPCW to the continuation of its IC programmes and the development of new such programmes based on a set of agreed criteria.

The importance of this decision cannot be overestimated. While the absence of such a decision had not prevented the OPCW from developing and implementing international cooperation projects, a lack of consensus between the OPCW membership about how to implement a core Article of the CWC has had significant political ramifications. But at the end, the decision was inevitable. Once the OPCW moved towards what it called 'results-based budgeting' and had agreed that among its 'core

---

[717] Report of the Organisation on the Implementation of the Convention (1 January-31 December 1999), document C-V.5, dated 17 May 2000, Section 4.

[718] For details of this and the other OPCW international cooperation programmes, see the OPCW website at <www.opcw.org>.

[719] Ibid., para. 7.108.

[720] Conference of the States Parties, Decision: Full Implementation of Article XI, document C-10/Dec.14, dated 11 November 2005.

objectives' was the '[e]conomic and technological development through international cooperation in the field of chemical activities for purposes not prohibited under the Convention in accordance with the provisions of Article XI',[721] taking a decision on how that core objective was to be met could no longer be avoided. Also, the OPCW had by now gathered a good amount of experience with implementing international cooperation projects that combined the benefits of international exchanges of information, people, chemicals, technology and equipment form the peaceful uses of chemicals with the non-proliferation objectives of the CWC. Confidence among States Parties had grown that the OPCW was capable of developing and implementing meaningful and effective IC programmes, and a decision that was long overdue could finally be adopted.

9. Universality of the Chemical Weapons Convention

A final word is due with regard to achieving the universality of the CWC regime. This is perhaps the most impressive result that the OPCW has achieved over the past ten years, building firmly on the work of the PrepCom which had been actively promoting ratification of the CWC during all its four years of existence.

Universality is one of the implicit assumptions which the CWC was built on – a stable global regime against possession of chemical weapons requires that all CW possessors and 'CW capable' States join the regime. The promotion of universal adherence had therefore been a priority of the OPCW since its inception, and the CSP adopts regular decisions that call for all remaining States that have yet to join to CWC to do so, with particular emphasis on those States that 'pose particular concerns'.

To promote universal adherence to the CWC, the Director-General, the Technical Secretariat and individually many States Parties conducted a range of outreach and promotional activities after the EIF. These included demarches, the holding of regional and sub-regional seminars to promote the CWC, and direct bilateral contacts with relevant States (for example in the margin of the meetings of the First Committee of the United Nations General Assembly). The OPCW also used its relationships with regional organisations such as the EU, the African Union, the OAS and the Pacific Island Forum to work towards universal CWC adherence. Adherence to the CWC steadily increased as a result of these activities.

When the First Review Conference assessed the situation, it had some reason for satisfaction with the results achieved so far. Two aspects were emphasised, however: the need to combine the quantitative aspect of universality (i.e., the number of States adhering to the regime) with qualitative factors (i.e., the efforts that these States Parties make to enforce the CWC), and the fact that there still remained too many States outside the regime (including some that were cause for concern).[722] The report of the First Review Conference stated that

---

[721] Conference of the States Parties, Decision: Programme and Budget of the OPCW for 2005, document C-9/DEC.14, Annex, p. 11.

[722] Ibid., paras. 7.12 and 7.13.

> there are important political, economic, and security benefits of becoming a State Party to the Convention. The First Review Conference recognised the positive effect of international cooperation among the States Parties on universality. Furthermore, their desire for increased security and their determination to participate fully in the global community were incentives for them to adhere to the Convention. The First Review Conference also recalled that States that remain outside the Convention would not be able to take advantage of the benefits that the Convention offers the States Parties.[723]

To further universal adherence to the CWC, the First Review Conference recommended that the EC develop and adopt an Action Plan to promote universality. This Action Plan was subsequently developed by the Council, and adopted alongside the 8th Session of the CSP in November 2003.[724] As with the Action Plan on Article VII, this Action Plan was a step into new territory. The OPCW started more closely coordinating the activities of the Secretariat with the outreach programmes of States Parties. Regional focal points for universality were established. Information on planned activities to promote the Convention was shared more extensively, and the Secretariat analysed each remaining State not party in detail so as to identify the reasons that had led to non-accession/ratification so far.

As the 10th Anniversary of the CWC approaches, the number of CWC States Parties has crossed the 180 line. By comparison with other global arms control and disarmament treaties, this truly is an accomplishment, also given the short time frame involved. When the Director-General reported on the universality issue to the Eleventh Session of the CSP in 2006, there remained only six Signatory States that had yet to ratify the CWC, and 9 other States that had not taken any treaty action on the CWC.[725] The CSP, in response to this report, reaffirmed the goal of reaching universality of the CWC by the 10th Anniversary of the CWC, and to review the status of any State not yet party at its 12th Session at the end of 2007.[726]

At the end of 2006, there remain few geographical regions that are not fully covered by the CWC regime: most notably the core of the Middle East, certain parts of Asia (Myanmar and North Korea), and parts of Africa and the Caribbean. The OPCW continues to work with these remaining States not party in order to facilitate their adherence to the CWC as early as possible.

---

723 Ibid., para. 7.15.

724 Document (EC-M-23/DEC.3, dated 24 October 2003), see Report of the Eighth Session of the Conference of the States Parties, document C-8/7, dated 24 October 2003, para. 17.2.

725 Note by the Director-General 'Annual Report on the Implementation of the Action Plan for the Universality of the Chemical Weapons Convention from 11 November 2005 to 25 September 2006', document C-11/DG.4 EC-47/DG.5, dated 29 September 2006, Annex. Note: among the 9 non-signatories was Montenegro, who has in the meantime assumed responsibilities of a CWC State Party as a successor State of Serbia and Montenegro.

726 Conference of the States Parties, Decision: 'Universality of the Chemical Weapons Convention and Further Implementation of the Universality Action Plan', document C-11/Dec.8, dated 7 December 2006.

10. Concluding Remarks

Ten years of CWC implementation have demonstrated that the PrepCom had given the OPCW a good head start. In only four years, and despite the large number of issues that it could not resolve, the PrepCom had managed to bring together all the essentials for the newly-formed international organisation to evolve and to implement its mandate with success. Ten years later, the OPCW has matured considerably and is respected as an independent and competent international disarmament agency. Despite several serious hiccups, it continues to receive the necessary political and financial support from its Member States, and it has demonstrated that it is capable of adjusting to changing requirements.

There are challenges ahead. Science and technology are developing at a rapid pace, which tests both the scope of CWC prohibitions and the way the verification regime needs to be implemented. The security environment has changed, and the OPCW (as other international organisations) has had to assess both its mandate and capabilities to identify how it could contribute to the response to new security challenges such as the threat of terrorism. There are internal issues that need careful monitoring, such as the impact of the implementation of the OPCW tenure policy that limits the service time of internationally recruited and professional staff at the Technical Secretariat to seven years aggregate. The demands for verification of CW destruction are still increasing, and will increase even further should there be more delays in destruction programmes. And any such delays in these destruction programmes will themselves be a challenge to the consensus of OPCW Member States, and require wise and careful political management.

But the OPCW has proven that it can meet such challenges, and it will go into its second decade of treaty implementation with confidence and resolve. The results of the work of the PrepCom were no small factor in ensuring this success.

Chapter 15

Lessons Learned

1. Introduction

Although several of the chapters of this book include concluding paragraphs discussing the success or otherwise of the Preparatory Commission for OPCW in their particular context, this work is a case study and it is therefore appropriate to try to pull together in one place some of the most important lessons which can be learned from the work of that body.

2. Need for PrepCom Process

The most important lesson is that a formal preparatory process, whether or not with the attributes of a Preparatory Commission, is an essential preliminary to the establishment and operation of an international organisation with a functional remit. OPCW was able to 'hit the ground running' and to meet all the initial goals set by the Chemical Weapons Convention within the timelines laid down.

3. Sound Start

The true test of the PrepCom was the efficiency with which the First Session of the OPCW's Conference of the States Parties functioned, the volume of decisions taken, and the subsequent ability of the OPCW to be operational from the outset – just as planned. The fact that there were unresolved issues is not completely a reflection of the Commission's effectiveness. Many of those issues were not politically ripe for resolution and needed several years of actual practice in the OPCW for their resolution. Others were discovered to be actually of no consequence to implementation of the Convention and could be dismissed, eventually.

4. UN Membership

The political decision was taken by the negotiators of the CWC that OPCW should be an independent international organisation and not part of the United Nations system.

I.R. Kenyon and D. Feakes, The Creation of the OPCW

Whilst this, in theory, left the Member States free to decide the details of the structure and rules of the new organisation without being bound by UN practice, in fact the UN model was very largely followed. A formal agreement with the UN was necessary so that OPCW inspectors could travel on UN *laissez passer*. If a status of association with the UN, such as that enjoyed by the International Atomic Energy Agency, had been selected the PrepCom would have been able to draw more easily on UN support in the early stages of its work when the secretariat were under considerable pressure.

5. Location

The new organisation experienced both advantages and disadvantages from its establishment in a different location from that where it had been negotiated, Geneva, and its establishment in The Hague where there were few other international organisations and none with a technical remit. On the one hand the authorities and the populace were very welcoming, took considerable interest in, and gave all the help they could to the new arrival. On the other hand, the diplomatic missions which had to represent their governments interests in the organisation were set up to operate bilateral relations between their home state and the Netherlands and in most cases had no staff with multilateral negotiation experience or technical expertise. Countries with large chemical industries or a history of military involvement with chemical warfare sent full time specialists to reinforce their embassies but most of the diplomatic corps of The Hague had to learn on the job.

6. Timelines

The timelines laid down in the CWC for provision of information by Member States (declarations); for initial inspection of relevant facilities in Member States by the OPCW Inspectorate; and for destruction of chemical weapon stocks and related facilities were all set during the negotiations as a result of political pressures rather than realistic calculation. In fact the initial inspection deadlines were only met because one of the major chemical weapon possessor states was late in ratifying, which enabled the work to be spread over a longer period. Many declarations were late, in some case by years, and the initial weapon destruction deadline is having to be extended.

7. Initial Admin Support

Any international negotiating body needs a minimum of administrative support from the outset. Personnel expected to service such negotiations need to operate in a suitable working environment, knowing that they have a contract of employment and that a salary cheque will appear at the end of the month. Also of vital importance is adequate insurance cover. (The Provisional Technical Secretariat (PTS), in its short existence, had one death and one case of long-term sickness.) The failure of the Member

States to either obtain initial support from the UN or to make alternative arrangements for a small cadre of administrative staff meant that the Executive Secretary and his first group of helpers, none of whom had specialist administrative experience, had to solve these problems for themselves in parallel with the substantive work.

8. Bilaterals

The CWC was drafted to permit its operation in parallel and in coordination with a bilateral agreement between the United States and Russia, which at the time of signature of the CWC had not entered into force.[727] In fact it did not enter into force but the PTS were instructed to continue to plan on the assumption that it would be in force at the entry into force of the CWC. This had a serious effect on the numbers of inspectors needed to be deployed in the initial inspections. Any such hybrid treaty arrangement in the future should be on a more secure foundation.

9. Unrealised Concerns

The implementation of the CWC since 1997 has demonstrated that many of the concerns expressed during the negotiations and during the PrepCom itself have proved to be unfounded. Perhaps the most significant relates to the protection of confidential business information which was a major issue in Geneva and, as described above, was probably the biggest issue in the PrepCom too. However, experience since entry into force demonstrates that the OPCW has been able to protect the information entrusted to it.

10. Importance of the Support of the Industry

The continuing support of the chemical industry for the CWC is dependent upon its close involvement in the process, from the beginning of the negotiations in the 1980s, through the preparatory phase in the 1990s, to the implementation of the CWC in the late 1990s and to the present day. This was recognised by the Director-General of CEFIC in 2000: 'An important lesson learned from the Convention is that the involvement of industry is essential, not merely during the negotiations, but also during the implementation process'.[728] The OPCW Director-General recognised the synergistic relationship between the CWC and the chemical industry in a report to the first CWC review conference: 'The Convention and the OPCW cannot function properly without the support and engagement of the chemical industry. [...]. Declarations and

[727] Ian Kenyon, 'The USA/USSR Arms Control Relationship and Its Impact on the CWC', *CBW Conventions Bulletin*, 72+73, September 2006, pp. 1-3.

[728] Alain Perroy, 'The contribution of the chemical industry to the Chemical Weapons Convention', *OPCW Synthesis* (Autumn/November 2000), pp. 4-5, p. 5.

inspections under Article VI, as well as the enforcement of export controls for scheduled chemicals, require a true partnership between the OPCW, the National Authorities, and the chemical industry. This will be even more important in the future, given the high pace of technological and organisational change in the industry.'

11. Informal Legal Basis

Given the relative informality of the legal basis for the Commission – an unpublished, unratified international legal instrument adopted by some but not all of those that participated in the implementation of its provisions – the ease which its operations moved forth is astonishing. The political willingness of states to carry the work forward can be the only explanation.

12. Use as Model for CTBTO/PC

The Preparatory Commission created the necessary infrastructure and legal arrangements necessary to make the permanent institution (OPCW) operational from the outset. The challenges that arose unexpectedly were dealt with creatively, determinably, and solved with a lot of hard work by staff and delegates. The extent to which it was navigating uncharted territory pales in comparison with the next preparatory commission created in the field, the Preparatory Commission for the Comprehensive Nuclear-Test-Ban Treaty Organisation. Nevertheless, it served as a model for much of the initial work of that later preparatory commission.

13. Caution in Negotiating Inspection Procedures

The negotiation of the detailed procedures for inspections covered in Chapter 7 was not easy and, on occasions, reaching consensus required considerable compromises by individual Signatory States. This was because the CWC was not in force and no inspections were taking place. As a result, many delegations had no knowledge of what, in practical terms, an inspection might involve and how much actual risk there was to their national and commercial sensitive information from such inspections. It was inevitable, in such a situation, that those participating in the negotiations would err on the side of caution and this often made for slow and difficult progress. Despite these difficulties, by the time the 'trigger point' was reached and the 180 day countdown to EIF began many of the key decisions had been made. Even where there was no formal agreement on an issue, sufficient text had been developed to provide the Technical Secretariat with a basis on which to work.

14. National Implementation

Neither during negotiations of the Convention nor during the initiation of implementation support during the preparatory phase 1993-1997, was it ever imagined the duration or depth of support that would be needed by states for effective national implementation. Even when the explicit obligations of Article VII have been met by all States Parties, it will form only the foundation for full and effective implementation at the national level. States Parties will continue to need to devote resources to enable a vital National Authority and the vigilant application and enforcement of the legislation and administrative measures they have adopted. Experience has shown – both during the time of the Preparatory Commission and in the OPCW today – the sharing of experience amongst States Parties is the key component in identifying and promoting best practice in national implementation. A partnership between the Secretariat and States Parties leads to effective implementation support and effective implementation. In the matter of national implementation complete reliance on the principle of *pacta sunt servanda* may not be enough. The Westphalian notion of the sanctity of sovereignty may need to be eroded slightly further.

15. Name Problems

An interesting problem arose over the name of the organisation. Everyone knows that 'CW' in OPCW stands for 'chemical weapons'. The 'P' is less well understood. One frequently hears it referred to as 'promotion' or (worse) 'production' rather than the correct 'prohibition'. There was public apprehension that the new organisation would be handling these weapons on its premises or transporting them through the neighbourhood. These misapprehensions were allayed and it is difficult to devise an alternative title for the OPCW, given its remit.

16. Envoi

In the end, the PrepCom lasted for twice as long as some people had expected. Rather than having everything wrapped up within two years, the process lasted for four with sixteen plenary sessions of the PrepCom. While this was partly due to 'internal' reasons, such as the technical complexity of the PrepCom's tasks and the re-opening of issues already negotiated in Geneva, it was also due to developments in the 'external' political environment and especially to the length of time it took signatory states to complete their national ratification processes. Two PrepCom participants wrote: 'Clearly, the negotiators in Geneva who decided upon this minimum two-year implementation period greatly underestimated the effort involved in setting up a completely new international organization of approximately 500 personnel, including 200 trained inspectors.'[729] While two years was clearly an unrealistic timeframe in which to achieve such goals, it is also quite remarkable that these goals were achieved in four years and that the OPCW was able to 'hit the ground running' to the apparent surprise of some of its Member States. Given problems such as the failure to resolve some issues delegated to it from Geneva, the uncertainty about ratification by Russia and the US, the delay in the construction of the purpose-built OPCW headquarters, the necessity to process declarations in hard-copy and so on, the PrepCom should be seen as a success in terms of its practical achievements. For example: over 400 individuals were interviewed around the world and almost 200 were recruited as inspectors; and procedures for the processing of declarations and carrying out of inspections were developed, and then implemented without any breaches of confidentiality or serious health and safety incidents.

Reflecting back on the preparatory work described in this book, there is a large amount of satisfaction ten years later to see the OPCW functioning in its beautiful building, inspection teams arriving and departing, meetings in progress to ensure implementation, delegates and staff suitably accommodated and working with national authorities in the 180 states actively engaged in the goal of a chemical weapons-free world. All of this was created by the Convention and is operating within the terms of the treaty as well as the subsidiary network of legal arrangements drafted prospectively during a brief preparatory phase.

[729] Robert Mathews and Antony Taubman, 'Preparing for implementation of the Chemical Weapons Convention: Progress during 1993', in JB Poole and R Guthrie (eds.), *Verification 1994: Arms Control, Peacekeeping and the Environment* (London, Brassey's 1994), pp. 111-128, p. 126.

About the Authors

DANIEL FEAKES was the Harvard Sussex Program researcher at the OPCW from August 1997 until July 2000. He has an academic background in history and political science. He is now a Research Fellow at the University of Sussex where he works on issues relating to the Chemical Weapons Convention and to the Biological Weapons Convention. Daniel has been the principal researcher on the project of which this book is a product.

IAN R. KENYON was the Executive Secretary of the Preparatory Commission for OPCW during its whole existence from February 1993 to May 1997. He was a member of the British Diplomatic Service from 1974 until his retirement in 1994, including serving as Deputy leader, UK Disarmament Delegation, Geneva from 1988 to 1992. He is now a Visiting Senior Research Fellow at the Mountbatten Centre for International Studies, University of Southampton, UK; a Visiting Research Fellow at SPRU Science and Technology Policy Research, University of Sussex, UK; and a member of the Advisory Board of the Harvard Sussex Program on CBW Armament and Arms Limitation.

SERGEI KISSELEV was the Resident Representative of Russia to the Preparatory Commission for the OPCW from 1993 to 1997. During this period, he also served as Chairman of two Expert Groups of the Preparatory Commission: of Chemical Engineers and on Inspection Procedures. He also served as Acting Chairman of the Committee on Relations with the Host Country for a period of six months. In 1982-1986 he was a staff member of the United Nations in New York. Following that, he was a member of the Soviet and then Russian Foreign Service. From 1991 to 1993, he served as Head of the Chemical and Biological Weapons Division in the Ministry of Foreign Affairs in Moscow and as Deputy Head of the Russian Delegation at the Conference on Disarmament and at US-Russian chemical weapons negotiations in Geneva. He joined the OPCW Technical Secretariat in 1998, serving in the Verification and International Cooperation and Assistance Divisions. He also served as Secretary of the Committee of the Whole at a number of sessions of the Conference of the States Parties to the Chemical Weapons Convention. He holds an MBA degree from Webster University, Saint Louis, Missouri, USA.

RON MANLEY joined the Provisional Technical Secretariat of the Preparatory Commission for the OPCW, as Head of the Chemical Demilitarisation Branch, in September 1993. He held this post until entry into force of the CWC, in May 1997, at which point he was appointed Special Advisor to the Director-General of the OPCW. In 2000 he became Director of Verification and held this post until his retirement from the OPCW in late 2001. Prior to joining the PTS he worked for the UK Ministry of Defence in a range of fields related to chemical weapons defence. He is currently a Visiting Professor at the Defence College of Management and Technology, Cranfield University, UK and a freelance consultant on Arms Control, and CBW related issues.

HASSAN MASHHADI was Head of the Government Relations and Political Affairs Branch in the Provisional Technical Secretariat of the Preparatory Commission from 1993 to 1997. Following the entry into force of the CWC and its ratification by Iran, he became head of the Assistance and Protection Branch from 1998 to 2006. Prior to his time in The Hague, he was head of the Iranian delegation to the Conference on Disarmament in Geneva from 1987 to 1993, during the last few years of the CWC negotiations. He is now working as a consultant for development of national response plans, establishment of response systems and training of first responders against chemical, biological, radiological, nuclear and explosive weapons and terrorism.

JOHAN RAUTENBACH was Deputy Legal Adviser in the Provisional Technical Secretariat of the Preparatory Commission from 1993 to 1997. After the entry into force of the CWC, he became Head of the Human Resources Branch of the Technical Secretariat. Prior to 1993 he was a member of the South African diplomatic service, representing his country at the Conference on Disarmament in the final years of the negotiation of the CWC. Since 2002, he has been Legal Adviser and Director of the Office of Legal Affairs at the International Atomic Energy Agency (IAEA).

PAUL RYAN, Group Captain, joined – on loan from the British Government – the Executive Secretary at the Provisional Technical Secretariat from the onset in February1993 and filled a number of senior administrative appointments pending the recruitment of staff members on Fixed Term appointments. Subsequently in February 1994 he assumed the appointment of Head of General Services Branch and in that capacity continued to serve as the Secretary of the Group of Experts on the OPCW Building and also of the Committee on Host Country Relations. He was the principal point of contact on building-related issues within the Secretariat from 1993 through to the completion of the building in 1998. Before moving to The Hague, he was the Military Adviser to the UK Disarmament Delegation, Geneva (1990-1992) and previously served in a variety of appointments, including NBC/CBW Staff Officer, throughout the world. He is now enjoying retirement, but missing the 'cut and thrust' of the conference room, continues to chair or serve as secretary on a number of public and Service committees.

LISA TABASSI was Senior Research Assistant in the Legal Division of the Provisional Technical Secretariat of the Preparatory Commission during 1993 to 1997. From 1997 to 2007 she continued in the OPCW Office of the Legal Adviser as the principal Legal Officer responsible for providing legal advice to States Parties on implementing legislation as well as the regulatory framework to administer and enforce the treaty nationally. During that period she contributed articles or chapters to a number of publications and compiled two books: *OPCW: The Legal Texts* (1999) and *Treaty Enforcement and International Cooperation in Criminal Matters, with Special Reference to the Chemical Weapons Convention* (2002). She has guest lectured at the law faculties of the universities of Amsterdam, Geneva, Leiden as well as Webster University on legal aspects of the OPCW and national implementation of the Convention. Previously she worked for private law firms in the Iran and the United States and as a researcher for the Iran-United States Claims Tribunal in The Hague. She holds an LL.M. cum laude in public international law with a specialisation in international criminal law. She is presently serving as Legal Officer in the Provisional Technical Secretariat of the Preparatory Commission for the Comprehensive Nuclear Test Ban Treaty Organisation (CTBTO) in Vienna, Austria.

RALF TRAPP was branch head (Industry A, then Industry Verification Concept Development, then Policy and Review) in the Verification Division of the Provisional Technical Secretariat of the Preparatory Commission between May 1993 and May 1997. A chemist and toxicologist by training, he had been with the GDR Academy of Sciences between 1978 and 1990, working on environmental and arms control issues. Between 1985 and 1987, he was a guest researcher at the Stockholm International Peace Research Institute (SIPRI). Beginning in 1982, he provided technical advice to the GDR, and later the German, delegations to the Conference on Disarmament. After the entry into force of the CWC, he served in a number of senior positions at the OPCW (verification policy and review, international cooperation, government relations and political affairs, preparation of the First Review Conference, and finally strategic planning). He is now an independent consultant on arms control and disarmament affairs. He is external member of the Academy of Sciences of Bologna.

Illustrations

1 18 March 1988, Halabja, Iraq. Large numbers of Kurdish civilians were killed during an Iraqi chemical weapons attack on the village. Pictures of the aftermath of the attack gave impetus to the CWC negotiations in Geneva. (Source: Iranian government)

2 23-24 August 1991, Prins Maurits Laboratory, Rijswijk, The Netherlands. During the Netherlands lobby for the seat of the OPCW, CD ambassadors were invited to The Hague. While there they visited the Laboratory. (Source: Netherlands Bid Book II)

3 13 January 1993, Paris, France. The CWC was opened for signature at a ceremony at UNESCO headquarters, presided over by French President Francois Mitterand (standing) and United Nations Secretary-General Boutros Boutros-Ghali (seated, to President Mitterand's right). (Source: HSP)

4 Laan van Meerdervoort 51, The Hague, The Netherlands. The office building which the Provisional Technical Secretariat occupied from February 1993, until the completion of its purpose-built headquarters in 1998. (Source: Netherlands Bid Book II)

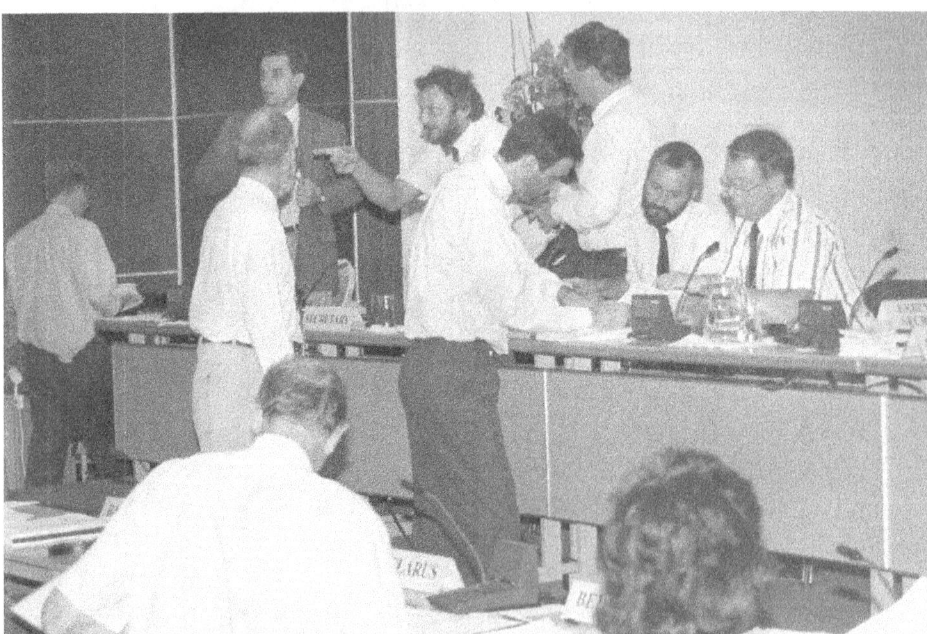

5 A meeting of an expert group during the Preparatory Commission. Although the date is unknown, this picture demonstrates the collegiate nature and the variety of nationalities involved, and it shows a number of key individuals. Standing behind the desk, from left: Mikhail Berdennikov (Russia); Ralf Trapp (Germany); Ron Manley (UK). Seated at the desk, from left: Sylwin Gizowski (Poland); John Gee (Australia). (Source: OPCW)

6 Visit by Provisional Technical Secretariat staff to a former Chemical Weapons Production Facility at Volgograd, Russia. From left: Mikhail Berdennikov; John Gee; Don Clagett; Ron Manley; Ian Kenyon; Pavel Castulik, Mechislav Remishevski. (Source: Ian Kenyon)

7 9 May 1996, Catsheuvel site, The Hague. The groundbreaking ceremony to mark the start of construction of the purpose-built OPCW building on Johan de Wittlaan. Executive Secretary Ian Kenyon leads the attendees down the steps. (Source: OPCW)

8 December 1997, OPCW building, The Hague. The OPCW headquarters building in the final stages of construction. The flat-roofed one-storey building is the Executive Council chamber, which was later named the Ieper Room in honour of the Belgian town where chemical weapons were first used. To the left of the site is the Netherlands Congress Centre, and to the right is the Bel Air Hotel. Across the road is the Prime Minister's residence. (Source: Provastgoed Nederland BV)

9 11 September 1996, OPCW Laboratory and Equipment Store, Rijswijk, The Netherlands. Following its conversion and fitting out for the OPCW, the laboratory and equipment store was officially opened by, from left, the chairman of the Preparatory Commission, Ambassador Marin Buhoara of Romania, the Mayor of Rijswijk and the Executive Secretary Ian Kenyon. (Source: OPCW)

10 11 September 1996, OPCW Laboratory and Equipment Store, Rijswijk, The Netherlands. Inside the OPCW Laboratory after its official opening, from left: Head of the Laboratory, Pia Bruce; Director of Verification, John Gee; Executive Secretary, Ian Kenyon; and Head of Chemical Demilitarisation Branch, Ron Manley. (Source: OPCW)

11 31 October 1996, Netherlands Congress Centre, The Hague, the Netherlands. The staff of the Provisional Technical Secretariat assembled beside the construction site of the new OPCW headquarters to mark the 65th ratification of the CWC which triggered the entry into force of the Convention 180 days later, on 29 April 1997. (Source: Ian Kenyon)

12 6 May 1997, First Session of the Conference of the States Parties, The Hague, The Netherlands. United Nations Secretary-General Kofi Annan (depositary of the CWC) and PTS Executive Secretary Ian Kenyon. (Source: OPCW)

13 May 1997, The Hague, The Netherlands. PTS Executive Secretary Ian Kenyon signs the assets of the Preparatory Commission over to OPCW Director-General Jose Mauricio Bustani. (Source: OPCW)

14 20 May 1998, OPCW Headquarters, The Hague, The Netherlands. HM Queen Beatrix of the Netherlands officially opens the purpose-built OPCW building. (Source: OPCW)

15 A view of the front of the completed OPCW Headquarters. (Source: OPCW)

16 13 February 2005, OPCW Headquarters, The Hague, The Netherlands. As part of the research for this book, the editors organised a 'witness seminar'. A number of former national delegates and PTS staff members attended. Front row (l-r): Ron Nelson; Lisa Tabassi; John Gee; Ian Kenyon; Chantal de Haas. Second row (l-r): Daniel Feakes; Heiner Staub; Hassan Mashhadi; Anil Wadhwa; Ian Mundell; Shmuel Limone. Third row: Sergei Kisselev; Ralf Trapp; Bunro Shiozawa; Sylwin Gizowski; Vladimir Iossifov. Fourth row: Brian Davey; Serguei Batsanov; Patrick Dewez; Graham Cooper; John Walker. (Source: HSP)

Index